Photos and collages by Hunter.

Photos by María Fernanda and Savana.

ROOKIE
YEARBOOK
FOUR

RAZORBILL
AN IMPRINT OF PENGUIN RANDOM HOUSE

Editor-in-Chief: Tavi Gevinson

Editorial Director: Anaheed Alani

Art Director: Tavi Gevinson

Art & Design: Sonja Ahlers

Designers: Kristin Smith, Vanessa Han, Maria Fazio, Maggie Olson, Anthony Elder, and Kelley Brady

Managing Editor: Lauren Redding

Story Editors: Anaheed Alani, Derica Shields, Lena Singer, and Amy Rose Spiegel

Publisher: Ben Schrank

Razorbill Editor: Jessica Almon

Razorbill Managing Editor: Vivian Kirklin

Copy Editor: Jerome Ludwig

Design Assistant: Ellie Kibbe

Cover design: Sonja Ahlers

Cover art: María Fernanda Molins, Erica Segovia, Rose Lichter-Marck, Rachel Louise Hodgson, Nafisa Kaptownwala, Siena LaMere, Sandy Honig, Tyra Mitchell, Eleanor Hardwick, and Chrissie White

razor bill

An Imprint of Penguin Random House
Penguin.com

Rookiemag.com

ISBN: 978-1-59514-795-0

Printed in the United States of America

1 3 5 7 9 10 8 6 4 2

CONTENTS

CONTRIBUTORS

Charles Aaron
Kelly Abeln
Madison Adams
Ahida Agirre
Sonja Ahlers
Leeay Aikawa
Anaheed Alani
Syar S. Alia
Hilton Als
Emily Beard
Tova Benjamin
Mithsuca Berry
Lucy Betz
Sofia Bews
Esme Blegvad
Seth Bogart
Ry Book
Dana Boulos
Lilly Bralts-Kelly
Krista Burton
D'Arcy Carden
Elvia Carreon
Pixie Casey
Hazel Cills
Greer Clark
Choy-Ping Clark-Ng
Maxine Crump

Emma Dajska
Tori Rae Davis
Camille Delaune
Stephanie Dinkmeyer
DeJ Loaf
Bridget Donegan
Devan Diaz
Anne T. Donahue
Caitlin Donohue
Ed Droste
Clare Drummond
Tewsdey Erickson-Million
Julianne Escobedo Shepherd
Alyssa Etoile
Anna Fitzpatrick
FKA twigs
Tyler Ford
Britney Franco
Kate Gavino
Ananda Gervais
Tavi Gevinson
Minna Gilligan
Briana Gonzalez
Emily V. Gordon
Meredith Graves
María Inés Gul
Ruchi Gupta

Vanessa Han
Eleanor Hardwick
Rachel Hardwick
Caitlin Hazell
Ana Hinojosa
Rachel Louise Hodgson
Beth Hoeckel
Sandy Honig
Akilah Hughes
Amber Humphrey
Devonté Hynes
Mads Jensen
Rashida Jones
Nafisa Kaptownwala
Ellie Kibbe
Camille Klein
Ezra Koenig
Kelli Korducki
Stephanie Kuehnert
Siena LaMere
Brodie Lancaster
Rose Lichter-Marck
Allegra Lockstadt
Marie Lodi
Lorde
Jerome Ludwig
James Lyons

Lisa Maione
Marah*
Meg Matthias
Cynthia Merhej
Anna Menasche
Tyra Mitchell
Annie Mok
María Fernanda Molins
Naomi Morris
Kaleemah Morse
Ryan Murphy
Ragini Nag-Rao
Brooke Nechvatel
Gabby Noone
Savana Ogburn
Chanel Parks
Lola Pellegrino
Elizabeth Perry
Alex-Quan Pham
Rian Phin
María Rangel
Lauren Redding
Simone Rembert
Sarah Rimington
Dylan Tupper Rupert
Isabel Ryan
Shriya Samavai

Roberto Sánchez
Hunter Schafer
Erica Segovia
Arabelle Sicardi
Lena Singer
Willow Smith
Amanda Leigh Smith
Brittany Spanos
Amy Rose Spiegel
Hattie Stewart
Emma Straub
Dylan Tupper-Rupert
Estelle Tang
Dario Villanueva
Florence Welch
Chrissie White
Alyson Zetta Williams
Jamia Wilson
Meredith Wilson
Chloe Wise
The Witch and the Glitter Badger
Leanna Wright
Suzy X.
Charli XCX
Kendra Yee
Allyssa Yohana
Jenny Zhang

Kelly Abeln DIY Instructions design.

Leeay Aikawa Backgrounds for Let's Do This for Real: An Interview With Alessia Cara, Something to Read While Debating Whether or Not to Call Your Ex, Creative Solutions, and The Hope for Connection: An Interview With Genevieve Liu.

Esme Blegvad Background for How to Tell Creepy Dudes to Leave You Alone.

Seth Bogart Lettering for How to Tell Creepy Dudes to Leave You Alone, For Every Sector of Humanity: An Interview With Harlo Holmes, Queens Every Day, and Trust Your Gut: An Interview With Marina and the Diamonds.

Emma Dajska Lettering for Empathy, In Excess, and Eyes on Me. Playlist artwork for Dueling Duets. Margin artwork for The Sex Crylebration: Part III, Ex-Girlfriends, and Call of the Wild. Backgrounds for Friend Crush: Amandla Stenberg and Kiernan Shipka, Always Listen to Yourself: An Interview With Jazz Jennings, Sensitive and Powerful: An Interview With Donna Tartt, Reveling in the Extraordinary: An Interview With Tracee Ellis Ross, Channeling My 15-Year-Old Self: An Interview With Solange, Teenage Bedroom Diorama, Jewelry Box, and Paper Fan.

Kate Gavino Lettering for Freestyle Joyride and No Apologies.

Minna Gilligan Backgrounds for The Sex Crylebration: Part II, What Is a Boy?, Approval Plan, Life Skills 401, We Mean What We Say: An Interview With TLC, Empathy Isn't Everything, How to Structure Your Days If You're Depressed, and Dear Zayn.

Briana Gonzalez Lettering, margin artwork, and backgrounds for Dear Diary and Just Wondering.

Vanessa Han Lettering for I'll Be Your Mirror, I Will Paint the Sky, When a Crush Is Enough, and Bathing Beauty.

Caitlin Hazell Lettering for Songs for Getting Ready to Go Out, Age of Consent, Songs for Exerting Control Over Your Sexuality Like a Boss Bitch, and Songs for Your Own Personal World-Conquering Montage.

Ana Hinojosa Background for Imagine Me & You.

Rachel Louise Hodgson Lettering for How to Make a Photo Diary, Hanging Out With Harriet the Spy, Sudden Death, and Selfie Esteem. Background for The First Day.

Beth Hoeckel Margin artwork for Approval Plan, How to Make a Photo Diary, Soft Power, Hanging Out With Harriet the Spy, Selfie Esteem, and The First Day. Backgrounds for When You Arrive, Change of Clothes, and Dress Up in You.

Allegra Lockstadt Lettering for How to Write a Celebrity Profile of Your BFF, Where My Girls At?, Slumber Party Games: A Taxonomy, Slumber Party Soundtrack, and How to Lose Your Best Friend. Backgrounds for I Will Paint the Sky.

Lisa Maione Lettering for We Are What We Love: An Interview With Laverne Cox, Girls Afraid, DIY Glitter Globe, Magical Creatures, Lyrics-Free Studying, Qui Êtes-Vous?, Take This Job & Shove It, When You Arrive, Change of Clothes, Elephants Can Forget, Both Sides, Life Skills 401, Allied Force, We Mean What

We Say: An Interview With TLC, Are You My Mom?, Empathy Isn't Everything, How to Structure Your Days If You're Depressed, Let's Do This for Real: An Interview With Alessia Cara, Your Creative Energies Must Be Released: An Interview With Sana Amanat, and How to Wear Flowers in Your Hair.

Cynthia Merhej Lettering for the book's cover, Addictive Personalities, Poem for Edgar, and Dear You.

Savana Ogburn Backgrounds for masthead, Table of Contents, Contributors page, Acknowledgments, and Welcome letter.

Sarah Rimington Backgrounds for Hero Status: Medusa, It's Not About You, Your Creative Energies Must Be Released: An Interview With Sana Amanat, and How to Wear Flowers in Your Hair.

Dylan Tupper Rupert Backgrounds for The Sex Crylebration: Part II and How to Lose Your Best Friend.

Isabel Ryan Margin artwork for Open All Night, Songs for Getting Ready to Go Out, Age of Consent, Songs for Exerting Control Over Your Sexuality Like a Boss Bitch, Stand for Something, The Sex Crylebration: Part II, What Is a Boy?, and Songs for Your Own Personal World-Conquering Montage.

Hunter Schafer Lettering for Hero Status: Medusa, It's Not About You, Something to Read While Debating Whether or Not to Call Your Ex, Creative Solutions, and The Hope for Connection: An Interview With Genevieve Liu.

Hattie Stewart Margin artwork for Don't Stay in School, I Can Do All These Things: An Interview With FKA twigs, and Change of Clothes. Backgrounds for Wild Disco With Charli XCX, Steps to Sonic Victory With DeJ Loaf, and Friend Crush: Hayley Williams and Joy Williams.

Leanna Wright Margin artwork for DIY Glitter Globe, Magical Creatures, When a Crush Is Enough, and Bathing Beauty.

Suzy X. Margin artwork for Have Your Freedom: An Interview With Danyel Smith and Take This Job & Shove It.

Kendra Yee Lettering for Stand for Something, Say Everything, No One Can Mess With You, Girls Afraid, I Belong With Me, and Everyone's Invited. Margin artwork for Don't Stay in School, The Importance of Music to Girls, When You Arrive, I Can Do All These Things: An Interview With FKA twigs, Change of Clothes, Life Skills 401, We Mean What We Say: An Interview With TLC, Field Day, Empathy Isn't Everything, How to Structure Your Days If You're Depressed, Dear Zayn, Hero Status: Medusa, It's Not About You, Let's Do This For Real: An Interview With Alessia Cara, Stars in My Eyes, Something to Read While Debating Whether or Not to Call Your Ex, Creative Solutions, Your Creative Energies Must Be Released: An Interview With Sana Amanat, How to Wear Flowers in Your Hair, and The Hope for Connection: An Interview With Genevieve Liu. Background for Allied Force.

ACKNOWLEDGMENTS

Thank you to…

Everyone who decided to make themselves vulnerable by writing/ drawing/photographing a piece of their soul and then letting us publish it. We would literally be nothing without you. Just a bunch of sad Editor's Letters, promising a bunch of content that would never come, to a readership of like, my dad, who is not even a teenage girl. Not only is it all so lovely to look at and interesting to read; it's personal, painfully familiar, and vitally important. Thank you thank you thank you.

Sonja Ahlers for beautifully collaging this book and for her blood-brother (sister) commitment to Rookie for the entirety of our existence. You've defined the visual language of a very specific voice, and I am continually thrilled to have you as a brain-twin.

Lauren Redding for wearing a trillion Rookie hats, managing this whole project as well as our site, and envisioning it with me. I am so happy to work with you every day.

Anaheed Alani, Derica Shields, Lena Singer, and Amy Rose Spiegel for bringing their invaluable eyeballs to editing the work in this book and on our site, taking such good care of our contributors and readers. Thank you to Anne T. Donahue for coordinating killer music coverage.

Tina Lee for editing and shaping these articles for print.

Ben Schrank, Jessica Almon, Vivian Kirklin, Elyse Marshall, and everyone at Razorbill for giving Rookie this space. Thank you to Razorbill's designers, Kristin Smith, Vanessa Han, Maggie Olson, Maria Fazio, Anthony Elder, and Kelley Brady, for helping to create and design a gorgeous book.

David Kuhn, Nicole Tourtelot, Jessie Borkan, and everyone at Kuhn Projects for matchmaking Rookie and Razorbill.

The illustrators who made new work just for this book: Kelly Abeln, Leeay Aikawa, Mithsuca Berry, Esme Blegvad, Seth Bogart, Maxine Crump, Emma Dajska, Alyssa Etoile, Kate Gavino, Minna Gilligan, Briana Gonzalez, María Inés Gul, Caitlin Hazell, Ana Hinojosa, Rachel Louise Hodgson, Beth Hoeckel, Allegra Lockstadt, Lisa Maione, Cynthia Merhej, Annie Mok, Brooke Nechvatel, Sarah Rimington, Dylan Tupper Rupert, Isabel Ryan, Hunter Schafer, Hattie Stewart, Leanna Wright, Suzy X., and Kendra Yee. There'd be almost no point in printing all this without you bringing it to life.

Kelly Abeln, Mithsuca Berry, Lucy Betz, Sofia Bews, Maxine Crump, Emma Dajska, Ed Droste, Alyssa Etoile, María Inés Gul, Dev Hynes, Rashida Jones, Ezra Koenig, DeJ Loaf, Allegra Lockstadt, Lorde, Isabel Ryan, Hunter Schafer, Willow Smith, Hattie Stewart, Florence Welch, Leanna Wright, Charli XCX, and Kendra Yee for contributing to our extra-special print exclusives. Thank you to Chloe Chaidez, Tyler Ford, Ariana Grande, Jazz Jennings, Sarah Paulson, Emma Roberts, Tracee Ellis Ross, Shamir, Kiernan Shipka, Solange, Amandla Stenberg, Donna Tartt, Hayley Williams, and Joy Williams for agreeing to be interviewed for that section.

María Fernanda Molins for taking our dream cover photo, and so many others. Thank you to Eleanor Hardwick, Rachel Louise Hodgson, Sandy Honig, Nafisa Kaptownwala, Siena LaMere, Rose Lichter-Marck, Tyra Mitchell, Erica Segovia, and Chrissie White for capturing the smiles/laughs/bitchfaces that make up the rest of our cover.

Cynthia Merhej for lettering our title and subtitle. They are just right.

Ellie Kibbe for assisting Sonja and laying out the marginalia for a series of stunning spreads.

FKA twigs for contributing her artwork to accompany her thoughtful interview.

Steve Gevinson for acting as Rookie's unofficial business advisor and my dad. Mom for BRINGING ME INTO THIS WORLD and giving me art supplies from a wee age and letting me wear the same shirt every day and have bad haircuts.

Grace: I love you.

Our readers. Whether you've been keeping up with the site since day one or just picked up this book to appear busy while avoiding someone you ran into at Barnes & Noble, thank you. Thank you for coming to our events, organizing meetups, finding each other, sending in your work, telling us what you want to see or making it yourself. You have made Rookie a living, breathing thing.

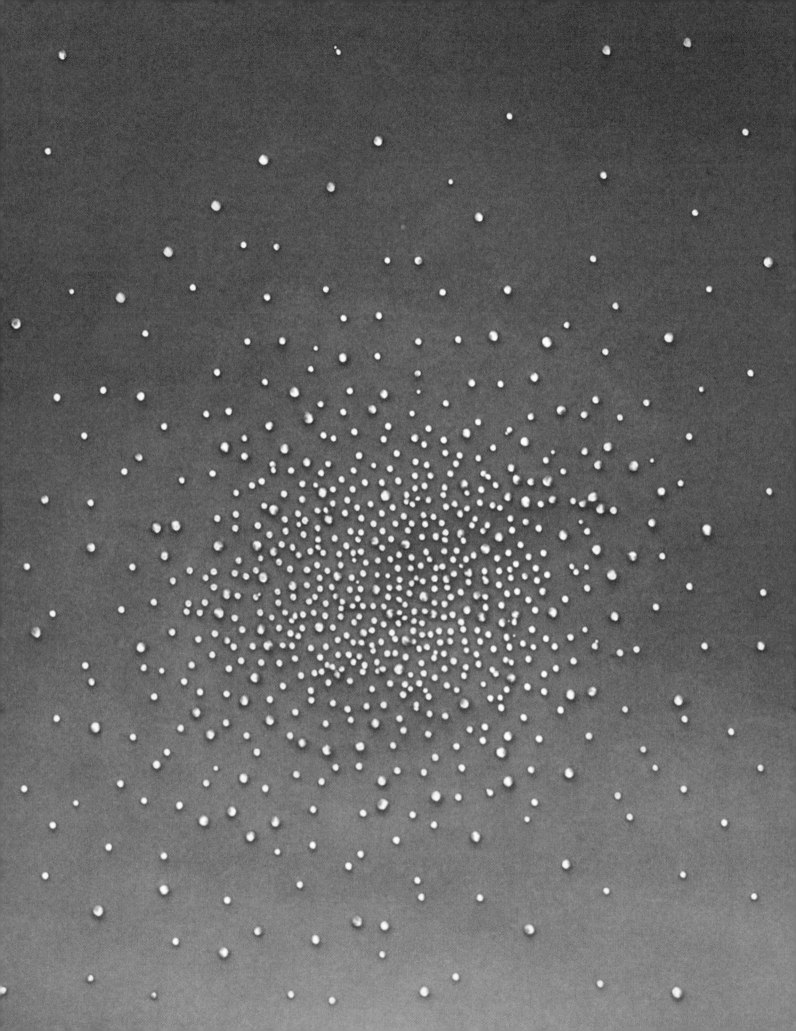

WELCOME

Dear Rookies,

Welcome to *Yearbook Four*! This book compiles the best of our website's senior year, and I've been graduated from high school and living alone in a new city for the duration of it. I am often asked if this transition into adulthood—of mine and our very first readers—means one for Rookie, too. Not only do I struggle to know what that would look like ("I came up with this month's theme while gazing out at the Manhattan skyline from my bedazzled fire escape when I said to myself, *Girl, you can vote, buy fireworks, and sign a lease. Now go take that city—and your residual standardized testing anxiety—by storm!!!*"), but I am also learning that while It *does* Get Better, some things get worse; other things just transfer "teenage" (human) feelings over to a scenario that is only more "grown-up" in some artificial sense. I always knew adults who said they read Rookie were not developmentally stunted weirdos; that what is at the heart of the work you see in all four Yearbooks is not a celebration of the glory days of high school but an earnest look at what it means to be a person, zeroed in on one's first encounters with such a question, which sometimes manifest as a history of slumber party games (page 108) or thank-you notes to Zayn Malik (page 244). There is life after high school and you can throw this all away if you so please (see: "Don't Stay in School," page 88), but I think what's truly special about this time in a person's life is that it's when you begin to code your own DNA. You're reevaluating what you learned in childhood, seeing adults in a more critical light, gaining agency in deciding who you want to be, and experiencing the joys of not knowing for sure. Some of these friendships are fleeting, some of these obsessions are "just a phase," but they are all important. And this time around, what's left is what you choose to keep. It's like an exercise playwright Annie Baker has her students do when they feel they've lost their writing voice, to transcribe a conversation from memory—"And that's it. That's you listening to the world," ("Just Saying," *The New Yorker*, February 2013).

 I wrote in the "Faith" editor's letter for *Yearbook Two* that the closest thing I have to the sense that someone, somewhere is watching over me is the knowledge that everything I could possibly feel has been articulated by another human being in art. Editing the stories that go up on Rookie every day is a daily practice in this religion, and going back to choose what would go in each book is a tortuous ritual. It was hardest this time around, knowing that, in the tradition of actual high school yearbooks, the senior one would be the last. But I am deeply proud of everything in here, and I really hope you love it, too. I tried listing my favorites but it turned out to be the entire table of contents. It also has way more print-only features than any of our other books, making it both way more special as well as economical! (*Ka-ching* sound, *100* emoji.)

 Rookie will continue to chug along in its many forms, providing writing and art that I hope can be of use to your DNA-coding. I can't thank you enough for everything you've already done to make Rookie not just a one-way stream of ideas but an actual community. From Solange's interview at the end of this book: "Opening up that support system and camaraderie becomes a force—it's invaluable." That's you. That's us. Thank you. Thank you. Thank you.

Love,
Tavi

Design by Sonia. Title lettering by Cynthia. Salt-N-Pepa, Abbi Jacobson, and Ilana Glazer portraits by Leanna. Photos by Shriya. De La Soul, Talking Heads, and ESG album covers and doodles by Isabel.

JUNE 2014: ACTION

SCHOOL'S OUT, ROOKIES! And, for me and any fellow graduates, it's out FOREVER!

I have nothing to reflect upon, no nuggets to share, no eulogizing to do. I'm just *done*! Like, on the left is a selfie I took the night before my last day of school, mindfucked by life and change and what it all means, and here I am on the right at the moment after the final bell rang, totally excited by life and change and what it all means!

I have appreciated this four-year chunk of life and the time I spent trying to understand it all more than I can express, but if I attempt to process any of it now, or even put on a song I used to like, I am overcome with guilt over the idea that I might be keeping myself from all the people I'm about to become and all the lives I've yet to lead, and I do not want to die with any of my potential untapped.

I don't know if I would be this hell-bent on being hell-bent if I didn't have the motivation of heartbreak. One poem I've written out a few times just to better ingrain the words in my 'tude is "You see, I want a lot" by Rainer Maria Rilke, which serves as a reminder that there is always time to explore your inner world, where life "calmly gives out its own secret."

I've also been finding comfort and fuel in Emily Brontë's "Remembrance," which acutely captures the temptation of indulging in nostalgia when an inevitable change is upon us. Then the poem basically becomes Fergie's "Big Girls Don't Cry" when Brontë says she will no longer "indulge in memory's rapturous pain," in other words, "I kind of just need to get on with my life, now, though." Two more I really want to share with you in case you don't know them and you too are in a transitional phase and need something that feels comforting and familiar but new enough to get you where you're going: "As I Walked Out One Evening" by W.H. Auden and "here's to opening and upward" by e.e. cummings. I've been writing out my favorite parts of these poems on notecards and posters and taping them up all over my room because I think that's supposed to help you know/feel something on an emotional level that you may currently know/feel on only an intellectual level. I get bashful when a friend sees my wall, and my sister teases me about it looking Pinterest-y, but seriously, it makes all the difference in the world to make a thought a tangible thing instead of expecting your body to learn *I am OK* just because the thought ran through your mind.

All of that is very much what this month's theme, ACTION, is about. For the most part, we just feel like Rookie already has so much content about reflecting on your past and preparing for the future; we wanted to do a month that's purely about NOW. But I also hope that, by the end of it, you too will come to feel a kind of unbreakable Bob the Builder determination to fill your brain and space with the things you need.

This month is about living in the moment in that way that only seems possible in the summer. Flirting with people you're shy around, really dancing instead of just doing the Social Sway, dumb but so important low-fi friend adventures, testing your own limits. The arcade. Roller coasters. Block parties. Showdowns and dance-offs. *Broad City*, Tom Tom Club, ESG, Le Tigre, Salt-N-Pepa and their devotion to a "don't think twice" lifestyle. Going for days without using the internet because you're just, like, sleepovers every night.

Action like sex, impulsive sex, purely physical, non-emotional sex. Action like being direct in how you communicate with others, be it in a get-what-you-want career way or in a romantic relationship or with a guardian. Action like the power of visibility, of existing as someone consistently silenced and how refusing to go away is a radical act in and of itself. Action like picking yourself up after an unfortunate experience or just a bad day. Action like ridiculous self-pump-up stuff that we should all be doing because there's no reason not to say "I'm a badass bitch" in the mirror every day (me) (besides feeling ridiculous, but WHO CARES?). Last year when M.I.A. played at Pitchfork, there were a lot of people from my school that my friends and I just could not get away from, and finally I had to decide that I didn't really care if I looked stupid dancing—and that, of course, is when my dancing got rlly good.

I will leave you with this: After graduation yesterday, I went to my first ever High School Party. This isn't a braggy "dude, I was so wasted" story so much as it is just an "I am an idiot, and maybe know your limits with this stuff, but this one thing that happened was funny" type of cautionary tale. There was dancing/talking/kissing/vomiting, and then I came home, and my mom helped me get water and get into bed. This morning she told me I had said to her, after all her maternal caretaking, "You are, like, such a good friend." I spoke to my mother like she was some other dumb intoxicated teen!!

HAVE FUN AND STAY SAFE.

LOVE,
TAVI

Open All Night

Another round of pancakes in the wee hours with strangers.
By Brittany, Anaheed, Jenny, and Amy Rose.

In what has become an annual Rookie tradition, a bunch of us camped out at the International House of Pancakes for an entire night and interviewed every teenager we could find to learn what's on the mind of American Youth. Read on for a lot of drama, love, and actual tears!

11:56 PM
GERALDINE AND JULIAN

BRITTANY Have you two ever gotten in a fight?

GERALDINE [*Laughs*] We did! 'Cause when someone messes with my friends, I'm gonna fuck that person up.

ANAHEED [*To Julian*] Did you mess with one of her friends, or did someone mess with you?

JULIAN Someone messed with me last weekend. [*To Geraldine*] You tell it.

GERALDINE We went to this party that I was invited to. We get there, and it's a lot of people, but probably only one or two black people. As soon as we go in we all need to pee, so we go to the bathroom, and then we hear something outside breaking, like a lamp.

JULIAN But we were all in the bathroom. We were all peeing and taking pictures!

GERALDINE Like, cute stuff! So I was like, "They're gonna blame us 'cause we're all black and Hispanic."

JULIAN She totally called it.

GERALDINE As soon as we get out of the bathroom, the owner of the apartment blames us for the lamp breaking.

JULIAN He's like, "You guys gotta go."

GERALDINE OK, so we leave. But my friend forgets her phone, so we gotta go back inside and get it.

JULIAN And the owner of the apartment is still bitching about the lamp.

GERALDINE So we're in there trying to find my friend's phone, and the whole time he's still like bickering in our ears about the lamp and how we broke it. We find my friend's phone, but as we're leaving, the guy's still bickering, so what she did was—

JULIAN She takes the lamp—

GERALDINE She takes the lamp and breaks it more. So everyone starts running. I'm walking 'cause I don't care.

ANAHEED Are you laughing at this point, or are you scared?

GERALDINE I'm dying at this point. Then [the apartment owner] catches up to us and he goes straight for Julian, even though he wasn't the closest one. He could have grabbed me or someone else [more easily].

ANAHEED Why do you think he chose Julian?

JULIAN Maybe because of the color of my skin, but [*sarcastically*] I don't know—we don't want to jump to any conclusions.

GERALDINE Because there was another guy with us too, and he didn't go for him. I'm drunk at this point, so I don't know what's going on. The next thing I saw was the guy choking [Julian]! As soon as I saw that, I grabbed the guy and pushed him off and started punching him in the face.

BRITTANY AND ANAHEED [*In unison*] Oh my god.

GERALDINE [The guy] took his cigarette and was like, "I'm gonna burn your face." I'm like, "Do it," and I kept punching him.

ANAHEED Wow. Have you gotten in a lot of fights?

GERALDINE [*Laughs*] This was the first time in a while.

ANAHEED You are a loyal friend.

JULIAN A hero!

ANAHEED Don't get on her bad side, though, man.

JULIAN I won't. Don't worry about that.

12:31 AM
DANITA, SAPPHIRE, AND SHAUNA

JENNY You guys have really distinct styles. Where do you shop?

SAPPHIRE H&M, Zara.

JENNY Can you tell us a little bit about your piercings, and your…what do you call those? [*Points to Sapphire's ears.*]

SAPPHIRE Gauges.

JENNY They look so cool. When did you get started on piercing?

SAPPHIRE My first piercing? I think I was 16. I got my belly. And after that—

JENNY You were addicted.

SAPPHIRE Yeah.

BRITTANY [*To Danita and Shauna*] Do you guys have piercings?

DANITA I just got my belly pierced. [*Lifts her shirt to show her piercing.*]

JENNY When I got my ears pierced, I was screaming for like 20 minutes.

SHAUNA Pain don't fear me. I like it.

BRITTANY Do you guys have anything you want to say to our readers?

DANITA Being a teenager is one of the hardest things to go through.

SAPPHIRE Just make sure to have fun. Do what you want.

DANITA Don't let anybody stop you.

1:19 AM
ISAIAH, LEMUEL, JULISSA, AND KRYSTIE

AMY ROSE How do you guys know each other?

ISAIAH He's my best friend since we were like 13. Do you wanna know how we met?

AMY ROSE Yes.

ISAIAH It was so funny. We were going to class, and I was like, "Oh man, what's your name?" This was like the beginning of freshman year. Me and him was like boys ever since. Even after we got out of college—I mean, we've drifted, but we still stayed in contact. That's my nigga for life.

AMY ROSE What did you see in Lemuel that you didn't see in other people?

ISAIAH Loyalty, honesty…

LEMUEL We talked a lot about girls.

AMY ROSE Like, you would talk about it if one of you had a breakup?

ISAIAH Yeah, serious stuff like that. I had his back when he broke up with girls and he had my back when I was going through things with girls. That's why he's my homeboy for life. I can't ever see him not being my best friend.

JENNY Awww!

ISAIAH 'Cause this is my guy, I'm not even gonna front.

AMY ROSE And what do you guys usually do when you hang out?

ISAIAH Well this is the first time we invitin' our homegirls Julissa and Krystie to party.

AMY ROSE What's your number one thing you like to do when you go out?

KRYSTIE Go out dancing.

ISAIAH Salsa. Merengue.

KRYSTIE We twerk together.

AMY ROSE What was the best night you guys had in the last month?

KRYSTIE Today.

JULISSA Today? You think so?

KRYSTIE Yeah! It was a nice time.

3:04 AM
JOHN, DEREK, AND DOMINICK

AMY ROSE How'd you guys decide to come to IHOP?

DOMINICK We come here every time we go out!

JOHN 'Cause Derek loves IHOP.

DEREK I'm annoying because I do, I love IHOP.

JOHN Listen to this: For his 20th birthday, he wants to go to IHOP!

AMY ROSE Do you think they'll put a candle in pancakes for you?

DEREK Could you imagine? I would cry!

AMY ROSE Where did you guys grow up?

JOHN In Atlanta. In the country.

DEREK I grew up in Baltimore, Maryland.

DOMINICK I grew up in Michigan.

ANAHEED Shut up! Me too! What school did you go to?

DOMINICK I went to University of Detroit Jesuit. It's an all-boys high school.

DEREK I would be very uncomfortable as an expressive gay male to go to an all-boys school. Even though there would obviously be other gay people there…DOMI-

NICK There wasn't. It was a big frat house!

DEREK Gross. I could never.

AMY ROSE [To Dominick] What was that like for you?

DOMINICK I mean, I'm just not the type of person who can be bullied, because for the most part I got along with everyone. I was part of the Christian Service Society!

ANAHEED Were you Christian? Are you Christian?

DOMINICK I am. My family's Baptist Christian. My grandfather's a Baptist minister. But I consider myself more nonreligous.

JOHN What does your grandfather think of you?

DOMINICK He doesn't. And that's sad.

ANAHEED Are you out to him?

DOMINICK Yeah. With much of my family, it's just not very talked about. Like, I have a great relationship with my grandfather even though he totally [thinks] gay people are on the opposite side of the spectrum from the whole Christian religion. I guess it is sad that we don't talk about it, but that's kind of how we both survive. And I can't blame him—he's a man of his time. He still loves me. He calls me every day. He considers me a son.

ANAHEED Were there really no other out kids at your high school?

DOMINICK There were a few other out people at University of Detroit, but…I don't know, I was like that "acceptable gay kid."

ANAHEED Do you know what made them see you that way?

DOMINICK I don't know.

ANAHEED Is it because you're so pretty?

JOHN He *is* pretty!

ANAHEED He's beautiful.

JOHN It's annoying. It bothers me.

DOMINICK What? Stop!

JOHN It does!

DOMINICK I don't know. But, as you know, Michigan is very segregated. It's very black and white. And I grew up on very much the white-privilege side, but I was black, and I had a black family. So I can talk to anyone and get along with anyone.

AMY ROSE [To Derek and John] What about you guys?

DEREK I didn't really have to come out, which was kind of relieving.

ANAHEED Why didn't you have to come

out? Did your family already know?

DEREK Um, the coming out…my mom was in the basement washing clothes, and she asked me to come down there. She was like, "Derek, I'm not gonna tell you how to live your life or whatever, but the one thing that I want for you is to be safe." And that's all she said!

JOHN Awww!

ANAHEED Aw, she's a good mommy.

DEREK You're gonna make me cry! [*Actually tearing up*] She's like, "I'll always support you, whatever you do." I guess that was 10th grade, so I was maybe 17, 16?

DOMINICK I came out to my parents one night sophomore year. I just told them, like, "Listen, I'm gay." Then they texted me like, "What's your Facebook password?"

AMY ROSE Ohhhhh no.

ANAHEED Like you're gonna fall for that?

DOMINICK But I'm such an upfront person, I just gave it to them. I didn't care. I felt like I didn't have anything to hide. And then I remember in English class I got like a fucking paragraph from my mom.

ANAHEED What did she find?

DOMINICK So, my parents are very conservative. They found out I was drinking in high school, and they saw a message from the guy I was seeing at that point. They were like, "Oh my god, I can't believe you hid this from us for so long." My grandparents drove down that night from Michigan. To Virginia.

DEREK That sounds stressful.

DOMINICK It was *very* stressful. I've [since] had boyfriends, but we don't talk about it. But of course they know. It's just something they're not fully comfortable with. They have to work on it.

ANAHEED When's the last time you cried?

DOMINICK Yesterday. I was just crying over school and stuff.

DEREK I almost cried during *Scandal* last night. [*Everyone laughs*]

DEREK I cried the other day because I was sick, and I feel like, with a lot of people who come to New York, you end up becoming very independent. And the one time you can't be as independent as you need to be is when you're sick—and there's nothing you can do about it. So I cried because I wanted my mom to be here to

SONGS FOR GETTING READY TO GO OUT
By Amy Rose

1. Queen of the Pack – Patra
2. Alex Chilton – The Replacements
3. Super Trouper – ABBA
4. Hybrid Moments – Misfits
5. Ça Plane Pour Moi – Plastic Bertrand
6. Floods – Flin Flon
7. Roxy Roller – Nick Gilder
8. Happy Song – Baby's Gang
9. Hungry Like The Wolf – Duran Duran
10. Whenever, Wherever – Shakira
11. Maniac Dragstrip – Nation of Ulysses
12. I Wanna Be Your Lover – Prince
13. A Minha Menina – Os Mutantes
14. Come on Eileen – Dexys Midnight Runners
15. Out of Sight, Out of Mind – Shocking Blue
16. Rapture – Blondie
17. Hold Tight! – Dave Dee, Dozy, Beaky, Mick & Tich
18. Hot Freaks – Guided By Voices

take care of me.

ANAHEED Awww! John, do you remember the last time you cried?

JOHN It was probably like four months ago. I don't cry a lot. I was crying because I was happy.

ANAHEED What were you happy about?

JOHN I don't know. Life. I'm a happy person, so I get excited about life.

AMY ROSE Was there a moment that brought it out of you?

JOHN Probably getting paid for what I do.

DOMINICK Because you're doing something that you're passionate about.

JOHN Yeah. It made me happy, so I just had a moment. I'm like, *Thank you.*

AMY ROSE When did you move to New York?

JOHN Three years ago. I moved to New York from Atlanta because I wanted to go into fashion.

AMY ROSE What is the biggest difference between the two places?

JOHN Well, Atlanta was much slower than New York. New York is way faster.

AMY ROSE New York, where people accost you in booths to talk about pancakes and your lives.

JOHN Yeah! I just like the randomness about everything about New York. Things like this—this would never happen in Atlanta. Where you could just leave your apartment and get interviewed. This is like amazing to me. ☆

PEOPLE REVIEWS

Reviews of real people we've known, observed, or heard about.
By the Rookie staff

MARY GOLDENBERG

In July, I got a text from my 22-year-old cousin that said her brother, who is nine, received his first love letter. He had been hanging out at the county fair in their small rural town. The letter was delivered to him by a girl from his school, but it was from a girl about his age whom he didn't know and had never even seen before: Mary Goldenberg. In the letter (written in pencil, on both sides of one piece of paper), Mary Goldenberg explains that she'd seen my cousin at the fair and developed a "secret crush" on him. What follows are the clearest words that have ever been strung together as declarations of infatuation: "I like the way you walk and talk and dress and act." I like the way you walk and talk and dress and act! It still leaves me almost speechless in its simplicity and radical nerve. Mary Goldenberg tells my cousin that her favorite ride at the fair is the Tilt-a-Whirl, and that he should meet her at the picnic table near it at 7 PM. My young cousin was thoroughly freaked out by the letter and her invitation. He did not meet *anyone* at the picnic table. This made me sad, but then I realized: Wherever she is, Mary Goldenberg is going to be fine. —Lena
★ ★ ★ ★ ★

MISS HAVISHAM

One bright day, we (Lola and Gabby) were driving on New York City's West Side Highway, discussing affairs of the heart. Lola was talking about how her romantic life seemed divided into periods of babes and periods of darkness. She was in a period of such pitch-black darkness that she wondered if her babe days were behind her, like those of Miss Havisham, the crone in Charles Dickens's novel *Great Expectations*. Miss Havisham is jilted at the altar and spends the rest of her life wearing her wedding gown, shut inside her mansion with her moldering, uneaten wedding

cake—and to Lola, this sounded like a prospect worth celebrating.

Moments later, we saw her: MISS HAVISHAM HERSELF. A ghostly older woman was standing in the traffic island wearing a long white gown, her head draped in a veil of white and blue streamers. "Oh my god, it's Miss Havisham!!!!!" Gabby yelled. Lola hadn't screamed that much in broad daylight in a while.

Gabby gives Real-Life Miss Havisham four stars, withholding one star for potentially putting us in traffic danger. Lola rates Miss Havisham three stars, for making a striking impression but ultimately leaving us puzzled. Was Miss Havisham appearing to say, "No, Lola, I'M Miss Havisham. You're just upset because you haven't made out with someone in like three months." Or was she a specter of glory, showing Lola that she too could one day have a bold daytime look and enjoy a solitary neighborhood stroll? —Gabby and Lola
★ ★ ★ ★ / ★ ★ ★

SPANDEX MAN

I work in an office with an open floor plan—there are no offices or cubicles, and everyone can see everyone else at all times (ugh). The company I work for also is pretty laid-back. If a dress code exists, you wouldn't know it—especially not if you observed Spandex Man. No matter the weather, Spandex Man bikes to work, snugly encased in a bodysuit of white, skin-tight spandex. (The suit unzips down the chest, has no sleeves, and ends in a pair of long shorts.) Spandex Man strides into the office each morning, helmet still on, cycling shoes clacking on the floor…wearing only the spandex leotard thing. He then spends up to an hour walking around. Imagine glancing up from your work to see two globes of man-butt sauntering past, knowing just a few atoms of heroic fabric stand

between you and a male co-worker's genitals. Imagine if a woman wore something like this to her office, even for one second. Spandex Man, after he finally changes into his work clothes, stores his spandex suit in the coatroom, and not a day has passed that I didn't walk by it without thinking of destroying it. "Soon," I whisper as I walk past its limp form. "Soon." —Krista
★ ★ ★ ★ ★

THE ULTIMATE DIVA

I was driving around Ojai, California, with my friend Shaun, and as we passed a bus stop, he asked me if I saw the lady sitting on the bench. I said no, and he replied, "OK, we're turning this car around." We circled back and there she was…an elegant elderly lady wearing a white fur coat, white leggings, and red boots. Her white hair was long and parted down the middle, and she had on hot-pink lipstick and vintage-looking red-rimmed sunglasses. She was the ultimate diva. I looked at Shaun and shouted, "ARE WE SEEING MY FUTURE GLAMOROUS SELF, OR WHAT!!!!!" —Marie
★ ★ ★ ★ ★

LITTLE BOY AT THE DRINKING FOUNTAIN

After a long walk around Lake Harriet in Minneapolis, I stopped for some water. As I approached a drinking fountain, a little red-headed boy ran ahead of me. I thought he was cutting. But: He was rushing so he could hold down the drinking fountain's button for me! In the cutest voice he said, "Drink up!" and kept pressing the button while I sipped. I imagine that he was hanging around the fountain waiting for people, so he could help them hydrate. My first impression of him was *What a cute little boy!*, then *This kid's rude!*, then finally: *He's the sweetest li'l guy in the world!* —Kelly
★ ★ ★ ★ ★ 🦋

AGE OF CONSENT

Sex involves a lot of "Yes" and "No" questions.
By Amy Rose

Sexual consent is a verbal go-ahead that tells someone, "What we're doing with our bodies is OK with me." It should be given before not only sex involving penetration, but so many other kinds of sensual scenarios, too. It's an important part of getting down with anybody, of any gender or sexual persuasion, every single time. In fact, it's probably the most important part: If you're in a physical situation where another person ignores you when you tell them not to touch you how they're touching you, what you're experiencing isn't sex (a catch-all term I'm using here for hookups of all stripes), but sexual assault. There is a plethora of ways to give and receive consent—and to refuse it. We'll explore as many of them as we can here today. Is that OK with you? (Look! We've already begun! I wish it were always this easy.)

While it may seem obvious that consent applies to far more than "Can I sexually freaq your bod, or…?" too many of us have been with people who don't understand that getting a clear go-ahead is as necessary for relatively low-impact activities, like kissing, as it is for sexual bod-freaqing. In moments spent with those people, the inside of my adolescent brain mostly sounded like *Wait, what the literal heck, I thought this person LIKED ME, so WHY IS HE TRYING TO HARASS MY LAP OUT OF NOWHERE, do I go with this weird crotchvasion or risk losing his company forever? Can we just go back to thinking that biting each other's lips a little was the craziest this was going to get, please? Plus, am I strong enough to overpower him if I have to?* This is not what the internal monologue of a person given over to erotic ecstasy sounds like, Alex from gym class whom I made out with because I was bored! Thanks for the panic attack!

When someone instigates sexual contact that you haven't agreed to, it can be tough to unscramble how you feel—let alone to figure out what to do. First of all, that's totally normal, and second of all, it has got to change, because I want you to have fulfilling, electrifyingly hot encounters *of the flesh* (ew, this expression) without feeling pressured, uncomfortable, or, heaven forbid, endangered along the way. Or like you're some kind of frumped-out killjoy for simply saying no, because YOU AREN'T. You know better than anyone else what feels good and manageable to you and what doesn't. (And this would be true *even if* Mark Ruffalo somehow merged with Sappho into a single entity, and that being was like, "…Hhhhello there, allow me to playfully lick you on the forearm, my dove.") You have the absolute right to broadcast these nonnegotiable preferences to every individual to whom you decide to affix your various and sundry (and sultry, my dove) body parts. No lap-harassment or weird crotchvasions necessary. Unless that's what you're into.

On the whole, my decade-long history of bod-freaqing, etc., has been wild enjoyable. (I know, I am a very cool sex-haver, CHECK OUT MY COOL-GUY HAIRSTYLE AND STYLISH DENIM JEANS.) I've also had some less-than-sterling, and occasionally downright fucking awful, experiences with partners who didn't seem to consider whether I was all right with what was happening between us. Here's an abridged list of illustrative quotations from *Remembrances of Bone Zones Past*, my mental encyclopedia of belt notches (this is not to be confused with Proust's classic literary masterpiece, which was definitely at high risk of happening here):

• "I didn't think you wanted me to use a condom."

• "Just relax. You'll like it."
• "You were OK with it last time."
• "I forgot you weren't into that."
• "This is the only way it feels good for me."

All of these are real-life toilet sentences, which were uttered by real-life toilet-worshippers, after I protested some dubious piece of the "action" we were getting. Sometimes these people were also actual rapists (because, straight up, anyone who disregards your not wanting to have sex, or coerces you into it after you say no, fits this description). Although these phrases were deployed in different scenarios, for ostensibly different reasons, each one says, "I don't care what you want, even though you just directly told me that it isn't this, and I don't respect you as a person more than I do my own horniness in this one moment." Taking on this attitude in any situation, but especially a sexual one, is *wholly unacceptable*, because it means you're trying to make someone else feel bad for *your* shitty behavior. (Not, you know, *you*, but some Alex-from-gym-class-style toilet loser whom I'm now itching to destroy even though he's a hypothetical person I just made up.)

I know *you* (real you, this time) wouldn't be the kind of selfish cretin who thinks that way, but if you find yourself in a situation where some scumbag is reciting a passage from this grisly chapter of my *RoBZP* to you, please understand that you have done NOTHING wrong, even though said scum is trying to make you feel guilty about the fact that they've decided it's OK for you to feel unhappy/uncomfortable/unsafe as long as they're getting off. The idea of even the potential of that happening to you makes me want to kick over seven trash cans, mail a congressperson a stink bomb, and yell obscene, hideous things at a beautiful phenomenon of nature—ideally a canyon, but definitely a majestic, centuries-old sycamore, at least—in addition to my previous crimes against fictional predators.

You are entirely within your rights to let anyone trying to pull that garbage know that they are acting like a human-shaped column of excrement, and then extricate yourself from the scene immediately. (We'll go into this more specifically in a bit.) I also want to halt for a sec and acknowledge that, in some terrible, wrenching situations, some of which I know firsthand, this self-extrication is not an option. (I have no denim-based quips about my experience this time, though. It was just awful and that's it.) As you hopefully know, rape and sexual assault are never caused by the victim's behavior—they are a result of the rapist's inhumane violence, and there is nothing you can do in this life to "deserve" or "invite" that. Another forever-true side note: You have an inarguable right to stop fooling around with somebody if you're no longer into it, regardless of how respectful the other person is being. You don't need a "reason" or "excuse" to not want to get with somebody, and you don't owe anyone a goddamn thing in that respect, ever. No one has any claim on your body but you.

It also has to be noted that there are circumstances in which it's not legally possible to give consent, no matter what you say or how you feel in the moment. This is a good thing. In the United States, you can't legally consent to sex if you're under a certain age (which varies from state to state) and having sex with an adult, when you're drunk or high, when you've been coerced into sex, or when you're asleep or otherwise unconscious. (And if you've been the victim of any type of nonconsensual sexual encounter, take a look at the website for the Rape, Abuse & Incest National Network [rainn.org], which has a slew of resources that you might find helpful.)

I don't want to scare you off sex forever with this talk—truly, most people are not angling to put each other in these kinds of scenarios, but if we're going to have this consent-versation, we have to talk about the fact that consent isn't always

a given, even in the most mutually loving encounters. I think that's partly because it can seem like a scary conversation to have. (This is a shame, since explicitly consensual sex is good, healthy, and the crowd favorite among highly skilled and respectful hookup candidates who want only wonderful, hot, and pleasant things for one another.) I've had myriad physical experiences with resolutely decent types who just didn't seem to know how to address the subject in a proactive and sexy way, *especially* not in the heat of the moment. I have also been this species of person myself! I don't think everyone who stumbles when it comes to discussing consent is a rapist/predatory beast—many have never even been told they have to think about it; others don't know how to bring it up without getting skittish, feeling prim, worrying they're killing some kind of moment/boner, or otherwise shutting down. This makes me sad, because I think avoiding the topic of consent because it's "uncomfortable" actually steers people into the exact awkwardness they're trying to avoid: It leads to situations where two hotties who set out to have a great time together end up snarled in a morass of anxiety, which is, at least from the maps I've drawn up in my *RoBZP*, not usually their intended destination. And it sincerely doesn't have to be like this—in most cases, it is so easy for it NOT to be like this! You just have to give each other some simple directions.

At its best, sex, or making out, or touching regions, or whatever affectionate physical contact you're enjoying with another personage, is communicative and instructive in tons of ways. Every person has their own motions, methods, preferences, and modes when it comes to all these lovely exercises. Learning someone's personal specificities—and having them learn yours—can (and will) be rad and edifying. One important condition on which all this is predicated, though, is mutual respect, which—guess what—comes from mutual consent.

You don't have to chuck spontaneity in the garbage disposal mid-hookup to instigate a heart-to-pelvis conversation about your entire sexual history and interior life

(although if that's what you need to do to feel comfortable about being physical with another person, *do it right up* without giving it a second thought). But no matter how free 'n' breezy (or otherwise reminiscent of a feminine hygiene–centric commercial) your encounter, you still have to pay attention to and interpret physical and verbal signals, respond to cues, and intermittently ask questions. Those are the basics (but, trust your girl, we'll delve deeper in just a moment). Speaking up is so much easier—and so much more effective—than wordlessly removing someone's hand from a part of your body where you'd rather not have it fluttering around (although, frankly, your partner should get the message from that alone).

Sex, for all its virtues, is weird (which is also frequently one of its virtues). It can be hard to know what another person likes, wants, or is thinking, or whether they're able to gauge what you like, want, or are thinking without an explicit, out-loud announcement from you (and vice versa). Such announcements can be especially hard for girls and women to make, because we've usually been taught that we should be "good," which means submitting to authority, which means not voicing our own desires or protests. This, in a sexual setting, can manifest as remaining passive as someone else does things *to* you, instead of allowing yourself to be an autonomous participant capable of gross, strange, amazing lustful passion just like everybody else. But, as you know, you are capable of all kinds of desires, and of voicing your concerns in the spirit of self-protection. What's more, your partner needs to be protected, too, and it's crucial to ask them the same consent-based questions that you require of them. Once you get into the habit of verbalizing that murky stuff, it'll be a massive relief and will lead to waaaaay more enjoyable, less intimidating *intimate encounters*.

The first tenet of consent: Each "yes" you give is one-time-use-only. By that I mean that since you are a person with mutable feelings, you might want to do something one day with one person in one setting, but you're not bound to want that same thing on any other day in any other

setting with that person or anyone else. You are not being unreasonable or prudish if you decide to (a) draw the line and/or (b) change your mind, at *any time*.

If you plan on having a sex life, you're going to be giving a LOT of consent, so it's time we delved into some specific ideas about HOW to give it—and how to clearly withhold it. The ideal time to talk about your sexual limitations is *before* you're embroiled in a physical situation where someone might be straining them. If you're able to have a conversation with the person you're potentially going to be intimate with prior to acting on whatever that means for you, you can tell them exactly what you do and don't want to do. When I started seeing my first long-term boyfriend, we spent a lot of time talking before anything beyond entry-level kissing took place, and while most of that conversation probably concerned our differences of opinion regarding what the best episode of *Curb Your Enthusiasm* was, we also asked each other plenty of questions about "how far we'd gone," that most classic of shy/sly high school sexual mile-marking systems. I told him that I hadn't ever had sex, among some other things that seemed intense to me at the time, and didn't want to until I was sure I loved someone and had been with them for a little while. In return, he told me about his history with sexual trauma, which made me rethink being rough with him in ways I would have otherwise thought playful. We knew each other's deals, and we didn't try to broker new ones mid-hookup. Learning to pretty much constantly ask, and respond honestly to, the question "Do you want to try [whatever new thing]?" and then actually respecting each other's answers was probably what made "losing" our virginities to each other after a few months so sweet and lovely—we were both stoked, happy, and comfortable, and totally aware that the other person was, too. We still had our Larry David–based differences, but all the other important stuff, we agreed on.

Not every sexual situation is going to be had in the context of a relationship, though. Soon after my first boyfriend became my first ex-boyfriend, I found that the same rules apply to scenarios where I attached my face to another person's whose middle (or even last) name I didn't know! (ESCÁNDALO.) These experiences taught me plenty of frank, direct, flirtatious, and gentle ways to make consent a part of every hookup, regardless of how well I might know my co-hooker-upper. How you decide to approach the babes of your consensual and highly sexy future is up to you, but here are some pointers on how to score and feel great about it, how to make sure these future-babes are equally jazzed about what's going on, and what to do if things take a too-intense turn and you want to set them back on track.

If someone is touching you in a way that feels like too much (how you determine this is, as with most things related to sexual desire, highly subjective), tell them to change what they're doing, or to stop, if you prefer. If you're all right with the former, pull away a little and say something like "Do that [more slowly, or gently, or however you'd like them to change it], please." No matter what you say, don't couch it in language like "I don't think I want to do that yet" if you're actually *sure* you don't want to do that yet. You don't have to water down what you know in your heart/parts to be true, and your boundaries are not up for renegotiation unless you say, and *mean*, that they are.

In one of my frenches of yore, nothing much was "happening" that wasn't kissing, on the surface, but the francophile in question had me pressed up against a wall in a way that I found a little too *impassioned*, even though I was otherwise enjoying the festivities. Getting specific about what wasn't working for me righted that weirdness: "Hey, can you back up a little?" goes a long way, and not in the sexually figurative sense. She got the message that I wanted to SLOW RIDE, TAKE IT EASY in that instance, although we had hooked up in explosive, grabby, and generally raunch-as-hell ways before. When dudes have rammed their tongues down my esophagus, which has happened a solid handful of times in my life, saying "Can you be a little gentler?" has been similarly effective.

If you say, "I like it when you slow down," and then that person doesn't, I advise you to bail—and this advice extends to not just kissing, but every kind of sexual contact. First and most important: Physically separate yourself from this person, since your comfort and safety come first, regardless of whatever the hell they're doing or saying to imply the contrary. Then, if you feel comfortable doing so, let them know *why* you're bailing, because they should be aware that their supremely jerky behavior is the reason they're about to be alone. Then, unless you have anything more you'd like to say, just *leave*.

Consent also includes protecting your physical health. You should always use some kind of barrier method that prevents STIs, like a condom, if you're having sex. To be extra-safe throughout your encounter, you should also periodically check to make sure that barrier method stays in place, too. People can be surprisingly and infuriatingly boneheaded about this! Once upon a night that started out promisingly, I caught someone I was with trying to remove a condom without telling me. What a nightmare, right? When he explained that he assumed I'd be "chill about it," I freaked. How dare anyone treat anyone else this way—and then be an idiot bro who tries to project his grossness onto me BY USING THE WORD *CHILL* AS AN ADJECTIVE. Yo, I became a banshee. I fucking hate that guy, and I wish I could tell the world his name so that he could see exactly how *chill* I am.

On the other end of the consensual spectrum, a recent hookup asked me if I'd gotten the Gardasil shot (an HPV vaccine). This sounds a lot less cool than it was, but trust me! I was kissing this person for the first time, and, even though it was unclear whether things would go further, he wanted to let me know before they did that he carried the virus, so any decisions I made that evening would be informed ones. "That's awesome of you to tell me," I said, a little too impressed. His response was even better: "It's not! I just think you have the right to know whether I could potentially be giving you something like that." That is exactly how to be! In case anyone tries to tell you that pausing a *sensuous sexperience* to ask questions, provide information, and/or make sure everything is cool with your partner "kills the mood," let me tell you, honesty made me like him even more, which is usually the case with any kind of sexual encounter—or life encounter in general.

Sex, like every other way of relating to another person, is at its very greatest when you and those you've chosen to hang around with are honest, listen to each other, and generally make a point of keeping kindness and respect at the forefront of your minds. I know that part won't be hard for you. I hope that, even though hooking up with other people can be unpredictable, you go into every situation knowing and trusting that, whatever your boundaries are, they're exactly the right ones to set. You know what you want—and so should anyone who has the privilege of being on the other end of whatever that means for you. Go get it.

SONGS FOR EXERTING CONTROL OVER YOUR SEXUALITY LIKE A BOSS BITCH
By Amy Rose

1. Cherry Bomb- Bratmobile

2. Switch- TLC

3. Romantic Call- Patra feat. Yo-yo

4. Contact- Brigitte Bardot

5. None of Your Business- Salt-N-Pepa

6. XXX- Helium

7. Partition- Beyoncé

8. She Bop- Cyndi Lauper

9. Muscles- Diana Ross

10. Cherry Bomb- The Runaways

STAND FOR SOMETHING

Checking back in with the Justice League.
Interviews by Jamia. Photography by Sandy.
All footwear by Dr. Martens.

Last year, we met these six lionhearted teenage girls, all of them committed to changing the world by standing up for what they believed in. I was curious about what they've been able to accomplish in the last 12 months, so I got back in touch. I learned that after a year of campaigns, graduations, and moves to faraway colleges, Diamond, Francesca, Nathania, Kisma, Alex, and Kodi are still bringing their determination and leadership with them wherever they go, expanding their reach, passing on their wisdom, and claiming their considerable power.

This generation—your generation—will change the world. You are not just our future, you are our here and NOW. You are the true inspiration.

 DIAMOND, 19

What have you been up to?

I left home for college—I'm at Bowdoin College, in Maine—and finished up my first year there. I'm a sophomore now. I've been continuing the work I did last year with the New York Civil Liberties Union, but on my college campus. Can I tell you about what I did over the summer?

Tell me!

My summer was really great. I received a grant from my school to work at the Children's Defense Fund. It was absolutely amazing! I did a lot of juvenile-justice and education-justice work there as an intern.

So, what are you standing for now?

Right now, I'm trying to get settled in with my classes, but I'm really trying to apply what I learned over the summer to my college. I've been trying to develop a concentrated support system for students with different passions, to help them create their own advocacy-based workshops where we can all learn from and support each other, and to raise awareness about different issues on campus—and outside the campus community, too. So I guess you could say I'm working on my own activist program!

What is it like being a woman of color in Maine, a state with so much less diversity than New York City?

It's different. If you come from an urban place like where I'm from—the Bronx—you don't really notice that you're black. Here, I do, because there are only a few of us. Sometimes you get self-conscious about how you act and how you talk. You keep yourself in check, in a way. But an upperclassman told me that's not my problem, and that I shouldn't care so much what other people think. You can just be yourself—you don't have to play up stereotypes, but if you fall into one of them, oh well, that's just you!

FRANCESCA, 18

What have you been standing for this year?

I stand for peace, equality, and having an awareness of the world around you.

How has being in college impacted your activism?

Since I've been in college, my activism has helped me stay balanced and grounded. And it taught me how to get involved on campus.

Last year, you were mentoring some girls, and you told me they taught you how to listen. Have you learned anything else about being a mentor since then?

I learned that being human is absolutely fine. In the past, I thought a mentor had to be Superwoman. I thought I had to be a perfect role model for the girls I was mentoring. Now I've found that by just being yourself, you can inspire other people to do the same. Your story can give people the opportunity to get to know you, and by telling it, you can encourage them to tell their own stories.

NATHANIA, 17

What are you standing for now?

I'm taking a stand against gender-based violence, school pushout, and street harassment.

Which of those issues are you most passionate about solving at this moment?

Street harassment. We've done a lot of work on it at youth rallies, but a lot of people still don't really think of it as an issue. I get harassed on the street every day. If I don't pay attention to the guys trying to harass me, they make threats. That is something I'm passionate about ending.

What is school pushout?

School pushout is basically young people not being able to finish their education because of a lack of resources, harsh discipline, or over-policing in the schools—factors created by the educational system that end up pushing students out before they graduate.

What does gender justice mean to you?

Gender justice means not worrying about being catcalled because you're a woman. Not being harassed or beat up because you're transgender. Or, if you're in school, not feeling like you can't try out for the football team because you're gay or transgender. It's about being comfortable in your own identity.

KISMA, 17

What are you standing for these days?

I'm taking a stand for women's health, because I want to be a nurse, and for women's education, internationally. Currently, I'm fighting to get women included in My Brother's Keeper [President Obama's initiative to give boys of color better educational opportunities]. And I still volunteer at Girls for Gender Equity.

Beyoncé donated $125,000 to Girls for Gender Equity earlier this year. What do

you think it means for pop culture figures to support gender-equity issues?

I think it's really inspiring and great, because a lot of females are afraid of the word feminism. There shouldn't be any fear of feminism. Feminism, on the basic level, is equality between males and females, and that's good.

How do you see your generation impacting the world right now?

I find that even though there's a lot of tension around [Michael Brown's shooting in]

Ferguson, My Brother's Keeper, stop-and-frisk, and other topics that affect young people, there's also a lot of activism happening around them. People are drawing attention to these things, which means they will inevitably change. I love that people are taking action, and I love that my generation is a generation that uses the internet to really fight for what we believe in.

What makes you feel most powerful?

The fact that I have knowledge that I can pass on to others.

ALEX, 18

What have you been up to since the last time we talked?

I kept working with the New York Civil Liberties Union's Teen Activist Project on recent issues around police brutality. There's been a lot of progress lately toward ending the stop-and-frisk practice in New York City, but there is more to do. In the spring, I worked on a photo project with NYCLU, documenting stories of everyday activism in New York City. It was sort of inspired by the Humans of New York project, but with a focus on activism. We talked to strangers on the street, found out what issues they were passionate about, and what they were doing to affect them. That was really fun. I also did some work with Hollaback!, trying to end street harassment of young people. And I'm still working with Teen Concerts NYC, which gives young musicians opportunities to perform in the city.

What are your plans for this coming year?

I'm trying to determine how I can still be involved in issues that I care about in New York City, now that I'm [going to college] in a very rural area in Massachusetts. How can I still be involved with improving police practices in New York, and ending discrimination against students in the city, from a distance? I'm still trying to figure everything out. Something I'm getting more involved in now is the environmental movement. I also plan on working on reproductive rights and issues around health and wellness.

Much of your work has been focused on ending discrimination against young people of color. What does being an ally—working on issues that may impact other communities more than your own—mean for you?

One thing it means is that I have to be constantly aware of the privileges I have because of my skin color. Another is to make sure that the people who are most affected by these issues speak first. Having thought a lot about these issues and having worked to try to end them, I have a lot to say about them, but the voices that are most important are always those of the people most directly impacted by them.

When have you felt most powerful in your activism?

When I've been passing something on. That feeling there's someone out there who's going to carry on your work, that it's no longer just "your project" but is actually going places—that's a really powerful feeling.

KODI, 18

What do you stand for today?

I'm speaking for the youth and speaking up for myself. I took a hiatus from activism, because I was working and getting ready for school, but then [the shooting and unrest in] Ferguson happened, and I joined a candlelight vigil to remember Michael Brown. That was very interesting, because I saw how youth are speaking up about current events and how passionate they are about making change.

How did those events get you back into activism?

They told me that I had to go twice as hard to stand up for my people, for boys of color.

What did you learn during your hiatus?

I learned that maybe I shouldn't take such a long hiatus! Because I've noticed that when you do that, you just come back with more things to stand up for.

What do you hope to accomplish this year?

Getting into more activist work, attending more protests, and speaking out more about the social issues that are happening now. Making my voice bigger, pretty much. ☺

the SEX CRYLEBRATION part II

Our resident embarrassment experts are BACK with all-new, queer-centric reassurances!
By Krista and Lola. Illustration by Esme.

This is our second Crylebration. Our first one, last year, was kind of a compendium of worst-case scenarios and embarrassing moments, designed to address your deep, lingering fears and rumors about all kinds of sex, and to answer questions like "What if I smell bad?" "What if my mouth gets tired during oral?" and "What if I fart/burp/bleed?"

This year's Crylebration focuses on queer sex, and is more of a beginner's guide (don't worry, we threw in lots of juicy, embarrassing real-life moments). Because if you thought hetero sex was mysterious, consider how much less often you see any other kind of sex in movies, on TV, in advertisements, etc. This time around, the questions were not so much nightmare-scenario paranoia; they were more basic, like "HOW???" So, here's how.

"I'M A GIRL, AND I KISSED MY FRIEND WHO'S A GIRL. AM I GAY NOW?"

LOLA The short answer is "nope." You can identify however you like, regardless of what physical action you're getting—or not getting. The only determining factor is *what you feel is true.*

KRISTA Nothing you do "makes you" gay. If you're a girl and you kiss another girl, there is not some invisible gay-radiation-filled ink that suddenly sprays all over you and turns you into lesbians right then and there. You are not a different person after

a non-hetero snuggling session, or a make-out, or even sex—you are still *you*, regardless of the gender of the other person, and only you get to decide whether or not you're gay (or whatever other orientation feels right!), and only if/when you're ready. There is literally nothing you can do that will lock you into a label forever.

LOLA Which is not to say that there won't be any rapids in the river. Claiming your identity can be a scary process, because then it suddenly feels *very real*, and *what if you change your mind?*

KRISTA When I first suspected I might be bisexual, or even (gasp!) a lesbian, I was 18, and I was terrified. I had this vague idea that being a lesbian was "bad," possibly a gift from my conservative religious upbringing. I'd lie in bed and whisper "lesbian" like 10,000 times in the dark, or repeat it alone in my car. I was trying to get used to the word, and the idea that that word could be me. "I'm bi," I practiced saying to no one. "I'm a lesbian." What did it mean? Could I be *me* while belonging to a huge, scary-seeming label like that? (I could, and I do.)

LOLA Between the ages of 13 and 23, I only partnered up with cis dudes. (*Cis* refers to people whose gender identity matches the gender they were assigned at birth.) This did not make me straight! Just like none of these True Stories "made me queer":

Thirteen: Made out with a girl whose house I was sleeping over at.
Fourteen: A classmate accused me of being

a "lesbo slut with scary friends" on AIM.
Sixteen: Had sex with a girl.
Twenty-two: Felt my heterosexuality was a book I had grown bored of, but was too far into to stop reading.
Twenty-three: Developed the distinct and unceasing urge to go down on a girl until I glowed in the dark.

Like the poet Andrea Gibson says in her poem "Andrew," "No, I'm not gay. No, I'm not straight, and I'm sure as hell not bisexual, damn it! I am whatever I am when I am it, loving whoever you are when the stars shine and whoever you'll be when the sun rises."

Figuring out your sexual identity can be a long process, which is how it was for my friend Heather, who was ultimately rewarded for her many years of trying:

LIVED TO BONE ANOTHER DAY: HEATHER

Growing up, I dumped boyfriend after boyfriend and felt absolutely nothing about it. While I occasionally entertained fantasies about my high school's head cheerleader, I never connected my failure to be "in love" with sexual orientation. Since being gay never occurred to me, I assumed I was some kind of unfeeling sociopath! In college (and only after many years of therapy), I realized I might actually be a lesbian. My hypothesis went unconfirmed until I met a totally great lady...and froze. What if I made out with her and I didn't

feel *anything*? Then I'd know for sure I was a sociopath. I'm happy to say I went for it anyway, and it was good (sometimes even great). For the first time in my life, I felt present and engaged in a romantic scenario.

"WHAT DO I EVEN DO IN BED IF I'M NOT STRAIGHT?!"

KRISTA This question is not so much "How do queer people have sex?" Na-uh. It's more "How *don't* we have sex?" We use our fingers, tongues, mouths, legs, genitals, butts, chests, and—most important—BRAINS. Fingers, tongues, and toys can explore the various openings, crevices, and sensitive areas on most people, and queer people, like all people, have sex by stimulating some (or all) of those places.

The word *sex* is not defined exclusively by a penis entering a vagina—hellllllll no. Sex can mean a lot of things, but best believe: Queer sex, however you're having it, is "real" sex. Nobody can tell me that hours of sweaty, hot, orgasm-after-orgasm-inducing mattress sessions with another person "don't count" as "real sex" because my partner and I are not having P-in-V sex.

LOLA Queer sex can include P-in-V, too—it just doesn't have to. But before we go any further, promise us you're not going to do *any* of these things without getting consent from your partner! Everybody involved needs to be 100 percent on board with what everyone's doing, 100 percent of the time. You're not waiting to hear a "no" from your partner before you stop what you're doing; you want to hear a "FUCK YES."

KRISTA But how do you know if you have enthusiastic consent from your partner? Lola and I will model it for you right now!

LOLA Krista, I'm so excited to be DOIN' IT with you for educational purposes. I can't believe that we chose matching sheer pink nightgowns! And yet…I can.

KRISTA Lola! SO THRILLED to be goin' at it with you in demo form as well! You look stunning in pink, my dear. Here are some sensual finger foods, such as grapes

and Gushers-brand fruit snacks, for us to snack on.

LOLA I consume these delicacies with gusto. Now, perhaps we may consume each other. Would you like to get started?

KRISTA Yes, darling.

[*Time passes…*]

KRISTA OK: We have now been making out for hours on your cheetah-print couch, and I have rubbed my face raw on your ruby lips. I have a feeling you'd like to take things to the next level. I am aching to have sexytimes with you, but I have never done this before.

LOLA Luckily, we've talked beforehand about how you've never really hooked up with a girl before, because we both know that the best time to deal with any sort of negotiation is before a decision is required. I got a good sense of what your boundaries are, as well a ton of hot ideas, from that conversation.

KRISTA [*Pops Gusher into mouth and chews in a sensuous manner*] I love how well we communicate. But, honestly, I'm still a little nervous.

LOLA So am I, because I approach each new person—actually, every new sexual encounter—the same way: with as few assumptions as possible about what the other person might like or want. Beyond a possible slight advantage in technical fluency/muscle memory, my sexual experience doesn't really matter. Krista, *you* matter. What do you like? Talk to me about what you want me to do for you right now.

KRISTA …I'm not sure? I dunno…um… OK I FEEL STUPID HELP ACKKKK! [*Starts freaking out and shutting down.*]

LOLA Yo, Krista, I can tell you're into me and want to consummate our demonstration, but even though you're not saying no, you're not saying yes, and just "letting" me do something isn't giving consent. Are you OK? Do you want to keep kissing for a while?

KRISTA Oh, Lola. I'm so glad you checked in with me. It's not that I don't want to move on to the possible glorious finger-banging/passionate oral sex portion of our

demo session, but I'm hesitant to say what I want out loud—I might need some time. Kissing you would be just perfect for now!

"WHAT IF MY PARTNER IS SECRETLY LIKE, EW, SHE'S DOING IT WRONG?"

LOLA (BUT HER HAIR'S ALL MESSED UP NOW) Whew! So, in summation, don't do a sex thing because you heard it works, or because you made an assumption about someone's body, or you saw it in porn. In what other domain would people do things exactly as they saw them happen in a movie once? "Oh, I took you whitewater rafting because I saw it in a movie." "But I hate whitewater rafting!" "Well, the girl in the movie kind of looked like you, so I figured you would like it, too." *I can't swim, this date sucks, and I want to break up with this person.*

Doing stuff with a real live person isn't going to be a face-off between your "weird" sex map vs. their "normal" one. Even in the most casual encounters, people shouldn't just be "having sex." They should be having sex with EACH OTHER, specifically! You've got a certain way of getting off, and so will your partner. Every single person in this world gets off in a different way! When you get there, how will you figure out what your partner likes, or help them figure out what you like?

KRISTA There is just no "right" way to have queer sex, except however feels really good. I mean, funny stuff and mistakes can happen during sex (and, trust me, we'll discuss those!), but rubber-stamping a whole encounter as WRONG? Nope! Not unless your idea of queer sex is, like, going to feed ducks at the pond. Thaaaaat might be construed as "wrong," from a sexual standpoint.

LOLA As an honest and intentional practitioner of celibacy right now, I'd like to respectfully interject my support for the feeding of ducks as an expression of queer sexuality.

KRISTA Interjection accepted—since every-

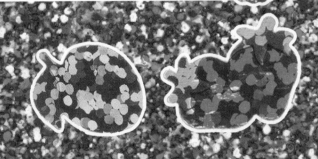

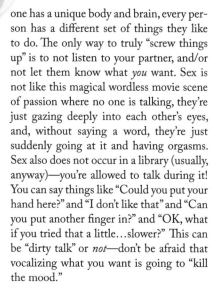

one has a unique body and brain, every person has a different set of things they like to do. The only way to truly "screw things up" is to not listen to your partner, and/or not let them know what *you* want. Sex is not like this magical wordless movie scene of passion where no one is talking, they're just gazing deeply into each other's eyes, and, without saying a word, they're just suddenly going at it and having orgasms. Sex also does not occur in a library (usually, anyway)—you're allowed to talk during it! You can say things like "Could you put your hand here?" and "I don't like that" and "Can you put another finger in?" and "OK, what if you tried that a little…slower?" This can be "dirty talk" or *not*—don't be afraid that vocalizing what you want is going to "kill the mood."

"WHAT IF MY PARTNER WANTS ME TO GO DOWN ON THEM, BUT I DON'T KNOW HOW? WHAT IF I DO ORAL SEX WRONG?"

KRISTA OK. You really, really, really want to go down on your partner. You have your partner's enthusiastic consent. And you are…nervous! What if you're bad at this?! Before we dive headlong (ha!) into this one, you know that oral sex isn't the be-all and end-all for queer sex, right? It's just one of the many, many ways that humans have sex. (Personally, oral sex is waaaaay lower on my list of likes than other stuff.) That being said: Should your partner be into having a tongue on their parts, it's hard to screw it up.

By now, you're probably like, "Cool, Krista, thank you ever so much for being vague! Also, this is the first time I've heard that oral is failproof—I don't even trust you, maybe," and you are getting ready to leave. Come back! I'll give you details, OK? Graphic details! We're mostly going to be engaging in vagina talk here, but a lot of this info applies to people without vaginas. First thing to know: It's totally OK to wait as long as you like to have oral sex. No pressure, y'all!

Next: *Wanting* to be good at oral sex is the first step! Enthusiasm is a huge turn-on for most people, so let your partner know how excited you are to go down on them! Now, if you have never seen or hung out with another person's undressed genitalia before, you may be a little bit scared. What if it looks weird? What if you don't like the way it smells? If you both identify as girls, what if you panic and FAIL LESBIANISM before you even start?

LOLA Like, WHAT THE FUCK AM I SUPPOSED TO DO WITH ALL THESE FOLDS? I'm sorry. Continue.

KRISTA Shhhh, my friend. Do not fear the vagina. It is your friend! It will reward you for your efforts. You simply cannot "fail" lesbianism, but if you're feeling a little overwhelmed right now at the thought of a naked vulva right in front of your face for the first time, there are a few things you can do to get a bit more comfortable.

One quick thing to know before we get into the nitty-gritty: Oral contact with another person's genitals can transmit things like herpes, chlamydia, gonorrhea, and in rare cases, HIV. Use a barrier method with anyone whose STI status you don't know.

On to oral sex! So you're down there, and it's go time. Go slow, and be gentle (at least at first). Don't be afraid to use your whole face, or to put your tongue on all different parts of your partner (unless they've specified otherwise). You're doing great! If your partner has a vagina, find their clitoris. Hint: If your partner is lying on their back, and you're between their legs, imagine everything between their whole undercarriage as a clock face—the clit is up at the top, at 12 o'clock. It looks like a little fleshy knob, about the size of the tip of your pinkie finger. (Some are bigger, some are smaller.) Sometimes it's hooded, with a little bit of skin covering it. Sometimes it's shiny and swollen.

What it isn't: a magical "make someone come" button that you can just grab and poke with abandon—it's a highly sensitive li'l bundle of nerve endings, so, again, be gentle! Lots of people like to have their clits played with, but some people's are so sensitive that they can't stand direct contact. While touching your partner, ask: "Does this feel good?" If yes, try lots of different licks. Try a long, sweeping, up-and-down lick on either side of your partner's clit, or flick it with your tongue—do they like that? And please, please, do not be afraid to ask, "Do you like that?" or "How's this?" no matter *what* you're doing!

Outside of straight-up *telling* you what they do or don't want, your partner will probably let you know in some more-subtle ways what's working for them. Keep in mind that most people don't make shrieky-excited noises like in the movies. A relaxed, pleased partner might lift their hips if they like what you're doing. They also might get wet, moan, and/or make other happy, sighing sounds. Again: EVERYBODY IS DIFFERENT!

In many cases, it's going to take longer than three minutes to make your partner come (if that's what you're both looking for out of the encounter). Your partner may not orgasm when you eat them out, or they may come like a ton of bricks. If they don't have an orgasm, you're not a failure—some people (hellloooo *waves*) have a hard time orgasming through oral sex. Also: Some people enjoy oral sex, but don't want to come that way, or at all. This doesn't mean it doesn't feel awesome!

"MY PARTNER ISN'T CISGENDER. WHAT IF I DO IT WRONG THEN?"

LOLA The best way to find out how to have sex with aaaannyyyy person is to ask that person about it and/or have them show you themselves.

KRISTA Just like in all areas of life: If you don't know, *ask*. Don't just sit there, quietly panicking. This applies to people of all genders, in all bodies, with any type of genitalia.

I asked my trans-identified friends MJ* and Tony* if they had anything to add, and they did:

LIVED TO BONE ANOTHER DAY: MJ AND TONY

MJ The first time with someone new can be stressful. The first few times a recent partner and I had sex, they didn't touch

---

* *These names have been changed.*

my bits, and it turned out that they were scared! But then there are people who don't ask if and where they can touch you *at all*, and they just go for it, and that can be bad, too. In general, it is always best to ask. With the caveat that everybody's different—sometimes trans-identified people get tired of explaining trans culture and history to newcomers.

TONY The worst sex I've ever had is with people who, instead of asking what they could and should do, didn't do *anything*. It's also really annoying when people comment on your body in an objectifying way. If someone is genuinely saying, "I'm so into this right now, this is so hot," that's great, but sometimes you can just feel when people are being creepy—like they're not into the actual *person* who is attached to all these body parts that turn them on.

If I could go back in time and give myself some advice, I'd say, "You will always be learning. Have sex with your friends."

MJ Yeah! Go slow, and be respectful of your partner—and don't put shit up about people on the internet.

KRISTA Hahaha, what?

MJ I just think that's important.

"WHAT IF I'M DOING IT RIGHT AND THEN SOMETHING SUPER EMBARRASSING HAPPENS??"

KRISTA Like what, boo? Like…getting your lip ring caught on your girlfriend's nose ring the very *second* her parents walk into the living room?

LIVED TO BONE ANOTHER DAY: KRISTA

My girlfriend's parents were in town, visiting her for the first time. They were *staying* with her, and my god, were they staying. They never left whatever room we happened to be in—*ever*. For days at a time, they were glued to our sides, never going out for a walk, never needing a nap. I was going home every night to sleep—even though her parents knew we were dating, at no point did I want them to think I was having *sex* with their daughter, no way.

Having them around all the time was

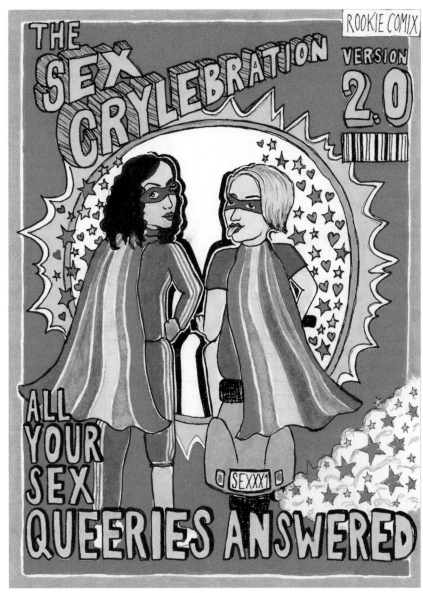

sheer exhaustion, compounded by pent-up new-relationship super-horniness. Then, miraculously, on Sunday afternoon, four days after they'd arrived, her parents *went to a coffee shop*. YES. It was just down the street, *but this was my chance*. I jumped on my girlfriend and we started making out hardcore, basically slobbering all over each other on the couch. I was on top of her, trying to eat her face, when it happened—the one thing my dad had warned me about when he saw my lip ring for the very first

time: "You're gonna get that caught on something and get hooked like a fish," he'd said. And he was right—I had gotten hooked, like a fish, ONTO MY GIRL-FRIEND'S NOSE RING. We were stuck! We couldn't detach our rings! Her parents would be back any minute!! We scrambled, frantically trying to unhook ourselves, in no little amount of pain. And then… THE FRONT DOOR OPENED. There I was, the person who was dying to make a polite and good first impression on my

girlfriend's folks, straddling their daughter on the couch, my lip hooked to her nose. *Of course*, as soon as her parents had taken in this whole scene, my girlfriend managed to detach us. I tumbled off of her. There was a silence.

"I think I'll make a cup of tea," her mom said. Then she walked into the kitchen.

…or when cooking a meal with Boo becomes a sensual recipe…FOR DISASTER?

LIVED TO BONE ANOTHER DAY: TONY (FROM BEFORE)

In the first month of my relationship with my current partner, she made us fish tacos at her house. After we ate dinner, we fooled around. Her hand was on my junk, and I started to feel this intense burning sensation. I didn't think I had suddenly caught an STI, so I thought, OK, I'm gonna just push through this, because I really wanted to have sex with her.

But then the pain got worse. I started to sweat, and every part of my vajay was on fire.

"You have to stop! My junk is burning!" I shouted. My partner was totally confused.

I asked if she may have handled anything spicy when she was making dinner. Then she said, "Wait…oh! I used cayenne pepper!" OH MY GOD. I don't know how this was my first reaction, but I was like, "Do you have any milk?" I was already in the shower by the time she returned with the carton. She handed it to me and I proceeded to pour all the milk over my burning junk—just loads of milk, it was so disgusting. But it worked! I was pissed for

a second, but then we went right back to fooling around.

…or finding out that the commotion in the hallway was your climax's personal cheering section?

LIVED TO BONE ANOTHER DAY: LOLA

My friend Z. was going down on me to terrific results, when, through my orgasm-haze, I became peripherally aware of the sound of movement and voices in the hallway. This was not unusual, as Z. lived with nine other people in an old-library-turned-feminist-art-collective with limited sound insulation. Later that night, Z. informed me that the noise was three of those nine roommates standing directly in front of her bedroom door, cheering me on and then, when I came, bursting into applause and celebratory high-fives.

What?

I never even considered this could happen and thus I was so mortified—as in mort, death, a corpse of embarrassment—that time slowed to a crawl. I reviewed my choices: *Should I apologize for being loud? Apologize for being born? Cry? Cry really hard? Laugh?* I laughed. And I was like, "That's right, I'm a fucking champion." And then she laughed too, and I barely ever thought about the incident again, except while fondly recalling great sex I've had in the past. If you're in a similar situation—confronted with a sex horror you could have never foretold—and you can muster a "That's right, I'm a fucking champion," even

if you have to imagine that you're in a movie about confidence, or that your convincing performance will save a kitten's eternal soul, even if you have to pretend you're ME, get a wig and do it, you goddamn shining star.

When you let it all out and just GO FOR THE GOLD, sometimes stuff like that is gonna happen. Or maybe even stuff like THIS:

(2) Krista Burton, lola pellegrino

i'm about to start the "What if something really embarrassing happens?" section
Krista Burton 10:17 PM
is there a more fun way to phrase that/?
me 10:17 PM
"What if my goddamn junk falls apart like an old jalopy at the crucial moment?"
Don't listen to me.
Krista Burton 10:18 PM
What if my privates crumble into dust or shoot out spiders
me 10:18 PM
"What if I'm secretly full of spiders?"
Krista Burton 10:18 PM
and someone looks up into my crotch and sees cobwebs????

Well…probably not that. But, hypothetically, if your privates were secretly full of spiders, what would you do? We'll tell you what: You would live through it. You hear us? You would live to bone again! Here's one last true thing about sex-having: You cannot die from embarrassment, even if you might want to. So go forth, young Rookies, and crylebrate! ♡

Remembrance of Bone Zones Past

By:

WHAT IS A BOY?

Show this primer on sexism, respect, and so much more to the dudes in your life.
By Charles Aaron

We are gathered today for a Rookie conversation of an uncommon sort: a no-scrubs airing-out of the ongoing struggle for boys/men to accord girls/women a baseline of respect, decency, awareness, and camaraderie from the guy's-eye-view, addressed to teenage boys, with the hope of reminding us all that we can be here for one another as loving humans if we just put our most empathetic brainwaves together.

Now, that jumbled, try-hard, not-sure-where-to-start introduction reveals a classic symptom of what brought us here in the first place. We dudes tend to have a hellacious time confronting our role in sexism. We defensively backpedal, complain, and brush the whole subject off as something bigger than all of us—*I, personally, am not the one refusing to pay women equally, after all!*—when it's actually all around us in not only obvious ways (like unequal pay), but in tougher-to-spot, more insidious ways, too.

Before we really get things started, let me assure you that this isn't about assuming that teenage boys have done something wrong. It doesn't do anybody any favors to generalize negatively when we're trying to honestly and openly deal with the forces that keep boys/men and girls/women in unnecessary conflict. But it's time for us guys to stop acting like we've got no personal responsibility here. It's not fair or right or even true to say, *Hey, this is how we were raised*, and, well, *our biology is beyond our control*, since *all this sexism stuff is a systemic problem anyway…*and, like, *we've got our own relationship problems to deal with*, so, yeah, *we're with you in spirit*. I hear all that (and have heard it for years), but real change can't happen without individual guys deciding to make good choices.

The goal here is not to be a Noble Selfless Martyr (boring! impossible!), but just to recognize the mechanics of how sexism hurts girls *and* boys, which can be tough to do amid the chaos of classes, jobs, and extracurriculars. This is about waking up and meeting the day with the genuine head-up confidence that comes from valuing your fellow person, instead of spending your free time building a flimsy, smirking, badass self-image that you know is bullshit.

I used to put this song called "We Are Each Other" on mixtapes. It was about a couple who had shared so many secrets as friends and were so much alike already that to be lovers felt almost weirdly redundant.

What that song always said to me was that boys and girls and men and women are mucking around in the same swamp of wants and desires. We are more alike than we know, and we need one another more than we care to say. And when you stop mucking for a second to think about that, it's actually a wonderful revelation!

Handshake agreement: Let's ditch the boys-will-be-boys, testosterone-made-me-do-it, no-harm-no-foul excuses. Instead, let's explore ways in which we can evolve from boys to men, but not according to some Don Draper version of manliness, e.g., knowing how to snap a left jab or efficiently change a flat or masterfully grill a steak or casually fire up a stogie, which, though all fine skills to have, are more suited to a picture of masculinity from a fictional 1959 than from the real 2014. This brand of manning-up will ask you guys to puff out your chests a little *less*.

I. I AM A CLICHÉ WHO LIVES NEXT DOOR

I'm not writing this because I'm some model image of a feminist man (which is impossible, anyway, since there's no such thing as a "perfect" feminist of any gender). I've spent my entire post-adolescent life wrestling with a very basic question: Why am I still such a sexist jerkus, repeatedly committing the same inane, hurtful blunders? I should know better. I *do* know better! Why am I regularly looking at women and immediately calculating their attractiveness on some bullshit scale that isn't even really mine? Why did I once, when leading a meeting of younger people who looked up to me for guidance, use the phrase "pussy out" to mean they shouldn't "lack courage" in some situation or another? There were young women in the room, and, yes, I did glance at them to see if they were laughing or uncomfortable. *Very funny.*

So, *why?* Why is sexism so deeply ingrained in me—in us—that it sometimes feels like we were born with it? Well, that's complicated (but we'll get to it). Please know that I write from a place of humility, not judgment, and that, as an adult, I'm still having to critique and adjust my own wack behavior. In fact, I've got no respect for people who don't embarrass themselves *regularly*—provided they learn from their screw-ups.

II. RAPE CULTURE 101

A quick crash course: "Rape culture" is not only about rape; it's the mindset that says boys deserve to have sex with any girl of their choosing, whenever and however they desire, and any girl should submit to those desires, or there's something wrong with *her*. Rape culture tells us that guys have a right to get mad when a girl doesn't want to sleep with us, because, hey, we flattered you by asking; and if a guy pays attention to a girl, she's required to at least smile appreciatively. Ummm, *no*.

Rape culture is why girls and women are told to ease up on the "revealing" clothing, to not accept drinks from strangers, to not walk anywhere alone at night, and, hey, maybe take some self-defense classes *just in case*. The thinking goes something like:

If women just got their shit together, this stuff wouldn't happen to them. This attitude leads people to make laws that blame victims and ignore the responsibility of *the men who are raping, harassing, and objectifying women.*

Let's be real: The premise that straight boys have some dudely entitlement to whichever female bodies they want to have sex with is sad and gross, and it's built on shaky, confining stereotypes that aren't good—or even possible to embody in full—for anyone.

Many people believe that boys are genetically coded to fight and hustle each other for the most desirable girls in the village in order to spread their seed repeatedly. I'm no scientist, but I've read enough to know that this theory (which is given perhaps its most nuanced, convincing defense in Robert Wright's book *The Moral Animal*) is in great dispute, to say the least. Do you really want to believe that we're all destined by natural selection to exist in a never-ending animalistic cycle of sexual manipulation and faithlessness? We can do better, guys.

I still cringe when I remember a scene that took place in a Miami hotel lobby many summers ago. I was sitting with a group of work acquaintances (including a couple of women), and I visibly leered at a complete stranger in a bikini and exclaimed, "God *damn!*" as she walked by. My female co-workers sneered in disgust, and I had to agree with them. I'd never even thought about catcalling a woman before, so why was I doing it now? When I think about it, that was around the time that I was really feeling myself for the first time as an adult— cool job, new girlfriend, all-expenses-paid business trip to South Beach. So, to celebrate, I guess, I decided to act like a depraved Wolf-Whistler of Wall Street, entitled to loudly assess a woman's body in public. Somewhere, I'd apparently learned to associate livin' large (at least my version) with acting like a colossal douchebag.

I've got no interest in blaming the broken-down scapegoat that is "society" for dumb behavior like this—it's important to accept responsibility for your own stupid decisions. But this d-bag impulse came from *somewhere.* It wasn't just a result of having grown up in a conservative small town in the South (though that was a big part of it).

Because I never really talked to family or friends about sex, I learned about it mostly from movies, TV shows, and music, which showcased grandiose, romanticized adventures about crass, bros-before-hos, hit-it-and-quit-it scenarios. I soaked in the exciting escapades of film Lotharios played by people like Tom Cruise and Sean Connery, who collected women like trophies, and the musical boasting of Led Zeppelin, N.W.A., and too many more to name. Porn also seeps into every part of our culture, and while it's not inherently "bad" as a stand-alone thing, there's plenty of it that makes sex between men and women look like a power game, and it's not too difficult to guess who's usually in power. After being fed these outrageous ideas about POSSESSION and POWER and PIMPS and GIRLS GONE WILD, it's no wonder that everyday life seems rather tame by comparison. I once wrote this in a diary years ago, and it hasn't aged much:

> You are not a pimp. You are not *like* a pimp. You are not up on "pimp game." Pimps are psychotic abusive creeps who live off the grid and get arrested a lot. No matter what Ice-T says, they ain't that smart. Snoop Dogg is not a pimp; he's a legendary, millionaire rapper whose music has gotten more boring the more he's talked about being a pimp.

To be blunt, no matter what the external world promises, the idea that you can possess women as a form of social currency, to gain power, to impress your friends, or as retribution for the time some other girl dissed you in elementary school...*anyone* who buys into any of that is probably a sad, lonely, injured person.

When you're a straight teenage boy who feels powerless and wants to lash out at a world that seems to be conspiring against you, one very popular reaction is to decide that the least you deserve is attention, comfort, and/or love from girls. It should be obvious why this is a flawed assumption. You're skipping past the girl's feelings, you're asking for a yes/no answer to a complex question, and you're actually setting yourself up for a variety of bad results, possibly including heartbreak or despair. Girls are not inanimate generators of self-respect, and sex, even with someone you love, will not magically solve your personal problems.

It's normal to mess up. It's also normal to adapt and improve your behavior based on past mistakes. We're all inclined, at some point or another, to play the blame game or go off the guilt-filled deep end, but when that happens, it's a way better choice to face the mirror, learn from your errors, and treat girls—and yourself—with more respect.

III. WHY WE DON'T KNOW WHAT WE'RE DOING (AND WHY WE'RE DOING IT)

So, yeah, *we need help!* But where and how do we get it? How many of you have positive, communicative male role models? How many have been sold out, jerked around, or embarrassed by older men in your lives? If you raised your hand at that second question, consider the fact that all the men you know used to be boys, too, and they probably never thought about the way they were raised.

For boys in America (and most of the rest of the world), the toughening up starts early. You're told that you need to be the independent master of your domain. You're strongly encouraged to close yourself off from others and to value traditionally "masculine" forms of power and success over being empathetic, honest, and communicative human beings. The clichés come fast and furious: "Be a man," "Stop acting like a baby," "Control your emotions," "You're a mama's boy." Even before elementary school, boys are discouraged from relying so much on their mothers, as if having a close relationship with a female parent is wrong. It's not hard to see how this could get a boy's relationship with the opposite gender off to a rather disorienting start. Shame can be a real motherfucker.

None of this is the fault of a certain set of musical artists, or movies, or our parents, or *any* one specific entity. These are all the

results of a bigger societal problem, which is that we live in a patriarchy—a system in which men hold the majority of powerful social and professional positions that shape our society. It's a totally shitty situation that hurts not only women, but everyone.

If you're gay or bi (or you might be gay or bi), you probably don't need me or anyone else telling you how harmful the pressure to be "manly" can be. In many groups of guys, the worst thing you can say to someone is that they're…*like you*. If you're not sure whether your friends will accept you as you really are, you might decide to secret away your feelings, or assume a personality other than your own to avoid suspicion. You might even laugh at homophobic banter. What better way to wipe away any doubt of your heterosexuality than by attacking other kids for being or "acting" gay?

At its core, homophobia comes from sexism: If women weren't seen as lesser, boys wouldn't bully one another for being "feminine." This is yet another way in which the patriarchy is such a bummer for everybody, of all genders and sexual preferences.

I've always had trouble with the idea that when guys get together, we're supposed to play sports, watch sports, talk about sports, talk about cars, and talk about sex in the dumbest and "dirtiest" of ways—all the things we supposedly "can't do" with women. When I was a teenager, hanging with *the guys* invariably made me feel awkward and out-of-sync. Mostly, I just shut down, saying as little as possible. Over time, I was able to develop a tight group of guy friends who hung out, talked on the phone, drove around listening to the radio, and played basketball together. None of us figured we had a shot to talk to girls outside of school, so we rarely talked about girls or sex, but when we did, it wasn't as a way to prove our manhood or wield power over each other or other kids. That kind of power trip can seem cool in the abstract— we're all tempted by the dream of being a suave asshole for *just one day*–but you usually just clown yourself.

High school doesn't have to be a hormonally apocalyptic cock-fighting pit where panic dictates every moment—not if you make your own rules. When kids try to push you into scenarios that seem hurtful to anyone (including yourself), be aware that you're being pushed, and stop, at least long enough to mentally push back for a second and figure out what you're agreeing to. One nonnegotiable scenario: If you see another guy acting shady, creepy, or aggressive with a girl, it's your responsibility as a human being to speak up or get help. If you're looking for a solid way to prove your manhood, not allowing a guy to be predatory with a girl is a pretty damn good starting point. Especially if that guy is you.

IV. ENTER THE FRIEND ZONE

One of the most ruinous and sad relationship-based myths of all is that straight men and straight women cannot be platonic friends. Dudes who believe this are essentially saying, "I am such a helpless beast that I can't control my urge to constantly paw women in a sexual manner, so I'm eliminating half the species from my friend pool." Or, in caveman terms, since that's apparently how they see themselves: "MMM. GIRL. GIRL HOT. ME WANT DO SEX WITH GIRL. NO OTHER REASON TALK TO GIRL. BURP. FART." I've heard guys claim that this is just "the way men think," that our brains are genetically encoded to be completely reductive and emotionally stupid. That's a bullshit excuse—it's not "the way men think," it's someone *choosing* to be a jerk. If we can't do better than that, we might as well just download porn in our parents' basements or carpool to the dinner buffet at the strip club for the rest of our sad, deprived lives. Stop! Turn back now! There's another way, my dude!

I've had crushes on female friends, sure, but the crush isn't the issue, it's how you react to it. As you spend more time on this planet and meet more and more people, you will be awash in crushes, some stronger than others, but you have to remember that they are *just crushes*. They are not commands to try to get in someone's pants by any means necessary, or to otherwise act like an ass.

Which isn't to say you're not allowed to respectfully make your romantic feelings known to a friend, whatever their gender. Just follow a few common-sense guidelines: Only tell them once (they will remember, you don't have to keep reminding them). No matter if they feel the same way or not, don't pressure them into anything or try to make them feel guilty about *your* emotions. If they do like you back in *that way* and you really value their friendship, you'll have to talk about some possible consequences. Could be awesome, could be tragic. If the two of you decide it's not worth risking your friendship for (usually the best course, IMO, if you're looking to keep someone in your life long-term), or if your freshly confessed feelings are not returned, congratulations! You are lucky enough to be in the "friend zone" with a person whose company you enjoy. You know where I learned most of this? From my platonic female friends.

Quite a while back, I was suffering through a devastating physical withdrawal from a nasty cocktail of antidepressants that a quacky psychiatrist had prescribed (free samples, whee!). I called a friend who had gone through similar problems, and she knew exactly what to do. She gave me room and permission to vent, shake with anger, and collapse completely. Then she built me back up, made me laugh, told me how she'd gotten through her issues and how none of that shit would ever work for me, and reassured me that I'd find my own way back. She told me that I should never feel embarrassed to call and talk about anything. I'm not saying that a male friend couldn't have played the same role, but I don't know if I could've been as open and vulnerable with a dude as I was with her—thanks, traditional masculinity!

V. THE DATING GAME

In the real world, honest advice about dating is hard to come by. You will come across myriad "instructive" books, how-to guides, and lists or rules that will purport to be "the secret" to "getting girls" to like you, but don't believe them. Each person you want to date will be different, so how can one set of instructions "work" for all of them? Maybe the worst offender in this category is the whole pitiful culture of "pickup artists," which casts women as nothing more

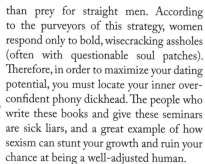

than prey for straight men. According to the purveyors of this strategy, women respond only to bold, wisecracking assholes (often with questionable soul patches). Therefore, in order to maximize your dating potential, you must locate your inner over-confident phony dickhead. The people who write these books and give these seminars are sick liars, and a great example of how sexism can stunt your growth and ruin your chance at being a well-adjusted human.

If memory serves me right, the number one resentment among so many straight boys in high school is "girls dating idiots." Why do guys who offer little more than passable looks and a smug demeanor seem to date more girls than an average or even above-average but quiet guy? One reason is probably that smug, confident people actually *talk* to people instead of hiding in the shadows and grumbling about how the girls they have never talked to aren't eager to date them. Listen: I know it can be hard to know what to say to someone you like. Don't overthink things. It ain't all that mysterious.

Here's what I wish someone had told me. It's a simple mantra that actually works in any social interaction, one-on-one or in a group: *Fall back…listen…question.* In other words, slow your roll, be respectful, listen to what someone's telling you, and then ask about some part of it that genuinely interests you. Don't interrupt. Don't try to correct her or argue with her. Don't force a joke. Don't laugh when you don't know what she or everybody else is laughing at. Don't jump in to add a story that's basically the same story someone just told you, except that your version involves something awesome that *you* did. *Fall back…listen… question.* Trust me, it works. Everyone on the planet, including girls, appreciates being treated like a person instead of as game to be hunted.

In no way am I saying that you should just shut up. But you do have to give other people room to speak, and really take in what they're telling you. If you ask questions, with any luck, the person you're talking to will feel comfortable asking you about stuff, too, and eventually you may get to a point where you both realize you're interested in each other as people. If that happens, it's a cause for celebration—and you can consider it a victory over the idiocy of "the game."

Now: What about when you're actually on a date, and it's going well, and things start to get physical? First, that's awesome. But don't get ahead of yourself. Proceed gently. Be sure that whatever you're doing is something you *both* want to do—yes, by asking out loud.

To be perfectly honest, consent is viewed by a lot of boys/men as a gray area because, for so long, we've been given the message that we don't really need to ask for it, nor do we need to be asked for it—which is unbelievable garbage. I also know that a lot of people, male and female, feel like checking in with someone to be sure it's OK to kiss them is just too awkward and embarrassing and, like, *fucks up the flow.* The flow of being unsure if you're both into it? Dude!

Asking for consent is obviously in both parties' best interest, considering the life-altering fallout that can ensue if one of you feels coerced, pressured, or just unable to vocalize what a terrible time you're having. And it's actually not that awkward or embarrassing—just a simple "This OK?" here and there is all it takes to make sure your partner's enthusiastic about whatever you guys are up to. CRUCIAL REMINDER: You can't just ask once, at the beginning of the proceedings, then clam up and expect the other person to, too. You've got to do periodic little check-ins, because someone's answer might change smack-dab in the middle of the action, and that's OK. This once-in-a-lifetime, "you only get one shot" attitude that a lot of guys I've known take when it comes to sexual encounters is not only potentially harmful, it's also awfully unattractive. In fact, it's easy to detect and to reject.

VI. WHAT IS A BOY?

Throughout my childhood, a framed poem hung in a bathroom in my family's house. Alan Beck's "What Is a Boy?" described the tyke in question with a killer combination of clumsy romanticized hokum ("Wisdom with bubblegum in its hair") and cutting, judgmental romanticized hokum (an "inconsiderate, bothersome, intruding" distraction).

Throughout my adult life, I've looked back on the character in this poem—this quintessential "all-American boy," this imaginary kid we're all supposed to emulate—and thought, (a) *Where did they get this shit?* but also (b) *What is a boy, REALLY?* Does that caricature really represent all we are? Or are we actually human beings who are capable of vulnerability, greatness, shame, joy, guilt, and humiliation—each in our own specific and subjective ways—just the same as anybody else? Perhaps if we encouraged more introspection, more responsibility, more consideration of others, more maturity about our failures, we could get the frickin' bubblegum out of our hair.

On the worst date of my life, I went out with a perfectly cool and interesting woman, had fun talking, and went back to my apartment, where things got physical. It's hard to explain, but the instant we started hooking up, I felt a wave of regret—I was detached and I shut down. I'd never felt like this before, and it scared me. My mind drifted: What was I doing, not here on this date, but with women in general? Why had I mentally checked out of relationships so regularly, and felt so disconnected from women? In my past relationships, one of which had just ended, I'd not been honest about what I wanted—because I didn't really know—and that uncertainty, plus my unwillingness to talk about it, had inflicted a lot of pain. I was so confused and closed off that I wasn't able to feel anything for anybody, and it was obvious to the people I was with. I didn't like how I was acting, and neither did my date, who pulled away as I stared blankly, immobile on the bed, unable to process whatever I was feeling.

The next day, something unexpected happened: That woman called me and asked if I'd like to have coffee to talk about what had gone down on our date. Well, no, but I guess I felt some desire to ask her for forgiveness—not real forgiveness, just the ego-salvaging "I'm really a good person" kind, where I could convince her that I wasn't really one of *those guys.* (By the way, who are "those guys"?) But that's not how the meeting went. She did most of the talking. When she asked me, "Do you really want to be dating right now?" I answered plainly: "No, probably not." Then, without any trace of recrimination, she told me that I really needed to work out my issues before going out with anyone else. Before I heard her say it, I hadn't admitted that to myself, but now I could no longer deny it.

In the years since then, I've thought about that conversation a lot. Not because it followed the worst date of my life (it actually wasn't), but because that woman taught me something incredibly valuable. The problem wasn't "women" or "people," it was *me*, and the solution was sitting down and listening to what this woman had to say without trying to defend my actions. If I'd been trying to prove to her that I wasn't really that bad, I never would've learned this lesson.

It's not like I instantly turned into a perfect saint after that day. But I became a far better listener, and it's probably no coincidence that I've finally been able to build a lasting, loving relationship with a woman I cherish and respect. Honesty is still a challenge (my nature is to hold things close until I figure out how I really feel), and I'm far from consistent, but I'm trying. The truth is that you work this shit out by making mistakes, asking questions, and being willing to accept the results. Maybe you'll get some answers from your father or your brother or some other male role model or mentor. Or maybe you'll get the answers you need from a girl or a woman. But you have to be ready to hear them.

Basically: Act like the good-hearted kid that we both know you are. Don't blame girls for your issues or failings, or get all wounded or aggro or call them "sluts" when they'd rather spend time with another guy. You will fuck up along the way, but you can come back from all of it if you realize that how you treat other people, including girls, is how you treat yourself. Whatever you put out there will come back to you, so put your best self out there. He's a great guy, and people deserve to know him. So do you. ✏

SONGS FOR YOUR OWN PERSONAL WORLD-CONQUERING MONTAGE BY AMBER

1. If I Had A Heart - Fever Ray
2. Container Park - The Chemical Brothers
3. Sunshine (Adagio in D Minor) - John Murphy
4. The Rains of Castamere - Sigur Rós
5. O Fortuna - Mozarteum Orchestra Salzburg and Kurt Prestel
6. Spider Pig - Hans Zimmer
7. In the House - In a Heartbeat - John Murphy
8. Teardrop - Massive Attack
9. Lux Aeterna - Clint Mansell and Kronos Quartet

SAY EVERYTHING

If you love someone, let them know.
By Amber. Illustration by Leanna.

So, you've finally done it! You've decided to let love lift you up where you belong and have plans to tell the remarkable, fascinating, deeply cute person you're smitten with exactly how you feel. It's been two overwhelming years/months/days/minutes/seconds since your beloved took up seemingly permanent residence in your mind, your heart, and your soul, and they brought with them some noteworthy changes: Whereas, not long ago, you had no opinion whatsoever about adult contemporary music, suddenly you've discovered that every soft rock and smooth jazz ballad is an extraordinarily accurate description of your innermost longings and fantasies. Even songs that have nothing to do with love, romance, or the sweetest taboo remind you of your crush (just recently you heard the *Law & Order* theme and got a little titillated).

You think about this person *all the time* and imagine the beautifully mundane life the two of you might build together: The kisses you'll share. The photo booth pictures you'll take. The burritos you'll eat. (Oh, the burritos you will eat!) Maybe you're currently friends with this person, or you've recently started flirting with them. Perhaps the two of you have exchanged sexually charged high-fives. Or maybe you've simply been pining for them from afar. All you know is that you'd like to be closer. Much, much closer. And so here you are, about to take the first step toward transforming this fervid infatuation into something tangible (and hopefully just as fervid).

Although you've passed the stage of neurotically wondering (and asking everyone you know and don't know) *if you should tell them how you feel* (and congratulations on getting through that torture!), it's perfectly understandable that you might feel a little nervous—maybe even a touch nauseated—about what's about to happen. Because to tell someone that you like-like them is to make yourself vulnerable to ridicule, rejection, embarrassment,

the works. Better to not say anything at all, or to couch your sincere emotions in fake irony, right?

Honestly, I'm not an especially bold person. Sometimes I struggle to stand up for my beliefs or just to articulate my thoughts to other people in casual, friendly conversation. Oddly, though, I am rather daring when it comes to these sorts of declarations. It might be because I watched too many Richard Curtis movies at an impressionable age, but I've never had too big of a problem being a girl standing in front of a boy and asking him to love her.

Of course, because I live in the real world, my affections routinely went unreturned. I've experienced some truly mortifying rejections—like, back in high school, when I wrote a love letter to a guy and later stumbled upon him and a friend reading my letter…and laughing. I've also had plenty of unremarkable but still unequivocal rejections where a guy I liked told me he wanted to "just be friends" or that he wasn't "ready for a relationship" or that he liked Jennifer Cooper and did not like me.

But do you think I let any of these experiences get me down? Of course I did. At least for a little while. Getting rejected always sucks, right? But there can be freedom in rejection! Freedom from obsessing over a person who doesn't reciprocate your feelings.

Or maybe—and this is a *big* maybe—you *won't* be rejected. And that's the really wonderful part about all of this, isn't it? Right now, as you prepare to make your big announcement, you just might be standing on a metaphorical railway platform, seconds away from boarding the express train to Makeout City (or Snuggle Junction—it's up to you).

I refused to allow the countless rejections I amassed over the years to keep me from wearing my heart on my sleeve. I once told a close friend that I had a crush on him by earnestly quoting the "to me, you are perfect" bit from *Love Actually*. This

schmaltzy plagiarized confession actually led to a brief romantic relationship, and even though we didn't end up getting married and acquiring babies and matching forehead tattoos, the experience was exhilarating—both because that dude was hella adorable and because, like Mulan, I had been true to my heart. I was being this unfiltered version of myself, and that by itself was exciting. I also learned that this guy was perfect as a friend or as the star of an erotic daydream, but not so perfect as a boyfriend. As the two of us eventually settled comfortably back into a friendship, I was happy that I could stop asking myself what it might be like to date him.

Maybe there's been a moment in your past when you allowed your fear of being vulnerable to stop you from chasing something. A dream? An opportunity? Love? And maybe there will be another such moment in your future. But this moment, right now, is different. In this moment, right now, you will do the difficult thing. You will say your piece, and it will feel strange and uncomfortable, but that's OK, because, regardless of the outcome, you will have been brave. You will have been true to your heart. And that's something you can be proud of.

So, as you brush your teeth tonight, mentally compose a love poem, practice your "I want to go on a date with you" interpretive dance, or do whatever it is that you have to do to get ready for this special event. And remember: No matter how things go, your declaration of love will enable you to move forward. Because when you choose to tell a crush how you feel about them, you are also choosing to embrace and be fueled by uncertainty instead of letting it smother your wonderful romantic, idealistic spirit. Anything is possible, right?

So maybe you'll get a date or maybe you won't. Or maybe, just maybe, sea shanties will be sung about your bravery on this day. There's only one way to find out.

JULY 2014: THE GREAT UNKNOWN

Dear Rookies,

July's theme is THE GREAT UNKNOWN. I'm writing this on my first day in my first apartment, where I am living alone for the first time. These facts are related, despite my usual attempts to not build these themes too much around my own life circumstances.

Near the end of high school I felt that so much had come full circle—that I had archived/documented/crystallized so many parts of my adolescence through my diary-keeping and through Rookie, that I had lived these years as fully as possible. Then my high school boyfriend and I broke up, and I graduated, and now I just feel overwhelmed by not knowing who I am now or what my Identity is or what my Core Me tools are to come back to when I feel sad. Going back to what used to be myself pulls me into a lot of painfully bittersweet memories, so I've been talking less and drifting more and actively testing a theory that reincarnation can happen to live bodies by trying to turn myself into a blank slate. It leaves me both terrified that I could become an actual monster and thrilled that I could become the exact person I ought to be, WE CAN BE HEROES Bowie-style. June/ACTION was a month of good, colorful fun, but July/THE GREAT UNKNOWN is black and white in anticipation.

I don't think this is an issue exclusive to having graduated and being my age, exactly. I had a series of these moments during high school, too. The most horrifying thing was realizing, early junior year, that I would have to be stuck with myself for years, and that you have to live with your own brain, and I felt like I had no surprises left in me (like, I felt OLD for the first time, but also mortifyingly young) and like it was becoming less and less fun to find myself, because my self suckkkked and what I needed was to become a new person, and I think I did, but that person was largely attached to a High School Boyfriend, and so now I feel like a weird fetus again.

And it is actually really wonderful.

"Ruby Tuesday" by the Rolling Stones. "Cactus Tree" by Joni Mitchell. "Like a Rolling Stone" by Bob Dylan. "Time Will Tell" by Blood Orange. "Still Sane" by Lorde, and how perfectly it captures the moment before you know everything is about to change. The delightful few seconds in "Hannah Hunt" by Vampire Weekend when the sound implodes and blooms and singing becomes screaming.

I made this month's moodboards backstage on break at rehearsal, in costume for the play I'm doing, *This Is Our Youth*, which is about three young people living in New York City in 1982. I love it because it's such an unglamorous depiction of youth, and of all the horror that having your whole life ahead of you can bring. Like, the characters all have these realizations and belief systems that they delusionally think are brilliant and original, and it's both pathetic and sweet. I loved going through the thousands of photos I keep for making these monthly moodboards and picking out ones that I felt my gal would gravitate toward. Unlike the guys in the play, she has somewhat of a trajectory for a future with school/a career, but she's also incredibly socially inept and unsure of herself and overwhelmed by the very basics of being alive.

That is something I've related to so deeply lately. Not feeling in my body. Not knowing how to talk to people now that I'm no longer an enchantingly eloquent kid, but just another adult. It's ultimately so much nicer to be spoken to as an equal, but it also makes me mumble more. It reminds me of a lyric my BFF Claire and I wrote sophomore year when we had a band for a minute: "You were so proud, with so much to say / How does it feel to just run away?"

From a 2014 interview with playwright Kenneth Lonergan in *Backstage* (I know this seems like a huge plug for this production but, man, if this is not all so relevant):

How do you feel the disillusionment of that generation relates to what the kids are experiencing?
Well, they are stepping into a world where there is no longer a place for their particular philosophy. They're full of opinions and beliefs and ideas, but at that very instant, their team—so to speak—has been not just beaten but totally dismantled—so they don't quite know what to do with themselves.

And some Joan Didion, from her essay "On Self-Respect" that I first read in *Slouching Towards Bethlehem* (1968):

I lost the conviction that lights would always turn green for me, the pleasant certainty that those rather passive virtues which had won me approval as a child automatically guaranteed me not only Phi Beta Kappa keys but happiness, honor, and the love of a good man; lost a certain touching faith in the totem power of good manners, clean hair, and a proven competence on the Stanford-Binet scale. To such doubtful amulets had my self-respect been pinned, and I faced myself that day with the nonplussed apprehension of someone who has come across a vampire and has no crucifix at hand.

Then there's this comment that Rookie reader "M" left on my June editor's letter:

Ho lee shit. I've been having this thought a lot lately: "What if I tried my hardest with everything in my power to do the things I really want to do?" It's kind of embarrassing to admit that I'm not already trying my hardest, and also that this simple thought has only recently popped into my head. Every time I think this thought, I start to feel nervous with excitement, though.

M is talking about June's ACTION theme, of course, but I think they tap into the exact exhilarating feeling that makes THE GREAT UNKNOWN truly wonderful, even if you can't stand unanswered questions. The anticipation of your newest incarnation is true excitement under all those nerves, and this moment is worth basking in all on its own. Looking out my window at my new view, I am immensely comforted by the neutrality of every building, like the world is just waiting for us to color it in.

love, Tavi

HELLO, DARKNESS

The sad parts of life are just as important as the happy ones.
By Jenny. Illustration by Kendra.

For my fifth birthday, my parents drove us to Disney World in a borrowed car with a cracked windshield. The whole time, even when I was sucking cotton candy off my fingers, giving my stack of quarters to Mickey Mouse–hatted employees to try and win a stuffed Minnie (only to have my father buy one for me—"This way, it won't cost me hundreds of dollars in quarters"), and hugging Donald Duck (my favorite because he sounded like a fun-ass baby with too much saliva in his mouth), and throughout so many joyous firsts—seeing palm trees, wearing a T-shirt in December, sticking popcorn in my nostrils and yelling, "Look! A new kind of eating!"—I had one disturbing thought that wouldn't leave me alone: *We are all going to die.*

Not like *right then and there* (although this was a possibility—riding Space Mountain made me think I was going to drop straight down to the last rung of hell). I was concerned with the idea that I would have to die *eventually*, and so would everyone I loved. My father, who carried me on his shoulders whenever I got tired? He would have to die one day. My mother, who smelled so much like flowers that I would think of any excuse to make her bend down close to me ("Is there something on my face?" was a favorite ploy) because sometimes, as she did, her long black hair would fall over my face and I could pretend it was my own hair? She too was going to die. Whether it happened now, soon, or later didn't matter. Once someone died, time was irrelevant, time was useless, time was over.

Other thoughts I had on the weekend of my fifth birthday in Disney World, Florida, included:

• I need more candy.
• Why do people have to die?
• Why did I have to be born into a loving family who will all die?
• Why do I have thoughts?
• I WANT TO WEAR CINDERELLA'S DRESS OH PLEASE OH PLEASE OH PLEASE LET ME.

• Is my mom afraid of dying, too?
• I wonder if we can have McDonald's for breakfast AND lunch AND dinner!

Thus began my lifelong tendency to see the bad, dark, scary, and sad parts of life just as vividly as the good ones.

I slept over at my best friend's house for the first time when I was 10 years old. Instead of being elated that my parents were finally allowing me to stay the night somewhere else, I was wracked with guilt. Why did I want to pull away from my parents? They'd say, "We wish you didn't have to grow up. We wish we could stay like this, as a family, forever," and it gave me tons of anxiety. My parents were so incredibly loving that I couldn't have fun with a friend without stressing out about making them unhappy by leaving.

"Do you ever feel guilty doing things without your parents?" I asked my friend. "Like, when we go to the mall, and they drop us off and go home and wait for us to call them so they can pick us up—does that make you sad at all?"

"You think way too much," she said. "I highly doubt our parents care what we're doing. They're probably excited to have some time away from us." But the idea of taking joy in their loss was terrifying. I couldn't sleep for wondering if *they* couldn't sleep, and worrying that they might be worrying about me.

My mother's motto was "Be happy. Don't worry." She said she woke up happy every single day. She trusted everyone and claimed that no one had ever lied to her in her entire life, and even though she knew that wasn't possible, she still believed it. In pictures, her smile was always so huge and uncontained that it appeared to be bursting at the seams, like she couldn't smile wide enough—like she could spend the rest of her life smiling, and it wouldn't be enough to express how happy she was to be alive.

"Your mom is a happy-go-lucky type," my dad said when I asked why she smiled like that in photos.

"I see that," I said, even though I didn't totally believe it. If she was so happy, why did she snap at me whenever I refused to pose in family photographs?

"Smile with your teeth," she would tell me whenever the camera came out.

"Just because you smile like that," I said, "doesn't mean everyone has to."

"Yes, you have to smile like that," she would say.

She also liked to say, "You will be happy if you strive to live a *normal* life." When I started high school, it angered me how her version of happiness negated mine. Her happiness seemed to work only when other people did exactly what she did; it left little room for other ways of being. Why did she insist that what I really wanted wasn't to be a writer, but to find a stable job as a dentist or a pharmacist, when I had never even once expressed an interest in cleaning teeth or learning about the chemical compounds in medicine? If she really valued my happiness, couldn't she let me decide for myself what sort of life I wanted?

Like other self-proclaimed optimists I knew, my mom made it sound like happiness was a choice, and anyone who was unhappy was simply *choosing* to be miserable, even though it was clear as day to me that if anything, *she* was *choosing* to ignore the things that did not fit neatly into her idea of happiness, and that was its own form of tyranny.

My father, for his part, saw my stubborn refusal to submit to happiness as a waste of energy: It was self-defeating, self-pitying, and utterly boring. Whenever I bitched and moaned about the trials and tribulations of the life of a teenage girl, whether it was how I didn't like or respect a single one of my classmates, or how some of my teachers were just as shallow, superficial, and popularity-obsessed as the kids were, or how unfair it was that the boys in my class shouted out the answers and talked over people like me, or how every other person my age was allowed to go to prom afterparties except me, his sympathies were limited.

"You love to feel bad," he told me. "It's your favorite feeling. Most people like to feel good, but not you. You love to make life hard for yourself."

"Forget you, Dad," I said.

"No," he said. "Go ahead. Keep feeling bad. Let me give you some more things to feel bad about. You can take some from me, since you love it so much."

Maybe my father was right. I sought out darkness and indulged in it while everyone else was trying to find the light. I saw so much misery in the world, and the elaborate lengths people went to avoid naming, discussing, encountering, or even having to look at it. (If anyone is looking to hire a professional bummer for their next party, I am available!)

I couldn't stop the voice in my head that asked me to examine every little moment of joy. And not just my joy, but other people's, too. I saw how certain girls in my school would gush and gush when they were dating someone, proudly declaring that they had already picked out a wedding dress, because "I seriously think I've found my soulmate," only to trash the dudes mercilessly once they broke up: "He had a small penis anyway, and I feel sorry for whatever poor sap gets him next." The extremes made my head spin. It seemed like, to most people, others were either angels or hellish monsters. Where were the in-between stages? What about honestly expressing your fears and your ambivalence and your uncertainty? Embracing darkness was a way to allow for nuance and contradictions and all the other messy stuff that has always made it hard for me to write someone off completely or fully idolize anyone. My darkness helped me see things—and people—on a spectrum.

I find that the people who insist on their resolute happiness and refuse to show any kind of negative emotion are often the DARKEST of all. (Cue the people you've blocked on social media for starting too many posts with "So grateful for my amazing boyfriend/girlfriend. . .I'm the luckiest person in the world!!!!!" Cue that one person who flits from person to person at parties, laughing the loudest and making joke after joke, but, weirdly, with whom you've never had a single conversation that lasted longer than three Tostitos Scoops.)

I made a friend in college who never seemed to see the ugliness I saw in the world. Where I saw an instance of vicious racism, she saw an innocent nothing-comment. Where I saw an instance of horrible mansplaining misogyny gone unchecked, she saw a guy trying to be helpful.

"He's a horrible person," I would say.

"He's so sweet!" she would retort.

Once, during a particularly frustrating conversation, I decided to get right to the point. "Do you ever have dark thoughts?" I asked her. "Do you ever let yourself get, like, really dark?"

She didn't even pause to consider the question before saying, "No. I'm a glass-half-full kind of girl. Life's too short to be negative all the time. I like people who face every day with a smile."

Then why are you friends with me? I wondered. Was I passing for an optimist?

"You're just like my mom," I said. "I wish I could be more like you guys." Why not face each day with a smile? Wouldn't I be happier if, instead of fuming every time someone said something messed up, I could just think, *They didn't mean anything by it. I'm sure their intentions were good.* Maybe, for me, it would take a certain amount of willful ignorance to be happy, but why not try? Instead of finding most things disturbing, I could find them cute or awesome or funny. It was too emotionally taxing to name and face all the things that disturbed me.

While I was contemplating jumping ship and joining the shiny, happy people, I watched my friend's upbeat veneer chip away. As I got to know her better, I started to see how she needed that cheerfulness to survive. One night, over cheap vodka mixed with orange juice, she confided that she had been abused by a family member as a child, and that she fundamentally did not trust men. She said that, deep down, she believed all men were brutes—violent and disgusting—and that, for this reason, she would have a baby only if she could do in vitro fertilization and choose the gender.

"I don't know if I could love a boy," she said, "even if it was my own child. I know that's bad. But it scares me to think about giving birth to a child who could turn out to be a monster, or a rapist, or a violent woman-hating psycho."

All along, I had thought I was the dark one, but that night, I saw why my friend couldn't allow herself to ever express sadness in everyday life, because when she did, it was *biblical.*

For a long time, I was the opposite way—I couldn't acknowledge a moment of happiness without a sad preface or rejoinder, which was, I admit, annoying as hell, but also the only thing that felt true to how I saw and interacted with the world. When I came back from six life-changing weeks volunteering as an English teacher in a Romanian mountain village a year after graduating college, I refused to describe what I did as "selfless," as some of my peers characterized their own experiences.

"If anything," I said to my friends, who were very likely tired of hearing me tear everything down all the time, "it was the most selfish thing I have ever done. I went and disrupted these people's lives, ate their food, slept in their beds, and learned about their world, which was ridiculously interesting to me and probably something I will write about one day and be praised for, and on top of that, I get to feel good about myself because *I volunteered*! It's more honest to say, 'You know what? I feel guilty about the privilege I was born into, which I do not deserve more than anyone else in this world, and I do very little with that luck to change the world for the better. I truly care the most about myself above others, and that is just something I have to live with.' Sorry. I think I'm ranting. What was the question again?"

"So you had fun," my friends joked.

"Actually," I said, "I did." And I meant it. I had the time of my life. I woke up every morning to the crisp mountain air and a bouquet of freshly picked flowers that my host sisters would eagerly present to me. Somehow, I found a way to communicate with an entire village of people without knowing their language and without them knowing mine. If anything, my skepticism about the virtues of volunteering made me more open to forming relationships with the people there. Instead of idealizing the villagers I met as poor, virtuous, salt-of-the-earth people, I was able to just see them as people, like you and I are people: flawed, messy, selfish, sometimes incredibly kind, and sometimes incredibly cruel.

Sometimes, disavowing the dark shit makes the world even darker. Last week, I was explaining to my friend Sasha that I had to watch all the U.S. World Cup matches by myself because I couldn't bear the thought of being in a room full of people chanting, "U-S-A! U-S-A! U-S-A!"

He said he felt the same way and told me that at one point in his life, he had wanted to get a tattoo of the American flag because, as he said, "I want to look at it every day and remember all the shit this country has done: the genocide of natives, slavery, the Jim Crow segregation laws, racist immigration policies, building a fence along the U.S.–Mexico border, criminalizing women's rights to make choices about their own bodies. I want to remember all of it because it tests my love for this country. I *do* love America, but I will not forget the blood on our hands." It was the greatest expression of national pride and love I had ever encountered.

"That's how I want to love this country, too," I said.

"That's the only way I can love this country," he said.

When Woody Allen fans crusaded to discredit Dylan Farrow's account of being abused by her father, it seemed far scarier to me that anyone would go to such lengths to prove that their favorite director could not possibly be a sexual predator and abuser than simply accept the possibility that maybe, yes, the person who made those movies that changed their life forever is a complete and utter irredeemable piece of shit.

My own paragon of optimism, my mother, won't watch any movie or TV show that isn't a straight-up comedy. When I was in high school, she somehow got sucked into watching *American Beauty*, a movie about repressed, disconnected, nihilistic, morbidly depressed people in the suburbs. She found it so deeply disturbing that she couldn't sleep that night. In the middle of the night, she came to my room and asked me to confirm her hope that everything in this movie is nothing more

than a twisted, made-up fantasy. She asked, "Are Americans really like that? You don't know anyone like that, do you?"

I wanted to say, "Yes, I do know people like that, and, actually, I'm kind of one of them. If only you weren't so afraid to see that, maybe you would actually see me and actually come to know me."

I want to be seen and known by people who are unafraid of seeing the admirable, the execrable, and everything in between. I'm not advocating party-pooperism, or defending the kind of person who's always bringing everyone down with them by, like, going to someone's birthday party and screaming at the birthday girl about global injustice, or showing up to a friend's graduation dinner and talking nonstop about how shitty their life is (but *congrats on graduating!*). Wanting to confront darkness doesn't mean being an overall negative person, a narcissist who is only interested in their own pain, or trying to find ways to downplay other people's achievements or invalidate their feelings. I'm just wondering if there's a way to acknowledge, every once in a while, the possibility that we are not always good people, that we do not always live up to the promise of who we want to be, that we may never get what we want, that sometimes we aren't as brave as we wish we were, that we're capable of being awful to the people we love the most, and we can act spitefully instead of honorably, and sometimes we're lonely and terrified. I know I just dumped a whole lot of sad on you, but what if it didn't have to be the saddest thing in the world to acknowledge that these are possibilities? What if acknowledging some of that stuff could feel like a moment of clarity, instead of one shrouded in darkness?

As I've gotten older, my desire to trace my dark thoughts to their fathomless origins has both diminished and bloomed. There are days and weeks and months when I binge-watch *Keeping Up With the Kardashians* or whatever other frothy TV show will give me a break from my brain (MAD RESPECT to any show entertaining enough to do that). I go through long stretches of time when the last thing I want to do is think about my hopes and

fears, my disappointments, my sensitiveness, my monstrousness. Mostly, though, I find that confronting my darkness isn't a choice I'm making. If it were, I could choose not to. But no one can ignore or outrun their darkness forever—eventually, it catches up with you, whether you choose to acknowledge it or not. I'm not sure if that's comforting or depressing, or if it just *is*.

Sometimes, I think it's easy for me to acknowledge that the world is a scary place because I've never really had to deal with anything that scary. I think maybe the reason I'm able to dwell in darkness is that my darkness isn't all that dark. When I'm feeling uncharitable toward myself, I think all of this is just evidence of my having had a fairly trauma-free, privileged life. And there I go again—seeing the worst in myself and focusing on that, while ignoring the good.

So *here's* the good: My darkness makes me more compassionate and better able to relate to others, because I'm not afraid of other people's suffering or sadness or pain. I think our little souls are capable of so much—they can handle the darkness with as much patience and grace as they do the sunnier parts of life.

Don't get me wrong—it's terrifying to be five years old and thinking about death between mouthfuls of cotton candy. But since that birthday I've learned that confronting what I'm most afraid of makes it way less terrifying. And when you realize things don't have to fall into either OMG SO INSPIRING or OMG SO DEPRESSING, you can give your responses to the world room to be complicated (but also legitimately OMG SO AMAZING).

There's no better time to set yourself on the PATH TO DARQUENESS than when you're a young doe. The older we get, the more we tend to fall into the habit of fearing our old friend and doing anything to ignore it. So go forth, my dark army of Rookies! Embrace your darkness! Or at least test it out? Be lionhearted, be happy, be sad, be vast, be honest, be compassionate, be open, and let the darkness set you on the righteous path—the path of the true lover who is not afraid to see it all, and to love despite all that they have seen. ◊

WE ARE WHAT WE LOVE: AN INTERVIEW WITH LAVERNE COX

The Orange Is the New Black *star and all-around superwoman on being yourself.*
By Kelli Korducki. Illustration by Kendra.

Laverne Cox has got it going on, in the sense that she's really rad *and* really, *really* busy. She's currently filming the third season of *Orange Is the New Black* while also finishing her memoir, and co-producing the documentary *FREE CeCe*. The movie tells the story of CeCe McDonald, a trans woman of color who was sentenced to 41 months in a Minnesota men's prison for defending herself against a life-threatening hate crime in 2012 and freed earlier this year.

In June, Cox became the first transgender woman ever to grace the cover of *Time* magazine, which anointed her "a public face for the transgender movement." Last week, she made history yet again when she became the first transgender artist to be nominated for an Emmy. As I found out when I met her at the Toronto International Film Festival's headquarters, Cox doesn't think of herself as a role model. She's just fighting the good fight, working hard (and looking good doing it), and hoping the patriarchy catches up.

KELLI KORDUCKI You're very vocal about the need to challenge the patriarchy and binary ideas of gender. What strategies have you found effective in that fight?

LAVERNE COX It's about what we teach our children, what we internalize, and how we challenge those things in our daily lives. For folks who might be in some sort of patriarchally privileged space, it's about being critical of that and interrogating it and not just blindly embracing that privilege. For people who are not, it's about being critical of and pushing back against patriarchy in our lives in a personal sense. It's *always* about changing people's hearts and minds—and then we need to look at public policy.

What drew you to CeCe's story and this project?

I say in the trailer for the film that I could've very easily been CeCe. There have been many times that I've been walking down the street in New York City and gotten catcalled when people realized I was trans. I was kicked on the street once. I've been called a man. I've been called a "he-she." I've been called everything but a child of God, actually. It's been a part of my life. So whenever I hear of a trans person experiencing violence, it's very close to me. It's palpable, and it's real. What was also deep, to me, when I read about CeCe's story, was how everyone talked about what a light she was to people around her. She was kind of a mother figure for a lot of trans youth in Minneapolis. Meeting her, I was like, *I get it.* She's this remarkable young woman who refuses to be a victim. I got goose bumps just thinking about that. I love her.

She's quite young, too. What advice would you give to trans or genderqueer kids who are trying to present their true selves to the world?

Define yourself in your own terms. In terms of gender, race, anything. We are not what other people say we are. We are who we know ourselves to be, and we are what we love. That's OK. You're not alone in who you are. There are people out there who will love and support you. It's about doing the work and believing and finding those people—if they're not in your local community, there's somebody online that you can talk to for support.

How are you balancing being an artist with being an activist?

I'm not! There's no balance in my life at all right now. I've had some conversations with my agent and my brother, who's a huge adviser of mine. There are some projects coming up that will hopefully help me to do that. But balance is something I'm working on. When it happens, I'll let you know! ✶

NO ONE CAN MESS WITH YOU
BY GABBY

1. GIRL TALK - TLC
2. I'M THE BEST - NICKI MINAJ
3. BRING THE NOIZE - M.I.A.
4. GO ON, GIRL - ROXANNE SHANTÉ
5. Q.U.E.E.N. - JANELLE MONÁE
6. WHO'S THAT GIRL? - EVE
7. THE JUMP OFF - LIL'KIM
8. SATURDAY NIGHT - NATALIA KILLS
9. DISPARATE YOUTH - SANTIGOLD

GIRLS AFRAID

BY ROSE

ON SOME RECENT WEEKENDS, I WANDERED AROUND THE SANTA MONICA PIER ASKING PEOPLE WHAT THEY WERE AFRAID OF. EVEN AS THEY DESCRIBED THEIR BIGGEST FEARS, MANY OF THE AWESOME GIRLS I MET LAUGHED AND POSED FOR MY CAMERA. HERE'S WHAT THEY SHARED WITH ME.

MELISSA (RIGHT), 16: DEATH. I'M SCARED THAT I WILL RANDOMLY DIE ONE DAY AND NOT FULFILL MY PURPOSE IN LIFE.

JENNIFER, 17: NOT ENDING UP HAPPY WITH MYSELF. IT DOESN'T MATTER WHERE I END UP, AS LONG AS I'M HAPPY.

SABRINA, 14: BODIES OF WATER. I DON'T SWIM.

TIANA, 14: INSECTS.

MARINA, 13: BEING IN FRONT OF LARGE CROWDS.

EMMA, 18: LOSING PEOPLE I LOVE.

JAY, 20: BUGS!

MIRANDA (FAR LEFT), 14: FAILURE.
TATIANA (CENTER), 17: THE FUTURE,
AND GOING TO COLLEGE.
MEGAN (FAR RIGHT), 16: NOT BEING SATISFIED.

QUIFEI, 14: NOT KNOWING HOW I WILL DIE.

ROSLYN, 15: REGRET.

YILINN, 13: DEATH.

KARINA, 9: HIGH PLACES.

LISBETH, 14: CLOWNS.

JESSICA, 18: DYING.

ALEXA, 14: FACING THE WORLD ALONE.

WAY TO SURVIVE

Learning to love my body after sexual assault.   By Arabelle. Photo by María Fernanda.

I'm going to start this story where the needles are, half an inch from my heart. I'm lying on my back with my shirt pulled up in a room full of people I don't know. My tattoo artist has just started his work. The pain hasn't begun yet.

He's only finished one word so far: IN

All tattoos come with stories, but sometimes you don't want to tell them, or can't, or won't. I'm grateful my artist doesn't ask me, but I'll tell you. It's a secret between you and me. No matter how many strangers might read this, I'll pretend they're all you, OK?

I've been sexually assaulted twice, both times by people I loved, and it took me a while to break off my relationships with them. I still think of the people who've hurt me with kindness. I did once love both of them, in different ways. The classic narrative of assault is simple: An unexpected stranger in a dark alley, or somewhere else disconnected from everyone and everything. But the truth is

heartbreaking in its complexity. In the U.S. alone, sexual assault takes place, on average, once every two minutes, according to RAINN (Rape, Abuse & Incest National Network).

I'm staring at the ceiling of the tattoo shop, counting the popcorn, an old habit that started as a way to pass the time I spent in bed with the people who assaulted me. I'd count the tiles and mold spots—the popcorn—on the ceilings of our rooms. I don't believe in God, so I count: I have been assaulted twice. There are 26 steps up the stairs to my bedroom, where I counted the minutes until my parents came home the first time it happened. There are eight window panes on my door. It has been nearly a year. Counting is my prayer. It is also a curse.

Before the artist did the placement sketch of where the tattoo would go, I stared in the mirror at home for hours, naked, bewildered at my body. I have always liked seeing bruises blossom into roses and purples and golds—I think of them as flowers. Unusually, I had no bruises that day. (My skin flowers easily.)

The artist is up to three words now:
IN A DREAM

Once, in one of my college classes, we raised our hands to count. You never think the ratio is real until it's sitting diagonal, horizontal, parallel, and adjacent to you. And then you all cry together. The numbers go up if you are trans, if you are a woman of color, if you are queer. Women are sometimes afraid to walk home alone, lest they become a number, but I became a number through lovers—other girls, incidentally—whom I had initially trusted. Nobody told me that could happen, and for a long time, I didn't believe it myself. But everyone is capable of cruelty.

It wasn't even the assaults themselves that hurt me the most. It was that I believed they were my fault somehow. I apologized in one way or another each time. *I* apologized. I kept returning to bad situations, which filled me with such self-loathing that I would sometimes take scalding baths, like I deserved to be burned. I was trying to wash it all off me, but the water was never hot enough. Inevitably, I turned the cold faucet on. I have to remind myself every day that it wasn't my fault, and I still don't feel like I'm telling the truth. Now, when I see something that reminds me—a word, a certain jacket, an old neighborhood—I have to keep my eyes on the ground. *It wasn't my fault.*

IN A DREAM YOU SAW A WAY

It was difficult for a long time. I told my closest friends, and they nodded, but they didn't seem to know what to say. I tried to reframe it as part of a political conversation. On Tumblr, I read about sex positivity, which champions sexuality and loving yourself so that you may love others. Positivity meant vocalizing everything, evidently, and so I swam in its vocabulary. I tried to love myself to emotional health with the help of these discussions, because talking about it meant I was *past* the notions of body terror and betrayal… didn't it? I tried to love my body. I tried to love sex, out of spite, and I couldn't. It was hard to when all I could remember was that the last time I was naked with someone, I felt like crying.

I felt like I was trapped into boning, talking about boning, and being "unafraid and unapologetic" about vocalizing my desires. I thought that being an "empowered" queer person meant fucking myself out of my traumas and the patriarchy, and if I didn't want to, I was doing something wrong. That it was my fault, all over again. I wasn't queer enough, or sexy enough, or empowered enough. The weight was all on *me*. The pressure was just *too much*.

I decided to take a break from sex. I shifted my focus onto everything *but* my love life. I chased after bylines in my favorite publications, took trips with my friends to cabins and beaches, and enjoyed a lot of friendly kisses when I felt like it, without worrying about what they meant. I sought a new version of intimacy in the kindness and love of my friends. Now, I get my intimacy from friendships and from my dreams (and yeah, I masturbate *a lot*). Not worrying about other people and what they want from my body has freed me in the ways I had thought sex would.

IN A DREAM YOU SAW A WAY TO SURVIVE

I came into this tattoo shop to remind myself that while you may always remember what has happened to you, your body will keep changing. A body can become unfamiliar to someone else's in time. Here's where counting becomes comforting: Red blood cells can live up to four months, white blood cells just under a month, skin cells a little over a month and a half. This means progress—my body is now all mine again. I survive my history by making my body new in other ways, too: I change my hair color constantly.

While I'd like this to be a neat narrative where I have gotten over my fears, my anxiety, my triggers, and my nightmares about sex after assault, I haven't entirely. But I've learned that, sometimes, you don't move on. You move through.

It took me a frustratingly long time to live with the aftermath of my assaults. Sometimes, I still get pulled back into nightmares, but I find comfort in the fact that I woke up. The sun is shining. There are dogs in the park. I woke up. I am not altogether my past. The bruises that bloomed faded away, too. Any body, with time, can be new. *And that is a blessing*. That is joy. That's why I decided to permanently ink a quote by the artist Jenny Holzer on my body: to reflect that.

Talking about this is difficult, and so I am out of my body again, hovering over myself like a ghost. Like Casper. I am a friendly ghost, telling myself (and telling you, too): *It wasn't your fault*. Our experiences as survivors are complicated. They come in many shapes and forms. But if you have been in a sexual situation where you were too scared to say no, or incapable of saying no, that was assault. And it was never, never your fault. I want to hold your hand and tell you this with utter sincerity: You owe it to yourself to survive, first, always, and forever.

The artist is finishing up his work—I have a new tattoo:

IN A DREAM YOU SAW A WAY TO SURVIVE AND YOU WERE FULL OF JOY.

I'm delirious with pain. I feel fuzzy and light, but I'm awake, and I'm not a ghost—*I'm alive, I'm alive, I'm alive*. The difference between this ache and the aches from before: I am safe. I could have told the artist to stop at any time, but *I didn't want to*. I decided. I chose to mark my body as my own territory. It's entirely mine, and, though it always was, I know that now, and I blossom, and I bloom. ◊

Design by Sonja. Title lettering by Lisa Maione. Playlist lettering by
Vanessa Han. Haim and Erykah Badu portraits by Mithsuca Berry.
THEESatisfaction album cover by Brooke Nechvatel. Doodles by Leanna.

AUGUST 2014: Enchantment

Dear Rookies,

Welcome to August's theme, ENCHANTMENT. Think summer witches and summer fairies. Astrology and general cosmic vibes. The combined etherealness and vindictiveness of *Speak Now*–era Taylor Swift and Stevie Nicks (s/o to "Gold Dust Woman," "Rhiannon," and every other song of hers that I've based my whole sense of self around). First Aid Kit. Erykah Badu. Cat Power. A scratchy, sun-stained kind of magic that life sometimes offers up and we sometimes scramble to write down, as in this month's poetry compilation, "I Will Paint the Sky." Or the glittery but deceptive kind of charisma that has been mythologized as the foundation of true love, as explored by Amy Rose in "I'll Be Your Mirror." Basically, ENCHANTMENT: LIFE SHOWING ITS TRUE COLORS, OR ALL OF US PROJECTING? Enjoy!

*love,
Tavi*

Summer Spells By Dylan

1. Hush - Deep Purple

2. King of Speed - Hawkwind

3. The Hunter - Blue Cheer

4. Nothing to Lose - Girlschool

5. Sunshine of Your Love - Cream

6. Love Buzz - Shocking Blue

7. Fuzz's Fourth Dream - Fuzz

8. Lady of Fire - Sir Lord Baltimore

9. Under the Spell - Uncle Acid and the Deadbeats

10. Roisin Dubh (Black Rose):
A Rock Legend - Thin Lizzy

11. Sunshine - The Gun

I'll Be Your Mirror

A cautionary tale from a former dreamgirl.
By Amy Rose. Collages by Shriya.

Both parts of my first name are associated with love: Amy comes from the French word *aimée*, or *beloved*. According to both the history of literature and most of the bouquets on offer at various florists/gas stations nationwide, roses are symbols of rrrromance. My last name, Spiegel, means *mirror*. For a long time, the combination of the three amounted to a fitting title for how I behaved in relationships. In high school, I tried to suss out what my partners considered the behavior of a DREAM-GIRL, then did my best to imitate it. This didn't require me to change my personality so much as to reduce it. While I made those subtractions, I was very quiet about my actual heart.

If there were some equivalent to porn for loneliness, the various fake-o ideal women I embodied would have been total stars of the medium. I got used to being Amy Rose: This One Dude's Fantasy Edition. She was a mutable character—she changed depending on whom she was talking to, but her lines always included something like: "Yes, Craig. I also think there is such a thing as 'the *good* Burger King' in town and also 'alternative comedy,' and I appreciate and agree with your strident views on each. *Do go on* about the history of every Eric Clapton album. I'm so impressed you know so much about him—*and* that you have the lung capacity to deconstruct his oeuvre for hours on end!" (Wait…I just realized there *is* an equivalent to porn for loneliness. It's called porn. Plus also maybe every inane movie where a female love interest's taste in a band is considered a majorly telling character trait. There goes THAT billion-dollar idea.)

Of course, refashioning yourself into someone else's idea of the perfect girl/partner/friend isn't a choice that you make all by yourself, even when you realize

what you're doing, which I did not at the time. Someone has to throw you a line, and you've got to catch it. This was easy enough—imaginary feminine ideals aren't all that dynamic, personality-wise. (This is because they are *pretend*.) Every time you feel an urge to talk about yourself, you just swallow that urge and go on imitating the preferences/opinions/personality of the other person.

With one high school boyfriend who idolized Trey Parker and Matt Stone, I would casually drop that I had won the official trivia contest they used to run on the *South Park* website each week. (NO AUTOGRAPHS, PLEASE.) The next dude, an adjunct literature professor with a hot, judgmental face, found the show "puerile," so he never heard an ort from my vast database of Butters-centric erudition—instead, he got Amy Rose: How True, Thomas Mann DOES Rule Edition. I was never all the way phony, since I meant these things when I said them, but I was…selective in what I chose to reveal, in a way I now find dubious and unnecessary.

On its own, choosing not to disclose that you know the name of the Christian rock band that some fictional children were in for one episode of a cartoon isn't a grave betrayal, but imagine editing out of your biography *anything* that might not be 100 percent attractive to someone else, including things far more complex in nature than *South Park* (maybe). It's bizarre at best and toxically insecure at worst.

Hearing that you are capable of making someone happy can be a dangerous comfort. Why would I want to be my ACTUAL SELF when I could be, as one boyfriend once described me, "a girl too wondrous to be of flesh and blood"? (At 15, this was a sterling thing to hear.) The only rule of being a dreamgirl: Do not

reveal your feelings or be vulnerable in any way. Since no one can totally obscure their selfhood, I allowed myself the occasional joke or wry comment, but I kept everything VERY light.

Between the ages of 0 and 17, sharing anything about myself was dangerous—sometimes emotionally, sometimes practically, sometimes both at once—because my "situation at home" was…perfect! (What if someone actually ended that sentence that way in a personal essay sometime? I would love them with my whole entire life, for the rest of my entire life, and not even in my ineffectual mirror way, either.) No, it was fraught and terrifying, because my parents were addicts, and I wasn't allowed to talk about how sad I was or anything else involving my feelings without upsetting them, because addicts, as a rule, do not "talk." This is still a very hard lesson for me to unlearn.

While being brought up to see communication as a form of weakness contributes to the urge to turn yourself into a mirror, anyone can do it! You don't have to have a grim "situation at home" to want to kowtow to that self-conscious "whatever YOU want!" impulse. You can just be a teenage girl going to high school, or walking down the sidewalk, or otherwise thinking and feeling and breathing among other thinking, feeling, breathing beings. Cool, huh? One afternoon when I was 15, I was in the car with some friends when the guy driving announced, "If Amy opens her mouth one more time, I'm pulling over." Was he kidding? He was not, he assured me. I walked home, reprising in my head a mini-quiz I gave myself each day, I guess to keep my insecurities nice and sharp: What had I done wrong, besides everything? I felt that way a lot, wherever I was.

By hiding all the potentially unsavory aspects of my character—grievous flaws like enthusiasm, curiosity, etc.—I got to be "a goddess," instead of the clumsy, ineloquent public nuisance I felt like. There was lots of power in that. There's a concept in game theory called backward induction, where you look at a result you want—for me, this was to be seen as an ENCHANTING BEACON OF PURE INTRIGUE, CAMARADERIE, AND TWINSHIP OF THE HEART, and, consequently, to never have to worry about being alone—and map out the steps, from last to first, leading to that desired outcome. Then you follow them in the regular direction. When a girlfriend I had as a teenager was super into Jewel, I took part in a ritual where we sat in the bath listening to *Pieces of You* for hours, which would have been fine, except that I privately thought Jewel was the aural equivalent of stale B.O. that someone had tried, in vain, to mask with patchouli. I had sex with guys in ways that didn't turn me on because I knew they liked certain things more than others. I periodically administered tea and painkillers to one dopehead boyfriend's terrible jam band as I sat through hour after hour of practice, nodding along to their guitar progressions. In every situation, I was agreeable, but mostly, I wasn't there at all.

Defaulting to this way of being in the world made me feel fernlike. I pictured myself like a time-lapsed recording taken in a forest. In the sped-up footage, we botany enthusiasts can see me reflexively extending myself toward the world, stretching as far as I can to touch it, then curling tightly back in on myself. Over and over and over.

Both tendencies—to open myself to others and to hide the whole of me from them—were, for much of my life, expressed in the extreme, sometimes simultaneously. I found that gulping back the things I really wanted to say, and learning to ride the ebb of whatever conversation someone else wanted to have instead, dramatically reduced the likelihood that I would lose or disappoint them. They, in turn, agreed to listen to me never, ever talk about anything but their interests, aspirations, politics, and creative endeavors. I'm disappointed in myself, reading this

back right now. I really hope you don't follow in my footsteps, because you are radiant and valid all by yourself, and if you knew how true that was, you'd be even more powerful than you already are. You would be a force to be reckoned with.

Because here's the alternative: You can try to be someone's dreamgirl, but this will require you to be secretive, calculating, and lonesome. Doesn't that sound like a fun trade-off? Or does it sound like a great way to architect a treacherous, self-punishing alienation-station of a life? If you picked the second option, you are correct—it is. And this bargain doesn't even get you a lasting relationship. There will inevitably come a time when you can't keep up the gambit anymore and the whole thing goes to pieces—either because you're scared of revealing yourself and flee (this is what I always did), or because at some point, late in the game, YOU show up in the relationship, and your partner goes, "I'm sorry, have we met?"

When I was able to pull it off, being Craig's dream date to Burger King earned me high accolades. Has anyone ever made you feel like the exception to every rule? My first boyfriend was great at that (as were all of his successors, but we'll get to that in a little). We can call this guy Roger. Rog was VERY into chewing on his thoughts with his mouth open. Contrary to every impulse I've ever had, there is actually nothing wrong with sharing the things that you love with a person that you love, but Roger seemed never to have learned that sharing involves reciprocity; he preferred to structure our conversations as lists of books he liked. That was cool by me, since I got to be around someone who told me I was smart and had "really good taste" in the way that people say it where you know the sentence ends "…because it's exactly like mine." In retrospect, it seems like he thought I was captivating because *HUH, how NOVEL, a GIRL can like the things that I like, except she has boobs?*

Some people, instead of wanting you to reflect their image back to them, want the total opposite. They see your personhood as accessibly wild 'n' wacky and they suspect it might help them look at their

own lives through an all-new magical/sexy/fancy-free kaleidoscope and become inspired as they *never have been before*. Such people appreciate you, but with a wink and a flourish, like they're doing a self-congratulatory magic trick. They want to be applauded for having the evolved sensibilities to think a total weirdo like you is hot: Sure, you're vibrant and gorgeous and perfect and everything, but who else could be *open* enough to see that? They're doing you a favor by wanting to be around you! But saving you from the caustic rejection of the rest of society (that place is the WORST, isn't it?) was, they assure you, worth it: Truly, it's *you* who hath rescued *them* from the humdrum routines they once shuffled through, when they were not yet INSPIRED by the thrilling, let's-be-honest-kind-of-unhinged abandon you've whirlwinded into their lives. They've finally found you. Hooray! Everyone is saved and gets matching tattoos. (The only thing: You want these people to get the hell away from you forever. They're dangerous, reductive creeps.)

What if, whenever someone complimented you, what you heard was, "You're weird"? What if hearing that were your exact fear, and you were having it reinforced on the regular? How would you feel then, besides delusional for ever having thought someone might want to hang out with you because you find each other mutually pleasant and rad, rather than because you're some kind of offbeat mode of deliverance from whatever ennui they felt about the way they live their life? You're not a person to them, you're a vehicle: an alien spacecraft that they'd like to drive as far away from their pre-you lives as possible. Who needs society when you can sublimate all your insecurities, hopes, and romantic/artistic/sexual idiosyncrasies into a dreamgirl? "Man, are you ever special. Just…you're almost crazy, aren't you?" (It is not an accident that the phrase Manic Pixie Dream Girl includes a word commonly used to refer to mental illness.)

All the comments I complained about earlier—"You're special/unique/whatever"—are, on their own, far from

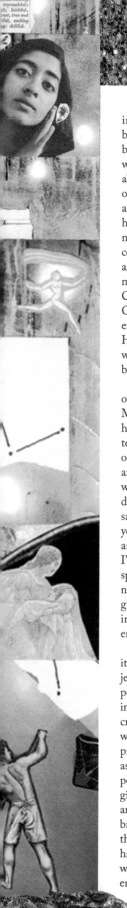

invectives. Remarks about a person's beautiful singularity can be lovely when backed by the right intentions. Recently, I was talking to a guy with whom I have just about zero in common. I'm low-key crushed out on him regardless, and vice versa. In a casual exchange about our days, I told him about some interests of mine that had nothing to do with him—a band I'm in, a community dinner I volunteered at. "You are so perfect," he replied. In the past, comments like that have come off like a threat: CONTINUE TO BE IDEAL, OR I'M OUTTA HERE. But this guy wasn't threatening me or thanking me for CHANGING HIS LIFE, he was just saying he thought I was cool! I was touched instead of horrified because his words felt sincere.

That's the deciding factor: Is someone making GRAND PRONOUNCE-MENTS about you that are really, at their heart, about themselves? Here's a simple test to help you spot a phony compliment of this type: Did it come right before or after a phrase like "You're the only person who gets me," or "I thought girls like you didn't exist"? Turn tail! This person is likely saying, "Our relationship is predicated on your willingness to make me happy exactly as I want to be made happy, because I'm insecure." They're saying that you're special because of how you *make them feel*, not because of how you *are*. While it's great to have both, the latter is way more important, and, alone, the former isn't enough to sustain a relationship.

Chronic dreamgirl-ization isn't limited to some strain of easily identifiable jerks, either—I've had it done to me by people I totally respect, admire, and am interested in. In these cases, I'd be all crushed out, we'd start dating, things would be really cool, and then I would be presented with this, like, model of myself as angel/savior/dreamgirl that I was supposed to live up to. I have dated guys and girls, and, in my experience, at least, guys are especially susceptible to turning living, breathing human beings into archetypes of the Platonic ideal of GIRL. I never would have said this to any of the dudes I dated way back when, but much of their reverence for me boiled down to "I thought

girls were STUPID, but *I'm* not stupid, and you and I have so much in common!" Of course, their logic didn't then go, "All genders are equal!" but instead "I guess you're"—wait for it, babybros, it's coming— "NOT LIKE OTHER GIRLS! IN FACT, YOU ARE NOT A 'GIRL,' BUT ACTUALLY AN EMBLEM OF DIVINITY PLACED ON THIS EARTH TO MAKE ME HAPPY." For those keeping score at home: *Words like these are never a compliment.* They are, rather, a way for people to disguise misogyny as love. And that's not a good foundation for romantic bliss, no matter how much you want it to be.

It seemed like even the coolest guys I dated wanted me to be MORE THAN A WOMAN. They seemed to think that a female human being with her own autonomous thoughts and life was ger-*oss*, so I didn't protest too loudly if I liked the person enough. Instead, I was evasive in the way I learned to be when I was younger—and, very brilliantly, expected a different outcome.

By the numbers, here's a truncated catalog of the fallout from my repeated escapes, having found myself trapped in yet another collaborative projection: two and a half broken engagements, four tattoos (I wasn't kidding about this before) bearing my name, initials, and/or handwriting, plus innumerable instances when I was the butt of that most abysmal of would-be compliments: "You're different from anyone I've been with before—you're the only girl I actually feel close to." I tried to interpret these "compliments" the way I did as a teenager—as the highest commendation possible—even though I knew better. But seeing them for what they really were would strip me of the feeling that I wasn't strange after all—I was SPECIAL. Even better, I was pretty certain that, despite an annoyingly persistent sense of churning sadness, I wasn't alone.

Except I was, more than ever. I wanted to be close to most of these people, and I couldn't grasp why I still felt totally lonely when I was with them, even though they claimed to love me so much. It's almost funny to me now: I didn't understand why, after sequestering my love life as far away as possible from the way I actually lived the

rest of my life, *I still felt so isolated*! HOW COME NO ONE COULD RELATE TO ME IN A MEANINGFUL WAY THROUGH THIS TENUOUS, UNREPRESENTATIVE SMOKE-SCREEN OF A LIE-PERSONA THAT I WAS CONSTANTLY CALIBRATING TO PREVENT JUST THAT?!!! I had all but handed them the keys to this here furtive nightmare heart!

As you've probably surmised, all of this pretending, and being rewarded for pretending, has completely fucked with my head and made me feel like no one wants ME (the "real me," whatever that may be at a given moment). They just want this mirage they've helped me create, and the minute I act differently, it's like I've ruined everything for them, since they can't continue to see me as their fantasy-hologram.

This finally came to a head after a particularly unhinged breakup a while back. I was dating (and eventually became engaged to) a guy not really named Brian. Like me, he was a writer, and he was pretty successful at it. I trusted and felt understood by him, even though he had the tendency to valorize me in that dreamgirl way. I don't know why I didn't find it alarming that I rarely felt the desire to bring him to shows with me or ask him to meet my friends or let him know if I was sad or angry about something or talk to him about my work. I kept our relationship closed off from the rest of my world and the rest of myself. So I shouldn't have been surprised when he started telling me I was the most immaculate bastion of womanhood who had ever lived, and didn't he see how I had saved his life, and would I marry him?

I wholeheartedly loved this guy, and I think that feeling was so consumptive that I said yes despite every reservation I had. Then, as our relationship neared the one-year mark, I started relaxing a bit. I got less insecure. Bit by bit, I let him see more of me—which you would think would be an optimal plan of action if you are GOING TO BE WITH SOMEONE FOREVER, but it did not go well. One example: For the longest time, I pretended to want fast food every time he was in the mood for it. When I finally confessed that I was trying to eat less meat, he acted betrayed. He scolded me, saying he had "always appreciated" that I was "one of those girls who don't have to be a vegetarian." I hadn't realized how important that had been for his Perfect Girlfriend ideal!

Here's another, more telling example: Brian supported my lit'rary aspirations and work (as I did his) until other people started to do the same. I got an editing job that I love and devote most of my time to (for transparency's sake: It's Rookie), started work on a book, and got a gig at a national music magazine. This last thing, which I was really excited about, incited a cataclysmic fight that let me know that Brian wanted me to be successful—as long as I was *way* less successful than he was. The day my first piece came out, Brian didn't even read it. Instead, he sulked all day, then had a screaming fit outside my bedroom door that ended in his breaking it with his fists. I went to a friend's house for the night, where I made the decision I had known was coming for almost a year: Having the life I had always wanted for myself seemed far more attractive than managing and coddling someone who couldn't handle that. Why, when I had my own pleasures and tastes and goals and friends and EVERYTHING, was I still agreeing to trot out the boring, supportive-muse archetype? I was over it, at long last. I broke up with him.

In the aftermath of that relationship, I wanted to learn to be more open with people, but the whole idea was shaky and hard to apply to reality. I wondered if it was even possible to be in a relationship where I didn't have to prioritize someone else, or become their compliant attaché, to be loved. I remember saying to a friend that I felt like a satellite, like I couldn't hope to be a part of the world, but only to kind of hang out *around* it by myself. I felt ragged and foreign and alienated from everything/everyone. Because being told you're "not like anyone else" all the time is, guess fucking what, very isolating.

But I wasn't ONLY a victim. I had a hand in turning myself into a SATELLITE OF LOVE by staying quiet—which, in these relationships, was kind of deceptive—and I had to figure out what parts of this mess I could change. I began with the most obvious potential curative I could: *talking*. That's it! Just opening my mouth and saying something that would be true even if the other person weren't there. I had to believe that whatever came out wouldn't shock my audience into permanently abandoning me. If they couldn't hang, that was their deal.

In my mad scramble away from my old DREAMGIRL default, I've had to be careful not to jump headlong into how exciting it is to be THE REAL GIRL. I have to keep reminding myself that treating me like a full person doesn't qualify someone for a HUGE REWARD—that's, like, baseline what I should have expected all along. A few months back, instead of committing myself fully to a brilliant weirdo with a heart of gold who helped get me through that last breakup just because he was kind, I acknowledged that I didn't want to keep seeing him—but I had to ignore the sizable chunk of me that was all, "But he's NICE to you!"

I'm only JUST starting to inch away from a lifetime of reducing myself to what others want me to be, and it's hard. I have no idea how to relate to great, cute people I actually like and want to be honest with. I had an anxiety attack the other night while I was out with my best friend and a new person I'm dating. Nothing was wrong. The standup we were seeing wasn't all great, but some of it was (I guess I DO love alternative comedy…OK, the guy was totally Craig, you got me), and I was excited for these two people to meet… or so I had thought. EXCEPT HOLY SHIT OK UH I HATE THIS WHY AM I EARNESTLY SHOWING THIS DUDE MY LIFE/TASTES/THE PEOPLE I LOVE AND TRUST? I didn't realize it at the time, but I think I froke out because I had let him *into my world*. I nearly blacked out in a comedy club, I felt so vulnerable.

I still apologize after saying anything with a granule of my real feelings in it—anything sad, or religious, or anxious, or hopeful, or otherwise related to the closed-fern part of me—but the vital thing is that I'm saying it at all. I'm changing the terms on which people can decide whether or not to love me, and while I harbor some fear that my friends won't be able to adjust…it's not that much fear. I used to blur the reality of who I was to make other people happy so they wouldn't abandon me, because I was terrified of being alone. But you know what? Loneliness makes me sad, but being alone is rad—not ONE person tries to talk about Eric Clapton with you! I frequently get knock-kneed about SHOWING MY HAND, but I have to keep reminding myself that the only way to "lose" is to go back to how I used to be.

And though I feel like the world's most pristine specimen of *Dorkus malorkusa* when I try to get to know people this new way, it's already proven itself to be incredibly worthwhile. It makes me feel warm and filled with actual camaraderie in a way that's entirely new to me. That's scary, but I am trying to be brave, because it's also pretty beautiful. Other people, when they like me now, are liking the real McCoy. It can feel so good—so certain and safe—to secret yourself away, I know. It is also the thing that allowed people to take advantage of me and blotted out any hope I had of straightforwardly loving another person for years. So I'm not going to do it anymore. I'm through living up to my name now. ★

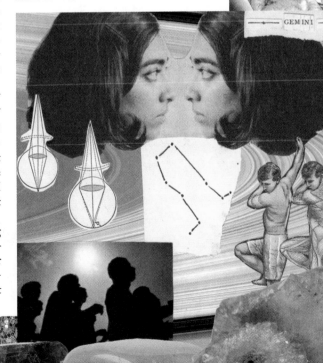

DIY Glitter Globe

A sparkly party in a jar.
By Emma D.

On one exceptionally hot summer day, I found myself going through boxes of Christmas decorations. I was looking for glitter the way you look for leftover ice cream in the freezer—I knew it had to be there, buried under everything else. I eventually uncovered a snow globe, and as I watched its shimmery flakes flutter around, I realized: There are so many things you could put in that magic liquid that would be even prettier than pine trees and tiny sleighs, and that could be enjoyed all year! After some experimentation, I learned that there are as many possibilities as you can imagine, most of them totally easy to make at home.

WHAT YOU'LL NEED:

- A clear glass jar with a lid. Any size or shape works as long as the surface of the glass is smooth.
- Decorations
- Water. Use distilled or bottled water if the tap water in your area has a high mineral content. (A telltale sign of "hard water" is if the drains in your house look rusty or chalky when they aren't clean.)
- Glitter in the color(s) of your choice
- Clear-drying waterproof adhesive, like glue-gun glue
- Liquid glycerin, which will make the glitter fall slower. It's available at most drugstores (optional).
- Enamel or acrylic paint to cover any labeling on the lid (optional).

What you put in your glitter globe (besides glitter) depends on the scene you want to set and/or where you see your globe on the cute-to-creepy spectrum. If you can imagine it, you can put it in a glitter globe! Even the ugliest stuff can look cool if you coat it with water-resistant paint. Rummage around the house or dollar stores for plastic and ceramic tchotchkes that will fit inside your jar. Collect seashells, rocks, and crystals for a fantastical seascape or find some tiny plastic cupcakes for a mini Marie Antoinette-esque banquet. Go wild, but whatever you decide to use, just be sure that it's made with a material that won't rust, bloat, discolor, decay, or dissolve in water. Unless you want your globe to look REALLY creepy.

Here's what I found in my house:

I wanted my globe to evoke something between Hieronymus Bosch's wild triptych, *Garden of Earthly Delights*, and the mutant toys from *Toy Story*.

STEP ONE

Plan your scene. Make sure the centerpiece, which you will glue to the lid of the jar, isn't taller than the jar or wider than the diameter of the lid.

TWO

Glue the parts of your centerpiece together and let them air dry.

THREE

Once the centerpiece is dry, glue it to the inside of the lid and wait for it to seal completely.

FOUR

Fill the jar about 90 percent of the way with water. Add a dash of glycerin, if you decided to use it, and a big pinch of glitter. Throw in any other elements (like small beads or plastic gems) that you want to float around in the water.

FIVE

Trace the inner rim of the lid with glue to form a watertight seal. Holding the lid, dunk the centerpiece into the jar (you might want to do this over a sink).

SIX

Screw the lid onto the jar as tightly as you can, then flip it over and watch the magic happen!

You can paint the lid or embellish the outside of your jar with stickers and ribbons, too.

Even a single figurine and a dash of glitter is enough for a perfectly realized water-filled world. If you end up with a lot of leftover material, make small installations to brighten the duller corners of your home—just keep in mind that you might accidentally creep the shit out of your family or roommates, like I did! ☺

I Will Paint the Sky

A glorious roundup of poetry by Rookie readers and writers.

May

Tori Rae Davis

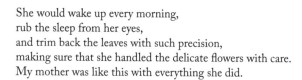

My mother used to grow red roses
the same color as her hair,
in the garden out back.

She would wake up every morning,
rub the sleep from her eyes,
and trim back the leaves with such precision,
making sure that she handled the delicate flowers with care.
My mother was like this with everything she did.

Her small hands twisting the petals through her fingertips
with a face that longed for something more than a garden
and a three-bedroom home
that wasn't even hers to keep.

Her hair just to her shoulders—
it never seems to grow any longer
no matter how hard she tries.

My mother is a woman who wants everything
and gets half of what she deserves.

She scrubs the floorboards of our home
till the splinters wear down,
unable to bury themselves in the soles of our feet
for at least two weeks.
Never longer though.
Our home so old that it's spitting up the wood

My mother can't stand this.
Her frail fingers unwilling to wrap themselves
around sharp edges in fear of coming up with a fistful
of thorns.

My mother used to grow red roses
the same color as her hair,
in the garden out back.

Her fingers twisting through the petals,
she stands in the neighbor's yard,
longing.

The Milk Poem

Ryan Murphy

Late, at the bottom of the field, my sister and I
watch the dairy cows turn in for sleep. They cry
in the barn. We hear them low across the grass,
each of them moaning: *moon, moon.*

My sister turns to me and asks if sky is animal,
exploded: I tell her yes, and also that she is matter,
compacted. Light hardens on her hands like prayer
as she stands beneath the moon. It's dripping milk.

In Catholic school, they taught us that all of creation
has only one heart. That it beats within us.
That cigarettes may clot God's will. That science
makes every human organ a milkless flower.

Sister Jamie poured a drop of red food coloring
into a bowl of milk and told us, as the veins branched,
that God moved both within and without us,
but that we infinitely absorbed Him. Sun

to Earth; cycles of dark. My sister and I know
that in the blue night, light is anything that can
be caught but never held. Spilled milk. Our bodies
set each other into bonfires: the moonlight makes us look obscene.

And yet we know this blind field exists only to collect milk
and meat. Each female cow swells with her own liquid
while my sister's hair rolls away from her like cream.
Our bodies answer to moons, not to milk—

each of us licks the shores of our skin
until we become banks of our own blood.
Here, in the clockless night, the only fluid
is white. God drips red. *Moon, moon.*

My sister tilts her head to the constellations—
her lips are pink, as the meeting of milk and blood.

Getting a Way

Madison Adams

Cigar cutter arms
Reaching, ever reaching
But are they mine
Or yours?
There's nothing to do
There's nothing I can do
Just leave me to myself

He emotes so hard
It's so hard to emote
Slammed doors
Shut mind
Heavy with pain
In his knees
In his brain
Pulls him under
Waves crashing, crunching
My body
Keeps getting thinner
He holds my head under
He is a strong swimmer

I attempt to align my aches with his
For every one of his nightmares
I have a memory
For every panic attack
A physical assault
I consider propping up his bruises with my scars
We could build a church
Or a bar
Structured out of bullet holes
Supported by columns of razor burns

I buy a plane ticket instead
I build wings from all my tickets
I build a house, a home, a car, a manicured lawn
A husband, 2.4 kids, a dog, memberships with Al-Anon
And yet I still have leftovers
To share
With all the angels of this city

But oh, what a pity
That audacity
Is not the same as love
Diseased pigeons don't count as doves
He said,
"Baby, it's all in your head"
I said,
"Yeah, well, that's what I'm afraid of."

I am a runaway woman-girl on the loose
Dodge bullets, dodge compliments
Slide out of my noose
There's nothing I can't do
I'll just leave you to yourself
I'll just leave you

I am notorious
Notoriously hard to get
I will always be the girl who finds a way
The woman who gets her way
The one who got away
Just in time

July

Emma S.

Breakfast is sausage and eggs, made
in house. The waiter has tattoos, sailors

turn towards your face. We are on the beach.
We are in the surf. We are mermaids

but only every other Monday. Potatoes
and cupcakes too. We drink rosé until our mouths

open up and the trees recede. They are sharp
exclamation points clinging to the side of the car

and dresses are what make the days change
on screen. I am in red, in blue, in gingham

though we hardly ever get lost. You are
a time machine and need no help and so

we lose time easily. Days even. Weeks
pass and our bellies ask for more

leaves in our tea. On the bottom of the glass
there are messages and we read, no translation

Yes! The ocean! We jump, shoes in hand,
conscious of the cold and the seaweed

which has wrapped our hands so tight.

I Close My Eyes When We Go Up the Hill

Meg Matthias

We ride the roller coasters after a four-hour drive,
putting our hands up upon reaching the summit,
smiling for the cameras
or pretending to be asleep—
we are too cool to be frightened of something so secure,
too intelligent,
too happy in our bravery to feel anything but elation//

(but when we have just been strapped into our restraints,
and the mechanical sounds of an uphill track
are grating in our feet and
in my mind
and in my stomach—)

We ride only the largest,
only the best,
and talk about branching out to metal
so our teeth won't vibrate
and our heads won't
crash together—
We put up our hands because
WE ARE BRAVE,
and we will proclaim it in this one single movement of triumph//

(But when the tunnels are coming closer
and closer
and enclosing us in gloom and water-slide born drips,
when it feels like we are miners underground—
and you know what happens to some miners,
don't you?
You know that some miners never come back?)

We have sent our canaries
ahead of time,
scouting out the site through vigorous research,
crunching the numbers
and watching others embark before us,
and come back whole.
We are not afraid,
because WE ARE BRILLIANT,
and in our genius
we have become invincible.

(But even though we are the
never-dying gods,
adding constellations to the sky left and right,
I close my eyes
so very tightly,
and I fold my arms
neatly in my lap
so I do not scrape the ceiling.)

The Czech Officer

Ry

He was the kind of man who liked the pay but not the job. He was the kind of man to whom integrity meant as little as the decorations on his uniform. He was the kind of man who called after the skinny Czech women in the street without wondering why he did it. He was the kind of man who would drown those women in his ocean eyes. He was the kind of man who would pour them large glasses of his cheapest red wine. He was the kind of man who waited until after they had glazed eyes and had let down their blond hair. He was the kind of man who said "I love you" before sex but not afterwards, when he would make her leave because he had work in the morning.

Sophomore Year

Camille Delaune

It passed without my permission: violently, quietly, with purpose.
Took my apologies with pride,
didn't give me a chance to grasp what it was running with.
Fed me remnants of newspaper articles by the spoonful
and thought that was enough.
Facts were never worth losing the night, but was it me who made
    you think so?
I meant to tell you that I'm still here, I'm still waiting.

Honey filled the swollen cracks around my nail beds.
I'm asking you to consume me. I'm asking you to be something
    real.

the left arm is warmer

Stephanie Dinkmeyer

the left arm is warmer
because it's closer to the heart
this isn't a poem about
love
or the metaphorical
red
heart
this is a science poem
that I want
you
to think about

windows

Greer Clarke

car windows
should be banned
all four

i hate having the windows down
i like being snug
i like picking the temperature
i like talking to myself and being able to hear the music without
    it competing
with the horns and tyres and air rushing beside me

which is why they should be banned

occasionally i put the windows down
and make myself feel like a teenage dream
a young liver of life
and i guess i can tell why other people like it

i can actually tell how fast i am driving
and appreciate the temperature of the air of the place where i am
    living
and deal with it

so yeah
ban car windows

paperclip

Tyler

he calls you
paperclip
not because you hold everyone together
when the wind tries so hard
to scatter souls
or because your eyes flash hints of silver
when you talk about your favorite song
or because your lip ring taints your kisses
metallic.

paperclip
because he can downsize you in an instant
replacing you with a version of yourself
that doesn't weigh his pockets down
your body now too small to hold your essence
and a mouth that will only open wide enough
to swallow.
you are easily forgotten
but somehow always end up
attached to his keychain.

paperclip
because he can bend you to his will
and you don't even notice
until everything else
begins falling out of your grasp.
every time he snaps you back into place
the world has only changed
but a fraction of a centimeter
and you're used to measuring your life in kilometers.

paperclip
because he is a staple
leaving puncture wounds in everything he touches
a few drops of blood in every corner of your mind
and when you learn how to extract him from your heart
no goodbye is successful enough to patch
permanent holes you fold yourself in upon
and pretend not to notice.
to this day,
that chapter of your life remains dog-eared
and you wonder
why you still have trouble
picking locks.

Pregnancy Scare

Anne Menasche

The moon is hollow as my body and everything
is fine. I press the shell of his shoulder to my ear

and listen. God, still the earth and let me hear the blue
tide of the television; the detective has just shut

the car door and stands on a dark street in Cambridge
and is about to knock, I can feel it. His breathing steadies

me. I want to know who did it. I want to know
what was done: In sleep I missed the beginning,

just as in sleep I missed the end of another mystery.
We knocked through the room from a long journey

and fell upon the rusted bed, drinking the smell
of Lubec, Maine, the most eastern point

of our good earth. As we drove north the world
undressed for us. Maples shook off their red wigs. Pines

got down on bended knee or, naked entirely,
lay on top of one another, shoulder to shoulder,

hip to hip and now, the field green and untrimmed
shrugs off her robe of fog. She waits with us

for morning. The door opens and the detective steps
inside, past a mist-green phone. I can taste the sea

on the back of his neck. He is the salt of my earth.
When light cradles us he will turn over and kiss

my elbow. The detective climbs the stairs. I have never wanted
to know anything so badly

as what will happen next. My sisters and I
were all accidents; our parents wanted sons to march

our last name down the aisle. Instead they got three
wombs. He stirs and I imagine that he has said

my name, asked me for a glass of water, but
it's the detective, calling for another Anne,

delivering different news.

For the Blond One

Stephanie

Tonight we walked to the edge of the world
And I finally pushed you off.

Uncertain, Texas

Hayley Grgurich

Uncertain hangs thickly in ambiguity
like the clouds of gnats that get stuck
in the unnatural green of the algae
that clings to the banks like
grits to your ribs.

It's a town
with its brow permanently furrowed.
Perpetually unsure of itself,
but thinkin' hard on the matter.
Nothing moves.
As if the air,
the grass, the moss, the lake
were stuck in viscous concentration,
the atmosphere abuzz
with ideas and horseflies.

Spanish moss fingers dangle
from the arms of dreamers
who sit cradled in the
hammock hands of live oaks,
staring into the sky,
wondering what to name their home.
And when you oar your way
through the vague waters,
you sweep those mossy fingers
to the side like the thick velvet of a quilt
as you tuck a sleeping child into bed,
never disturbing a thought,
uncertain of the power
of thoughts
born in sleep.

V card

Elizabeth Perry

"lost it?" an earring? yeah, one of my best
must have come out when he pulled off my dress
but other than that i think i'm intact
not sure i can say the same for his back
i had nothing to lose—or have you forgot
you're whole when you're fucked and whole when you're not

will i see it again? like a long lost friend?
does it come back around like a spring/summer trend?
will it be handed in if it's lost on a train?
is it lost like the loss of a football game?
did he take it from me? did i give it away?
if it's meant to be mine why don't i get a say?

i'm still the same weight, all my organs are there
nothing gets popped 'cause it's just tissue tear
i don't feel any different, though you say that i should
nothing goes missing, though you said that it could
(apart from my earring which I've already said
and potentially one of the springs in his bed)

i'm still good at cooking and i'm still pretty smart
i still love my parents, still try to make art
still have my principles, i still see no stain
my worth is untouched and i feel no shame
perhaps it is you that had something to lose—
control of my body and of my right to choose.

The Sea is a Reflection

Choy-Ping Clarke-Ng

Ninety-five percent of the world's oceans
are yet to be explored by humans—
as is my body (my ocean);

it's an expanse of pale canvas,
occasionally route-marked by old scars, old freckles
and new bumps.

Every contact with this skin / sea sends
R I P P L E S throughout and sometimes storms.
I never drown though—I never let her.

Whoever Fights Monsters

Stephanie

Some people drowned
I waded out into the deep,
Closed my eyes and let go
But I couldn't keep from breathing
I couldn't keep from swimming
(Just keep swimming)

Some people surrendered to the darkness
I liked it there, too, for a while
But I fought monsters
I didn't slay them all
Just enough
So I could sleep
And dream them vanquished
(Just keep dreaming)

Some people crawled,
Buried themselves under ground
But I painted my heart the color of the sky
And made it to this misty milestone
And now I will paint the sky
The color of my heart

when the end result is nothing

Stephanie Dinkmeyer

in writing,
when the end result is nothing,
the only possibility
is that you have
too little
or
too much ☼

Magical creatures

Pictures from a charmed life.
By Eleanor

Styling by the Witch & the Glitter Badger.
Thanks to Hannah, Louisa, and Rachel for
modeling.

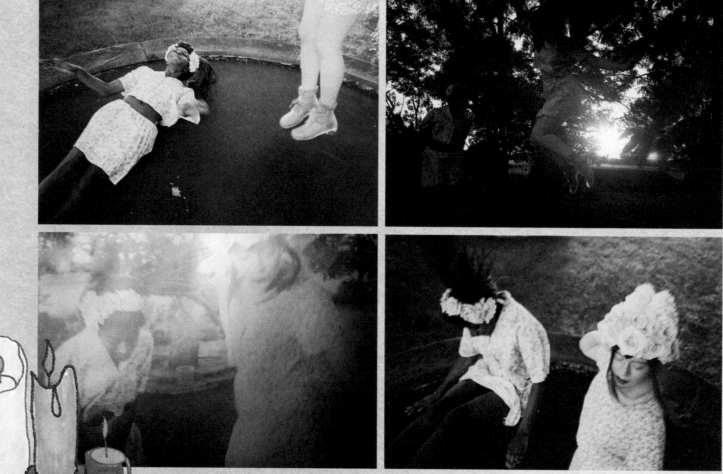

When a Crush Is Enough

I think of unrequited love as a daisy field of me time.
By Dylan

My love career has so far consisted of mostly crushes, occasionally requited, and some light experimentation with commitment. That's pretty much perfect for where I am right now. I've spent my prime crush years busting my ass at school and at work, growing up, learning stuff, and having a life full of community and culture and so many different kinds of rewarding relationships. These life zones take up lots of time, and a lot of myself. Love does, too.

It reminds me of a passage from the Bible of Babes, from the Babe God:

> There is a time to admire, and a time to pursue; a time for flings, and a time to commit; a time for me, and a time for relationships; a time for snacks, and…actually all of the times are for snacks.

Now I don't take this entire scripture literally, but there's definitely some truth there. There is, indeed, a time for crushing—a time to admire and dream but to leave it at that. Sometimes, crushing is enough. Sometimes, it's perfect.

A crush has an expected narrative. It goes like this: First you like someone, then they like you, then you love someone, then they love you, and then you become each other's someones, more or less. But keeping crushes in that first phase—liking a person—and letting go of the rest of the story is, quite often, *the best thing ever*. There are billions of humans out there for you to crush on. Think of the possibilities! Filling up your life bucket with crushes—whether it's a total-fantasy-celebrity-person or the babe who makes your coffee every afternoon—has distinct benefits, especially for someone like me. Maybe for you, too.

Unpursued crushes have been small miracles of self-rescue in my life. When all else turns to shit, isn't it nice to remember that there are beautiful and extremely likable people on the planet? A crush can be a golden, glistening nugget of joy in your pocket, no matter what else is up in your world. Sometimes crushes flash into your life like bolts of lightning and sometimes they develop over time and you just can't help it. When you're open to having those feelings, and can lighten up enough to allow them to just *exist*, they can make you really happy. For me, it's almost always worth it, especially when life gets weird.

My most important crushes have happened during times of transition. During one such period, when a lot of stressful change was doing a number on my self-confidence, I had a see-you-across-the-room-lock-eyes-weak-knees encounter with a boy at a party. No grand romance ensued, unless you count some late-night online chats, but it's exactly what I needed in that moment. Not affirmation via the attention of a dude, but a nudge to get out of my head and remember that I'm not the worst, after all, and that life is really fun when humans make contact with other humans instead of sulking around solo-style!

More recently, there's been a boyperson who dropped in from another town. He arrived right after my college graduation, a milestone that made me feel like I had busted open a pair of huge French doors overlooking an epic valley while wearing a silk kimono, declaring, "LIFE, I'M READY FOR YOU NOW!" Crush status: ongoing. It isn't poised to go anywhere, though—for one, we live in different states. But having him to think about reminds me that having feelings about a person is really nice, and those feelings can be a bigger part of my life now that I'm not constantly doing schoolwork. After all the stress and sleeplessness leading up to graduation, it's *rad* to be newly available for adventures involving cute faces.

Because, as much as having a crush is submitting to a mind-consuming, phone-checking obsession with another person, it actually has almost nothing to do with anyone else! It's a hobby you pursue alone. I think of it as high-quality me time. It also gives me a reason to step up my game a little. Can we all admit to the process of self-checkout once a crush establishes brain residence? You check your hair game, internet presence, record collection, and personal accomplishments to convince yourself that this person might be impressed with you; and, by taking inventory of your own radness, you remind yourself what a baller you are. This is a great thing to do every once in a while, and crushes give us a nice little daisy field of time and focus to do it in.

When I look back on the party-crush I mentioned earlier, I think about the time we spent trading videos of favorite live versions and B-sides of glam-rock and power-pop songs from the '70s. I was already low-key into that kind of thing, but the hours I clocked being into him turned into hours clocked trying to find things he, apparently well-versed in these subjects, had never seen before. I came away with a whole library of personal favorites that now make up my DJ playlists and LP collections. While I definitely don't credit dude with getting me into that music, I do thank him for inspiring me to spend so much time discovering new-old stuff, which was *totally* worthwhile. Both self-love and other-love are projects and practices—not just feelings—and I like crushes for wedging open a block in my mind for such activities to go down.

My newest crush started during a mixed-feelings time. Following my graduation, I've been partly elated and confident about the future and partly self-doubtful and confused because, suddenly, nothing about life is certain or defined like it was in school. Who are you when a huge part of your life is over? When crush-of-late and I started talking, I, like always, dove deep into my social-media data: How was I coming across on Facebook? What kind of person did I look like in my pictures? Was I still slaying on Twitter? I found my answers real fast: I'm a bomb-ass lady with cool clothes, fly friends, and a whole lot of awesome and promising things going on. And sometimes I'm funny, at least to anyone who's into dad-type puns. Thanks for the reminder, self!

I know that not everyone gets a jolt of confidence from a crush. Sometimes, unrequited love is agonizing, frustrating, and just TOO consuming. I feel you, and can confirm that those vibes continue post-adolescence (sorry). But I've found that certain strategies help me make the most of any crush. Maybe they will help you, too, tenderhearts?

• **Let go of any expectations about the outcome.** If your M.O. is to enjoy this phase, *let yourself enjoy it*. Easier aid than done, I know, and how you accomplish that is a journey of personal discovery. What do you do if you can't get there, if you find yourself stuck feeling like if this relationship doesn't happen, LIFE is a sham? My advice in such cases is to…

• **Ride it out.** You are probably going to feel this way for a while. You're already in the deep end of the unrequited crush pool, and, in my experience, you don't just pop out of there and dry off and run along your merry way. Last time I was mired in these waters, crushing on a person who had no interest in entertaining my heart-flutterings, I finally, begrudgingly accepted that he must be a big dumb-dumb, because why else would someone not want to get with me???

• **Try to detach feelings of need and/or acquisition from the person you are obsessing over.** Attempt to change the impulse of MUST HAVE to JUST LOVE. Focus on appreciating what's cool about that person without the self-torture of wondering why they just won't be yours. Instead of thinking, "This human is a perfect angel, and if they aren't mine, then I give up, goodbye planet," try, "This human is a perfect angel, and it gives me hope that other perfect angels must be out there, too, I can't wait to meet them!"

It gets easier to maintain these perspectives after you've clocked some years pining for many a human (a really boring Older Than Thou statement, but hear me out). You realize that, *Hey—I'm going to have a lot of these feelings in my lifetime. Some are more light and fluffy, some are torturous, but they all come and go, thank goodness.*

Because in the end, isn't it a special kind of fun to consider love in a million different places, with a million goofy faces? Crush feelings are always there for the taking, even if they last only five seconds. It might be all in your head and heart, but those are important places, and about as real as it gets. ♔

Bathing Beauty   By Eleanor

1. Tomorrow New Knows - The Beatles
2. Anemone - Brian Jonestown Massacre
3. Come Down Softly to My Soul - Spacemen 3
4. Daydream - Ash Ra Tempel
5. It's Choade My Dear - Connan Mockasin
6. River Man - Nick Drake
7. Alla L'aa Ke - Alhaji Bai Konte
8. Ladies of the Canyon - Joni Mitchell
9. Dark Star - Grateful Dead
10. Golden Hair - Syd Barrett
11. Space - Thurston Moore
12. Delius (Song of Summer) - Kate Bush
13. Daffy Duck - Animal Collective
14. Landmines - St. Vincent
15. Stay the Same - Bonobo
16. Incense - Erykah Badu
    (feat. Kirsten Agnesta)
17. Trek Mountainous Heck - Flamingods
18. Harken Sunshine - Sun Araw
19. In Here the World Begins - Broadcast
20. 1983...(A Merman I Should Turn to be)
    - The Jimi Hendrix Experience
21. Journey in Satchidananda - Alice Coltrane
22. Charm - Four Tet
23. Piano Days - Teebs
24. Biggy - Warpaint
25. Apply - Glasser
26. Endless Shore - Melody's Echo Chamber
27. An Orphan of Fortune - MGMT
28. Welcome to the Now Age - Prince Rama
29. Ice Sheets on Feet Prints - Dustin Wong
30. Mountain of Needles - Brian Eno and David Byrne
31. City of Love - Blues Control and Laraaji

HELLO
MY NAME IS

SEPTEMBER 2014: **WORK**

Hi, Rookies!

First things first: This month marks Rookie's three-year anniversary! Thanks for sticking around this long, or for joining us recently. We begin our senior year with the theme WORK. Schoolwork, job-work, self-care-work. I just watched *All About Eve* for the first time, in which Bette Davis as Margo Channing talks about the "career […] of being a woman." In the movie, the speech is horribly antiquated and actually about the work of keeping a man, but when I first heard her get ready to discuss the work of "being a woman," I projected a lot onto it and was like "SING IT, SISTER!" This is because, lately, I have felt like a crucial part of my jobs both at Rookie and in the play I mentioned in July's letter is to spend time every day working on just my CONFIDENCE. Believing in myself, being able to trust my instincts, not letting my work suffer due to girlish tendencies to recoil or to get myself down. In the early run of the play in Chicago, I had a very specific routine for self-care before a show so that I would be able to go onstage and think just about the other actors in relation to my character instead of about what the *audience* thought of *me*. It involved listening to Eve and Lil' Kim and dancing in my dressing room and running around it touching everything and following my instincts so that I could achieve this total, physical self-trust. And I would write down and say out loud—because that's when things become true, when an intellectual emotion becomes a physical knowing—that I am awesome and mighty and cannot be made small. So when Margo gave her speech, before I really heard what she was saying, I was like, OH TOTALLY, THE WORK OF BEING A WOMAN, HAVING TO FORCE YOURSELF TO BE A MEGALOMANIAC JUST SO YOU CAN REACH A BASELINE OF CREATIVITY! I guess for me it's a matter of picturing my life's work without confidence/stamina/GUSTO, and then picturing it WITH, and the WITH one is much more full and real and plentiful. Think of how many incompetent assholes are successful just because they are *confident*! Or of how many competent people hold themselves back! If you can master both competence AND confidence, then you ought to be able to do anything you want. And as humiliating as it might feel to write the words "I AM MIGHTY" down in a Moleskine…who cares about that, I guess. There is a bigger issue at hand.

So that's all about job-work and self-care-work, but before I hand off this month to the rest of our contributors, I would like to share with you three games I played with myself in high school to make schoolwork more bearable:

1. Keep an ear out for any amusing dialogue that could one day make for a good TV show and write it all down, seeing every class as *research*.
2. Make outfits in your brain by combining stuff different people in your class are wearing.
3. Bring a bag of your candy of choice to class and eat a piece every time the same student interrupts the teacher.

Have a solid back-to-school, and thank you again for being here with us as Rookie becomes a SENIOR. (Expect a lot more bullying and penny-throwing.)

LOVE, TAVI

SONGS FOR CUTTING CLASS BY TAVI

1. SHE'S LOSING IT — BELLE & SEBASTIAN   2. STREETS OF FIRE — THE NEW PORNOGRAPHERS
3. BABY JUST BREAK — KING TUFF   4. ME AND JULIO DOWN BY THE SCHOOLYARD — PAUL SIMON
5. RUN, RUN, RUN — THE VELVET UNDERGROUND   6. GEOMETRY OF TWIGS — SKINNED TEEN
7. TROUBLEMAKER — SHANNON AND THE CLAMS   8. BAD SEEDS — BEAT HAPPENING
9. CHERRY BOMB — BRATMOBILE   10. WHAT A DAY TO DIE — SHOP ASSISTANTS
11. TIME KEEPS TIME — NEO BOYS   12. TEENAGERS FROM MARS — THE MISFITS
13. BAD REPUTATION — JOAN JETT   14. JUDY IS A PUNK — RAMONES
15. PARKING LOT — THE COATHANGERS   16. TIME OF HER TIME — RIDE   17. PACER — THE AMPS
18. CATHOLIC EDUCATION — TEENAGE FANCLUB   19. UNFAIR — PAVEMENT
20. CHEERLEADER — ST. VINCENT   21. WHITE TEETH TEENS — LORDE

There's kind of nothing better than fresh school supplies.
By Shriya   Thanks to Claire Christerson for modeling.

Opening Bell

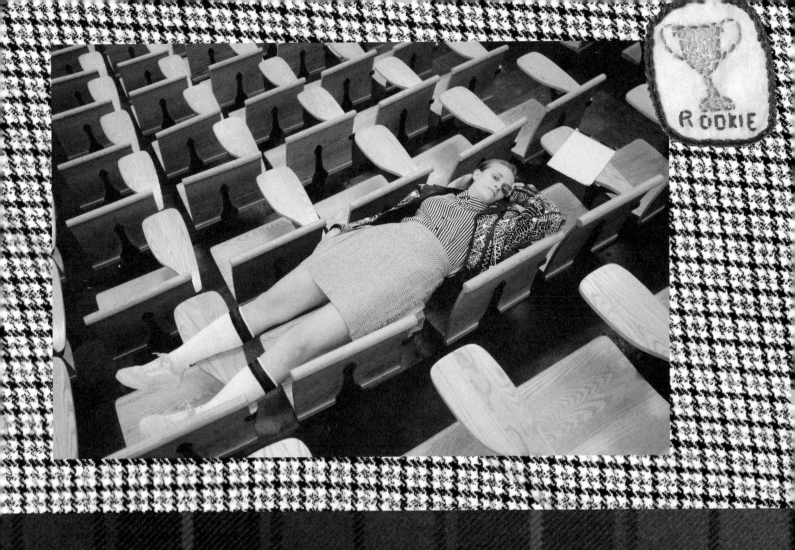

SPRAY

SORRY

How to Write a College Admissions Essay

Do as I say, not as I did.   By Gabby. Illustration by Emma D.

You know the saying "Those who can't do, teach?" I delayed completing the essay for my application to the college I currently attend for so long that I didn't turn it in until 30 minutes before the cutoff; yet here I am trying to tell you how to write a college application essay. Now, if you'll just hand over three easy payments of $69.95, we can get this seminar rolling.

My under-the-wire approach to my academic future was not the result of extreme procrastination, but of extreme deliberation. I started my college essays about six months before they were due, but with every draft, I felt increasingly inadequate. I spent the first few months of my senior year of high school complaining about my applications to everyone who would listen. I probably got seven hours of sleep during that entire fall season, most of which occurred in the middle of class. I got a weird stress-induced rash on my arms and stopped washing my eye makeup off before bed, which really enhanced the existing bags under my eyes for an overall glamorous look. Every time I sat down to work on my essays, I imagined a conference table lined with faceless academics in beige suits who'd scornfully stare me down and murmur to one another, sounding like the adults on Charlie Brown cartoons.

What's great about college application essays is that they give you a chance to show a school facets of your personality that test scores and GPAs can't convey. But it's really frustrating to have to summarize what makes you so special in 1,000 words or less. (I once asked my guidance counselor if I could just link to my Twitter instead of submitting an essay. She didn't stop laughing until I looked her in the eye and said, "That wasn't a joke.") I didn't have perfect grades or standardized test scores in high school, so I felt like my essays would make or break my chances of getting into the schools I really cared about.

No one ever told me that college admissions are mostly nonsense. But it's true: It won't ruin your life if you don't get into the college of your dreams—unless you let it. So shake that imaginary group of stuffy adults out of your head and write what feels good to you. Right now it's just you and, if you want, me, your incredibly glamorous yet somehow still down-to-earth and approachable admissions-essay-writing guide. Here is a timeline to follow that will hopefully be helpful and save you from any weird stress-induced rashes.

1. PICKING A TOPIC

You've mustered up the courage to sit down and finally write that essay. You've opened a document and titled it "My Great Big College Essay." And now you're like, *OK, cool…hmmm, yeah that's enough for now. Maybe I should go check the fridge to see if anything new has materialized in there since I last looked?* Hey! Stop right there! Before you take a break, I want you to set a timer for 20 minutes and force yourself to come up with ideas for your essay for those entire 20 minutes. When time's up, you can check the fridge as much as you want.

While you're thinking, keep in mind that most schools require that you submit a main essay of 500 or so words that will give them a glimpse of who you are, in addition to shorter pieces based on specific prompts. In America, a lot of institutions use the Common Application, which offers five different personal essay prompts. A few from this year are:

- Reflect on a time when you challenged a belief or idea. What prompted you to act? Would you make the same decision again?
- Describe a place or environment where you are perfectly content. What do you do or experience there, and why is it meaningful to you?
- Discuss an accomplishment or event, for-

mal or informal, that marked your transition from childhood to adulthood within your culture, community, or family.

The thing about these prompts is that they make me feel like, *Yawwwwwwn* and also like, *OMG, I have no answers for any of these! What's so interesting about* me*? The only place I've ever traveled to is Disney World! How am I supposed to compete with kids who've lived in 17 different countries and probably invented an app that cures cancer?* Maybe you feel this way, too, but the truth is, even if you've never left your hometown, you still have something to say. Never having left your hometown could in itself be your essay topic! I ended up writing my essay about how, even though I was totally underwhelmed by high school, I loved watching movies about high school, and that, in part, is why I want to write TV shows and movies for teenage girls. I never even left the couch, but I had a life experience right there that was worth writing about.

Think about the stuff that gets you excited and see if you can find a way to fit it into one of these prompts. Try to come up with half a dozen or so potential topics for each prompt you've been given. Write down anything that comes to mind, even if you think it's stupid. Totally forget your audience and the fact that this essay will help determine where you go to college. Once you've got a big list of ideas, take another 20-minute session to reflect on your best personality traits, what you're good at, and what your ambitions and goals are. These are the things you want to get across to a college. If you get stumped, ask a good friend or your parents or anyone else who really knows you what they think your best qualities are.

Now, look at your two lists. Can any of the ideas from your first list be used to illustrate something you mentioned in your second list? Maybe a "place where you feel perfectly content" is the mall, because you love people-watching—and this totally ties in with your desire to study psychology because you're interested in how minds work. "A time when you challenged a belief or an idea" could be when some boy in your class said something really sexist and you stood up to him. You can use this story to illustrate how important your personal political beliefs are to you, and talk about how you'd like to develop them even more.

2. WRITING YOUR FIRST DRAFT

So now you've got a third list: ideas that combine elements of lists one and two. Look over this list and pick the topic you feel most excited about. Don't worry, this isn't your final essay, so if you end up not liking it later on, that's A-OK.

Sometimes I like to create an outline before I write, and sometimes I end up being more productive when I just start writing in any random place. Since your essay will have to be pretty short, an outline can be useful to keep you on track. Now, you're definitely old enough to know this already since you're old enough to be applying to college, so feel free to roll your eyes here, but the basic shape of your outline should go like this:

Intro: Set up what are you talking about.
Body: Exemplify that thing.
Conclusion: Don't just summarize what you've already said—come to a new thought about it.

Your essay doesn't have to be super serious if you don't want it to be. Even though lots of people warn against using humor in college essays (because, they say, humor is subjective—but so is everything else!), I think being funny and good-natured in your essay is great, because even the most terrifyingly faceless admissions officers are actually human beings who want the students at their school to be capable of joy. Think about favorite essays you've read. What do you like about them? Try to channel those qualities without parroting anyone else's writing. Just write honestly and don't try to mold yourself into what you feel is the ideal candidate.

3. EDITING

Over a period of a few weeks, try to write three or four different first drafts. If sitting down to write feels overwhelming, force yourself to set a timer for 20 minutes every day and write for at least that long. Once you've got a few drafts done, wait another day to read them. If you can spare it, spend that day not writing at all—just print out your essays and carefully read each one. Which one do you like best? Which do you feel best shows off what you like about yourself? This is the one you're going to edit. But first, since you've already come a long way, take a moment to celebrate! Do whatever that means to you: Teaching yourself all the words to Nicki Minaj's "Anaconda"? Wasting an entire bottle of glue just peeling it off your hands over and over? Eating a roll of cookie dough?

Now to edit. Don't skip this step! Editing what you've written is just as important as writing it. Since college application essays have to be short, every sentence has to count. As you read over your draft, examine each sentence and ask yourself:

1. Is this sentence really necessary?
2. Does it add to the point I'm trying to make about myself?
3. Can it be said in fewer words?

Go through the essay like this, sentence by sentence, at least twice. Then proofread the whole thing for spelling and grammatical errors.

4. PROOFREADING

By now, you're feeling pretty good about your essay. So good, in fact, that you might be like, "But Gabby, can't I just mail this fricking thing already? I'm sick of looking at it!" The bad news is, no, you can't send it off just yet. The good news is, you don't have to look at it again—now's the time to get someone else to look at it.

Find someone to proofread—someone with a good grasp on writing, spelling, and grammar. I recommend an English teacher, current or former. Most teachers are happy to do this, especially because it earns them the right to brag about you when you're a world-renowned whatever-it-is-you-want-to-become. Be sure to ask them way in advance so they'll have enough time to do you this favor—and it *is* a favor, something they're doing in their probably rare free time, so you should probably get them some sort of thank-you gift, too.

You can also ask a friend, parent, or guardian to read what you've written, but I'd hold off on that until you've gotten help from a teacher. Otherwise, you might take what the people you love have to say a little too much to heart. My dad edits technical magazines for a living, but I didn't ask for his opinion on my essays until I felt confident with the state they were in, because I didn't want to end up arguing with him over stuff like my use of the word *literally*.

5. SENDING IT IN

That's it, babe. You're done! But wait—before you pat yourself on the back, GET THAT THING UPLOADED. You wouldn't want to throw away all the hard work you've done by blowing your deadline.

All right, NOW, toss back that cookie dough and sing your heart out. You've earned it. ✎

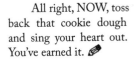

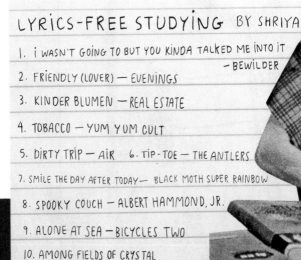

LYRICS-FREE STUDYING BY SHRIYA

1. i WASN'T GOING TO BUT YOU KINDA TALKED ME INTO IT
   — BEWILDER
2. FRIENDLY (LOVER) — EVENINGS
3. KINDER BLUMEN — REAL ESTATE
4. TOBACCO — YUM YUM CULT
5. DIRTY TRIP — AIR   6. TIP-TOE — THE ANTLERS
7. SMILE THE DAY AFTER TODAY — BLACK MOTH SUPER RAINBOW
8. SPOOKY COUCH — ALBERT HAMMOND, JR.
9. ALONE AT SEA — BICYCLES TWO
10. AMONG FIELDS OF CRYSTAL
    — BRIAN ENO AND HAROLD BUDD
11. AVRIL 14TH — APHEX TWIN

C'est cool, baby.
By Erica Thanks to Sara Skinner for modeling.

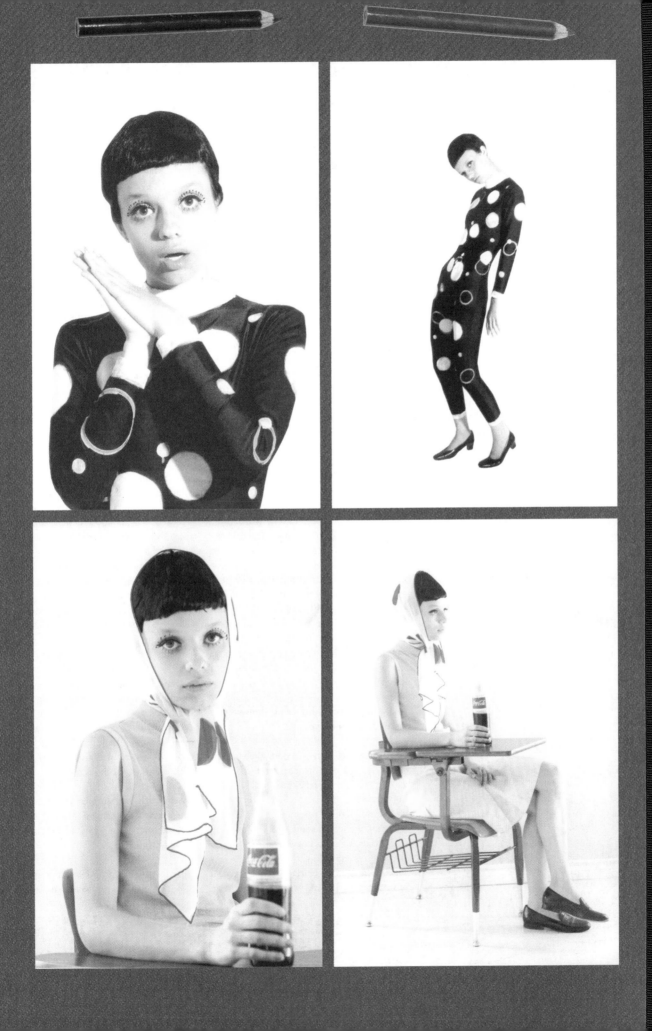

Have Your Freedom:
AN INTERVIEW WITH DANYEL SMITH

"Don't always be going to the party—*give* the party." By Julianne. Illustration by Suzy X.

The first time I met Danyel Smith, she was interviewing me for a job at *Vibe* magazine, where she was editor-in-chief. I went in being pretty intimidated by Danyel, who struck me as basically what you think of when you think of an EDITOR in NEW YORK CITY: powerful, fiercely intelligent, full of energy, and eminently cool.

She lived up to that image, too. I walked into her giant, pristine office, which was filled with modern-looking white furniture, and was introduced to this impeccably dressed woman who radiated authority. I'd had editing jobs before, but the energy in that office, and the legacy of the magazine, felt so much more *real* to me. I felt like I had finally *made it* just by sitting in that room, talking to that woman—whether or not I got the job.

Of course, I already knew all about Danyel Smith. She was, and is, one of my favorite music critics, novelists, journalists, and editors. I knew that she grew up in Los Angeles and Oakland, California, and was one of the first nationally renowned hip-hop journalists at a time when the mainstream media couldn't be bothered with that genre. She went on to become the editor of *Vibe*, *Vibe Vixen*, and *Billboard* magazine, to write two novels (*More Like Wrestling* and *Bliss*), and to teach writing at various colleges in New York. She has interviewed and/or written about almost every pop and hip-hop star you can think of, from the 1990s to now. And she has written *so many* great pieces of music journalism that I don't even know what to tell you where to start reading! Maybe start with *HRDCVR*, the new "book-shaped magazine" she is launching with her husband, the writer and editor Elliott Wilson.

I ended up getting that job at *Vibe* (thank you, Danyel!), and ever since then, Danyel has been a beacon, awesome advice-giver, editor, mentor, and friend to me. I am still in awe of her. She inspires me and so many others to accomplish our dreams.

JULIANNE When did you know you wanted to be a writer?

DANYEL SMITH Early second grade, third grade. I had this teacher named Mrs. Gibbs who was very into us building books. We could write little storybooks and draw pictures to go with our stories, and then we would staple the whole thing and make a cover. I was like, *This is the freshest shit ever.* I just knew that every time there was a creative writing class, a newspaper to be on, yearbook, anything,

[I would do it]. I was making a newspaper for my neighborhood called *The Fifth Grade Daily Arrow*. It had a circulation of six. We were strong on the block.

Do you remember some of the stories you published in *The Fifth Grade Daily Arrow*?

Definitely. There was a movie review, and [we would tell you] where you could see the movie in the neighborhood. I was doing that Moviefone shit before anybody! [I wrote about] what different families were doing on Hi Point Street in L.A. There was this one family, the Gardens, that had adopted kids, and for some reason I felt that it needed to be known that they were adopted! I don't know if they appreciated that. I had a sports section; I would write about what was going on with the baseball team at our elementary school. I think our lead story, like the best one—like straight "breaking news," right?—was the car accident on Pico and Fairfax or something like that. I was there taking notes! Not good notes—just like, "There's a blue car and a tan car. They had an accident. Everybody is OK." All bylines, Danyel Smith. I was like 10. I thought I was so fresh. I would literally hand [the paper] out to people on the block, like, "Hi, Mrs. Garden. I know everybody's adopted in your family, so here's a story." Steven, Michael, Renee—those were the three kids. I'm still friends with them on Facebook.

By the time you were in high school, did you already know you wanted to make magazines, since you had already been making them?

I totally did. I don't know a super nice way to put it, but I did not have that family that

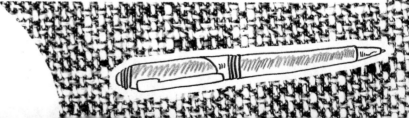

was super interested in everything I was thinking. I had to make up my own mind about a lot of things at a very early age. So in junior high, we could take electives, and I knew I wanted to take creative writing. Also offered as an elective was to be on the school paper, and I took that shit mad seriously. I just wanted to write all the time.

When you want to be a writer, at least when I was younger, there is a lot of romance attached to that. My mother used to give me Nancy Drew books and *Nellie Bly, Reporter* and all these biographies. I started to see that if you wanted to do stuff, you had to *do stuff*. And I did. When I got to high school, I went to an all-girls Catholic school, and I was voted "most involved in school activities." I don't know if I have ever stated that publicly before, because it's so herbish! But that included being photo editor of my yearbook, among other things. I think I always put myself in those places where I would get positive feedback, because that wasn't always forthcoming in my family. I've never really been, even to my detriment, that much of a complainer. I've always tried to find a way to fix my situation.

I was always around creative shit. I like the whole process of "We have nothing, but at the end of the month, we're going to have something," whether it's a play or a newspaper or a magazine or a book or even a fucking relationship, you know what I mean? We're gonna have *something*.

In high school, I was always trying to get grades good enough to get into college, and I had jobs. I was a junior lifeguard; I was working at the police academy as a proctor. This was my plan: *I'm going to have my own money. I'm not going to do drugs, because I'm scared of them. I'm not going to drink until I get to college. I'm not going to have sex, because I know as soon as I have sex—the moment I have sex—I know I'm going to get pregnant.* I didn't want anyone to have any reason to say shit to me about anything. When my mother or grandmother would be like, "Where are you going? You need to be home by midnight," I was like, "That's cute. That's super cute. Because, number one, I'm not smoking, I'm not drinking, I'm not pregnant. My GPA is as close to 4.0

as you can get without actually being a 4.0. So this is rather arbitrary, and I'll see you when I see you." And so, that's how I was living as a teenager.

Did your love for music inform your writing early on?

We had a pretty musical household. There used to be these things called record clubs where you could—I don't know how the economics of it worked—it seemed like you paid $10 and got four records a year for life or something like that. It was a big deal in our household. I got to pick one [record], my sister got to pick one, and my mom got to pick two. Then the vinyl would come. I was such a huge Rick James and Prince fan. Also, I was coming up in Oakland, at a time when Too Short was new and blowing up, and Tony Toni Toné, and En Vogue, MC Hammer, Digital Underground, and Tupac, of course. All these groups were coming out and I was interning at the *San Francisco Bay Guardian*. I was writing stuff about the mayors' convention and the history of olive oil (because the olive-oil convention was coming to town) and thinking, *This is mad boring. I don't care about any of this.* So I pitched this rap story about…I think it was MC Ant. When I started reporting it, the story just kept getting bigger and bigger. I started going to all these shows, people started giving me music, and as a future critic, I started feeling very respected.

I was serious when I went to shows. I wasn't partying when I was working. It was mostly dudes, so I would climb up on top of the speakers—for safety, for views, and so I had some peace to take my notes. I just began to love it. When I turned in that piece, it ended up being 3,000 words, with six sidebars! It was a cover story. I remember my editor, whom I love still to this day, Tommy Tompkins. Tommy is such a confidence booster in addition to being kind of a genius. He was poking me in my arm. I was like, "What, Tommy?" He said, "Be careful with this rap shit. Someone's gonna think you're an expert." I love Tommy to death. I'll always remember that. He was the one who gave me a column. It was called "What Time It Is."

I was like, "I'm not the movie critic, but you want me to write about movies. Who am I to say that?" Tommy was like, "You're Danyel Smith."

So around that time, you were emerging as a prominent hip-hop writer. And there weren't too many then. Was there a feeling that you were pioneering?

I think I tried to create a world where all that mattered was the work. It's not about me, it's about the music. I thought, *If I just do the work really well, then everything is going to be all right.* And that's just not true. Would that it were! In frankness, the readers of Rookie should probably know that it's a struggle when you're in these fields that aren't well-populated by girls—and even when you are in fields that *are* well-populated by girls. But when I was in my 20s, I was constantly strategizing ways to make [my gender] matter less. Frankly, I think my name helped. I still get mail to Mr. Daniel Smith. And back then, before the internet, everybody couldn't just see you, so people didn't know.

Me being the music editor [of *Vibe*] was such a weird thing for male critics. They honestly didn't want to believe that my job was what my job was. And that has continued throughout my career. A lot of times men find it difficult to believe that I'm the editor of a situation. They also find it difficult to believe that I'm at Madison Square Garden and reviewing the Neil Diamond show. So, what can I do that you will believe that I am?

How do you counteract that?

I think, honestly, it hurts my feelings. But, as my mother would say, "Did you melt? Did you die? Well, then, you should probably continue doing what you're doing." I don't know how nurturing that is, but I use it all the time. I just have to work. I like my career. I like writing. I like editing. I like making stuff. I like being the girl who is reviewing the Neil Diamond show. I like being the girl who is in the studio with Gang Starr. I like being the girl who is going to see Drake for the first time and not knowing how she's going to respond to

it at the age that she is. It's really amazing, and I don't want to let people who don't believe in me have that much effect on me. But they want to.

At *Vibe*, when you were my boss, you put together a staff with so many women, and people of all ethnicities, backgrounds, knowledge spectrums, and it really worked. That's still very unusual for a magazine staff.

As a kid, I lived in a very segregated neighborhood—it's still very segregated. I was in East Oakland, and as much as I love East Oakland, it's still East Oakland. When we moved to East L.A., we lived on a very integrated block. We had a lot of Jewish people, black people, Mexican Americans, Asians. It was a little magical block on Hi Point Street. Frankly, it was hell for me in other ways, but in terms of friends on my block, we were a tight group. My elementary school was a magnet school that brought in kids from around the city, so I had kids in my life from all races and stuff. When I got to St. Mary's, an all-black school, I still had that mentality of "gotta have class diversity." I mean, I wasn't using the term *class diversity*, but seriously, we can party together!

It still matters to me. The best content comes out of those situations. Sometimes, [these situations] aren't comfortable. Sometimes inappropriate shit gets said. But I'm a big fan of being slow to take offense; I'm a big fan of trying to respect everyone's opinion. I don't know why I'm so into it, but I just really am. I think it's fair. It's fucking fair. I also feel like women…we just don't get enough positive reinforcement in general, and especially in the workplace. I don't like that, so I try to give back.

There are age-related preconceptions, too. At Rookie over the past year we have talked a lot about how adult journalists will write trend pieces about "the selfie generation" and how young people supposedly don't care about anything, as if "the selfie generation" isn't reading, or isn't totally aware of how they're being perceived.

It's hater-y. It's very hater-y and very prejudiced and very ignorant. It reminds me of what people used to say about hip-hop. I don't like it when people make broad judgments, like "Millennials are this way." First of all, do you even know any of these kids? Do you know them at all? Kids are smarter than we think they are. The kids I see on Tumblr, at least, open and passionate individuals with these amazing, articulate kind of opinions and snappy-ass backtalk about everything! They are so aware of their identities and their place in the world. I'm so jealous of that, in a way. It took me so long to say, "This is who I am."

Everything is so accessible now, but when you started, hip-hop culture was never the dominant culture.

We were fighting, Julianne. There was a time when rock ruled and hip-hop was the underdog and nobody believed in it and nobody thought it was real. And every article that came out in the paper or *Time* or *Newsweek* or whatever was "It's negative" or "They're killing people" or "It's a fad, it's not real, it's not worthy of real criticism or love" or anything like that. One of my first big stories at *SF Weekly*—I thought I was so investigative and so deep—was about how club bookers told me off the record that there was a de facto ban on booking hip-hop in clubs in San Francisco. We were fighting all the time. To me, it was a fight for our humanity, for our place in culture. We had to constantly say, "We're here, we're rap, we're an art form, we're graffiti, we're dance, we're breakdancing, we're rapping, we're creating music. If you won't book us in your stadiums or nightclubs, we'll have parties in parks." It was the greatest time ever, frankly. It's so amazing to be part of a movement. As a journalist, it's a complicated relationship because you don't want to be totally fanned-out, but I was straddling the line, because I believed so hard that hip-hop was real and I felt that people were not giving it a fair shake. I felt committed to making people understand that it's a thing, and it's our thing, and it's going to be even bigger than this. It's going to take over.

It was an amazing feeling, like you were always working for the culture. If you are 16 or 14 right now, if there's something that you believe in, don't hang back! Put on your stomping boots, put on your sassiest dress, and be at the *center* of that shit. It's just the best to be part of something as it's happening. Then on those faraway days when you're like, "Oh my god, I'm thirty-threeee!" (it happens, young Rookies, it happens), you can look back and say, "I was major, and I'm going to be even more major in my 40s. I have experience in how to change the world." If you don't do that, you're going to be mad. "I was doing *what*? Homework?!" "What? I was high? Too high to enjoy it?" No—put on your cutest shit and go to the fucking party and *run it*. Not to get too preachy or anything, but don't always be going to the party, *give* the fucking party, you know what I'm saying? Curate it and make that shit as fresh as possible. It's all good to be invited, but it's a lot better to be the inviter. It's all good to be the reader, but it's way better to be the creator, the editor. It's just fresher, I'm sorry. And no shade to the community of people that are on the side of reading and just coming to the party, because maybe you're curing cancer, maybe you're raising amazing kids, maybe you're just going to work every day stunting off fools as the dopest receptionist ever at the dentist's office, because that's fresh, too! But if you're really into culture, *own* that shit. There's nothing like starting your own shit. There's nothing like moving on up, being like, "I was writing, now I'm editing." "I was editing, now I'm editing a whole section."

Do you have any other advice for young women who would like to be writers, editors, or just bosses?

I can only think of what I would tell my niece or tell myself when I was 12, 13, 14 years old: Relish in the independence that you do have. You don't have a lot, usually, when you're that age, but relish it, work it. Also, whatever fear you have, try to put it in the backseat.

I used to say to myself when I was 12, 13 years old: "What's the worst that could happen if I did this? What's the worst that could happen if I made a decision that everybody else wouldn't agree with?" Right or wrong, that's what I did.

I think it's important that you realize that you can manage your own life and 18 isn't the magic number where you can manage your freedom. You can manage your freedom as a teenager. One of the best things I did when I was 11, 12, 13, 14 years old was ride my bike. I lived in Los Angeles and I rode my bike all the way to the beach, me and my sister. We would have $5 and split pizza and Sprite and ride back home. It was like 12, 13 miles round-trip. But the freedom of just being able to be on your own, the lessons you learn of being with people, and talking with people, and knowing who's good and who's bad and who's fresh and who isn't—these are all lessons for the future. The more you start learning who you are and who other people are, the better off you will be.

The world is a dangerous place, there's no doubt about it, for women especially. You're always dodging bullets of a certain kind, but we can't let that make us scared to be free. Watch your back, but have your freedom. Just do it. Be wise. Cock your head at *everybody*. Side-eye *everybody*. Watch out for the weirdos who want to push up on you and touch you when you don't want to be touched and all that shit that's real fucked up, but have your freedom. It's the best thing ever. And when you're free out there, just think and think about what you can build with your friends and your siblings. Don't let people make you smaller than you are. Ask your parents, in the nicest way, "What do I have to do so I can have some freedom? Is it grades? Is it cleaning the apartment? What do I have to do so I can have freedom?" Because from that freedom will come everything you are going to be. So work it out. ✳

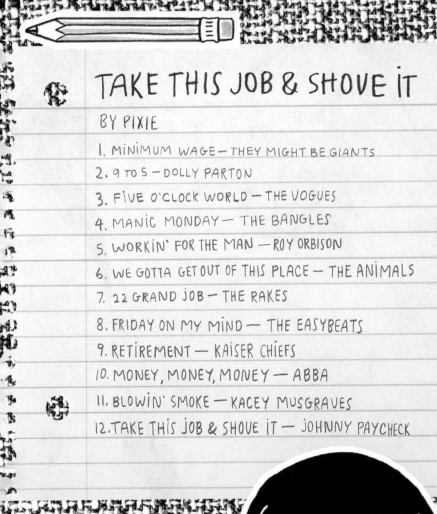

TAKE THIS JOB & SHOVE IT
BY PIXIE

1. MINIMUM WAGE — THEY MIGHT BE GIANTS
2. 9 TO 5 — DOLLY PARTON
3. FIVE O'CLOCK WORLD — THE VOGUES
4. MANIC MONDAY — THE BANGLES
5. WORKIN' FOR THE MAN — ROY ORBISON
6. WE GOTTA GET OUT OF THIS PLACE — THE ANIMALS
7. 22 GRAND JOB — THE RAKES
8. FRIDAY ON MY MIND — THE EASYBEATS
9. RETIREMENT — KAISER CHIEFS
10. MONEY, MONEY, MONEY — ABBA
11. BLOWIN' SMOKE — KACEY MUSGRAVES
12. TAKE THIS JOB & SHOVE IT — JOHNNY PAYCHECK

Darkness on the Edge of Town
By Caitlin H. and Naomi

1. Hold On, We're Going Home- Drake feat. Majid Jordan
2. Team- Lorde
3. Champagne Coast- Blood Orange
4. Rest Your Head- Bat for Lashes
5. Night Light- Jessie Ware
6. Lights On- FKA twigs
7. Salvation- Scanners
8. Neighborhood #1 (Tunnels)- Arcade Fire
9. Hiding Tonight- Alex Turner
10. So Nice So Smart- Kimya Dawson
11. I Am a Rock- Simon & Garfunkel
12. Half a Person- The Smiths
13. I Know Places- Lykke L
14. Darkness on the Edge of Town- Bruce Springsteen

Design by Sonja. Title lettering by Lisa Maione. Playlist lettering by Kendra. FKA twigs portrait, *X-Files* poster, and landscape illustration by Brooke Nechvatel. Photo by Allyssa.

I WANT TO BELIEVE

OCTOBER 2014: THE OTHER

Hi, Rooks!

This month's theme is THE OTHER. Alienation, ostracization, and isolation—in high school and society, and with ourselves, and the subjects we outcast when we are afraid to examine them.

The Other takes place in the kind of world created in Lorde's album *Pure Heroine*, specifically the song "White Teeth Teens" and the video for "Team"—buzzcut adolescent congregations with their own little murky green/black/gray highway kingdoms, with hierarchies and conflicts and romances all their own. There's also the look and feel of the shitty rainy town in the 1986 teen movie (but not really a Teen Movie) *River's Edge*, and the graphic novel *Black Hole* by Charles Burns, where a mutant STI goes around a town of teenagers in the 1970s as a metaphor for Othering. There's FKA twigs's new album, so self-Othering that it has the sterile name of *LP1*, slow and dark and mayyyybe what it would sound like if blisters had tiny cartoon faces and sang when you popped them. (In a good way.) I think part of my love for her music is that I've never before come across an album that has such a sexual current but doesn't LEAD with sexuality, and also isn't just about sexual *pleasure*; is also about how its primal-ness can make it feel Other; how it can be creepy, uncomfortable, upsetting, or freakish. Acknowledging the Otherness makes me more comfortable with it. ILY TWIGS.

There's the Othering people do at our age to other people our age. Like, I entered middle school with the Daria/Holden Caulfield/Liz Lemon approach of rejecting other people before they could reject me, and suffered for it, and limited myself, and was probably sort of mean, and teased girls I thought seemed "dumb," because clearly I was "smart," because I...had blue hair? Felt sorry for myself all the time? Martyring yourself as an Other not only makes you rude, it also keeps you from understanding other people! Were any of those girls mean to me? No! Did I still operate on the assumption that BLOND = MEAN (even though, hi, I was blond until I dyed my hair blue)? Yes! Am I really embarrassed, still, two graduations later? Very! Not to lecture from a rocking chair on my very elderly *18-year-old* porch, but please do not repeat my mistakes.

Moving outside of the high school bubble, there's the way Otherness is appropriated and fetishized until it has real-world implications, a cycle perfectly summarized in this tweet from @locoernesto about the killing of Michael Brown: "I have yet to hear anything about #Ferguson from Miley or Bieber. Katy? Iggy? Everyone wants to be black until it's time to be black."

Buzzfeed also published a really good piece about *The Mindy Project*, beauty, and Othering ("A 'Mindy Project' Roundtable," April 21, 2014):

AYESHA SIDDIQI I remember having to learn that being different wasn't dope, because for my first few years in the U.S., I thought it was. I was like, "Y'all are mad basic," and when I felt like it, I wore a kameez shalwar to school just to stunt and I was funny and smart and got away with it. But then 9/11 coincided with middle school, when issues of romantic desirability become salient. Suddenly being different was the worst thing you could possibly be. The first time I was sexually harassed based on race was first grade, by another classmate. All the times since have also been rooted in my perceived "ethnicness." I'm saying a lot of things here that I'm saying for the first time in my life.

DURGA CHEW-BOSE That's how I've felt about this chat series we've been having and it's been so important to me.

HEBEN NIGATU Sameeeee. I feel known.

AS Such a rare feeling.

DCB I think I've always felt desirous, but in the Othering sense of the word. Desirous, Desi-rous, like, "Ooh, foreign beauty."

AS Yeah, that. It doesn't make me feel beautiful, it makes me feel consumable.

DCB Right, but, like, that's what I thought desire was: to be consumed.

AS Peace to bell hooks's "Eating the Other."

This month is for fleshing out one's multitudes and creating space to be plain human people.

love,
Tavi

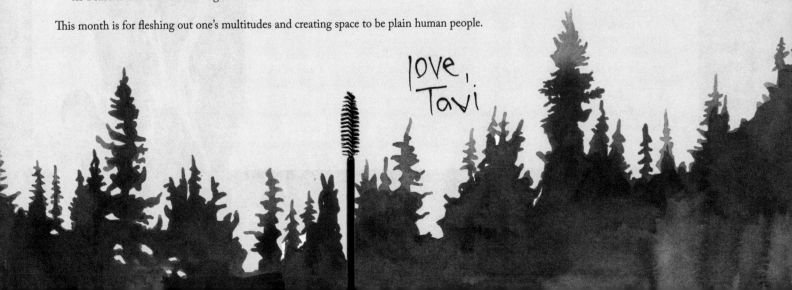

DON'T STAY IN SCHOOL

You don't have to be defined by four tiny years of your life.
By Hazel. Illustration by Cynthia.

When I was in high school, all I wanted was to not be in high school. My classes and teachers were OK, but I hated my peers and could not wait to never see them again. I'd come home each day loudly complaining to my parents or Twitter or my dog that everyone at my school was a "total jackass," that they didn't get me and I didn't get them and I didn't want to. I wanted out of that hellfire ASAP.

Now that I'm in college, I see that whole time differently. I thought I was such a weirdo in high school, but I wonder if I wasn't just trying really hard to define myself that way, based on my musical tastes and my interest in art. I would do anything to differentiate myself from my peers—the people who had bullied me in middle school, told me I was ugly, and tortured me on the bus with anti-Semitic and misogynistic jibes. I was so desperate to distance myself from them because I was scared that whatever it was that made it fun for them to torture quiet girls like me was a disease I could catch by standing too close.

Very little made high school bearable, but one reassuring thing was that everywhere I looked, popular culture told me that these people, who made me so sad as a young'un, would be the real losers one day. The message was that if you were afflicted with loserdom (shyness, singleness, ugliness, dorkiness, whatever), you'd eventually be redeemed, because you had earned it by suffering for so long. Get through the gauntlet of high school on the bottom of the popularity scale, and the world will owe you: girlfriends, boyfriends, power, fame, etc. But high school for me was never nerds vs. jocks, or theater kids vs. popular kids, or whatever other subcultures movies have but real life doesn't. I was never sure what *popular* meant. The term suggested glossy pretty-girl threesomes or football jocks who ruled entire high schools with terror. Nobody terrorized my high school. The "nerds" were as rude as the theater kids, who were as rude as the football stars.

Since my mom's high school days, the "geeks shall inherit the earth" message has only gotten louder and more obnoxious.

Now, the nerd who spent four years being alternately bullied and ignored will not only turn out to be hot and get the girl/boy, but will build your smartphone, write the next great American novel, and direct your favorite films. It's no longer possible to see nerdy kids as the underdogs. Saying you were a nerd in high school is tantamount to bragging. Jennifer Lawrence, Christina Hendricks, and Justin Timberlake are just a few of the countless celebrities who point out that they were picked on in high school in seemingly every interview they give. If being bullied makes you cool, then "losers" are the new popular kids, bullies are the new losers…and nerds are the new bullies! ARGH, CRAZY UPSIDE-DOWN WORLD!!!

In her 1976 essay "Memoirs of a Non-Prom Queen" for *Rolling Stone*, Ellen Willis wrote, "High school permanently damaged my self-esteem. I learned what it meant to be impotent; what it meant to be invisible. None of this improved my character, spurred my ambition, or gave me a deeper understanding of life." This was my experience, too. High school leaves everyone with scars. Some of them may look like glitter you can never totally scrape off your skin, but your teenage years are bound to stick with you in horrifying or bittersweet pieces no matter what. I'm not arguing that high school isn't important, because it is, but only if *you let it be.*

I hate the idea that what you were or weren't in high school defines what you'll be for the rest of your life. The prom queen is not poised for failure because everyone liked her, and the bullied, nerdy girl isn't poised for greatness because she was spurned. High school, like any part of your life, is a stepping-stone to another point in your life. This is how time works!

Can you forget high school? Maybe. Maybe not. Like I said, it's gonna stick to you a little bit. But you are allowed to try. I know what it's like to be 14 and think that high school is the whole world. What I needed was not someone to tell me that the mean kids would get their due when we graduated, but someone to tell me that one day I'd learn not to care. Because when you

do, you will laugh. You will laugh at how much you cared! And when you go back to your hometown and hear about your old mean classmates who have flunked out of college or were arrested for stupid crimes, you won't feel good, you'll feel sad for them.

I am currently 20 years old. This year, I cut ties with nearly everyone I went to high school with, including someone who had been my absolute best friend. We had known each other since sixth grade, and, no matter how many times people told me that my friendships would change when I went to college, I never believed it would happen to us. We were going to the same university— surely, we would be inseparable.

But gradually, we became (or maybe we revealed that we always were) different people. As she chased a music career and grew closer to her boyfriend, I made some great new friends and made New York my home. Over time, it seemed like our friendship had been based more on high school situational ease than long-standing connection. It was just over.

And that feels weird! There's something strange about realizing that you've grown out of an era of your life that used to feel all important. I can no longer remember the boys who made fun of my clothes. I can barely remember gym class, even though it made me hate myself. What was once traumatizing just *isn't* anymore. And *that* feels good.

When high school is over, it can, if you want it to be, be over forever. 🕷

THE IMPORTANCE OF MUSIC TO GIRLS

You could do a lot worse than sharing a teenager's taste in music.
By Brodie. Illustration by Ana.

Earlier this year, in Belfast, Ireland, Miley Cyrus covered the Smiths' "There Is a Light That Never Goes Out."

This performance was immediately all over the internet. Friends of mine, and rock critics that I follow, called it "offensive" and "sacrilegious."

A month earlier, Lorde was hand-picked by Dave Grohl and Krist Novoselic to join them in a rendition of "All Apologies" in honor of Nirvana's induction into the Rock and Roll Hall of Fame (with Kim Gordon on bass!). I thought this was a pretty badass tribute, but it seems I was in the minority. Chris Schulz's reaction in the *New Zealand Herald* (April 2014) was typical: "Kurt would have hated that." And it wasn't just rockist old dudes who objected: Iggy Azalea did, too, telling *Billboard* (June 2014), "I think when you're doing a tribute to someone that's dead, generally it should be the person's peer. Lorde is not Kurt Cobain's peer. […] I just don't think it's appropriate."

What is going on here? Nirvana, in their heyday, were never known for their loyalty to the Church of Rock, that questionable institution made up of music-industry people, critics, and fans who worship guitar-driven, mostly male bands for their "purity," while dismissing pop music as superficial fluff. Kurt Cobain was 18 when Nirvana formed and was an outspoken feminist—I'm sure he would have

loved a 17-year-old girl covering his band's poppiest hit. And Miley's version of "There Is a Light" is arguably darker and mopier, even, than the Smiths'.

But the wave of hate that follows any attempt by a pop artist to cover a song by a (usually male) rock band, with a (usually male) rock fan base, is, by now, both totally predictable and deeply depressing. The reason is as obvious as it is sad: plain old sexism.

I'm not saying that Miley and Lorde are targeted for this criticism for their gender. In 2013, when One Direction released "One Way or Another (Teenage Kicks)," a combination Blondie/Undertones cover they recorded for charity, the *Guardian*'s Adam Boult was prompted to start a list of songs that "must never be covered." Never mind that 1D's medley got a seal of approval from Blondie's Debbie Harry herself; Boult said it was an "abomination" that "tarnished" the originals (February 2013). So it's not about the gender of the artist doing the cover—it's about the gender (and age) of their fans. Think about it: Young, poppy acts have largely young, female fan bases. I believe the reason rockist dudes feel so dang uncomfortable watching these artists cover songs by bands they love is that it points out that they might have something in common with fans of Miley, Lorde, 1D, etc. They might have something in common with *teenage girls*. What could be worse than that?

I say to these people: You could do a *lot* worse than sharing a teenage girl's taste in music. The pantheon of acts who couldn't have gotten famous without the support of teenage girls includes a lot of people and bands you probably respect a lot: Michael Jackson. Elvis Presley. The fricking BEATLES. When Nirvana was around, most of their fans weren't 50-year-old rock critics; they were kids.

Here is something Kurt Cobain once wrote, with his own hands, published in his 2003 *Journals*: "I like the comfort in knowing that women are the only future in rock and roll." Now tell me he wouldn't

have "approved" of Lorde, Kim Gordon, St. Vincent, and Joan Jett covering his band's songs.

I get it. I understand what it feels like to love a band with your entire soul and then discover that the people who feel the same way you do about them are people you have nothing else in common with. People you don't even like. At this taste-crisis juncture, you have two choices: You can get angry, and distance yourself from those fans and everything they stand for; or, you can realize that the people you thought you hated are not as different from you as you once thought, and you can feel a new space for them grow in your heart. The choice is yours!

This defensive barrier constructed around certain rock acts doesn't do anybody any favors. Isn't it actually great if a new generation of musical performers and music lovers connects with something in the back catalogs of Blondie, the Undertones, Nirvana, or the Smiths? Does it matter how they got there? Whether it was a dusty vinyl LP ferreted out from the depths of the world's last brick-and-mortar indie music stores, or a One Direction cover, something introduced these fans to this old but new-to-them music, and isn't that cool, no matter what?

My first exposure to the Ramones, whose music provided the soundtrack to my teenage and young-adult years, was the teen soap *The O.C.* I saw the band's posters in Seth Cohen's bedroom and read an interview with Mischa Barton where she raved about them, which led me to buy their anthology. That led me to seek out and adore music by other punk bands, which created a rock-solid, foundational love in my heart.

My punk-music fandom is no less valid because I wasn't alive to see those bands play at CBGB in the '80s. Music, whether it's rock or pop or rap or new wave or whatever, is meant to last for ages. All ages. If you love music as much as I do, let people like me discover it our own way. You would have wanted the same when you were young. ♪

WHEN YOU ARRIVE

A cautionary tale about letting other people's opinions shrink you down.
By Ragini. Photos by Eleanor and Caitlin H.

Falling is the first fear I ever had. In my dreams, I'm constantly being sucked downward, past clouds and skyscrapers, by inexorable gravity. The weight of my body, its bulk and clumsiness, will not let me float. I'm falling.

This fear has a memory: I'm holding on to my grandparents' bedposts and slowly, carefully hoisting myself up on unsteady feet. I must have been a toddler, which makes me wonder how real this memory could be. At some point, my memories merge with family stories, with myths of my childhood that were passed down to me, all of which shared a single plot point: Ragini, at some point, would fall. Ragini was too fat and too scared to walk. Ragini crawled everywhere until she was old enough for nursery school. Ragini was so fat, too fat to stand, much too fat to run or walk. Did I ever run as a child? Really *run*, fearlessly and unself-consciously? If I did, I have no memory of it. As fearless as I was in my imagination, where I regularly traversed the world performing feats of undimmed glory, in life I was cautious, calculated, slow. They told me I couldn't run, and I believed them, so I never did.

Instead, I read and wrote and painted and drew. Every evening, I watched TV, where one of the only two channels we got would inexplicably broadcast swimming competitions from Germany. In their racing suits and with their swimmer's legs, the athletes seemed like gods. Sometimes, when no one was watching, I'd lie on my bed and practice strokes. The swimming pool's blue depths seemed so mysterious, a world away from the darkness of my bedroom, my desire, and my shame.

One day I was watching TV with my grandparents, and a water ballet came on. Glittery mermaids in fantastic headdresses splashed, writhed, and twirled in perfect synchrony in the greeny blue water, their faces glowing eerily in the underwater lights.

My deepest desire, formerly an inchoate longing, found form: *This* was my dream. I wanted to be a mermaid. I wanted to swim.

When I begged my parents, their dismissals rang with finality: "You can't. You're too fat." "You'd look ridiculous." "You'd catch a cold—you know your lungs are delicate." That summer, my best friend's mother signed him up for lessons at the local pool. I was consumed by envy.

I hated school back then and alternated between calling it "a prison" and "a factory" that manufactured high test scores, but, strangely enough, that's where my body got brief chances to feel free. We had 40 minutes of gym class every week—a parboiled mishmash of calisthenics, yoga, rudimentary scouts training, and basketball. Basketball is what saved me. Out in the school courtyard and dribbling with my friends, I could forget to be self-conscious. I could ignore the jeers about my body and focus instead on how my body *felt*—the energy coursing through it, the physical power when I jumped to make a basket, the heat of summer sun, the sweat rolling down my face, and the delicious exhaustion after a game. My proudest moment was the time one of my gym teachers stopped me in the middle of a game to ask if I wanted to be on the rowing team, indicating that my size and strength would be an asset. I caught myself beaming before I had to mumble, "I don't know how to swim."

"That's a pity," the teacher said, giving me a once-over. "We could really have used you."

When I was 11, I started playing cricket, a sport that not only accommodated my size and the ball of resentment in my stomach, but made good use of them. I could hit better than any of the boys I knew, and I was stronger. Even so, I'd always get picked last. So, I channeled my anger into each hit. I smashed egos and windows, I fielded with grim determina-

tion, and I practiced catches against my father's bedroom wall for hours on end. Still, I was picked last.

I got my first period on the cricket field, sitting on a broken concrete bench, waiting for my turn at bat. I remember sitting there, praying that the blood wouldn't soak through my pants, my head a jumble of confusion about my changing body and what it meant, and about the childhood I was leaving behind. Not long after that, my grandmother saw me playing basketball outside in my shorts. She told my mother, who put an end right then to my cricketing. Shorts weren't "seemly" for me anymore, she said. My body was too "developed" to be so exposed. I gave up athletics altogether and took to hiding my shameful body under baggy jeans and oversize T-shirts.

It was a strange limbo: My breasts and hips, my swelling body, my fat, were deemed too female for "male" pursuits like sports. But, I was considered too big, too awkward, too loud and outspoken to count as desirably "feminine." No matter what the standard I was judged on, I was "too much." I'd always been too much. Too big, too fat, too tall, too manly. I felt like a freak.

The next year, when I was 14, I was taken over by an eating disorder, and my life began revolving around the toilet bowl. Hunched over it, I'd bring up my meals, trying to purge not just my dinner, but every last bit of my freakish mannishness. I drained my soul into the toilet, thinking, with every finger I shoved down my throat, *I'm a freak, I'm monstrous. Girls aren't supposed to be "strong"; girls are* feminine. *I need to be smaller…I need to be a girl, I just want to be a girl.*

I longed to be weak, fragile. I wanted very badly to be able to faint. Fainting seemed the essence of girlhood, as it meant you were weak and vulnerable and in acute need of male protection. I wanted my body to succumb to utter helplessness at the slightest trigger. I wanted to be "a girl."

That was all a long time ago. Now, I'm struck by how brutal I was with myself, and how brutal we are with girls in general. How we limit girls to these strict narratives of girlhood, a state defined by negatives, by an endless series of "nots," a Venn diagram of exclusion. We teach girls to be not this or that, and not to be too much of anything. We train them to trim away the "excess" from their bodies, their desires, their dreams, their strength.

It doesn't stop once we've grown up. These narratives bind competitive athletes, too. Media coverage of women's sports remains concerned with the physical appearance of athletes. When I looked for information about Victoria Pendleton, Great Britain's most successful female Olympian, Google helpfully completed my search with "hot." Reporting on the 2012 Olympics, the Melbourne *Herald Sun* saw fit to run side-by-side photos comparing what swimmer Leisel Jones's body looked like that year with what it had been in 2008. Body shaming comes with the territory for female athletes.

Just ask Sarah Robles, an Olympic weightlifter, who recently wrote on her blog, Pretty Strong, about the hateful internet comments she gets. Such comments center on Robles's body and perceived lack of femininity—and subsequent lack of attractiveness. In her post, Robles addressed these remarks by saying: "I will not ever apologize for the way I look, and I never expect anyone else to […] If I have acne or small boobs, or big feet, or calloused hands, or smeared makeup, or messy hair, etc. That's no one's business but my own. […] What matters is that I did my best for the day." In other words, there's no one way of being a girl or a woman, because how you choose to express your femininity depends entirely on you, and no one else.

At 14, I had a choice. I could reject other people's ideas of "femininity" and become the person I wished I was: an athlete, tall, strong, and proud. Or I could give in to society's ideals and embrace the toilet, trying to shrink myself into what people told me a "girl" was. I chose the toilet. I chose it because no one told me that being a girl didn't mean being *less*.

~*~*~

I was 18 the first time I swam. I took a step into a sectioned-off part of Calcutta's biggest lake, and I was scared. Floundering in the murky water, weeds tangling in my feet, gawked at by a rabble of children and old men, I felt self-conscious and clumsy.

For some reason, I went back the next day and tried again, with the same result. I found a teacher. I kept trying. It took me five days to finally swim on my own—awkwardly, gracelessly, my belly swollen with the water I had drunk, but I was *swimming*!

The water transformed me. A body I'd felt shame in inhabiting became a source of pride. My swimmer's legs, my tanned arms, and my endurance helped me see my body as a beautiful, powerful instrument. I'd never thought I could wear a swimsuit in public, but, once I was swimming, I no longer cared. The cellulite on my thighs was irrelevant compared with their tireless motion.

Nothing about you is too much; you are exactly enough. When you feel the power coursing through your legs while you run, a burst of pride when you cross the finish line first, the thrill of seeing new bands of muscle in your arms, or the speed with which you cut cleanly through water like a seal, that is you, too, and it is wonderful and amazing. Your body is *your* instrument—and you get to use it to do whatever you want. Don't diminish or reshape or neglect it for anyone else. Silence shamers by showing them what you're capable of. Leave them all behind. What they tried to shame you for, take pride in. Your moment has arrived. ♥

I Belong With Me

By Shriya

1. Chum - Earl Sweatshirt
2. Don't Cry - Deerhunter
3. Eros' Entropic Tundra - Of Montreal
4. Honey Bunny - Girls
5. Xerox - Julian Casablancas + The Voidz
6. Boom Skit - M.I.A.
7. Why Won't They Talk to Me? - Tame Impala
8. Millstone - Brand New
9. Be Normal Frankie - Frankie Cosmos
10. Where Is My Mind? - Pixies
11. Creep - Vega Choir
12. Accept Yourself - The Smiths

I CAN DO ALL THESE THINGS:
AN INTERVIEW WITH FKA TWIGS

On not listening to what anyone else has to say and doing whatever the hell you want!
By Julianne. Collages by FKA twigs.

FKA twigs is a lightning-don't-strike-twice kind of musician: Her music combines realism and the avant-garde, abrasiveness and vulnerability, intellect and instinct. Born Tahliah Debrett Barnett, she got her stage name during her career as a dancer, from the way her joints cracked when she was warming up (the FKA stands for "formerly known as"). She danced professionally through her teen years, then she quit to make music full-time. She taught herself to produce music and to direct videos; today, she produces most of her songs and controls all her videos and imagery. The fruit of her hard work is a very personal world that is completely magical and unique, as heard on *EP1*, *EP2*, and her latest, the excellent *LP1*.

This is the second time I've spoken to twigs, and each time I've been struck by how cool she is. In conversation, she's a little shy and quiet, but very honest and thoughtful, and when she gets more comfortable, she talks and jokes like you're family. This time around, we talked about being a lifelong professional artist, body image and beauty standards, and what becoming an adult means to her.

JULIANNE **You started dancing when you were a kid, right?**

FKA TWIGS Yeah. I was just really drawn to it in a really bizarre way. I begged my mum to take me to ballet class for years, but she was a dancer and she didn't want me to get, like, sucked into that whole world. But she gave in when I was eight, and I got into ballet and jazz. Eventually, I realized that I couldn't really be a ballet dancer, so I took it into my own hands to discover the style of dance that suited me.

Why couldn't you be a ballet dancer?

I don't have a ballet dancer's body. My bum sticks out, my pointe isn't great. I'm sure if I were brought up in New York or London or another city in which they cater to people of different ethnic origins, it wouldn't have been a thing. I would have just been able to dance and look beautiful within my ability. But I grew up in the country [in Gloucestershire], and, back then, when I was 12, you had to be, like, white and blond and a rake and not have an ass and have a pelvis that could tuck under for days. And my body's just not made like that.

Were you dancing professionally when you were a teenager?

A bit, yeah. I'd gotten my first professional dance gig when I was 13, and I guess there was that fear that my mum had—that world kind of sucked me up, and I spent the years between 13 and 16 going to London to do dance jobs and modeling jobs that were based on dancing and music. By the time I got to, like, 15, 16, I was very disillusioned about what I wanted to do. I was feeling really lost, and thinking that *I just wanna be normal. I just wanna be a normal person, and not do all these things.* So I just stopped. Because I wasn't that kid—I never wanted to be on *The Mickey Mouse Club* or get that type of attention.

So I gave it up. I went to Croydon College, did my A-levels, and started singing in youth centers and doing youth work, teaching other young people how to play music and write poetry and how to sing. I was a youth worker for like two or three years, then the government cut the

funding, so I got sacked, basically.

I was really upset, because that was my job! I wanted to be an art therapist, I wanted to work with youth and work in the social sector. When it stopped, it was devastating, but it also made me realize I could do things myself, on my own terms. I can dress how I like and make the music that I like, and I can produce it if I want to. I can be a video director as well. I can do all these things.

I think there's this perception that if you're a studio geek—if you know loads about production, or you know loads about cameras and can direct all your stuff, or if you're a songwriter who knows loads about lyrics and stuff—then you can't get your nails done and you can't get your hair done and you can't, like, dress like this. And I realized that that wasn't true. So when I started making music and videos, it was on my own terms. I'm 26, and that's not old for what I'm doing, but it's not young, either—there has been this whole idea for a few years that to be a female artist you have to be, like, 21, but I don't really feel like that. I feel like I know *exactly* what I want, and no one can tell me to do anything I don't want to do or pose in a way I don't like or make a song or write something I don't want to. I guess I got to the point where it's all me, and only I am to blame, and that feels really great. And if something goes wrong, I am to blame as well—it was *my* stupid decision, you know what I mean? It feels great! To know that everything is *of yourself*. Every single decision that I've made to become the artist that I've become is because I really know what I want, I'm really ambitious, and I really want to be in charge of everything creatively.

FKA twigs

I dance feelings like they're spoken

Who was your best friend when you were growing up "in the country," as you say?

I did have a best friend, but [growing up in the country] was hard. I went to an all-white school, and I still remember so many things that people said to me. You know when kids say things and they don't realize that one sentence might stay with someone for years? I'm mixed race, and my hair is either two things: It's either beautiful—curly and shiny and suited to humid weather and I feel like the girl from that Michael Jackson video "The Way You Make Me Feel"—or it's a nightmare, frizzy

and dry and all over the place no matter what I do. I spent most of my teen years in that [latter] stage, because I didn't know how to do my hair. I would try to straighten it, and it just wouldn't hold.

I remember when I was maybe 13, I went to London, and I saw a girl on the Tube who had really nice hair. She looked mixed race, so I was like, "How did you do your hair?" She was like, "You have to moisturize it and put loads of oil in it and only wear your hair out when it's a special occasion." I went out and got some coconut oil, and I put my hair in two braids, and I felt good about it. You know when you're

young and you start to take pride in your appearance? It's not necessarily in a vain way, it's just, like, *I'm getting older, and my mum doesn't do my hair anymore.* You just start to become more independent.

So, then, I'm in history class, and the girl who was supposed to be my best friend turned around and was like, "*Ew*, your hair's so *greasy*." Like that. It hurt my feelings so bad. It was really hard, because I just didn't fit in. I remember when I was 12, they made fun of me because I had a mustache.

Oh my god, I'm sorry. Kids can be so mean!

I'm over it! It's just really funny. I guess as you get older you learn to embrace things. I always think to myself, like, *Neneh Cherry has a mustache!* Whenever I see her I think, *That is so cute!* That's the way I see stuff like that now. But when you're a teenager, it's harder.

In my last year or so of secondary school, when I was about 16, Beyoncé came out with "Crazy in Love," and Christina Milian came out with "AM to PM." Before that, it was about Britney, Avril Lavigne, Christina Aguilera—all these really cute white girls who defined what the boys were fancying. Then, that year, there was this boom of all these light-skinned black stars, and all of a sudden I was *the shit.* I was hanging out with the popular girls; I'd gone from people literally scribbling out my face in school photos and writing **UGLY** next to it, to two years later, having everything be fine—all of a sudden I was really cute. At the time, I was super androgynous—I had short hair and I dressed like a boy— and suddenly it was cool to dress the way I did, and I was the most desirable thing on earth. I always called bullshit on that!

It was right after that that I left my hometown with my mum and moved to London and completely started a new life. And then from, like, 17 to 22, I went back to having no friends.

It seems like London would be a place where you could thrive!

I was *so* shy. And the kids in London were so

much more cultured. I was just Tahliah—a shy, mixed-race girl with a farmer's accent.

What does it mean to have a farmer's accent?

Where I'm from, it's really rural, and people talk in a country accent. When I moved to London, people would be like, "You're a farmer!" I was like, "No, I'm not a farmer!" [*Laughs*] When I say I had no friends, literally, I knew like four and a half people in college. It was just me and my mum hanging out every day.

Were you lonely?

I don't really believe in being lonely. I believe in being alone, but if you're lonely, that's just bringing some extra emotions into it. Loneliness is self-indulgent. There's always something to do when you're alone.

But then, I met Carri Munden by chance—the girl who started [the fashion label] Cassette Playa. And Carri completely and utterly changed my life. It was crazy. I met her at a concert somewhere. We spoke briefly, and I was like, *Oh my god, that girl is SO COOL.* I started stalking her on Myspace—I messaged her all the time and she'd write me back with messages that were like one-third the length of mine [*laughs*] and I'd get so excited! I didn't have a computer, so I'd go to the internet café and check to see if she'd written me back. She was styling Billionaire Boys Club at the time, and she used me for something, and then she used me for her lookbook a couple of times. Then she introduced me to basically everyone who helped start my career: Matthew Stone, who did the *i-D* cover; Grace LaDoja, with whom I did my first film work; Sharmadean Reid, who does WAH Nails—she had me play her WAH Nails party in New York, and that was the first show in New York that I'd done as twigs.

When I met Carri, I was a confused 19-year-old, not knowing how I wanted to be, but knowing I had so many ideas and so much inside me, and she was the first and only person who saw it. One time she said to me, "Who are you going as for Halloween?" I was like, "I think I'm gonna go as Edward Scissorhands." And she was like, "You should go as Tank Girl." I was like, "Who is Tank Girl?" And she said, "*You're* Tank Girl. Just google it." So I googled Tank Girl, and I was like, *Oh my god, I am Tank Girl*. From that point on, everything clicked into place: how I wanted to dress, what type of woman I was, and how I wanted to be.

The thing I really loved about Carri was that she was really productive and forward-thinking, and really prominent in the scene, but she was also very vulnerable, very kind, and very sensitive. She's still one of my best friends.

You said you met Carri at a concert, but you were so shy back then—do you remember how you started talking?

It's really weird! I was there alone, and she was standing next to me, talking to her friend about how to make your pussy taste good. [*Laughs*] I knew how, so I spoke up: "Don't eat asparagus, don't eat too much red meat, and drink pineapple juice." I just came out with it! And I remember her being like, "Whoa!" She started pissing herself laughing, and that's how we started talking.

What concert was it?

I think it was Kanye West!

I'm curious about the tomboy style you mentioned earlier. What was your choice to wear menswear about?

I am very petite, and my build is very athletic, from dancing and running. In the '90s, you had to be this size zero to be considered beautiful, then in 2010 it was like, "Real women have curves," but I wasn't like that, so I basically rebelled by wearing only Uniqlo menswear or, if I was going out, a suit jacket from a charity shop. I felt really awkward about myself and about my body, so I just had to have everything really covered all the time. My body basically

hasn't changed since I was 16 years old, everything is basically the same.

I just did this video for "Pendulum," and I full-on look like an adult! I'm like, *When did that happen?* I don't even know! I only figured out in the past year that I'm not skinny, and I'm not curvy, I'm just really strong. That is me, and that's really beautiful as well. People don't really talk about athletic women. It's a whole segment of women who are completely missed out.

You know my music video "Hide"? That is me, too, and nobody really knew that was me. I made it when I was 23, and that was the moment when I thought, *Well, if I'm basically naked in my first music video, then I just can't really feel insecure.* Does that make sense? "Hide" is objectifying of women, because that's how I was feeling at the time. It's about breaking up with somebody and feeling like shit about yourself, so I thought it would be really brave to be naked but not have a head! Because as soon as you have a face and you smize into the camera, it becomes really sexy, and I didn't want it to be sexy. I wanted it to be awkward. I really thought people were going to say horrible things, but they never did.

Something else I've learned, though, is that you can't please everybody. Not everyone is gonna find you attractive! I'm not the most beautiful girl in the world—I'm just *not*, and I'm never gonna be, and I don't even know how to help you with that! I'm small, and my eyes are too far apart, and I've got two weird front teeth. When I first came to America, my then manager was like, "We'll have to get your teeth fixed." I saved up all my money to get these veneers, and I had all the initial work done—they have to do all this work on your gums—and then I was like, *Oh my god, what the fuck am I doing? This is an awful, terrible idea!* So I paid for like half the treatment but never got the veneers done. I wasted about £900 [about $1,450].

I am very glad that you did not do that!

It would not be me! You just have to be yourself. It's really not that hard! You just need to stop going on Instagram so much, because that shit is not real. I do not look like that in real life! It's a professional photographer and Photoshop!

Is that why a good amount of your artwork, like the "Water Me" video, is sort of exaggerated and blown out?

Yes. I want everyone to know it's not real. But even on my Instagram, people will say, "Oh my god, ILY, twigs, you're so perfect, I wish I could be you." I tell them that I'm *not* perfect, it's not true. I hate the way young girls think sometimes, it's so depressing. They'll write, "Why can't I look like FKA twigs?" I'm just like, no, you don't understand—I cried in the mirror as a teenager.

Another thing I want to talk to you about is this idea of learning. Basically, you have to keep on learning—it will distract you from all the bullshit that we're talking about. Two years ago, I couldn't produce [music]; I learned how to do it in literally two years. I found it really difficult to program when I started, then I had this leap of confidence to actually get in front of the computer and learn how to do it. It was a massive challenge, because I am not a very logical person at all. It's about facing your fears. If you do that, you realize that you can actually do anything you want to do! It's been the most liberating experience.

Last week, I bumped into a very famous music artist. She started talking to me about her nails and her hair extensions, and how getting this stuff done makes her feel like a woman, and she has to have so much money to get this stuff done because she's a woman and that's what being a woman is. I thought to myself, *That's very interesting, because what makes me a woman is when I know I've produced a song myself*—when I've found an artist to work with, given him a beat to work on and told him what I wanted, and he's given it back to me and it's what I'd envisioned as a producer. Or when I've made a video and released it into the world. That's what makes me feel like a woman. Like, fuck anything else—fuck how tall I am or how long my hair is! This is the absolute epitome of what makes me feel like an adult, and like I'm handling my business. I've sat in front of my computer at three o'clock in the morning and I've made something myself that I had to learn how to do that was very difficult. When you find something easy, that's a talent, but when you find something difficult, that's when you get to really work and push and challenge yourself. I'm not saying that [that artist's] image is invalid, because that might be where she gets her power from. Everyone is different. But for me, there's something about learning that makes me feel the most adult I've ever felt.

I'm so happy as well, because I'm not crying about stupid shit! I'm busy, I'm doing things, and it's an amazing feeling. If someone's stupid or someone's mean, I'm just like, *OK, love and light, go do what you need to do, I'm busy!* It feels amazing to be this way. ✥

You've got me, under your skin

Everyone's Invited

How to make people feel included.
By Krista. Illustrations by Kendra.

For one of our sixth-grade Fun Fridays (a once-a-month reward for good behavior and zero missed assignments), my middle school teachers took us to Wheels N Motion. Back then, Wheels N Motion was Green Bay, Wisconsin's only roller-skating rink, and everyone in town loved it—we kids had grown up spending every Saturday afternoon there. It had blue lacquered floors, a disco ball, and unbelievably cheap candy behind the counter where you rented skates. Full-sized Laffy Taffy sticks! Sour Punch Straws! Ring Pops! Everything was *25 cents*! There was a live DJ who took requests, and the walls around the rink were thickly carpeted, which took the fear out of showing everyone how well you could "skate backward." (You could not skate backward. No one you knew could ever skate backward.)

So, that Friday, I was having a great time, skating it up, when Kate*, a very popular girl, pulled me into the bathroom with Annie, another popular girl, and urgently whispered that when she hugged Aaron after their couple-skate, she had "felt his boner," and it was, she pronounced, wide-eyed, "*really* hard." Annie gasped. I tried to look appropriately impressed. I had no idea what she was talking about.

"Don't tell anyone, OK?" Kate pleaded, and I nodded solemnly, basking in the warm glow of a popular girl talking to me. As we were leaving the bathroom, a slow song started playing. The lights dimmed. The disco ball turned on, spinning light flecks onto the darkened rink floor. A boy named Jared, clumsy in his slightly too-large rented skates, made his way to me across the carpeted off-rink area, and asked me to couple-skate with him.

Jared was a boy in our grade everyone was mean to, for no particular reason that I can now recall. He was just universally agreed to be "gross," and that meant he was banished from all social groups. I knew Jared was actually a nice guy; we had

* Name has been changed.

been partners in science once, and I found him a little geeky but nothing major—he'd just never learned the right things to say to other kids. And here Jared was, asking me to couple-skate with him *in front of Kate and Annie*, two of the most popular girls in school. They were *right there*, watching me. I knew I should say yes, because I had spent my entire life being trained to correctly handle this exact situation by my parents and our church. Instead, I looked to Kate and Annie for a clue on what *they* thought I should do. Their expressions were blank. Then I laughed, tossed my hair, and said in this INCREDIBLY NASTY VOICE, "Um, *no thanks.*"

Jared's ears turned red. He turned to look at Kate and Annie, then turned back to me. "Oh, OK," he said. His cheeks were flaming. He turned around and skated away, stumbling a little in his skates. Kate rolled her eyes at me. "Gross!" she said, giggling. "Why is it always the gross ones?" She grabbed my hand and pulled me to a group of "cool" girls to tell them what had happened. Everyone laughed as she re-created the scene, exaggerating Jared's awkwardness with her talent for spot-on mimicking. I was popular for a minute. It felt…gross.

I'm not trying to be dramatic, but this incident haunts me *to this day*. I remember everything super vividly: Jared's face, his red ears, his too-big skates. And I remember how it felt to do something really shitty to another person. Later, I went home and prayed for forgiveness for a long time, kneeling in front of my bed. I knew what I had done was wrong, and I was sorry. I was *so* sorry.

What I had done was not only nasty, it was in direct violation of almost every lesson I had ever learned at church. I was raised a strict Mormon, a member of the Church of Jesus Christ of Latter-day Saints, and, from the moment a Mormon can walk and speak to when they die of old age, they are taught to be thoughtful to others and to include people. YOU AL-

WAYS INCLUDE EVERYONE. You are nice and kind to everyone; you do not leave anyone out, ever, for any reason, or make fun of someone more vulnerable than you, ever. If someone asks you to dance, you say yes, no matter who it is, because (1) it's just one dance, and (2) it took a lot of courage for them to ask you. If you're having a party, *everyone* is welcome.

Mormons go hard on inclusion. Does someone look lonely? Invite them along. Is someone new? Go sit next to them. Is someone in your group not talking much? Bring them into the conversation. A popular Mormon youth magazine called the *New Era* even published posters that instructed readers on how to do all those things.

At the time I was mean to Jared, I had five of these posters taped to the walls in my room. So I can't say I didn't know better. And after seeing with my own eyes the damage I was capable of, I never did something like that again. (I did apologize to Jared at school the next Monday. He said he didn't care and wouldn't look at me. He transferred schools a year later. I am still so sorry.)

These days, as an ex-Mormon, I have a lot of problems with some of the ideas and attitudes of the Mormon church in general, and I suspect that the heavy emphasis on including people was partially a tactic to recruit more members, but I will say this: The extreme focus that was placed on making people feel welcome has served me well in my life. Because those lessons were drilled into my head pretty much constantly for as long as I can remember, I now have a fine-tuned radar for detecting the odd person out, the person who feels uncomfortable in a social setting, the person who wants, very much, to be included but doesn't know how. Because of all that training, I also know how easy it really is to include people who feel left out, and how great it feels to do so. You also get some amazing results: You make a lot more friends, which is the actual meaning of being *popular*, contrary to what any

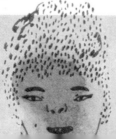

teen movie made between 1980 and 2010 would have you believe.

Mean Girls. Heathers. Grease. Jawbreaker. She's All That. Carrie. Clueless. Never Been Kissed. None of these movies are about popularity, per se; they're about *cliques.* And cliques are, by definition, about excluding people. I wanna talk about how to be the *anti-*clique. An anti-clique is a group of friends that is not closed off. An anti-clique is openly friendly and doesn't prey on the weak.

Lots of us have felt that familiar heartstring-tug when we see someone who is clearly feeling awkward at a party where we know everyone, and we feel that tug because *we have been there.* But not everybody knows what to do with this feeling, especially if we're already really comfortably ensconced in our own social group. How exactly do you include other people without making everyone feel uncomfortable? Well:

First, you spot the signs. People tend to feel left out when they're in or near a group of people and no one is interacting with them. There are rare exceptions who have a highly defined sense of self and *love* to be alone in public places, but most people don't like to be alone when our culture dictates they should be with friends. Too vague? Think of the cafeteria at school. Society says you should be eating with your group of friends in the cafeteria. Hence, someone eating alone is quite possibly someone who is currently feeling uncool.

At a party or gathering where you already know a lot of people, body language is a big deal. It's really easy to be caught up in your own social life, talking with your friends and having a good time in a tight cluster, and that's not a bad thing! But every so often, look at the people outside your warm 'n' happy group. Is there someone kind of hovering on the periphery of you and your friends? Maybe shifting from foot to foot, making brief eye contact with the people who are talking, then quickly looking at the floor or scanning the room? That's most likely a person who wants to be included, but does not know how to go about including themselves. This is where you come in, with your socially smooth moves. Such as:

Make some subtle changes. If you want to make someone sitting alone in the cafeteria feel welcome to join you at your table, try catching their eye. When they look up, look at them and smile. Do they look a bit surprised, then smile back? Cool, looks like they don't bite and might be friendly.

To help the person hovering around your group at the party, shift your body a bit to open the circle, making room for them to join you.

Or, go big. If you're feeling bold, go sit with the person in the cafeteria yourself! Believe me, when you're feeling like a friendless loser, it is *such* a relief when someone comes to talk to you. You can make someone feel that relief! And maybe you'll make a new friend who is completely awesome! YOU SEE HOW THIS IS A CIRCLE OF GOODNESS?

Let's go back to the party. Some bold ways to help that shy person out: You could leave your group momentarily to introduce yourself to them, or you could try the technique my friend swears by in this situation. (You don't have to be friends with the person for this to work, but you do have to know their name and at least one fact about them.) I asked her to explain it to me:

I think a great way to welcome someone into your circle is to shoot them a quick compliment. Like, you go, "Shelby, come here!" and then say to the group: "Shelby just adopted the most adorable dog." When Shelby comes into the circle, lured by your command, you say to both Shelby and the group, "Shelby, how's your new puppy doing?" And, BOOM, you have a new person making conversation in the group.

Isn't that so good? You could adapt this technique to use on total strangers, too, by talking to or (sincerely!) complimenting them and then asking their name, like this: "Hey! Those are cool earrings. I haven't met you yet. What's your name?" So easy!

Including people does not have to be this big, obvious gesture, and it doesn't have to be—and it really shouldn't be—

charity or pity work. It can be little things: People light up when you catch them up quickly on what your group is talking about, so they don't have to stand there, clueless, until the story is over. People feel warm and included when you draw them into a group by touching their arm or shoulder and gently guiding them into a tight-knit circle.

You can smile at a new person at school, introduce yourself to someone pretending to study the books in the bookcase at a party, ask a person you vaguely know if they want to grab a bite after school. Hell, try just saying hi when passing someone in the halls, instead of ignoring them and looking somewhere else. Try casually sitting next to someone who's alone at an assembly. Once in a while, pick someone to be your partner who always has to be partners with the teacher. You don't need to become friends—this is just about helping others feel noticed, like they are not invisible and they have a right to be in the same room as everyone else.

Why, exactly, should we do any of this? Because that's what most of us would like someone to do for us. I know I am astronomically grateful when someone helps me out in a social setting where I feel awkward. I try to repay my gratitude and pass the good vibes on by doing the same for someone else when I can.

You have social power when you are not the new kid at school, because you already know people there. You have social power when you have a core group of friends. You have power by being your confident and friendly self! *Use your power for good.* Most people will be very, very grateful for this kindness, and they will not forget it. It's a rare occasion that you'll be sorry you included someone.

You can be the person you've wished would come talk to *you* when you've felt awkward at a party. You can be a lot cooler than I was at 14—you can be the kind of person who says yes when someone like Jared asks you to couple-skate. It's not like you're getting married, and it may have taken a lot of courage for them to ask. ♥

CHANGE OF CLOTHES

Rei Kawakubo pushes me to be my full freak self at all times.
By Arabelle. Illustrations by Kendra.

There are certain moments of my life that, as they're happening, I know I'll remember forever. My mind drowns out the rest of the world: *Pay attention*, it says. *This is something you won't ever forget.* One Sunday afternoon in high school, I was lying on the floor of my old bedroom, flipping through the book *Style Deficit Disorder*, which included four pages dedicated to the clothing brand Comme des Garçons. The spread featured two models wrapped in gingham padded dresses from the 1997 Spring/Summer Collection. One wore what looked like a lumpy mutated tablecloth as formalwear, and it *thrilled* me. I'm not exaggerating when I say it changed my life. It made my life.

I had never seen anything as bizarre or beautiful (and still haven't). I imagined how the clothes felt to their wearers—how walking in those padded, humpbacked suits, so removed from others, must have been so strange and so comforting at once. I fantasized about the vital power and self-confidence their wearers must have had to be able to pull them off. And I wanted it. In those pages, I instantly recognized the person I wanted to be: the girl in misshapen Comme des Garçons, standing tall and unafraid, unbothered by what others might think of her. (Three years later, I became her when I replicated CdG's swollen tablecloth look at home, but that's getting ahead of ourselves!) In my obsessive research

about the brand over the years, I became totally smitten with the singular voice and design identity of Rei Kawakubo, the founder of Comme des Garçons. Rei K. lives to stand alone. She's one of the rare designers who owns her company entirely (most of the famous ones—like Dior, Louis Vuitton, and Marc Jacobs, to name just three—are owned by the luxury conglomerate LVMH). She answers to no one but herself.

Many Comme des Garçons dresses have no traditional patterns. Many merely suggest where your head should go instead of having a clear neckline. Two jacket armholes are not always enough for Rei Kawakubo—sometimes, she includes four for just one garment. I have some pieces she's made like this, and it's wonderful to be able to take one off as I walk, flip it over, and wear it in an entirely different way. Rei Kawakubo's clothes reek of the knowledge that she is utterly unconcerned with external validation. She does not provide much explanation into her process. She hardly even gives interviews (I can count the ones she's done in the past few years on both hands—and probably recite them from memory, too).

In the beginning of Rei Kawakubo's career, some critics didn't like her designs. When her first Paris collection debuted in 1981, the fashion trade magazine *Women's Wear Daily* declared it "Hiroshima chic," and called her the "samurai geisha of fashion" in 1984 (she was born in postwar Japan, and fashion likes to fetishize both the unfamiliar and the tragic in a way that makes them most comfortable). Kawakubo was pigeonholed as a purely Japanese designer (always the Other, always some kind of "Asian sensation"). Decades later, she's one of the most loved designers in the world—but she is never satisfied when her work is too warmly received, because, then, according to her scant interviews, she feels

like she didn't push hard enough.

Kawakubo's insistence on total independence was intoxicating to a socially awkward 14-year-old. Before I discovered CdG, I lived under the impression that the utility of clothing was absolutely only to fit into other people's ideas of what I should be. I would wear a new identity every day to fit in: Ralph Lauren cargo pants to play with the boys on my block; a knee-length velvet dress to go to charter school and read horse books. If I was feeling snobby, I wore my one label-stamped article: a scratchy, beige sweater with the logo DKNY the size of a small child on the chest.

But that was all before Comme. One glance at Rei K.'s creations quickly dismantled everything I thought I had known about fashion. She challenges you to think critically and keep moving. Sometimes, her clothes make you do the latter in a literal way. The first CdG dress I bought took me 10 minutes to figure out how to get on; the second took two other people to help me into. I wear it once a month now, a different way every time. It keeps surprising me: I shift it a little to the left, and the shape changes entirely. It's breathtaking to know that every way you wear a piece is right simply because you've chosen it. You're perpetually becoming something different, something other than you've ever seen before. Something *more...* because of clothes!

At the Museum of Contemporary Art Detroit's retrospective of her work in 2008, her one-liners were pasted on the walls and on pedestals made of bubble wrap. These included a design manifesto representing the opposite of what I used to think clothes were for: In 1983, Rei Kawakubo told the *New York Times* that she makes clothes "for the woman who is independent, who is not swayed by what her husband thinks."

Clothes hung from the museum's ceiling and on abstract mannequins that didn't resemble humans in the slightest. There was no glamorous spotlight, no immaculate woman-figure to idolize. There were just the clothes, floating, hung, empty of a body but artistic in execution—daring you to fill in the blanks. Become part of the art and story. It wasn't exactly glamorous, but it was beautiful.

Rei's wheat-pasted commentary and genderless presentation of the clothing at the MOCAD show became my casual introduction to a kind of feminism where you can be enough—you can be whole in your difference from others. You have a story to tell in all your particular quirks and singularities, and no one can take that away from you. There's so much strength in being able to stand alone and say, "This is all of me. Take it or leave it. I will not apologize for my existence. I will not explain myself for your comfort."

I have a feeling that without Rei Kawakubo's clothes, it would have taken me a much longer time to realize I was queer. I identify with her designs because she queers fashion by destabilizing the meaning of clothes and creating her own ideas of what they stand for. I queer sexuality through my incapacity for picking one gender to be attracted to, or assign to myself. Kawakubo's clothes made me feel brave enough to accept the parts of myself I otherwise thought were too strange to explore. Now, exploring those parts keeps me going. *She* keeps me going toward a future where I only answer to myself.

Like Rei Kawakubo, I want my work and identity—how I explore the space I take up, how I connect that space to others—to challenge people and make them think harder about the world around them. I want, and enjoy, to make people uncomfortable with the status quo. I want to soak up all my potential and make something bigger and better out of it. I want to change the world, and I want to do it *on my terms*, without apology. So I slip on a four-sleeved Comme jacket, I keep it moving, and I know I can conquer anything. ♪

Design by Sonja. Title lettering by Lisa Maione. *Girlband* portraits by Kendra. Bus illustration by Isabel. Pointe shoe illustration by Brooke Nechvatel. Background by Brooke Nechvatel. Background by Shriya and Clare Drummond.

NOVEMBER 2014: A WORLD OF OUR OWN

If October was about being defined in opposition to other people, this month is about connection: specifically, one-on-one friendship, and how intense that can be, especially in these days of high school/hormones/firsts. We'll explore the mostly magic, sometimes toxic third thing that is created between two people when they come together. It was Amy Rose's idea, who described it as:

> The private world you architect with a best friend or lover—like how you have your own jokes and language and things you love to do together. I'm thinking of my favorite moments with my friends, when I was a teenager and still now: the two of us posted up on a sidewalk, hella laughing and telling each other secrets, not going anywhere, not looking at a clock, being late for everything because we're busy SAYING OUR LIVES and TELLING JOKES and doing weird impromptu dance routines and leaning on each other in this useless/purposeless space.

And Anaheed added this counter to the dreamy side of friendship ('cause this month will also be about when friendships go awry, even if it's not, um, in the form of murder):

> The movie *Heavenly Creatures* really captures this thing we're talking about, how a teenage-girl friendship can be so intense that it gives birth to an entire WORLD. It's based on a real thing that happened in the 1950s in New Zealand. Two teenage girls, Pauline Parker and Juliet Hulme, developed an obsessive best-friendship that worried their parents, who decided to separate the girls and forbid them from seeing each other. The girls responded by murdering Pauline's mother. So, teenage girl love is one of the most powerful forces on the planet. It can create and destroy with alarming ease.

This is a diary entry I wrote when I was 15:

> I wish Claire had been there. I thought of that a lot throughout the trip, and at some point realized I'm in love with her. I can't verbalize any kind of equation to quantify all the wonderful things about her and our friendship, to simplify the million little colorful components wouldn't do them, her, or it justice at all. It's something in the air, it's not at all tangible. Because there are the technical and obvious reasons why we work well together, but then this sacred unspoken bond, colored purple and hazy and the warm light of our rooms. I hope we take a road trip together one day to her hometown of Frog Town, Arkansas, where she says 12-year-olds ride pink motorcycles. I see Claire the same way I see my version of god in my favorite movies and in *Twin Peaks* and in the moment where Kim Deal's voice cracks in the song "Oh!" and in amazing teachers and friends and basically whenever one human makes/creates/says/does something and another receives it in a way that feels like the first person had a puzzle piece to their soul.

I am 18 now. I am not that far out of high school. But everything changed pretty quickly: I moved to New York, live in an apartment alone, and already feel years away from those private worlds. Although it's wonderful to now have friendships with older people, and friendships that are based purely on connection and without the necessity of finding companions in a dreary high school, I don't, like… have sleepovers anymore, you know? Nothing is wrong or bad or tragic, but there's something I miss about being 15 and feeling so confused and hateful at all times and just wanting to give yourself over to another person and find yourself in them instead of in yourself. I'm sorry I don't have a more complex take on it all. But that feeling alone, remembering it, has me in tears right now. And it's why I have noticed that since I was maybe 13, I had trouble cuddling with friends, because I know I love them too much, and might even be in love with them, but I still don't want to deal with that, and I definitely didn't when I was 14, so I would curl up like a puppy at arm's length instead.

I am reminded of a comment on a blog post of mine from freshman year, a compilation of photographs that captured all of the above that I put together after running home from school because "So Far Away" by Carole King got stuck in my head in the last class of the day and it drove me nuts until I could listen to it: "I guess I'm the only one who found this post pretty damn sad. It reminds me of having a crush on my best friend in high school—makes me really miss her."

Love,

HOW TO WRITE A CELEBRITY PROFILE OF YOUR BFF

Because you're their biggest fan! By Gabby

Do you ever imagine what a magazine profile of you would sound like if you were a celebrity? You know, one of those cover stories where you hear how a famous person is learning to *live, laugh, and love* in the limelight. I've held up enough grocery store checkout lines browsing the latest issue of *Vanity Fair* thinking, *What if they were talking about me?* that I should be embarrassed, but I'm shameless. So far, the best theoretical magazine profile of Gabby Noone starts like this:

"Bossy" by Kelis begins to play throughout the restaurant as Ms. Noone, a vision in a holographic jumpsuit, saunters toward me and slides into the booth. She slams down her purse, a pink bedazzled clutch that's part of her capsule collection for Home Shopping Network. "Funny," she says wryly, "this is the third time this week I've heard this song as I've walked into a room."

The magazine's called *Lowlights*, an imaginary spin-off publication of the educational children's magazine *Highlights*—but about former child stars. Oh, also, I'm a former child star in this fantasy.

I love celebrity profiles because they're not only a glimpse into what a famous person will order off some upscale hotel restaurant menu or how pore-less their real-life, un-Photoshopped skin looks—they're a glimpse into their *soul*. Maybe that's an overstatement. Maybe I really like hearing descriptions of what people eat and look like in general. (You will never hear me complain about someone posting too many food pictures or selfies, because they bring me too much

joy. Like, I really do want to see that delicious sandwich you ate for lunch and how good your hair looks today. I'm happy to know you're thriving!) I also realize that these interviews are usually nothing more than a thinly veiled excuse for a famous person to promote whatever movie, album, or other project they're working on, and in turn, for the magazine to put that person on the cover and sell a lot of copies. I'm not hating on that, but more often than not, this kind of piece feels like a futile attempt to paint an intimate portrait of a person whom the writer has barely met.

Wouldn't you rather read about someone you know? If stars are just like us, why aren't there elaborate profiles of us, huh? I say we take this matter into our own hands and start writing glowing essays in praise of our friends! *But isn't that friend fiction?* No! Well, maybe—but this is another way of manifesting your friends' dreams into meaningful documents.

I've broken down the celebrity profile, and its most common tropes, into step-by-step instructions on writing your own (using myself as an example because you've got to be your own best friend to get to the top).

1. INTRODUCE YOUR FRIEND'S ACCOMPLISHMENTS

What, exactly, does your friend *do* in this imaginary article? Think about their current hopes and aspirations and then spin them into a future occupation. Maybe your friend is the first Vine star to make a full-fledged movie, or a

groundbreaking talk-show host/scientist who creates a toothpaste that makes orange juice taste *better*. Perhaps they're your run-of-the-mill triple threat. For example:

Reality TV stars who attempt to cross over into music careers rarely get any respect. One only has to look at the bevy of Real Housewives who've released pop singles and failed to get any recognition beyond ironic listening. However, Gabby Noone, star of Bravo's hit reality show, Noone Cares, *could be the game changer. Her first single, "Oops, I Don't Want to Do It Ever," debuted at Number One on the Billboard Hot 100.*

2. THEN BRING THE FRIEND BACK DOWN TO EARTH

This is the part where you compare your friend's future dream-self with the person you know and love right now. The person someone might find after typing your friend's name into a Google image search with the phrase "before fame." Like, think about something that embarrassed them recently, and then bring it into a better light—something they'll laugh about years from now, when they're popping champagne while relaxing in their gold-plated Jacuzzi:

You may know Ms. Noone as the world's most elegant competitive hot-dog eating champion, but not so long ago she was a simple girl who couldn't get through the day without spilling food on herself. "It's true," she says. "I had to keep a stain-remover pen in my backpack. I was so messy, and, to be honest, I still kind of am!"

3. PICK A SETTING

Where's this interview taking place? A fancy hotel? A chain restaurant that lets the reader know that, despite the fame, your friend is still soooo down-to-earth? A skate park? Perhaps a restaurant that doesn't even exist yet, like an upscale pizza boutique that makes your perfect pizza by scanning your fingerprint and mining a database that knows what you'd like? Essentially, think about their ideal place to hang:

When Ms. Noone sails into the cozy diner in New York City's West Village on a Thursday morning, her presence is like a disco ball's in a darkened ballroom—partially because her coat is embellished with fragments of an actual disco ball. At the sight of the star, children's eyes widen in delight and adults in suits pause their serious breakfast meetings to gape. We're led to a table in the back and she orders banana pancakes without even consulting the menu. "Everything's good here!" she declares.

4. DESCRIBE YOUR FRIEND'S PHYSICAL APPEARANCE

At this point, detail a dream version of your friend's outfit—something glamorous or outrageous that, so far, they've only wished they could wear. Compare their physical features to inanimate objects for the ultimate celebrity-profile effect:

Ms. Noone looks flawless, with lips as red as a cherry Icee and eyes as blue as a… blue-raspberry Icee. In fact, she's wearing a crop top and skirt printed with all sorts of—you guessed it—Icees. "Look," she laughs, "I really love frosty fruit-flavored beverages. I can't help it!"

5. MENTION THEIR IDEAL PARTNER

A key moment in any juicy celebrity profile is when the writer slips in a question about the subject's rumored love interest, and they respond with a coy, non-definitive answer. Now is a good time to mention your friend's ideal soulmate, too. You can have them respond however you'd like, but bonus points for vagueness:

When I mention Ms. Noone's rumored house-husband, Mark Ruffalo, she simply rolls her eyes. "Can we please talk about something more interesting?"

6. PAUSE TO DESCRIBE THEM DELICATELY EATING SOME KIND OF INDULGENT OR LUXURIOUS FOOD

The secret is to use any verb to describe eating that would make you uncomfortable in everyday conversation. Examples:

She glides her fork into a heaping bowl of spaghetti Bolognese.

She pops an oozing morsel of brownie into her mouth.

She claws at a buttery brioche with her sharply pointed, exquisitely manicured fingernails.

7. END WITH YOUR FRIEND MENTIONING SOME VAGUE LIFE PHILOSOPHY

Conclusions are as tricky for journalists writing celebrity profiles as they are for someone writing a paper for English class. You never want to end too abruptly. The trick is to leave readers with a quip from the celebrity that could easily double as an inspirational quote:

It's easy to wonder whether it gets to be too much—balancing her talk show, her love life, and her chain of lobster-restaurants-slash-nail-salons (Nails 'n' Tails). "Life is a gift," Ms. Noone says, "and I'm unwrapping it very slowly."

Congratulations! You've written your first celebrity profile. Get ready to deliver it to your favorite person this holiday season, because you're their biggest fan. ☆

WHERE MY GIRLS AT?

BY JULIANNE

1. BO$$ -- FIFTH HARMONY
2. I'M GOOD -- BLAQUE
3. WHERE MY GIRLS AT? -- 702
4. SALUTE -- LITTLE MIX
5. THE STORY OF BEAUTY -- DESTINY'S CHILD
6. SITTING HOME -- TOTAL
7. HOLD ON -- EN VOGUE
8. HEY MR. D.J. -- ZHANÉ
9. RIGHT HERE (HUMAN NATURE REMIX) -- SFW
10. JUST KICKIN' IT -- XSCAPE
11. 9 TO 5 -- ELECTRIK RED
12. 'TIL I SAY SO -- 3LW
13. ALL HOOKED UP -- ALL SAINTS

Sister Pact

Snap and pop, give it what you got.
By Nafisa Kaptownwala

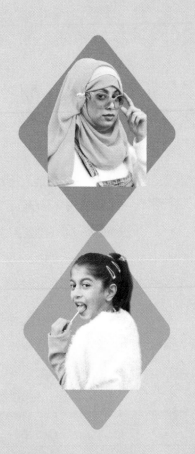

These images are part of an ongoing series called *Sister, Sister*, in which I pay tribute to the Morocco-born, U.K.-based photographer Hassan Hajjaj. I love the way his work creates an interplay between North African and Western cultures. I tried to achieve a similar effect when making these images, while using clothes and brands that are relevant to my life.
Thanks to Lubna and Shaheema for modeling. Special thanks to Lorde Inc.

SLUMBER PARTY GAMES: A TAXONOMY

Six sleepover rituals, explained.
By Gabby. Illustrations by Allegra.

Have you ever thought about how an anthropological essay on the typical teenage sleepover might be written by a stranger to the phenomenon? Or, how someone could try to explain its rituals—slumber-party games—to the uninitiated? Like, we know that a pillow fight is all in good fun. But to the untrained eye, it could easily look like a riot where girls laugh maniacally and thrash cloth containers of feathers over one another's heads.

I grew up taking slumber-party games for granted. Where did they even come from? What do they mean?! Today, I attempt to find out.

1. TRUTH OR DARE

This game is the fastest proven method to take a slumber party from zero to *Oh my god, we need an hour-long series on the CW to document all this DRAMA*. It requires players to 1) answer any question honestly or 2) agree to perform a physical challenge when it's their turn. The catch is that you have to pick "truth" or "dare" before you

know what either option might entail. It works best with a group of people who are creative and have a high tolerance for embarrassment.

Truth or Dare's origins are murky, but it's similar to an old English game, Questions and Commands, defined by the 1898 *Dictionary of Phrase and Fable* as "a Christmas game, in which the commander bids his subjects to answer a question which is asked. If the subject refuses, or fails to satisfy the commander, he must pay a forfeit or have his face smutted." In the modernized version, the equivalent of having your face smutted is being dared to like your crush's oldest Instagram photo.

2. LIGHT AS A FEATHER, STIFF AS A BOARD

Light as a Feather, Stiff as a Board exemplifies what a sleepover should be: spooky, slightly dangerous, and, most important, all about teamwork. During this game, one person lies on the floor while everyone else kneels around them and puts two fingers from each hand beneath their body. The people in the circle start chanting, "She's looking ill," then, "She's looking worse," then, "She's dying," and finally, "She's dead." The idea is that, somehow, the body of the person in the middle of the circle becomes light enough, and boardlike enough, for everyone else to lift using only their fingers.

This game dates back to at least the 17th century, when Samuel Pepys, an English naval administrator, recorded a story his friend had told him in his diary:

Four little girles [*sic*], very young ones, all kneeling, each of them, upon one knee; and one begun the first line, whispering in the ear of the next [...] and putting each one finger only to a boy that lay flat upon his back on the ground, as if he was dead; at the end of the words, they did with their four fingers raise this boy high as they could reach.

Between this and Truth or Dare, big ups to the British for laying the foundation for the modern slumber party.

3. PILLOW FIGHTS

Much like a food fight—but less messy and wasteful—the pillow fight is the international expression of soft anarchy. The origins of pillow fighting are unknown, but I am sure that the first person to initiate a cushion battle could not believe the power they suddenly wielded (much like our ancestor who first discovered fire).

The world's largest pillow fight happened this past September, when more than 4,000 college students at the University of California, Irvine gathered to swat one another. But is a pillow fight *really* a pillow fight if it doesn't happen at a slumber party? Apparently they played "Break Free" by Ariana Grande during the brawl, so I will give them credit for doing their best to create a sleepover-like environment.

4. SPIN THE BOTTLE

You're probably familiar with Spin the Bottle, the game where everyone sits in a circle, someone spins a bottle in the center, and then that person has to kiss whomever the bottle eventually points toward. But did you know that before this game was christened by Americans in the 1950s, it was impossible to convey sexual tension between teens in movies?! OK, that's not entirely true, but next time someone suggests playing Spin the Bottle and you feel deeply embarrassed, remember that at least it's not a game of life or death. Maybe the worst thing that could happen is your braces get stuck to someone else's?

5. THE HAND-IN-WATER TRICK

This is a single-player game of unknown origins that, if we're being honest, is more accurately a prank. The logic is that if you stick someone's hand in a bowl of water while they're asleep, the sensation will stimulate their bladder and they'll wet the bed. The show *MythBusters* proved that the only things that can make you pee in your sleep are drinking too much liquid before bed and a loss of bladder control.

I find this to be one of the most deeply cruel pranks—when you wake up the morning after a sleepover, your number-one priority should be perfecting your Toaster Strudel frosting technique, and not having to deal with a pee-soaked sleeping bag.

6. THE FROZEN BRA PRANK

As far as slumber party activities go, this is the least chill (metaphorically) but also the most chill (technically). Traditionally, it is a punishment given to the girl who falls asleep first. You're supposed to sneak into her bag to steal her bra, and then soak the bra with water, put it in the freezer overnight, and discreetly stick it back in her bag in the morning, just before she puts it back on. I don't know who first tried this and have never heard of anyone seamlessly pulling it off. Why do people do it? Should you?

The answers to these questions are up to you! Remember, next time you're playing this or any other slumber party game, you're not just having fun—you're carrying on traditions passed down by generations of girls in pajamas. ✈

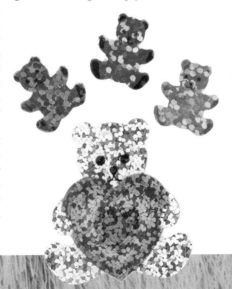

ON LIKING GIRLS

Some notes on bisexuality.
By Amy Rose, Lola, Meredith, Mads, Krista, and Suzy X. Illustrations by Isabel.

AMY ROSE As a teenager, I knew I wasn't a lesbian because I really liked guys…but I also really liked making out with Cara C. on a lark one day in seventh grade, and Rebecca B. outside of a Baptist youth group I went to every week to see her (although we were asked to stop coming when it became clear that our idea of fellowship wasn't in keeping with the pastor's), and all my girlfriends in freshman year of college after promising to "teach them to kiss," a move which might have been lecherous if they hadn't suggested we go over that particular syllabus first.

Bisexuality seemed like the rightful territory of people who dated guys and girls (and, sometimes, other genders) in equal measure, and that certainly wasn't me. (Yet.) I didn't want to step on the toes of an identity that didn't "belong" to me by claiming it when I didn't know what I was. I didn't make a point of identifying as anything other than straight until I was 17, when I got to college and told people I was bisexual for ease of girls knowing they were welcome to enroll in my vehemently unaccredited private frenching seminar (and there are plenty of otheridentifying names, among which you might find just the right title[s] for your particular sexualité).

Basically: My pervhood knows no limits!!! I'm actually not a perv, though, no matter how sprawling and manifold in scope my crushes may be. I'm just a person whose heart and anatomy are primed to love up my personalized bracket of multi-gender crushes, and I never understood why that was supposed to be confusing, wrong, untoward, or indicative of any fact about me besides "not straight," if it even meant that in the first place. Something tells me

more than a handful of you New Romantics out there can relate to this feeling…and that something is, rather than any extra-special adeptness on my part, you yourselves! Some recent letters from you, to us:

I've never considered myself bisexual, as I've only ever been attracted to two girls, but, for the first time in my life, I'm starting to think I might be. I have always found the female body far more attractive than the male body. When I watch porn, I'm only aroused by lesbian sex. I've never been in an official relationship, so it's difficult to see if I am attracted to girls, not just physically, but emotionally. I am 100-percent positive I am attracted to men, but I'm not sure if I'm really attracted to women. —Kelly, 18, Texas

I recently realized I'm bi-sexual. I've never been with a girl, and, though my boyfriend is my best friend, I feel like I'm missing out on the opportunity to be young and experimental. Girls sometimes express interest in me, and I fall for them, too, but that feels like I'm cheating on my boyfriend! I don't want to end our relationship on a bad note—I don't really want to end it at all, but I don't know how I'm supposed to sleep with girls and stay with him. —Anonymous

I've known I'm bisexual for almost two years. In the beginning, I was so focused on coming out to myself, but now I want to come out to my

friends. I'm afraid of becoming "a bisexual individual" instead of "an individual." My friends have said some biphobic shit (talking about "what a trend it is right now"; saying that a bisexual girl at their school has been "showing off," etc.). At moments like that…I just want to cry. I feel so lonely. What on earth should I do? —F., 17, Sweden

In these situations, here's what you should do not only on earth, but also if you happen to discover other planets on which multi-gender romances and sexual congresses are de rigueur:

Look at your hands. Take one of them and put it on the other. Think, *I am always going to be this person, so I had better be kind to them/me.* (Take a minute to laugh at yourself for being so EARNEST and SELF-HELPOID as you do this.) Then, think about how egregiously lovely it is that you are equipped to lust after/love/otherwise appreciate mad people in this world, and how many other people feel the way you do, or will see it for the A+ part of you that it is, if they aren't personally attracted to more than one gender.

If, after reading that, you're steaming up on some tip of *These girls just wrote that they DON'T see that yet, and I, as someone in a similar situation, don't, either, and you're telling us to LITERALLY hold hands with OURSELVES and pretend we do, anyway? How…dare you? How very dare you*, look, I understand. But! The evidence above is only the wispiest sliver of a shadow of the scads and scads of notes we get about same-gender attraction. There are so many of you who are furtively hurting or self-conscious on this front because you're not yet aware how much of a community is around you—though you will be. This is further proven by the Rookie staffers who offered their own tales and advice about liking GIRLS, GIRLS, GIRLS…in tandem with whomever else you're into, too.

LOLA When I was a freshman in college, I identified as bisexual…but my darkest secret was that I was "fake bi." I saw myself as all talk, no walk, because I had only made out with a couple of girls a couple of times, years before, and I was terrified of doing it again, because, *What if I'm bad at it, or a disappointment, or…*

At 19, I experienced a specific moment that allowed me to identify as whatever I felt like without feeling like the Sex Label Police were going to serve me a court order for felony charges of Inauthentic Identity. In a gender and sexuality class discussion on the sex researcher Alfred Kinsey's grading scale, ranging from 1 ("exclusively heterosexual") to 6 ("exclusively homosexual"), I learned that Kinsey created that classification because he found that many people's sexual experiences weren't entirely reflective of their desires. Many stops existed between gay, bi, and straight! So what if you were a girl and always wanted to kiss a girl, but you never did it because the idea was terrifying, and instead had sex with dudes your whole life because they were there and it was pretty fun? (ME ME ME!) Maybe I was a Kinsey "5" for desire and a "1" for IRL action, and that was fine—just more complex than I thought.

Don't feel like there's something you need to do RIGHT NOW to figure out what's right or wrong for you. Take your whole experience into account (fantasy, history, desire, lived experiences), accept that this is where you're at, and go from there. You don't need another person to be "what you are." Look no further for proof than my friend Z., who, when I stated my recent decision to identify as a "sex weirdo," responded, "Can I identify as someone who just wants to be left alone?" The answer is yes! I love what Rookie writer Tyler wrote in "Flying Solo": "The best thing about all these labels is that they're not definitions so much as tools that we can all use to think and talk about ourselves, and we can pick up different ones as we need them."

MEREDITH I always joke that I never "came out" because I was never "in." When my friends started gossiping about their crushes, it always felt normal for me to express interest in boys and girls right back. It didn't always play out that way in real life, though, and up until high school I had romantic contact exclusively with hetero cis boys. When I was 15, I met someone special enough to change my perspective on relationships and gender in total. At the time, I had a high school sweetheart—a wonderful older boy from a different school, but this new person—a girl from the Catholic school across town, whom we'll call C.—fanned the flames of my desire for non-boy people in a way that felt beautiful and dangerous.

At my first summer job at a coffee shop, C. often came in and wrote love notes on brown paper napkins, which she wadded up into balls and tossed at my head while I made cappuccinos. Because of my hazy relationship status, the two-CD mixes she gave me prominently featured Sonic Youth's "Shadow of a Doubt." I had that same feeling the Rookie reader with the boyfriend describes: falling so hard that it feels like you're cheating, even though you're only getting to know someone. By the end of that summer, the fire had grown large enough to collapse the foundations of my extant relationship. C. and I fell into a tremendous, melodramatic love affair. When I had what I really wanted, that feeling of missing out and any emptiness that came with it went away. Yes, I missed my boyfriend sometimes, but I felt so fulfilled: Not only had I met someone wonderful, but I had validated and subsequently asserted a crucial part of my identity. It helped me understand better who I was, and made me stronger.

If you feel like you're missing the boat— if you're falling for girls and want to be young and free but your boyfriend is impeding you— it's time to really take a long, hard look at what will benefit you most in the long run. In relationships, you always have a choice: You can stay with him now, because it sounds like he's very important to you, if you don't really want to break up with him. Once the desire to be with other people becomes too overwhelming, reassess. Or, you can re-evaluate and redefine your relationship to allow for each other's presence while not putting pressure on either of you to be romantic, so you can still enjoy his company while freeing yourself for that youthful experimentation you're after. You will have the rest of your life to experience other people, starting right now. It's up to you to assert your needs and decide what—and who—will be best for you in this moment.

MADS This past summer, I reunited with my long-distance boyfriend after spending a year apart. We started dating sporadically when I was 15 and he was 18, meeting up for casual makeouts in the student body officer lounge or his Prius. We continued dating when I moved to North Carolina for my senior year, and when graduation finally came, I moved back to where he lived. I was expecting our romance to reach some sort of cinematic climax when we met again, but really I just stood in his doorway awkwardly, unsure if I should shake his hand, hug, or kiss him. (I wound up doing a strange combination of the three.) The next few weeks, there were times that I felt ZERO attraction, but 100 percent affection, toward him. I spent over a month trying to convince myself that I needed to stay with him because there was no logical reason why I shouldn't be into it. (Obligation is a good reason to stay in a relationship, right? WRONG.)

I reconnected with one of my best girlfriends from high school. We started going to arcades, meditating in the mountains, and walking around parks, sometimes holding hands. During one hangout, she surprised me by leaning over and kissing me before we parted ways. Riding my bike home, I felt fluttery, partly because I really liked the innocent kiss, but also because I felt really guilty. I called my boyfriend immediately.

"A. and I KISSED!!! I'M SO SORRY BUT I THINK I MIGHT BE LESBIAN OR BISEXUAL OR SOMETHING. I NEVER MEANT FOR THIS TO HAPPEN and I DON'T WANT ANYTHING TO CHANGE, BUT ALSO KNOW THAT I DON'T FEEL RIGHT ABOUT OUR CURRENT RELATIONSHIP!"

What followed took me by surprise: My boyfriend laughed and told me that I was free to be with any woman I wanted, so long as I didn't kiss another man. I find this somewhat wrong now: That he was OK with me kissing women but NOT men made me feel like my boyfriend didn't take my attraction to women seriously, which felt belittling. That said, I did appreciate how much he understood and encouraged my sexual-identity journey, which is a journey that I think never really ends.

Since then, A. and I have remained friends, but we've never been able to discuss what happened in depth—I never took the time to process and communicate what I felt. I spent months in this confusing gray area, stressing myself out over morality, sexuality, and not wanting to hurt my boyfriend. I could have saved myself so much anxiety if I had just communicated with him at the start. For me, an essential component of relationships is to be free to talk about anything and not feel judged. Blurting out my feelings over that phone call really helped me, because afterward, I knew my boyfriend was my ally and would understand if I ever needed space to sort things out and explore my feelings for women. It's totally normal not to know where you land on the spectrum of sesssuality, and I slide all over the scale depending on the person/month/situation. Maybe one day I'll be able to state a stance with certainty, but for now, I'm enjoying the exploration.

KRISTA When I was 20, I had a fantastic boyfriend whom I loved and who was one of my best friends, but I also harbored crush-type feelings for several girls, including one very special one. My most major girl-crush at the time was a mystery to me—she smelled like incense, she had never been to a church service in her entire life, and she smoked clove cigarettes in patently inappropriate places, like restaurants, daring someone with her eyes to come and tell her to put it out. No one ever did. She casually kissed me when she felt like it, and I WORSHIPPED her, even though I suspected we would never actually date. Instead, I sensed my crush for this girl who didn't even love me was bigger than anything I had ever felt before, and I also sensed it was a sign of *things to come.*

I tend to be a steamroller about things I want to do, and when my boyfriend didn't appreciate the idea that I might want to do more than make out with other girls while he watched, I broke up with him, because I was young and free and DON'T HOLD ME DOWN IF YOU LOVE ME. I needed to know who I was, and it turned out I was a person who was sooooo queer, and sooooo happy about it. I wasn't "bi" or "gay" or even "queer" when I was experimenting with my sexuality. I was simply me, unsure and trying things out—and having a wonderful and heartbreaking and dramatic and totally fun time doing it.

SUZY X. Here are some words of encouragement from a 10-year queer:

• Don't ever let anyone tell you that your sexual desires are only legit when they become sexual experiences. Most people know they are straight long before they indulge in any hetero sexy time, if they ever indulge. Just like you already *know* you desire women, please understand that it doesn't make you a fraud or a poseur if you're happily dating a man. Your sexuality isn't defined by whomever you happen to be dating at the moment.
• Talk to your partner, if you have one, about your feelings. Do they know you've had feelings for other girls? Have you ever explored the topic of casually seeing other people (e.g., an open relationship)? If that doesn't seem like the right thing for both of you, that's cool—don't force it. Just have a talk about what levels of exploration you'd be comfortable with, if any.
• Should you and your partner decide it's the right time for you to explore seeing girls, try your best not to think of your experiences with other ladies as your scientific experiments. I know, you know: Girls rule. But it's a bit Bummertown when what should be a *mutually* satisfying moment with another girl comes down to *your* moment of self-discovery. Many lady-loving ladies agree: Be up-front if you're playing it super casual or noncommittal. And, of course, be honest if you feel a little shy or anxious. Anyone who gets put off by any of the aforementioned things isn't right for you anyway.
• If you're already in love with your boo… enjoy being in love! If it's there for you, relish it. Be as present as you can be. You are so very lucky to have what seems like a great connection with someone. You have your whole life to experiment and try new things.
• Reach out to other queer/bi/pansexual people. There are plenty of us out there! We're often mentoring one another on Tumblr (find your own crew by searching the bisexuality and pansexuality tags and following the conversations you find there), dating one another, or working through our dating woes over brunch. Some of us have romantic and sexual preferences for men, women, and/or anyone in between, and MANY of us have had the same anxieties you've had. Once you talk to more like-minded people, you may feel a little less disoriented…and more like yourself! ☻

SLUMBER PARTY SOUNDTRACK BY LUCY

1. THE SAME THINGS HAPPENING TO ME ALL THE TIME -- TEEN SUICIDE

2. OLD HAUNTS -- MEMORY HOUSE 3. FADE INTO YOU -- MAZZY STAR 4. BABY BLUE -- KING KRULE

5. TAKE ME SOMEWHERE NICE -- MOGWAI 6. LITTLE TROUBLE GIRL -- SONIC YOUTH

7. SWINGIN' PARTY -- THE REPLACEMENTS 8. MOON DREAMS -- DESOLATION WILDERNESS

9. ON THE SEA -- BEACH HOUSE 10. NEW HOUSE -- DIANA 11. RIBS -- LORDE

SLEEP OVER

*Nothing feels more like home than holing up
with a bunch of blankets, perfect tunes, loads of snacks,
and a pile of your best friends.*
By Allyssa

Thanks to Arabelle, Gabby, Hazel, Quinn,
and Shriya for modeling.

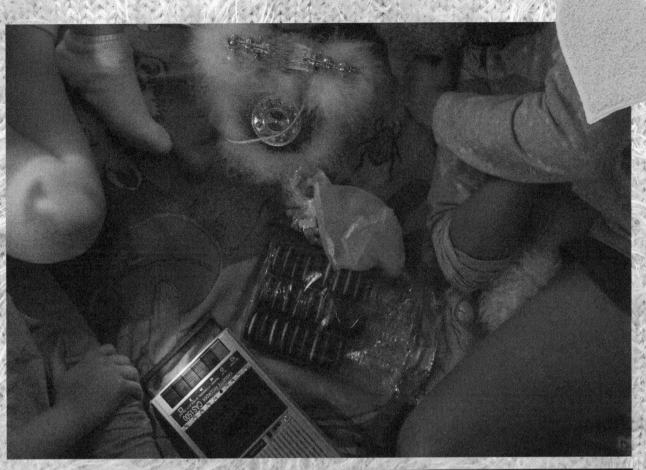

A guide to crushing on your pals. Written by Emily. Illustrated by Ana.

It can be the best of times, and it can be the worst of times. It's pretty much the most inevitable of times! Most of us out there have fallen victim to developing a hardcore crush on a friend.

There are a few reasons why we do this!

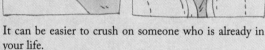

First, you have great taste in friends.

It can be easier to crush on someone who is already in your life.

Sometimes our hormones make us easily attracted to LITERALLY EVERYONE.

The vulnerable feelings that come from friendship can be intimate, and while intimacy is part of a romantic relationship, intimacy doesn't automatically mean a romantic relationship will occur.

Potential relationships can sometimes be better than the realities of actual relationships.

Being quietly infatuated with a friend is bittersweet, but exciting. You're carrying on a regular friendship with a heart full of delicious secrets, like some sort of spy. You wonder when will be the day that he/she will realize that you're *the one*. You long for deep, intimate talks that turn into deep, intimate makeout sessions. It's beautifully excruciating.

But it can't last. It's not healthy for you to long for someone without making a peep. It closes you off to relationship opportunities with other people.

STEP ONE

Prepare yourself for possibly losing your friend. It's a bummer, and it's no one's fault, but it's sometimes necessary.

STEP TWO

Pull your friend aside one day. Tell your friend how you feel. Keep it simple, unadorned, and short. I won't give you a script: Just say how you feel as if you were telling a stranger about it.

This step is going to be hard. You risk rejection and losing your friend and the fantasy of a romantic partner you've had in your head. But you can't go on in this limbo state forever!

STEP THREE

Give your friend space to sort out their feelings. They may tell you how they feel, or you may have to read their behavior. If they start avoiding you, that's a sign that your feelings are not reciprocal. If they start straight-up making out with you, that's a sign that they are! If someone wants to be with you romantically, they will make it known in broad daylight.

BOTH ARE GOOD!

If you end up in a romantic relationship with your friend, great. If you don't, give yourself and your pal some time, and in that time, pursue other people romantically. If your romantic feelings toward your bud have died down a bit and you still want to be friends, let them know. Accept the answer they give you. Friendships, like romantic relationships, require both parties to be enthusiastic participants and not doing so out of pity or obligation. Either way: GOOD FOR YOU for making your feelings known and being honest with your friend/maybe now significant other! Anybody would be lucky to have you as either. ♥

HOW TO LOSE YOUR BEST FRIEND

BFF breakups are hard, but you'll find a way to keep on jamming.
By Chanel. Illustration by Camille.

Sixth grade was a big year for me. It's when I met one of my best friends, whom we'll call Claire. We were nearly inseparable—when we weren't dicking around together at school, we were in each other's rooms talking about the boys we wanted to kiss, the people we mutually hated, and everything else in our lives. When it was just her and me, it felt like nobody else mattered. We were two halves of a whole, and we would always have each other. Or so I thought.

At the dawn of eighth grade, I sensed a new distance in our relationship. One day, I realized that Claire had seeped into the crowd at the back of the lunchroom rather than sit next to me. I had run into her talking to her new friends in the hallways or after school, but when I saw her at their table, I realized she was joining a new circle. Without me. We continued to talk for a while after that afternoon at lunch, but after it became clear that I wouldn't be joining her new crew (they were into drugs; I wasn't), our conversations dwindled.

Eventually, Claire stopped picking up my calls. At school, the hallways seemed to narrow anytime I saw her in passing. When I nervously raised my hand to wave or tried to muster a "hello" at our lockers, she looked the other way, and I'd get this feeling that my chest was filling with air, then suddenly emptying, like I was about to do one of those hiccup cries. (Later in life, I would realize these were panic attacks.) It took me a while to figure out that I was being left behind. After a few of these heavy-breathing fits, it dawned on me that her strange behavior wasn't just coincidental. It was a dismissive, purposeful disinterest in our friendship. I felt that I had been not just ditched, but recklessly betrayed, without warning or explanation. How was I going to live without the person I'd confided in so deeply, and so often?

It was hard for me to come to terms with losing her. I thought I was this untamed monster who couldn't control her emotions. I cried on my walks home from school, while watching TV, and under the covers. I was grieving, and while it felt horrible to deal with the feelings that came with that, it also helped me cope. Because being sad about a breakup with your best friend doesn't mean you're an *untamed monster*. It means you're a human being who is reacting to a hard situation, and almost everyone goes through this particular heartache at some point. If that point, for you, happens to be RIGHT NOW, here's what I learned about handling those feelings fairly and helping yourself feel better. Because you WILL feel better!

And now, the seven stages of best-friend breakup grief:

1. Becoming Irrationally Concerned About the Well-Being of Your Bestie-No-More.

When I first found out my BFF was hanging with what I considered a rough crowd, I thought she was going to *die*. That might sound melodramatic, but I really thought that something really bad was going to happen to her, and that I wouldn't be there to have her back if anything came crashing down for her. I thought that our friendship's absence was going to be fatal. In a deeper sense, though, I was really scared of our not being friends anymore, so I conflated these two fears instead of fully owning up to the latter one.

If you *can* get ahold of your friend, don't try to "save" them. Ask them what the deal is, and if everything's all right. They might refuse to answer or shrug it off…and that's their right! Their life is their own, and while you can tell a parent, guidance counselor, or other trustworthy adult if you're seriously concerned, you have to accept that you don't get to make their choices for them—just as my friend couldn't convince me to get involved with the new friends and experiences she was pursuing. Sometimes, a person needs to try new things with different people. In most cases, this doesn't mean they're in mortal danger—just that, as a teenage person on planet earth, they're growing up and changing, and that's OK.

2. Badgering Your Mutual Friends.

When I talked to the friends I shared with my ex-BFF about how I was concerned (and "concerned") for her, I got the impression that everyone, including her, was gossiping about me. I heard from one girl that my ex-BFF called me a poseur—the ultimate diss at 13, when I was trying so hard to seem "authentic." Another told me that I was lame for not doing what everybody else was (read: living that rebel life), so they didn't want to be associated with me. It was like nobody cared about my feelings. While this was wrong and mean of them, I wasn't *totally* innocent. I was kind of sabotaging any possibility that someone could be on my side, since I kept pestering them, which was probably annoying. Again: Let the person breathe a bit, and don't try to invade their privacy about things they clearly don't want to share with you. It might help you catch your breath, too. (This is especially invaluable if you're having panic attacks in front of your locker!)

3. Bargaining with Your Ex-BFF.

After a couple of weeks, I drummed up the courage to sit at Claire's lunch table and ask her what was going on. Unfortunately, it was a lost cause—we were in front of other people, and I think she was surprised by my plopping down across from her, so she just mumbled something vague instead of giving me a definitive answer. If you feel like you HAVE to try to repair the friendship, approach your friend without being accusatory. Ask her questions about what's going on with her instead of telling her what you think her deal is—focus on how you're feeling, and try to examine whether you had a role in the breakup. Try something like "I miss you and I feel like we're not as close as we used to be. Our friendship is really important to me, so I wanted to make sure everything's all right with you, and that I didn't do something to hurt your feelings." Be warned that, if your friend wants to take this opportunity to be mean and answer, "You did…BY BEING A POSEUR!!!" instead of telling you her real feelings, the distance between you might stretch exponentially. At least you tried, despite how difficult confrontations can be, which is a little victory to *sort of* celebrate, before…

4. Getting Totally Fucking Pissed Off.
It's been weeks, and your ex-friend is still giving you radio silence. If you're not thinking, *Fuck them!* over and over, you're loudly letting other people know that you really don't care "what the deal" truly is, as long as you don't have to be a part of it. Deep down, however, everything is hurting. I was hurting so much that, when I thought about Claire, it felt like a sharp physical pain piercing my insides. Even when I wasn't explicitly thinking about our crumbling relationship, a duller version of that pain lingered, reminding me that it could strike again at any time.

5. Cryyyyyying Your Eyes Out and Asking, "Why? Why? Why???"
Thoughts that are likely bombarding your brain day and night during this stage: *What's wrong with me? What did I do? Was it something I said? Where did we go wrong?* I asked myself these questions every day for a couple of weeks, mentally cycling through a number of possible answers:

• *I wasn't a good enough friend to Claire.*
• *She's embarrassed by me.*
• *There's something she doesn't want to share with me, so she's avoiding me.*
• *She wants to start a new life that doesn't involve me—which is totally fair, I guess.*

The thousands of other hypothetical reasons splintered off from those ones, which made me reconsider every single minute I'd ever spent with her, wondering, if all along, there had been evidence of the problem that I was too wrapped up in our friends-forever vibes to see. I kept revisiting my memories of Claire and casting them in a bad light, instead of seeing them as they actually were: good.

6. Crying Again. And Again. And More. Wah.
I used a lot of my crying time to reflect on my life and my individual worth. That made me feel better in the end—it helped me realize that I had other friends who supported me and would always be down to talk to me.

7. Blowing Your Nose and Moving On.
It may be hard to believe right now, but even if your friend never talks to you again, your life will keep moving forward, and you'll continue to survive. (Solid proof of this: You already are!) My constant pain about Claire diminished over time. Eventually, it came to a point where when someone asked, "What's with you two?" it took me a moment to remember why they would even ask that in the first place. Where, right after the breakup, my answers were bitter because of course I was still upset about what happened, later on, I was more composed: "It seems like we've grown apart, but I'm OK with that."

Acceptance doesn't come easy. When my mom periodically brought up Claire, pangs of that needling internal pain went through me. It was unsettling, but I tried not to confuse those reflexes for weakness when they were natural, valid sadness. It was hard to see and hear mementos of our abandoned friendship, like silly photos or songs we jammed out to together. With time, I learned to love them on my own. I could still jam without her, and I could certainly still smile at those silly photos without her.

If you're not quite there yet, hide your ex-BFF from your Facebook feed (if you're brave, unfriend them altogether) and put away your keepsakes and old photos in a box high up in your closet (or burn them, if you like, although you might regret it when you're less angry). When you leave behind the pain of your loss, which you will, no matter how long it takes, you'll replenish what you thought was dead; maybe with another loving friend, a significant other, or even the same best friend you grew apart from in the first place. But, if you remember one thing during the hysterical fugue state of grieving, coping, and moving on, it should be that you start with you, you end with you, and you survive as you. And, unlike some friendships, that's a real forever guarantee.

It will get easier to see your ex-friend around without being overwhelmed with WOE. You'll find someone else who'll jam with you in your car in the high school parking lot, and other people will be there to help you pick up the pieces of a seriously bad day. Maybe, later on down the line, you'll even become friends again (like Claire and I did—years later, I seriously love her, which is something my 13-year-old self could never have imagined saying again). This time, though, you'll have a better grip on yourself, and you'll be well acquainted with what really makes you whole (*pssst*—it's *you*, with or without a best friend). ✶

Dress Up in You

My muse, my mirror, my mate.
By Rachel
Thanks to Misha for modeling.

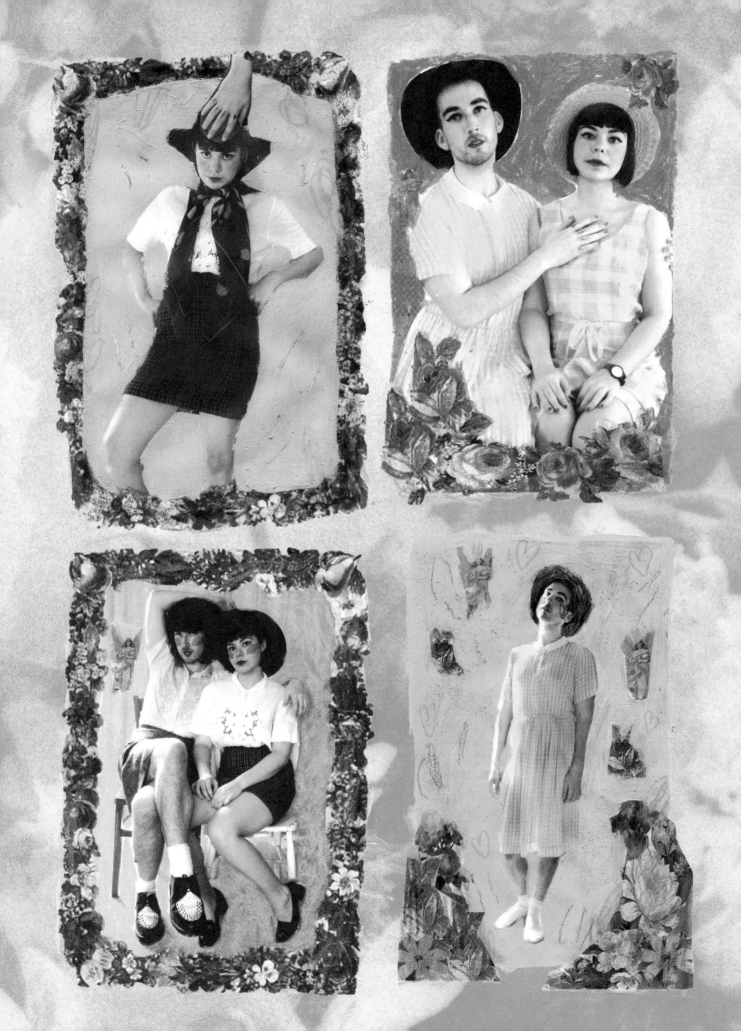

Imagine Me & You

A short story about a real friend.   By Pixie. Illustration by Ana.

Lately, my mind has been on my mind a lot. Do you know what I mean? Like I can't stop thinking about the way I'm thinking, and I'm worried that all of the thinking I'm thinking about might drive me to the point where I'm not able to properly think anymore. Does that make sense? I think it does.

I need to break up with my imaginary friend. It's harder than that might seem.

I don't even remember "meeting" Olly. He's just always been there, sitting next to me on the couch, or critiquing my sandcastle architecture at the beach, or gratefully eating the piece of imaginary cake I made my mother leave out for him at every one of my childhood birthday celebrations. My parents thought Olly was adorable—a figment that I'd come up with to help me navigate life and express myself. They'd ask me about him every day: *How is Olly this afternoon? Does Olly want lemonade? Is Olly excited about going to Grandma's this weekend?*

Olly made faces at me while I made up stories to please them—and tease him: *He feels great! He does NOT want any lemonade, thank you! He is very excited about Grandma's house, because she has crystal doorknobs on the bathroom doors, and he finds that very glamorous.*

In reality, Olly never showed excitement about much. He was just hanging out. He seemed to enjoy the impossible process of existing more than anything else. Sometimes, he'd cheer me up by walking through walls or changing his hair color mid-conversation, brown to green to purple to blue and back to brown. But it was on me to present him to the outside world, and though the two of us could talk for hours and hours, he never had much to say to anyone but me.

My parents stopped asking me about Olly once I started elementary school. Whenever I brought him up, they immediately asked me about my school friends,

as if to emphasize that my "real" friends were more important than the one they couldn't see. I started to understand that imaginary friends were a phase—my "real" friends laughed about theirs, embarrassed that they'd ever let themselves get so carried away:

I used to pretend I had an invisible friend named Muffin Febreze.

I used to pretend a lion named Albert protected me from the monsters under my bed.

I used to pretend I had a friend named Caroline who used to steal all of the cookies during our tea parties.

That was the common link throughout: *I used to pretend, I used to pretend, I used to pretend.* I listened to their stories, fascinated, wondering how they moved from active to passive. Olly listened, too, as he sat beside me, wide-eyed and smelling like gingerbread, soaking in the tales of the imaginary kids who didn't last.

"Where do you think they all went?" he once asked me, and all I could say was "away," as if that were a vacation destination and not a deep dark place that nobody returns from.

I've noticed that people don't like talking about imaginary beings unless they can be sure that you're not being serious—that you recognize the split between fantasy and reality. When you're four, it's adorable to have an imaginary friend. But when you're 15, it's a little creepy, I guess.

By age 10, I had stopped telling people that I still saw Olly, and I don't now, either. They'd think I was crazy, and, to be honest, I have enough to deal with right now. I have to write a 10-page essay on the psychological aspects of *Hamlet* this week and I don't have time to terrify everyone by casually mentioning to my parents over dinner that, *Hey! My childhood imaginary friend never went away, no big deal, pass the chicken, please!*

A few weeks ago, I told Olly that I thought something might be wrong with us. With me, really.

"Like, I think I might be crazy," I told him. "But not necessarily the *bad* kind of crazy?"

"I don't think 'the *bad* kind of crazy' exists," he said.

"Most people don't think you exist, though, in fairness."

"But you do," he said.

"That's kind of the problem, kid."

And then Olly said what he always says, what he's said since he first appeared: "Remember the rules."

When I was little, I asked Olly all kinds of questions about himself. Like, was he dead? Was he actually a ghost this entire time? Is that why he stuck around when everyone else's imaginary friends disappeared? He always replied the same way: "Remember the rules." The rules, according to Olly, are:

1. I exist because you allow me to exist.
2. Which means: I don't know anything you don't know.
3. No oatmeal raisin cookies, ever.

Olly claims that because he comes from my imagination, I get to control everything he thinks, says, does, and essentially *is*. And he is always quick to point out that, so far, our coexistence has not hurt anyone.

"It's not like I show up like some demon and tell you to burn down the supermarket or something," he says with a shrug. "I just want to hang out."

The problem with hanging out with Olly is that he ages at the same time I do, and somewhere around 13, I noticed that he was absolutely beautiful. Kudos to me, I guess, if indeed he did spring directly from my mind, because he's absolutely perfect-looking, with black hair and brown

eyes and a smile that shifts to the side when he's embarrassed about something. He does that smile a lot lately. When I'm embarrassed, I pretend I'm chewing gum. Now that we're both 15, there are a lot of crooked smiles and invisible pieces of gum floating between us.

Prior to this weirdness, our relationship hadn't changed much over the years: Olly showed up in my room while I did my homework, I'd give him an imaginary slice of pizza, and we'd talk about whatever. But he started acting weird a few months ago when I kept gushing about this kid named Alex who sits in front of me in bio class and sometimes smells like evergreen trees and Gatorade, and how that's both intoxicating and nauseating, kind of like the feeling itself.

Olly doesn't have much to say about Alex. He doesn't come to school with me, so that part of my life stays out of his reach. But when he does say something, it's usually something like "He sounds nice." Or, "Which kind of Gatorade? Because there's a major scent difference among flavors." He is both encouraging and disconnected, like he wants to say the right things but doesn't have the heart to back them up.

When I see Alex at school, I wonder what he's like when he's alone with someone. I wonder how his brain works and how he feels about oatmeal raisin cookies and if he ever accidentally spits when he talks, the way Olly used to when we both had braces in seventh grade. I am still living on the fumes of Alex telling me he "liked my brain," last week after I read a poem about that garbage island in the ocean (title: "Waves of Waste") during biology class.

"I like how you made the garbage island seem both scary and pretty," he said. (That is EXACTLY what he said, I will never forget it, I could have it tattooed on my face.)

"Oh, thanks. It's not supposed to be pretty," I stammered, making fleeting eye contact between long stretches of staring at linoleum. "It's a garbage island."

And then he smiled at me and said: "I like your brain, Laurel."

I don't really remember what happened after that because my brain turned into a pinball machine and all of the lights and bells were going off at the same time. But it was a good day in biology class.

I rushed home to tell Olly about it, how Alex had talked to me, and not only that, but had said the most romantic thing in the world. But he wasn't interested in talking much.

"I told you, you shouldn't worry so much about your brain," he said.

"Yes, but you're saying that because you come from my brain, right? Or do you not? Because I need to know if my brain is OK, and I think it may be? But you never give me an answer about anything, so I also think maybe it isn't. What do you think?"

"Remember the rules," he said.

Olly has only stopped by twice this week. On the other nights, I've been texting with Alex, who always starts with a biology question that I'm pretty sure he knows the answer to before turning the conversation to whales or Saturn's moons or some band he wants to ask me about. I've also been hanging out on my own, without either of them, and I'm coming to find that I like my brain just as much as they do.

I used to be afraid that I'd forget Olly if he ever went away for good—that certain parts of me would get locked up and I wouldn't be able to get to my own secrets anymore. But, lately, I don't worry about him as much, and I don't think he worries as much about me. We allow each other to exist in our own ways. I can exist without him, and it's not because I like a boy who smells like a sports drink. It's because I feel like I'm ready to exist on my own now, Alex or no Alex. I'm learning to space out and enjoy being myself instead of having someone—imaginary or human—to help me with that.

Tonight I have to study, though, so I'm trying not to think about that stuff. Olly is visiting, but he quietly glides around my room while I finish my biology homework. My assignment is all about cells and other little floating things that make up lives that are invisible to the average eye. When I finish, I notice that he's standing by the window, looking at the street.

"Anything good out there?" I ask him.

I walk over and stand next to him, and together we stare out at the pavement, lit by streetlights and porch lights and a sliver of moon. He turns to me and smiles. "I don't know," he says. "Just trying to see if there's anything good out there." I don't have to say anything, because he knows what I'm thinking: *There is, there is, there is.* And then he's gone again. 🐎

CONFESSIONAL SONGS
BY ANNA F.

1. WEREWOLF - FIONA APPLE
2. WHERE IS MY LOVE - CAT POWER
3. GIVE UP - FKA TWIGS
4. TREAT ME LIKE SOMEBODY - TINK
5. I LOST SOMETHING IN THE HILLS - SIBYLLE BAIER
6. LOVERS IN THE PARKING LOT - SOLANGE
7. HI-FIVE - ANGEL OLSEN
8. L'AMOUR LOOKS SOMETHING LIKE YOU - KATE BUSH
9. ALL THINGS GO - NICKI MINAJ

Dear Diary

LIFE: THE BEST OF

LIFE: THE BEST OF

CINEMA

POEMS

Design by Sonja. Title lettering by Lisa Maione. Playlist lettering by Rachel. Fiona Apple and Lauryn Hill portraits by Kelly. Marquee illustration by Esme. Diary illustration by Camille.

DECEMBER 2014: FIRST PERSON

I had my aura read in a jewelry shop a few weeks ago and nodded adamantly as the woman told me I was "removed, observant, in [my] own castle." It is very likely that other parts of her reading were far less accurate and that I seized only on what resonated with me, but that itself is innate to being removed/observant/in your own castle: picking what you'll remember later, curating moments, architecting your own narrative, as opposed to being open to the possibility that she could've been telling me something that did not already fit my idea of who I am. She said, "There is something between you and the rest of the world," and gestured as though to indicate a screen in front of her face.

This year, I graduated from high school and moved out of my parents' Midwestern home into a New York City apartment and started acting in a play every day, wondering, constantly, what it feels like to bring down that screen. This was for the sake of being onstage, but also because I was trying to start my life: How does it feel to exist in a moment, connected to another human being and to the world, without thinking about what it signifies, what it'll look like in memory?

To be able to consider these questions at all is not only a privilege afforded by a life with time to think about HOW EXACTLY to FULLY APPRECIATE these *MAGICAL MOMENTS* I am #blessed with *CoNsTaNtLy!*, but also just how my brain works. I started a blog when I was 11, and every day after school, I came home and took photos of my outfits for it. I was very picky about the setting and the colors and the lighting, not out of any interest in photography so much as a desire to draw connections between things and delight at the order of it all. I didn't feel like they were self-portraits, although I'm in every picture. They felt similar, instead, to doing plays at camp and community theater, or sitting at our family's piano going through a Bible-thick Broadway songbook and shifting among my favorite characters.

When I stopped writing my blog halfway through high school, I began keeping journals just for myself, each one cycling through a different personality as I had with fashion and with acting. For the duration of each journal, my handwriting would change, I'd dye my hair, I'd hang new posters on my wall, I stuck to a narrow selection of my wardrobe and my music, I chose a new route for the walk to school. I am similarly strict about the monthly Rookie themes, dictating to our illustrators and photographers which colors, motifs, and types of lighting to use in their work for us. (Have you seen the book you are holding?) My friends get annoyed with me for how often I try to art direct our hangouts instead of seeing where the night takes us—*Can we all wear these colors, walk down this street, listen to this song?* That cohesion frames the moment and turns it into a scene from a movie. I don't quite know how to let experiences unfold and be surprised by how they affect me; I want to know that I'll write down the aesthetic details of an event later and be pleased at how they fit together. All of my journals: *We dressed like teen rebels from the '50s, sat at the train tracks, listened to Hunx and His Punx.* I have no clue what we talked about, who these people were, or what this actually *felt* like.

Sometimes, this quality veers into the realm of vampiric hubris. Like: I sat on my roof on opening night of the play with a perfectly nice fellow who put on "Astral Weeks" by Van Morrison and his arm around me. Why did I let the love-y part of the song go over my head, but hear "to be born again" over and over, marveling before the skyline at my personal reinvention over the past few months—at how *perfect* it was that I was wearing my fuzzy pink *moving-to-New-York* jacket—instead of returning the embrace of a person I liked?

There is a terrible YA novel cliché of a girl who lives her life looking for *movie moments*, and I recently defended her/myself in my journal:

1. Why worship a life that is movie-esque?
2. Why should something be significant for feeling movie-esque?
3. Isn't life the real thing itself?

No. Movies are what make life real to us, because they pay attention to and crystallize emotions, colors, movement, human behavior, etc. (When I say movies, I also mean TV, I also also mean plays—even though a play is not recorded, it's crystallized in that it lives on in the minds and memories of its audience.) Movies are like "LIFE: The Best Of." "LIFE: The Essential Collection." "LIFE: Not Dead Yet!" So saying a moment is like a movie is how we comprehend its beauty and grant it significance.

I can defend the art direction and the obsessive documentation, but I also know that different answers to the above questions exist. I know there are infinite moments that could take place and affect me in ways I can't conceive of, if I could only put down my notebook once in a while and actually live my life instead of trying to immortalize everything. But, for now, this is where this month's theme starts: the combined beauty and danger of inventing yourself, owning your experiences, putting yourself on record.

love,
Tavi

Party of One

Dressing to impress myself.
By Rachel

Styling by Ahida Agirre. Hair by Bronwyn Gardiner with Kevin Murphy products. Thanks to Naomi for modeling. Special thanks to Maria Pizzeria from Coffin on Cake PR and Nico the cat.

APPROVAL PLAN

Knowing you're allowed to love your body is only the first step.
By Brodie

Before I was exposed to "fat acceptance," a movement that advocates an end to social, medical, and political discrimination against fat people, I felt awful in my skin. Even in my happiest times, I could never shake the sense that I was too much in size and not enough in every other way—that my fat body made me unacceptable and unworthy. But this new community, which I stumbled on online, turned my self-perception on its head. I started to see my body as a political weapon, and one that I could be proud of. Society wanted me to cover up, hide, or shrink? I'd show everyone how powerful I was by wearing short skirts, demanding that people notice me, taking up space, and refusing to apologize for it.

After the initial, revelatory wave of self-confidence settled in my bones, I was surprised to learn that there were still days when I woke up feeling awful, when I didn't want to look in the mirror, or couldn't feel good about myself, no matter what I wore or how high I held my head. I was filled with shame—but this time it wasn't because of my body's mere existence. It was because I wasn't feeling great about myself *every second of every day*. Now that I knew what it meant to *not* hate my body, was I being a phony, or betraying my fat sisters, when I had negative feelings about it or wished I could look like someone other than me?

I can be the most body-positive person in the world, but that doesn't mean I will always feel good, or that other people's projections or prejudices won't

bother me. Since stripping the word "fat" of its power, I've encountered other people who are so afraid to confront it that when I've described myself as such—never as an insult or anything derogatory, just as a description of my body that feels more right than "curvy" ever did—they've jumped at the chance to assure me that "No, no, you're not fat, you're beautiful!"

I'm here to assure you (and myself) that you can be both, even on the days when you don't recognize the latter. Every body is worthy of self-love; every body is cool and great and powerful. Having to remind yourself of that sometimes does not make it any less true. Here's how I do it:

1. I LET MYSELF ADAPT

My approach to fat acceptance has changed and grown as I've gotten older, just as my views on feminism shifted as I molded them to fit the person I became. I figured out that the label "body-positive" suits my outlook more accurately than "fat acceptance"; while removing the negative connotations from "fat" was an important step in my self-worth journey, it was equally important to me that all bodies are seen as good bodies, and that none are given more prominence or respect over others.

In the first few years after I discovered fat acceptance, I felt like people were either with us or against us; that you could only be unhappy with your body (like I was before F.A.) or happy being fat (like I

was after F.A.). I know now, though, that someone saying they want their body to be smaller or different is not the same as them saying, "I don't want to look like you." Another person's decisions have nothing to do with me, and they certainly are not making those decisions to rub them in my face. When Beyoncé worked hard to shed her post-Blue baby weight, I once would have interpreted it as a slight against her bigger sisters instead of what it actually was: someone doing what she needed to do to feel like her body was right for her. It took time for me to understand that no women are safe from having their bodies policed, and that it's not thin women who are the adversaries of the fat-acceptance movement, but rather the structures that enforce ideas about what bodies are "good" or "right."

2. I TUNE OUT

Here's something I wish I was told the second I could comprehend language: What other people think about me and my physical self—"good" or "bad"—ultimately does not matter. Their tastes and opinions about me should not inform my own. When I first spoke openly about my newfound acceptance of my body, a guy I knew congratulated me on my positive outlook before assuring me that he would "always be a chubby-chaser." All of a sudden, I saw myself the way this dude saw me: as a personality-less thing he could fetishize. And he thought he was *complimenting* me!

I was so shocked and grossed out by his comment. More than that, I was furious that I had worked so hard to get to a point where I could finally share how great it felt to accept myself, and he elbowed in and made it about him (and how special he was for not being "like other guys"—the ones who are so superficial that they're only attracted to women for the way they look). I didn't confront him about what he said, but I've encountered dudes like him since—men who make a show of being attracted to fat women and expect me to fall over with gratitude that they're paying attention to me. I've found that a clipped "Good for you," or, "That's nice," says everything I need to: I heard you, but I do not care what you think.

Whenever someone tells me that my worth lies in how attractive my body is to them or anyone else, I try to remember one thing: that other people are irrelevant to my mission, which is to be the flyest version of myself at all times. The only person who has a say in how I look, or how I feel about how I look, is me.

3. I IDENTIFY MY TRIGGERS

Checking in with myself when I sense that my self-love is starting to slip has helped me pinpoint *why* it's happening. Over time, I've been able to identify a few common triggers:

My period.
Like a frazzled lady in a tampon commercial, I always feel bloated and irritable a few days before I get my period. As *wrong* as I might feel at that specific moment, I know to remind myself that it will pass, and that after my hormones level out, I'll return to my old self. Until then, you'll find me wearing leggings, eating chocolate, drinking peppermint tea, watching *Kourtney & Khloé Take the Hamptons*, and not giving a fuuuuuuck.

Conversations about diet.
I'm all for people doing what they need to do to feel healthy and happy, but more often than not, talk of cleanses and significant dietary changes digresses into talk about weight loss, which can make me feel like shit. I'm happy to talk about new recipe ideas or tricks for adding more green veggies to my dinner, but when calorie restriction is the topic at hand, the message I hear (even if it's not said explicitly, or even the person's intention) is: "I would rather drink this disgusting lemon water than look like you." I've been in this situation enough times that I want a button that says, "I survived the ubiquitous green-juice trend of 2010," but it's also taught me that the best course of action for me is to remove myself from such conversations. If my two instincts in life are fight or flight, I find it best to just GTFO.

Trying to fit in—literally.
Nervous breathing and cold sweats sometimes grip me when I have to do things that put my body at the forefront of people's minds. Things fat people are often criticized heavily for—going to the pool or the beach, eating in public (particularly when it requires sitting in a tiny booth), traveling on an airplane or other cramped spaces—will increase my levels of discomfort tenfold. I've learned to dial up my self-awareness when I start being down on myself and question where the self-criticism is coming from. Some people will never stop having issues with my body's existence in public, so even if I hear their sighs as I squeeze past them on a plane, or feel their eyes on me as I grab a burger on my way home, I pretend to be oblivious. Usually "just ignore it and it will go away" is the least-helpful non-advice ever, but I hold fast to the belief that people's

reactions to my body are theirs to deal with. The times I was most critical of other people's bodies coincided with the lowest points of my self-esteem, and I truly believe in the link between feeling good about yourself and being kinder to others. Until they join me in my "all bodies are good bodies" mentality, I'll be over here, blockin' out the haters.

4. I'M KIND TO MYSELF, AND I LISTEN TO MYSELF

Sometimes, thinking so much about my body distances it from my self—like when I sit down and write about it and find I'm thinking about it as a subject to dissect (metaphorically—no scalpels involved) rather than everything from my mind to the fingers that type these very words.

When I feel myself dissociating from my body in this way, I watch a video of fellow Rookie Meredith, from the fashion site StyleLikeU's "What's Underneath Project," and listen carefully to her closing words: "In my body is a good place to be, because, functionally speaking, I know at the end of the day, it's the only home I've ever had, and it's the only home I ever will have. So no matter how much I argue with it, at the end of the day I have to treat it like my home. And home is where you're supposed to feel the safest. And home is where love happens. And home is where you're supposed to feel best about yourself. And, uh, welcome home."

Trust me when I say that once you accept yourself, not even the low points can make you forget that. Knowing you're allowed to love your body is just step one. After that comes the hard part: practicing that love when your instincts/other people/ your hormones tell you to do the opposite. But I promise you, it's worth it. ✿

hOW TO MAKE A PhOTO DiARY

A step-by-step guide to taking pictures that will matter to YOU.
By Allyssa and Shriya.

CHOOSE YOUR WEAPON

If you're gonna take pics, you need a camera! There are countless options, and there's no "best" one. To find the camera that is right for you, it helps to experiment a bit with different types to figure out what you're comfortable shooting with, and which ones make photos that fit your aesthetic. The two of us have shot with a lot of different film and digital camers, and here are some of our favorites.

1. Disposable Cameras

2. Point-and-Shoot or Single-Lens Reflex (SLR) Cameras

3. Digital and Smartphone Cameras

Disposable cameras are super accessible and cheap options for keeping a photo diary. You can usually get one at your local drugstore for less than $10, and most drugstores can develop the film, too. To take pictures, you just point and click. The photos tend to be pretty grainy, but the colors are typically bright and saturated. Because you can't focus the lens, you might get some blurry pics, but the blurriness can give the images a nice, fleeting feel.

ALLYSSA This is a photo of my little brother Kaleb, after a long day of swimming in the summer. I took it on a disposable camera that I picked up at a pharmacy. The soft focus and overall fuzzy quality of the photos reminded me of my childhood. It made the images even more precious, no matter how blurred or silly they were.

SHRIYA One of my first memories of taking photos is from fifth grade, when I went to camp. My folks sent two disposable cameras with me, and I clicked away as my friends and I ran around the woods. Using disposables was an easy way for me to document what I was seeing.

Point-and-shoot or single-lens reflex (SLR) cameras give you a little more control over your images. These cameras also use film, but unlike disposables, they allow you to adjust things like shutter speed, aperture (which determines how much light gets in), and focus. You can find cheap film point-and-shoots, like the Olympus Stylus, which has a good lens for its price, on eBay or in thrift stores. You can buy more expensive, high-quality film cameras, like the Contax G2, in camera shops. Cameras with high-quality lenses make sharp, precise images. Film SLRs, like the Canon AE-1, allow you to change the camera's lens, which gives you even more control over the aesthetics of the photos you take.

SHRIYA When I was 15, I talked about photography nonstop—so much so that my viola teacher's husband gave me his old film SLR, a bunch of lenses, and a bunch of film, too! I experimented a lot with this equipment—shooting with the zoom lens at concerts, using the 50-mm lens to take portraits of my friends (like this one of my friend Connie getting her first tattoo). These days, I also shoot with a variety of point-and-shoot cameras that I've found for cheap in thrift stores. It can be a little risky to buy a used camera because you never really know if it'll take good photos until you get the film developed, but I like that it's an adventure. Every time I get a roll of film developed, it's like Christmas morning.

ALLYSSA I got my first film SLR camera, the Olympus OM-10, by saving up a bit of money and racing over to my local thrift store. It taught me to work more slowly than I did with the little snapshot cameras I used before, because I literally had to FOCUS on what I was looking at.

Digital SLR (DSLR) cameras run about $350 on the lower end, if you have more money to spend. But using a digital camera doesn't necessarily mean the photos will be better—it's just a different style to work with. The photos won't have the dreamy, grainy quality that photos taken on film tend to have. Shooting digitally usually means the images will be clearer and sharper. There are myriad digital cameras out there, and higher-end digital cameras can cost between $1,000 and $3,000. Higher-end cameras tend to make images that have a huge image resolution, which means you could blow up the photos super big and the quality would not be pixelated or fuzzy. But if you're

just starting out, it's probably best to not invest in such a high-end camera until you really know what you want from your photos.

SHRIYA When I was 15, I took this photo of my best friend, Clare, in her living room on my Nikon D40, the first DSLR I ever had. Shooting digital photos can be nice because it gives me unlimited tries to make an image. With film, I have a finite number of exposures on the roll. With a digital camera, I can keep trying until I feel like I have the photo I'm trying to get. This can be both a blessing and a curse, because having infinite frames can drive me crazy! Sometimes, it's important to set a limit for yourself.

ALLYSSA I've never been much into the DSLR realm of picture taking, mostly because the grandma in me stresses out over all the functions! I've always resorted to my phone's camera to digitally document my life. Whether it's been a flip phone or a more fancy iPhone, I've gotten instant satisfaction and photos that come with their own aesthetic charms.

I'm a pretty socially anxious person, and photography provides a way for me to try and break out of that. Making myself go to a new place or hang out with a group of people to try and CREATE a romanticized document that I can enjoy later is sometimes more valuable than the time spent in the moment. I can't tell ya how many times I've had a completely shitty experience in a space, or was super nervous hanging out with a new pal, but the photographs I took gave it purpose and made it worthwhile.

This is one of the first photos I took of Elaiza, a good friend. I didn't know her very well when this was taken. I was staying at her house in Purchase, New York, and was feeling really nervous—as I do when I'm getting to know anyone. Taking this picture helped me feel closer to her. It also gave me the comfort of having the camera as a grounding tool, which kept me in the moment and less stuck in my head.

TAKE PHOTOS

**1. First and foremost:
Bring your camera wherever you go.**

**2. Find spots in town to explore—go alone
or bring a pal to take pictures of.**

**3. Tell yourself you're gonna take X photos in a day, whether
it's three pictures or 30, and whether you're at home
or out gallivanting around.**

**4. Put yourself out there and don't be afraid
to take a photograph.**

IT'S GONNA BE OK

Remember that this diary is for you. It it not meant to please anyone else, so all that matters is that you are taking the pictures YOU want to be taking. Not every photo is going to be "great" or "perfect," but they're all significant because they are all made by you and are documents of your life. The more you practice and shoot, the more you will grow into your own style and find comfort in the images you've made. You might cringe at the photos you take, but that comes along with keeping any kind of diary. We're all constantly changing and developing, and sometimes you might feel embarrassed when you look back at a photo you took. These images chart your growth. Sometimes an old photo can evoke sad feelings, but a lot of times it will make you feel a certain fondness, and there's something really beautiful about that.

SHRIYA I discovered light painting (taking photos with a long exposure and a light) when I was 15, and I took this picture of my Ron Weasley action figure "casting a spell." Yikes.

ALLYSSA A photo diary can seem really self-indulgent, or even sappy or cheesy, but you deserve the space in history that your photos take up. Embrace the sap! Break out the cheese!

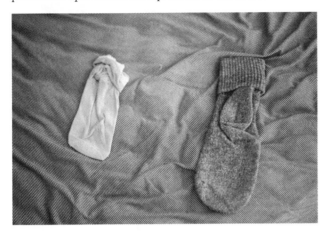

I am no stranger to the Cheese, and this photo is what I would consider its definition. It's a picture I couldn't help taking, no matter how goofy it seemed, because it came from an earnest place. This was my sock and my partner's sock found snuggled up together on the bed. It makes me turn into a tomato just looking at it.

I'm a real sensitive bug, and in the beginning of my photo-diary-keeping existence, I was entirely too apologetic for that. I've learned more about how and why I use photography to express myself—and it's very much a way for me to spew L-O-V-E into the world. I realized I have nothing to be sorry for! Know that everything you create/document introduces a blip of beauty and positivity to the universe, and that is one of the most powerful things you can do!

SHRIYA I go through highs and lows with my photos. Sometimes an image will capture exactly what I was feeling or experiencing, other times it doesn't do the situation justice whatsoever. But one thing I always have is the memory of making a photograph: getting just the right angle, waiting for the sunlight to be in the perfect spot, sneaking up to someone—like a sweet old man holding flowers—and snapping fast. Those added memories make even the imperfect photos special.

CATALOG YOUR WORK

There are a lot of different routes you can take in archiving and sharing your photo diary—choose whichever one works for you.

You can get your photos printed and throw 'em in a photo album or even paste them in a notebook or journal. There is something intimate in being able to physically hold evidence of your experiences, and there's nothing like flipping through real-life pages of photos!

ALLYSSA This is a photo that I keep in the pocket of my journal. I took it on an Instax instant camera, which is a good tool for taking snaps for a physical photo diary.

I'm still a bit wary about putting my photos on a blog, so most of my diary images either remain in organized folders on my computer, or are shared on Rookie. Keeping my images in little places—groups on my computer, printed zines, or just photos stuffed in the pockets of my journal—makes them feel like an even more secret, special thing for myself. Sharing my work is exciting and nerve-racking, but at the end of the day, this is a document of MY life. As long as my photos are special to me, that is what matters most.

SHRIYA I have a photo blog where I post work (like this picture of furniture on a sidewalk in New York) every few weeks. Between college and freelancing, my life can get pretty hectic, so having a photo blog helps me organize and remember what I've been up to. I also am a big Instagram fan; I love posting daily images, like one I took on my phone of me skating, or of a great piece of pie. It's an immediate way to share an image, serious or silly, with your friends in one step. I have to remind myself often to not measure my self-worth through Instagram likes, though. It's nice when people appreciate my work, but it's important for me to remember that a photo can still be great even if no one else thinks so. 📷

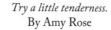

Soft Power

Try a little tenderness.
By Amy Rose

When we say someone is "being vulnerable," we mean that they're not self-censoring. This phrase, however sensitively we dispatch it, also connotes that they're exposing themselves to be attacked: The Latin root is *vulnus*, which translates to *wound*. Some of us grew up learning that hermetically sealing our thoughts inside ourselves is a way to self-protect. At the risk of sounding logically flimsy: This is right and wrong.

Of course, it *doesn't* always serve us to be vulnerable, especially as members of a gender often dismissed as shrill, hysterical, and frivolously heart-motivated by those who would like to see their own MALE-ASS PROFESSIONALISM AND STOIC SELF-CONTROL as an indication that they're better leaders. Not only men do this—how many times have you heard a would-be sister in arms say, "I can't hang out with other girls. Too much DRAMA," as though Henry VIII didn't straight-up decapitate his wives when he didn't get his way, not a single college-football Man Fan has ever rioted in the streets because a ball didn't go the direction they wanted the ball to go in, and every song by a dude on the radio isn't called, like, "Bitch (I Think You Are One, and I Want to Kill You Because You Don't Love Me—Hurt Feelings Remix)"?

Still, it's women who are condemned in high school tropes and maligned in studies on professional affect and in novels, for being TOO GODDAMN TALK-A-BUNCH, JEEZ, LADY, STOP CRYIN' ON MY HYPER-ASTUTE DICK WHILE I'M TRYING TO BE SMARTER THAN YOU!! Those who buy the lie that dudes are the sole containers of the world's power and intelligence also buy into a male selfishness that says "Your inner knowledge doesn't matter. Shut the fuck up, you oversharer—you have no right to talk about your own life." That selfishness comes from the fear that only one kind of experience can exist in

this world and that, in talking about lives deviating from that default as valid, the dominance of that default will be toppled. This is exactly why you need to do it. It's the opposite of "self-indulgent," the main criticism that is often leveled at people, and especially women, who speak. It is an agitation for more room for everyone, men included, to live freely as their exact selves. The idea that talking frankly about feelings=bad implies a distrust of the people in your life, and life on the whole—it expresses the thought *How could anyone POSSIBLY have the empathy or wherewithal to get the staggeringly complex work of genius and cool-guyism that is* me? I don't doubt that you ARE a complex person, but that's because so too is everyone else.

No one starts out as a kid *wanting* to be cruel or lacking in understanding for others, and many of us (I hope) still valorize kindness. So, when we think of love and friendship and how to be a decent, empathetic person, are we thinking, *I got it! Relationships should be a petty system of slamming the crypt door on a potentially edifying/sweet interaction with an acquaintance, methodically not texting someone I care for back to convey that they aren't my priority (even though they are), and/or subtly insulting a person in my friend group to place myself on the winning side of a power imbalance?* Or are we thinking, *I would like to find someone who understands me (and vice versa), to whom I can be helpful and sweet (and vice versa), and who makes me feel happier and more supported just by virtue of being themselves (and vice versa)?* The latter…r-right?

The problem is that the examples of LOVE: A USER'S GUIDE some of us are given as children and teenagers by our friends and families so often evince the former. That is so sad to me. I always assumed I would be hurt by other people rather than understood by them, so I preemptively shut down those I wanted to

impress or prove myself to—these were known, collectively, as "everyone on earth." I decided that I would never lay my tender or "deviant" truths open to potential besiegement—even to myself—after a particularly bad raid on my fifth-grade journal. One day in class, a jerkulux swiped my notebook and performed a recital of my innermost thoughts at the front of the room, giving an exciting theatrical voice to my mammoth, private terror about some… *trouble* my family was going through.

Rather than an egregiously cruel breach of privacy, this was considered the most uproarious revue that had ever taken place at Washington Elementary, based on my peers' reactions. As the room howled over the idea that my family was reeling from sadness and trauma, the message was clear: *You are a puny feelings-haver who can't hang—plus, you come from bad stock, and your dented-up life is worthy of our scorn and hatred.* I felt really fantastic!! Nah, I ran out of the class and cried myself ragged in the girls' room, much to everyone's horror and embarrassment. This, of course, only amplified their laughter—like, THAT'S what happens when you cop to having an emotional response to hardship? I GUESS I HAD BETTER JEER REALLY HARD AT IT SO THAT I NEVER HAVE TO STANCH THE FLOW OF MY OWN TORMENTED CRYFEST WITH SCRATCHY TWO-PLY.

From then on, I hid. As an adolescent, I cultivated the nasty habit of gulping back whatever it was I was feeling when it would have served me well to be a little more forthright. When I was 15, I went to a party at a nearby college, where, stoned out of my gourd, I leaned against a pitted pool table in someone's basement. I was intimidated by how easily everyone else could access the fun going on and enjoy one another, but instead of risking being unveiled as The Girl With the Perpetual

Nervousness, I didn't try to engage with anyone, lest I fuck up. Of course, this has a certain draw to it—when you hang back at a social function, some find fun and sport in trying to FIGURE YOUR MYSTERI-OUS 'N' BROODING ASS *OUT*, especially an aloof female to whose attentions they feel entitled. This is not a method of hearing your truth as a matter of allowing room for it, but instead, of harnessing and owning it. This person wants to be its sole master, as though you are an impetuous horse to be broken.

But...I still think that the guy who came up to me that night and started a conversation was just being gregarious and trying to draw in the drugged little cretin examining a cue ball as if it would suddenly swirl with the truths of her fortune. I probably want to give him credit because his face was an arrangement of perfect, wrenching geometry, and I was realizing, watching it swim up to me, that I didn't actually hate math. He said: "How do you know the guys in Sea Creature?"

High and insecure (how I spent my teenage years before I realized that the two conditions were in bed with each other and stopped smoking pot), I had no idea what to say. Instead of responding simply—"the singer is my friend's brother"—I was terrified of sounding facile. I decided to clam up, an oversimplified sea creature myself: "I don't."

He persisted as I locked my bloodshot eyes to the pockmarked topography of the pool table's dirty green felt and put up my hair with my hands (a nervous habit that I decided was sultry-looking as a kid and now understand, too late to break it, is a semaphore to my own skittishness). Finally, Math Mouth tilted his head and said, with a crescent or parenthesis of a smile (I was seeing the connections between the shape of the universe and the mathematical order of operations SO HARD, you guys, fuck a cue ball, this was an EPIPHANY and also I was so so *so* faded): "You hold yourself a certain way. You're always *posing*."

It sucked that he was right. I was literally hitting marks as I mimed the construction of a ponytail! "What a weird thing to say," I drawled, but we both knew the

conversation was over. I couldn't break out of my clamshell—the hardened part that seals away the living thing inside. I might have had a nice time that night, but instead was relegated to watching an atrocious band and some billiard balls by myselch. How laid-back and not-at-all pathetic, to choose to spend the ever-winnowing amount of time that you get to be conscious on this planet that way!

In retrospect, this interaction was... real hackneyed, and Math Blaster seems like a presumptuous dick for trying to break down the truth of me, to me. Sadly, he had something of a point: There was the un-jazzed-up truth of my misleading and cowardly brittleness, at last. I wasted so much of my life misunderstanding this kind of "ONE DAY I'LL FIND SOME-ONE WHO CAN SEE *THE REAL ME*" revelation as the inborn closeness and affection I pined for—in friends; in family members; in undergraduates with celestial-grade Golden Ratio faces. I didn't realize that, nah, everyone *can* see the "real you," and that my standoffishness and gruffness was coming from fear. Justifiably, no one *wants* to love someone who's always posing (unless you are a glamorous fashion model who makes your living doing just that—then people probably want to date you). Intimacy isn't, after all, "inborn"—it's carefully, reciprocally earned.

Recently, a woman I know told me how horrid she was to other girls in high school. "I had to let them know who was boss," she said, as she nostalgically recounted the times she made people cry or bleed, "because, otherwise, they would have fucked with *me*. I was scared of someone being mean to me first, so I wanted to look tough." What a lovely outlook! This affixes to friendship—an ostensibly affectionate and pleasant conceit—the idea imposed on politics and professionalism that SURVIVAL IS AGGRESSION, THEY'RE ALL GONNA GET ME. That philosophy is already destruct-o-max, right where it is.

When it's demonstrated to you that the way to "get ahead" in your social groups is by policing, mocking, and gossiping about your cohorts, it is fucking IMPERATIVE

that you do not internalize it, or you end up perpetuating that same hardness of heart yourself. As my acquaintance illustrated, it's a sham of illegitimate, wussy origins—why would you want to work in the service of that? When *everyone's* shuffling through that dishonest foxtrot, rather than being kind, everyone's sorta-right to make the sad and sick assumption that we're gonna dismantle or disregard or WOUND them, despite their good hearts and intentions. When people explain that others can be brusque, reticent to speak honestly, and/or plain unkind because they're insecure, it sounds like a moldy self-help trash trope. Unfortunately for our collective cynicism about all things that are sincere, banal, and moralistic at once, it's such a moldy self-help trash trope because it's incontrovertibly real.

This is true in less overt ways, too. I met my platonic life partner, whom I'll call Eddie, at 19. I was writing my first novel in the front booth of where he tended bar, so we got to know each other pretty well, and we ran in concordant social packs, orbiting each other affectionately over the next few years. Eddie was the star of the show no matter where it was being staged, and he delighted me and every cast in which he appeared. He was a font of interesting positions on literature and music, physically riveting beyond his handsomeness (ask me about all the times I've seen him swing dance acrobatically, spinning cackling strangers over his head), rife with endearing, haywire autobiographical anecdotes, and committed to sharing authorship in the serialization of those excellent stories with each venture into others' company.

We hung out a ton as pals and party dates through the first iteration of our long pairship, but we only acknowledged each other as best friends/forever-squad recently. Eddie was running late to meet me at a restaurant one night, so I posted up at a table thinking about him. Throughout all the years that I had found him to be an ace human being, we had never really talked about our treu-bleu feelings as co-members of our species. I wondered if raffish, charismatic Eddie had ever felt as alone as I did. So, when he got there, I asked him.

"I have often felt like a beautiful statue," he said. That wording is a little lunkheaded, but also kinda ideal (cf. "You're always *posing*"). I knew exactly what he meant, which intensified as he went on: "I locked myself out of my apartment the other day and I just stood outside my door because I didn't think I had anyone to call."

"I live around the corner!" I said, dumbfounded, trotting out information he has known for years. "You could have just buzzed!"

"Right? But I panicked—I was convinced I didn't have any friends and that no one would want to help me," said one of the most roundly well-liked and popular people I've ever met.

I told him about my hatred of being seen as a person who needs things from others: If I wasn't totally self-sufficient in all moments, about EVERYTHING, then I was a blight on the happiness and good opinion of whatever person might witness that. If EVERYONE wasn't 100 percent dazzled by my constant, harmonious social and professional capability, then of what use could I be to them, or to anyone? The worst thing in the world was to be a burden, so I didn't want to share any of my problems with others, no matter how small.

The size of a key, I understood, was gargantuan in that sense. We laughed: Did he really think I would say, "No, friend—stand in the rain; you're clearly not the bastion of radness I've thought you were, good job fucking up your whole worth to me by forgetting something you needed in your other pants?" and then dispose of him? Yes, in a way, and I understood perfectly.

We made a pact to get ahold of each other when we needed anything—to let each other come crash if the situation calls for it, to pick each other up before we go out together if we feel nervous, to let the only immutable thing about our friendship be, instead of the immobility of our statue-selves, the commitment to being weirdo, ungraceful people living in front of each other honestly, and to love whatever that looks like. And we do! Shared, our private wreckage transforms into a victorious and sweet point of communion. Seeing Eddie as he is, with all of his context, only

contributes to my affection for him. The exact situation I was afraid of—shunting my NEEDS onto someone; being typified as vulnerable—has been a mitzvah.

A Rookie contributor explained this brand of closeness to me on the phone last week. I was calling about work, but she knew my grandfather had died a few days prior and offered her condolences. We ended up having a remarkable dialogue about grief and how to be there for your people when they're hurting, as I was trying to be for my family, and then caught ourselves opening up. "I hope this is OK," I told her, slightly mortified that our professional conversation had mutated into a painfest of my moaning, "I! Will miss him! So much!"

"Yes!" she said. "I have a hard time with it, but I'm coming to terms with the fact that sharing with others frees them up to do the same. You have to lead by example. It's still tough, though—even now, I feel like, *Did I say too much? Am I too much? Is this a bad idea?*"

It wasn't. In telling me about her own life, she made me feel understood and cared for, although we don't know each other that well, and guess what? We still got our work done, and done perhaps even better and with more understanding, even though we had been QUELLE EMOTIONELLE. That reassurance came when I couldn't have needed it more. I want to do that for the people I like and want to support in any sense, whenever I can.

My colleague is right: A lot of the time, showing people they can trust you means treating them, first, as trustworthy. Part of being kind to other people is accepting kindness from them. Because how hollow might it seem if someone said, "You can confide in me!!" without giving you any real sense of why that could be true? It would be like me introducing myself to someone as a VERY good MLB pinch-hitter and expecting them to just believe it, without seeing me play. Talk about clumsy oversimplifications…but I'm pleased to report that, these days, I truly see my "home team" as the "all-stars" they are because they really know how to "home run" when they "show up at bat!!" (Punch me in the face, right now.)

Vulnerability isn't just about hairy shit like the death of a grandparent or the fear of being eminently friendless. Zealously liking things is scary, if not more so! A phenomenal man I'm seeing, whom we'll call Rad-xotic Fantasir, occasionally points out that, when I'm really into a Sibylle Baier song, or going off on the writer Patricia Highsmith's well-documented love of snails, or stoked on a writing assignment, I froth over like a dishwasher that someone accidentally put bubble bath inside of. Then I catch myself, study the other person for approval, and unconvincingly susurrate, "It's whatever. I don't care. It's not a big deal." When this happens, he laughs: "Yeah! Pretend to think this thing you love isn't cool!"

Rad-xotic Fantasir makes me feel more soundly cared for than many other people do, and it's not because he's the only one who's there for me. I just like the casual way in which he's always showing up at the ol' baseball plate. Once, we were sitting on my couch and I hesitated mid-conversation as I was telling him something that seemed personal to the point of goriness. Familiar with my pride and apprehension, he leaned back and smiled. "It's chill—I'm just going to use it to hurt you later."

Save for the deployment of "chill," that was just about the best thing I'd ever heard. (Look how, as in that sentence as when I was talking about Eddie's statue simile, I had to distance myself from a special and heartfelt thing that meant a lot to me by blandly mocking it. Please know that is symptomatic of what we're talking about here, and that I wish I didn't have to do it, but I'm afraid of you.) First, it demonstrated that Rad-xotic Fantasir saw and understood that I was scared, and then it pointed out the implausibility of seeing those fears expressed—but didn't pressure me to keep going if I didn't feel ready. The joke wasn't on me—he was instead showing me that he got it. I told R.F. what I was thinking about, and he listened, and now we do that all the time. What a great precedent to set for someone.

Being vulnerable, our nation's anti-pastime, will not always be an immediate celebration of the generosity of the human spirit, should you undertake that brave

task, which you should. Not everyone is a Rad-xotic Fantasir. It can backfire, and it can backfire hard. Some people will hurl a violent silence back at you, or, worse, ridicule you about something that was excruciatingly difficult to force out of yourself in the first place. A month ago, I had a friend who saw my self-concealment as a personal affront. This person's constant refrain: "I want you to trust me! You can tell me anything. I just want to be *there* for you." I should have heeded the empirical evidence to the contrary in front of my dunce face: If this person was so into the idea that I would fork over the grand truth of my innermost feelings, why were they only saying what THEY wanted from that, instead of asking me questions about it, or trying to make me *feel* at home enough to spit 'em out? Why was I surprised when, after I finally stammered out a shrapnel of a malignant secret that's been lodged somewhere in my lower intestine for over a decade, their eyes went cool? They said, "Wow. You know, you should really talk to someone." I thought that was exactly what I was doing! I thought I was being mad mature and EMOTIONALLY AWARE and, like, using *I* statements and that! They clarified: I should talk to a *therapist*, and they were saying it to make me feel like I was wrong for feeling as I did. SO GLAD WE HAD THIS TALK, BUD!

I am learning to employ "selective vulnerability," which sounds counterintuitive, but is actually good for self-protection. This means, wield your vulnerable feelings with respect and consideration for the specific person to whom you're speaking. Ask yourself, "What am I looking to accomplish by telling this person this thing? Am I in good hands with them?"

If the first answer goes, "Because I want them to feel sorry for me," or, "Because I want them to do me a favor that I don't feel is fair to ask for, and I think telling a story about How Doggone Bad I've Had It will coax them into giving me this thing out of pity," or, "I want them to make me feel like a good person and validate something I've done wrong," you are in EXCELLENT SHAPE. Just kidding—none of that stuff sounds like the work of a caring friend. It

sounds like untempered manipulation; it's skeevy to "use" feelings for some insidious other endgame. Do not exploit your own vulnerability to take advantage of people, my tender triceratopses. That's part of what gives it such a lousy stigma. If you actually, factually want to be heard by someone else, regardless of what they can then give you, go ahead and spit it out.

When it comes to WHO can handle your whole prodigious truth: You are allowed to be what you're like every single moment, and it's up to others how they deal with that. If you're very courageous, you'll sail forth regardless of their opinion. If, like me, you'd rather start a little slower because you're green as hell at this: Understand that vulnerability can make people uncomfortable if you're expressing it in a maudlin or un-self-aware way or constantly redirecting conversations to yourself and your problems, or if you've simply misjudged your audience. Here's how to tell if someone will be receptive to your confidences: Like Eddie, do you respect and enjoy them without their having had to insist that they are a GOOD AND WORTHY PERSON to you? Would you feel comfortable asking them about their own lives? Better yet, have they offered details of that autobiography to you unbidden? Tell 'em what's on your mind. You don't have to have experiences in common to care about each other. You just have to usher in the possibility of manifold truths, instead of just your own, or just the one you think you see most frequently.

It was dispiriting to finally try and extricate a part of the jagged flotsam in me with a person I thought would handle it with care but instead made it pathological. That encounter handily demonstrates how not to go about courting a person's fledgling attempts to be honest about their feelings. Don't IMMEDIATELY try to help, tell them they're wrong, or otherwise fix or administer to their "problem." Just listen and love them empathetically, and ask questions if it seems like they're faltering in telling you on their own.

I can't allow the miscalculations I made in the past to impede the goodness and closeness that can come from presenting the truth of your heart. As a veteran

posturer, I can tell you that if someone manhandles or maligns that, that's their failing, not yours. You've still done something incredibly kind by demonstrating that someone they know is capable of revealing themselves, even if they're afraid. That will stay with them, as it has with me each time it happens. They'll know it's an alternative option to "LEMME NEVER OPEN MY TRAP ABOUT THINGS THAT MIGHT BE CATHARTIC TO GRANT FREEDOM FROM THEM." Maybe, down the line, they'll remember when you did that and try it themselves.

If you don't feel safe being vulnerable with others, even selectively—if there's no one around to whom you can spill— at least be vulnerable with yourself. Find some way of squaring off with your feelings and employ it whenever you can, even if it's just in thinking through them critically yourself, or writing about them in a diary (but don't leave it on your desk unattended if your classmates are mercenary, shitheel jackals). I would rather be, like, Morrissey Jr. trying not to cry all alone in the cafeteria than a stunted fuckbag who's convinced that outwardly caring about anything is a crime punishable by knuckle sandwiches.

The earlier we at least TRY to buck the hardened, cynical ways of relating that le monde seems so dogged in imposing on us, the better chance we have at dispelling them, and of being thoughtful, self-aware, and UNDERSTANDING people in that same monde. Which, I think, is the preferable way to spend your time on/in it. God, see how wimpy that sounds? My teenage self wants to introduce my face to some toilet water via the gnarliest swirly ever committed! It's true, though, so 2 BAD, even if it means I'm a loser and an off-putting, effete heart animal instead of a cool, physically aggressive ruffian or ruthless multibillionaire/politician making my scrilla/policy on the backs of other people's pain. I'm the sucker getting too worked up over getting chosen last for badminton. I'm an acoustic guitar getting sand kicked in its face by a hot babe at the beach! WANNA READ THIS SONNET I WROTE REAL QUICK? I honestly think that's a more courageous goal, personhood-wise,

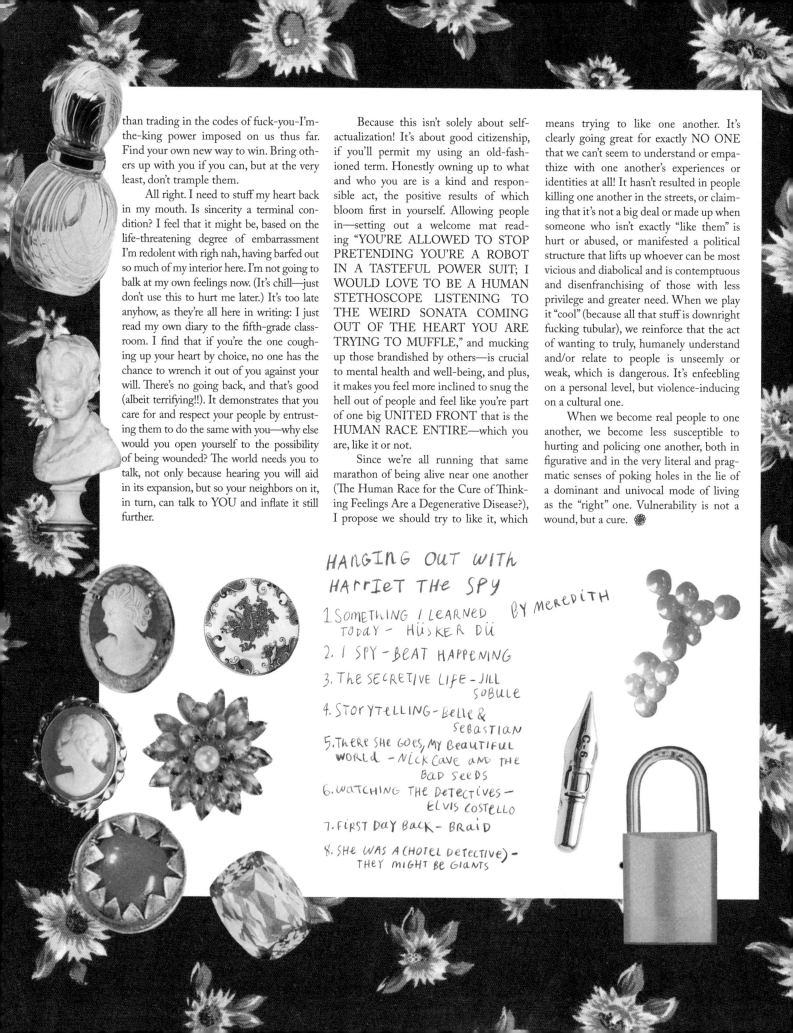

than trading in the codes of fuck-you-I'm-the-king power imposed on us thus far. Find your own new way to win. Bring others up with you if you can, but at the very least, don't trample them.

All right. I need to stuff my heart back in my mouth. Is sincerity a terminal condition? I feel that it might be, based on the life-threatening degree of embarrassment I'm redolent with righ nah, having barfed out so much of my interior here. I'm not going to balk at my own feelings now. (It's chill—just don't use this to hurt me later.) It's too late anyhow, as they're all here in writing: I just read my own diary to the fifth-grade classroom. I find that if you're the one coughing up your heart by choice, no one has the chance to wrench it out of you against your will. There's no going back, and that's good (albeit terrifying!!). It demonstrates that you care for and respect your people by entrusting them to do the same with you—why else would you open yourself to the possibility of being wounded? The world needs you to talk, not only because hearing you will aid in its expansion, but so your neighbors on it, in turn, can talk to YOU and inflate it still further.

Because this isn't solely about self-actualization! It's about good citizenship, if you'll permit my using an old-fashioned term. Honestly owning up to what and who you are is a kind and responsible act, the positive results of which bloom first in yourself. Allowing people in—setting out a welcome mat reading "YOU'RE ALLOWED TO STOP PRETENDING YOU'RE A ROBOT IN A TASTEFUL POWER SUIT; I WOULD LOVE TO BE A HUMAN STETHOSCOPE LISTENING TO THE WEIRD SONATA COMING OUT OF THE HEART YOU ARE TRYING TO MUFFLE," and mucking up those brandished by others—is crucial to mental health and well-being, and plus, it makes you feel more inclined to snug the hell out of people and feel like you're part of one big UNITED FRONT that is the HUMAN RACE ENTIRE—which you are, like it or not.

Since we're all running that same marathon of being alive near one another (The Human Race for the Cure of Thinking Feelings Are a Degenerative Disease?), I propose we should try to like it, which means trying to like one another. It's clearly going great for exactly NO ONE that we can't seem to understand or empathize with one another's experiences or identities at all! It hasn't resulted in people killing one another in the streets, or claiming that it's not a big deal or made up when someone who isn't exactly "like them" is hurt or abused, or manifested a political structure that lifts up whoever can be most vicious and diabolical and is contemptuous and disenfranchising of those with less privilege and greater need. When we play it "cool" (because all that stuff is downright fucking tubular), we reinforce that the act of wanting to truly, humanely understand and/or relate to people is unseemly or weak, which is dangerous. It's enfeebling on a personal level, but violence-inducing on a cultural one.

When we become real people to one another, we become less susceptible to hurting and policing one another, both in figurative and in the very literal and pragmatic senses of poking holes in the lie of a dominant and univocal mode of living as the "right" one. Vulnerability is not a wound, but a cure. ✹

HANGING OUT WITH HARRIET THE SPY

BY MEREDITH

1. SOMETHING I LEARNED TODAY – HÜSKER DÜ
2. I SPY – BEAT HAPPENING
3. THE SECRETIVE LIFE – JILL SOBULE
4. STORYTELLING – BELLE & SEBASTIAN
5. THERE SHE GOES, MY BEAUTIFUL WORLD – NICK CAVE AND THE BAD SEEDS
6. WATCHING THE DETECTIVES – ELVIS COSTELLO
7. FIRST DAY BACK – BRAID
8. SHE WAS A (HOTEL DETECTIVE) – THEY MIGHT BE GIANTS

SUDDEN DEATH

I dealt with mortality at the ripe age of 13.
By Sandy

It was around 10 PM when I got home from gymnastics practice and my dad sat me down at the kitchen table. This was odd: He usually left dinner out for me and was in bed by then, but that night he waited up. He told me he got my blood test results from the doctor. I had tested positive for Wegener's granulomatosis, an uncommon and incurable disorder that causes inflammation in the blood vessels, and that sometimes leads to organ failure. I asked him what that meant. Specifically, I wanted to know if *I was going to die*. I already kind of knew the answer. He said that I might, and that was that: no other questions.

You'd think a 13-year-old would have a goddamn conniption after learning that kind of information, but I didn't feel afraid. What I felt was massive gratitude toward the universe. The disease was a mouthful and would be a bitch to handle—meds, MRIs, a CT scan, and blood tests every two weeks—but I was alive. Before that moment, I was scared of the possibility of dying from an unknown problem. Learning that I had Wegener's granulomatosis, which could ACTUALLY KILL ME, was mostly a relief. Coming face-to-face with death gave me a shock, for sure, but, more than anything, it made me think about my time on earth, and what I wanted to leave behind. But this isn't an inspiring story about a girl who realized her days were numbered, and then set out to do everything she'd ever dreamed. This is about confronting my own mortality, and at a younger age than I'd ever expected. *This Girl Faced Death at 13. You Won't BELIEVE What Happened Next.*

Though ol' Wegener could (and still can) spread to my vital organs, he seemed happy to take up residence mostly in my eye: About a year and a half before the conversation with my dad, my left eyelid, which had been slightly swollen for a couple of weeks, ballooned like a bug's eye the day of my gymnastics team's state championships. Within hours, it had swollen shut and turned a nasty reddish purple. At school, I wore sunglasses to hide the bulging mass on my face, but SOME teachers (whom I will NEVER FORGIVE—Ms. P., you know what you did!) made me take them off. The other kids, including my friends, asked me things like "What's wrong with you?" or, "Why does your eye look like that?" I hated those questions because I had no answers. All I could say was "I don't know." It was mortifying: I was in the seventh grade. I was busy trying NOT to be noticed!

So, after the diagnosis, I wasn't going to jump up on a desk, throw my sunglasses across the room, and yell, "HEY, GUYS! I HAVE WEGENER'S GRANULOMA-TOSIS, AND I'M MAYBE GONNA DIE FROM IT!" I didn't say anything to anyone. I retreated from my friends and became very solitary. No one called me on it, and I don't know why, but maybe it was because I had been drifting away for a while, with nonstop medical problems occupying my time and energy. The way I saw it, and still see it, is that we enter and leave this world alone, and there are times when no one can help you but yourself. My mom and dad were constantly worried, and so was my older brother, but I didn't know the extent of it until later. I didn't reach out to them, and they gave me my space. No one could console me about my possible death—mostly because I didn't need consoling.

I set out to be the best I could be in whatever I was doing. And I wanted to do everything. Gymnastics was my life, but I started acting in school musicals, writing my own plays, and basically trying everything. I was going through the classic crisis of "Who am I?" and, "Who do I want to be?" but I took the time to figure it out. There was no one I was actively trying to impress—I was busy trying to outrun death, my only competitor.

I took a photography class because it was something I'd always wanted to learn, and I quickly became obsessed with it. Documenting my life through photos made me feel present and immortalized. My images took on their own life. I was photographing everything in my world and doing gymnastics four nights a week. I was on Sandy time!

Relationships with other people are necessary and beautiful, but I couldn't relate to other people unless I first knew myself. I was my own companion—no one else knew what I was going through. People at school noticed I would miss weeks at a time, and they all whispered about my hospitalization, but I never confided in any of them. Why should I live with them if I wasn't going to die with them? If my years were limited, I wasn't going to spend them at parties with people I didn't like.

It's been almost 10 years since I found out I have Wegener's granulomatosis, and I don't actively worry about death. I have to go to the doctor more than most people, and I get blood drawn every six weeks. I still have that sense of urgency, or ambition—though others might call it obsession. It might seem unhealthy, the degree to which I obsess over both photography and now comedy. I look at it as finding my voice and vision.

I am a full-time photographer, which I probably wouldn't have accomplished by 22 without my sidekick Wegener and his pal granulomatosis. I don't make friends with people unless I *really* want to. Ultimately, I want to make the most of my life. I'm not going to waste time with formalities. I'm on Sandy time! And I'm lovin' it! No one can tell me what my life is about. I'm gonna do that myself. ✧

Selfie Esteem

Taking your own picture is an act of bravery.
By María Fernanda

Taking a selfie is an act of bravery. You expose yourself to other people's opinions of you, and to take one requires self-confidence, which I think is a beautiful thing. This is a series of photos that celebrate self-love, and it starts with a story.

When I was 15, some kids from my school decided it would be fun to change the lyrics of "Stacy's Mom" by Fountains of Wayne to "Fernanda's mom has got it goin' on." My mom IS super hot, and they just couldn't handle it. I can laugh about it now, but back then I struggled with an unhealthy image of myself, thinking I was fat and ugly and so not like her. I told my mom about the song incident, and how it made me feel, to which she replied, "If you thought you were ugly, you wouldn't be taking pictures of yourself all the time!"

But photography was my *thing*. I argued that I took photos of myself to have more pictures, and to practice what I really loved doing. Sometimes there weren't enough people around to take photos of. "You can take pictures of everything around you," she said, "but you choose yourself because you like what you see."

She was right. Since then I've looked at self-portraits as something really special—a proclamation of one's own freedom and empowerment. I like having a record of my life so far, and I don't see anything wrong with reminding myself that my looks constantly change, and that I'm growing up and getting to experience every moment. Anything that can make you feel better about yourself while not harming others is worth a try. With a selfie, you always end up owning something new that matters to you, and that you can share with anyone you'd like.

I took these selfies over a weekend, and each shows how I felt for a moment. This was the first. I was with Zaid. We'd just gotten new tattoos, and we were talking and having a good time. I decided to take a picture, and that was that.

That night at our house, Zaid and Adrián were cooking (in the kitchen, of course), and I was next to them taking photos with a tripod, which was awkward. Eventually, I closed the kitchen door and went to the next room, and that was better. There's something kinda uncomfortable for me about taking selfies when someone else is watching.

The next morning after I woke up, I wanted to take a simple-looking picture of my new tattoos, but because they are in such different places, I had to strike this dramatic pose. So here they are—my new tattoos.

I was working later that day, and the light was really pretty. I felt like I was in a movie. It was nice.

This one was an accident. I was actually trying to find the right position, but then the camera did her thing and it was OK. Sometimes (all the time) I don't like my hair, but I like how it looks here.

This one is really weird. When I look at it, it doesn't look like me. After I took it, I went to the mirror for a very long time. I'm not sure how I feel about this picture. It's like I'm someone else.

Sunset is my favorite part of the day. I went to the roof, and there it was. Sunsets always make me feel good. We are moving, you know; we are moving all the time.

I stayed on the roof for a while. The moon was there already, looking good and bright. I felt the same way.

The city lights were pretty, and I started to think about stuff. I'd read too much news that day, and I'd had a fight with someone. When I went downstairs, I suddenly felt sad.

The next day was better. I'm glad I have a job, but working from 4 AM to 6 PM is NOT FUN. I was tired, and I look tired—I am tired—but I'm fine. I feel good. ✿

JANUARY 2015:
dedication

Dear Rookies,
We embark on 2015 with the theme DEDICATION.
To yer passionz, to your loved ones, but mostly to your
beliefs—and what happens when youthful idealism
is met with the horrible realities of the world you're
inheriting. Jamia talks about making yourself heard,
Tova feels out the moment when your beliefs clash
with your family's, Julianne interviewed TLC about
their years devoted to making music as a sisterhood,
and everything else here is TOPS, too, duh.
  Happy 2015!

love,
Tavi

Design by Tavi. Title lettering by Lisa Maione.
Illustrations by Meredith Wilson.

Elephants Can Forget

Being "thick-skinned" doesn't mean bottling things up.
By Jamia. Illustration by Caitlin H.

Books and cartoons about Babar the Elephant captivated me when I was a kid. In a practical sense, I had little in common with Babar, a fictional, tennis-playing pachyderm, but I wanted to be like an elephant, so I felt a kinship with him anyway. In my family, elephants were metaphors for being thick-skinned, thoughtful, and intelligent, like Babar, who was also regal, well traveled, and educated—the personification of dignity. He came to stand for many of the things I wanted to cultivate in myself. (At the time, I didn't know enough history to understand the neocolonialist critiques of the storybook and the underlying themes about so-called civilization. What I took from his story was that he was independent, brave, and perpetually optimistic.)

Being elephantine came with trickier qualities, too: My family often teased me about my elephant-like steel trap of a memory. This cognitive superpower was celebrated when it came to academics or trivia nights, but also reviled when I harped on with exhaustive explanations and rebuttals about past conversations and events I remembered long after my parents or teachers forgot them. This inability to forget became a challenge when an ex cheated on me with a close friend, a co-worker tried to make me the scapegoat when he violated policy at our work, and a boss unleashed a tirade on me for being "too nice" to interns and junior staff. Each of these instances was hard to let go of as I tried to make sense of how to navigate my relationships and boundaries. The same mind that made late-night cramming for tests easy also made it difficult to erase even the most intricate and detailed components of painful memories. My elephant memory has been most well defined by what a fortune-teller in New Orleans's French Quarter said three years ago, upon laying eyes on me. "Gal, you are so sweet and kind, but what most don't know is that, for you, it's never easy to forgive. Why? 'Cause you don't forget a thing." No matter how hard I've tried to compartmentalize—to shrug off hurts and microaggressions—my mind keeps my shoulders tight with righteous anger, and the only way to shake it is to talk about it, which has been very hard for me in the past.

The basic human act of accepting your feelings may seem normal to many people, but I grew up in a family of scientists who challenged me to prioritize facts, which made me feel alienated when I tried to process hard emotions out loud. I was discouraged from "wasting time" speaking about sadness or other feelings that could not be "solved" and taught to support my views and needs with logic. I feared being perceived as hysterical or weak, so I questioned my ability to be both emotive AND strong—and the inherent value therein. Throughout my teenage years, I was relentlessly teased for being "too sensitive" by some of my extended family members after I called them out for unsolicited and often rude comments about my weight, hair, skin, accent, or relationships. My dad sometimes described me as "fragile" when I complained about these comments. He thought I should "toughen up" and keep it moving—that their remarks were a part of our culture, and that there was no changing that, so why make a big deal out of it?

His mindset was that I was wasting time by reacting to other people's actions: I was told that I could only be responsible for what was within my control, so the blame should only be on me for responding with anger and sadness. It was as if being treated with disrespect and dismissal as a result of cultural problems didn't make it personally hurtful, which wasn't, and isn't, true for me. Being racially profiled in boarding school by some of my elite classmates' parents who talked down to me during Parents' Weekend because they assumed I was on scholarship; being told by my white, male English teacher to stop writing so much about feminism and race because it is "expected" from a black girl—shards of the pain I felt when they happened still remain in my elephant brain, and sometimes they dig into it sharply.

My mom lent a more sympathetic ear when I expressed individual pain over injustice, but she was also a stickler about the need to be tough—and I understood why. Both of my parents love me fiercely, but the hardships they grew up with drove their protective responses to my self-expression. Like a lot of elders from historically marginalized groups, they encouraged me to work harder to accomplish twice as much as people with privilege. They grew up during a time when exposing your fear or feelings could literally cost you your life, and their number-one priority was to arm me with tools for simple survival. In the Jim Crow South, Mom endured violence at the hands of racist aggressors during lunch-counter sit-ins to end segregation. I grew up hearing stories about her and fellow student organizers learning how to remain still while being attacked by white police officers and hecklers who targeted women to provoke the men sitting in with them to fight back and compromise their nonviolent protest.

Mom didn't know how crying or talking about someone mistreating you could really help anything because of experiences like those. While she always encouraged me to express myself and acknowledged that she understood my need for release, she discouraged me from crying because she thought it had no productive result. For her, tears were reserved for funerals (if they were even shed then) and private spaces. During breakups, work drama, or my receipt of rejection letters from colleges, she asked me to ask my therapist how to make myself "less sensitive."

At least my parents' feedback came from love, unlike what I faced from co-workers and bosses. After I entered the workforce, I sometimes found myself facing similar naysaying and undermining about my "sensitivity" regarding workplace bullying, racism, online harassment, and the culture of complacency in the face of adversity. After occasionally silencing myself due to external pressures, I learned to continue to speak up anyway: When I worked at a campus computer lab when I was 17, our older, white boss told me and another black staffer that we would be "up a tree" if we didn't meet his expectations on a project. I called a meeting with him about his use of harmful language, which he said was making a big deal out of a phrase that he would use with any staffer. Instead of backing down, I outlined the historic implications of his words, and my concern that he had alluded only to staff of color. After I spelled this out for him, he kept his distance and was much more thoughtful about his language. I trusted my own outrage, and I won.

When I was faced with situations like telling a different boss that I wouldn't accept being spoken to with a hostile tone, or even standing up for myself and my friends by reporting a racist restaurant manager who made disparaging comments about Muslims to her company president, the feeling of owning my power and being true to myself was rewarding even in the face of potential retaliation. It turns out that the cost of my soul doesn't have a price tag—even if someone thinks I'm too sensitive.

Throughout my life, I've *never* been motivated by feedback that advises me to move forward without acknowledging disfavor and reflecting on it. The difference today is that I'm feeling unapologetic about rejecting resilience as defined by others. The biggest hurdle for me to overcome has been to fully embrace and accept the way I personally practice resilience without needing validation from the people I love the most, or view as authority figures. When I apologized to my therapist recently for belaboring a point about something that was bothering me, she stopped me and told me to stop apologizing for having human emotions and a healthy response toward releasing them. When she said that my biggest lesson was to believe her when she said I'm one of her most "balanced and thoughtful" patients, and to recognize that people who call me oversensitive have their own issues, something clicked. Now, I'm focused on treating my dedication to my personal truth like a superpower I can use to create wonderful things.

I wonder what it would look like if we moved away from defining resilience and dedication as endurance through suffering by any means necessary. Last year, Hillary Clinton spoke at New York University about the need for young women to "grow skin like a rhinoceros" to ascend into leadership roles. At the same time, I was advised by my former executive coach to adopt a "Teflon" skin, and, in both instances, I thought about my former idol, Babar. Babar may have a so-called thick skin, but it's natural to him—not a buffer against the rest of the world he created intentionally.

Sacrificing my mental health to make others feel more comfortable has never been worth the modicum of respect we get for "keeping calm and carrying on." When we focus on perpetuating a narrative that places less emphasis on systems, culture, and toxic people to change, we imply that we must change. Righteous anger and the desire to process our feelings are as honorable as brushing something off, as long as they bring you back to yourself. The challenge is that we have a limiting (and sexist) definition of what it means to be strong and powerful. Truthfully, I have never seen anything as simple as a stiff upper lip fix such a complex, widespread problem, and neither will channeling all of my energy into changing the composition of many of the things I love about myself to suit others. So, I've decided that I've aspired to thicken my skin for too long. I've embraced that I am not a pachyderm. I'm a *person*. I am tender, I am soft, I am gentle, I have feelings—and that actually makes me strong. ♥

Both Sides

My family's beliefs are the unbridgeable distance between us.
By Tova

1. How to live with people who have political perspectives and religious beliefs that make you feel distant and helpless, that distort the space between your body and theirs: Hold your breath at the dinner table and concentrate on the lyrics to your favorite song until the noise around you dissolves. Push your teeth under your fingernail and chew off the edge, chew until the anger churning through you stops warming your cheeks and filling your eyes, blurring everything you are told and everything you believe in. Spend every night somewhere else: at friends' houses, at boyfriends' houses, wandering the neighborhood until your house is asleep. Find your baby pictures and study the faces: your face, your mother's face, her hands wrapped around your tiny body. Notice the resemblances: My mother and I have the same hair. The differences: She covers hers with a wig. When you finally find yourself alone in a bed, swaddle your body in blankets until you've built a home in your house and try to fall asleep.

2. How to love the people who have political perspectives and religious beliefs that make you feel distant and helpless, that distort the space between your body and theirs: When they speak to you, about you, don't argue. Let the anger web between your fingers and your toes, and when you finally get away, remind yourself that webbed fingers and toes do not affect your ability to walk, run, or swim. It's only something you notice every time you examine your body, every time you examine the ways your anger

has settled—the crooks it has found to inhabit. When you feel your identity slipping away, when you finally argue, try not to be afraid of the new distance your words create between the space your body stands in and the spaces inhabited by those you love. When you can spread your fingers wide apart and see how the face of your father looks like the face of a stranger, gently ask how much you weighed when you were born. Remind him of the things you can agree on: that he carried you out of the hospital and you weighed eight pounds and four ounces, much heavier than your older brother. Try not to sound desperate. Evade all conclusions. Try not to make lists.

3. I told a friend I was writing a piece on staying dedicated to your beliefs while staying dedicated to the people you love, and whose beliefs you disagree with almost entirely. I was going home for winter break and my parents asked me to respect the household, wear skirts, keep Shabbat, and be an example for my siblings. I grew up Chassidic, and when I left, I left most of it behind: the laws, the customs, and friends. I left it all, except for my family. And they know how I live my life—or, at least, that I live my life differently from theirs. They know that I don't pray in the mornings or keep kosher or keep away from boys. But when I'm home, when I exist in the context of their home, they want me to wear skirts, keep Shabbat, watch my language, hold back any critical perspectives, and bite my tongue until it bleeds.

   My friend wanted to know why my family's views mattered so much. She wanted to know what wearing a skirt or wearing pants had to do with my beliefs, with theirs. I didn't know how to explain the ways religious views make the air thick, or make people lie behind rituals. How the skirt I put on over my pants is the skirt that keeps me in the kitchen, the skirt that made it harder for me to go to college. "It's easy," she said. "Just wear the skirt for a week and then it's over. Put up with a few upsetting comments for one week. And then you can go back to where

you live, go back to your life." I didn't know how to respond. Most of the time, I don't know what to think.

4. The first thing my mother says to me when I arrive home is "Put on a skirt." I tell her I don't have any. Not exactly true. I just don't want to wear a skirt, which is as good as not having any. She stares at me, and I look away. We both stand there, wary of acknowledging the things we want each other to be, thickening the air between us. The moment is a moment that is happening this week, right now, but it could have been happening last year or the year before that or every morning most of our lives.

5. I thought I was balancing it: the two worlds I lived in. My family, the house choked with people I love. The family I created outside my house, the friends that felt like family, the boyfriend I could see forever with. My parents weren't asking me to fake. They were asking me to respect. We loved one another, so we made it work. And then they found out about the boy I was dating, that he wasn't Jewish. We stood on opposing sides of the kitchen counter and I suddenly realized that I was looking at the rest of my life. That compromising wasn't an option anymore. My pants, my major in college, my radical politics, they could work around. But a non-Jewish boyfriend would end everything—there would be a cutting off. They would still love me, I know that. But I am not hopeful that they would ever meet him, invite him over, ask about him, or acknowledge him. There are choices I don't want to ever have to make. We haven't spoken about him since.

6. Tips for breathing steadily when you realize you hate the political perspectives and religious beliefs of the people you love: *Remind* yourself to breathe. It is easy to forget the obvious things, things that are remarkably regular, even during sleep. Take long walks to ease the pain that throbs in your lower legs, the strain that spreads through your body when

you try to straddle both worlds. Remember the time your father told you he was proud of you, and you smiled at the other end of the phone. Ball up all the love you feel and insist that it stay complicated because you can't imagine your life without the people who raised you. Remember that there are no real tips. Writing *you* instead of *I* is an old trick that makes it easier to feel.

7. I spent more time talking about the piece than I spent writing it. Something to do with the fact that I was home, and the immediacy of it, prevented me from saying anything about it. Something to do with the warmth that coursed through my body when my family clustered around the Shabbos table, how much I loved us all together, talking about farts like we always used to. I told my sister about the piece and she said it sounded like I don't love being with the family. "That's why I'm writing in the first place," I tried to explain, "because I *do* love you."

8. How to avoid your chest collapsing during arguments with your parents: Ignore the invalidation. My father asks how it could possibly be difficult, growing up as a woman in our traditional community. At first, it feels as though there is no right response. Insist on your experience. Insist on your feelings, on their weight. Spread out your palms like surrender, because they have palms, too, and we meet by clasping palms. The softest and most vulnerable parts of our hands, which are the first to gather sweat. Once, a friend asked me about my parents. "What are your parents like?" *Not like yours*, I thought. Not like yours, but that doesn't mean they're wrong. "I love my parents," I told her, "but I can't ask anyone else to." Everybody's parents are different, and mine were with me the first time I left home. They came with me to my new city, and told me I would do well. They helped me move my couch to my second-floor apartment, and hung mezuzahs on every threshold: thin silver scrolls on my doorposts, watching over me, making sure I am safe. ☺

ADDICTIVE PERSONALITIES

Thinking about drinking.
By Lucy

My mom puts the car in park and yanks out the key. It's June in New York; I'm nine years old. My butt is sticking to the seat and I'm dreaming of being somewhere else, preferably a pool. Mom gets the bundle of flowers from the backseat. The peonies, big and puffy, are my favorite because they remind me of pink clouds or marshmallow pillows. We're on a trip she makes once a month.

We place the flowers at each gravestone, and she tells me about each person we visit: her grandmother, friends of her parents, childhood friends. I can't remember how many family deaths she attributes to cirrhosis, or liver failure—at least 10. We stop by the graves of a cousin of hers, or two, or three. They died of overdoses. I don't show it, but I am shaken.

I'm 11. We visit my mom's family often, but I've only met my dad's mom, Grammy, and her wife. I know that Grammy left my dad's dad many years ago, but I've never met my grandpa, or my dad's brother, who isn't in contact with my dad. I never wondered why until today, so I ask my mom about it as we drive home. "He doesn't really talk to his dad or his brother anymore," she says. "His brother likes alcohol a lot—more than he likes his family. Sometimes people try it, and they like it so much, they don't care about anything else." I fall silent, tense, and listen to the air conditioner as I watch the glowing yellow lines on the road.

I am 14, and my mom tells me she used to be an alcoholic. She describes the euphoria she felt when she first tried it and recites the values she learned at Alcoholics Anonymous, the organization she joined to recover. She tells me how she used it as self-medication, how she can't remember so much of what she did when she was young, and how sad that makes her. I learn that we have what she calls "the gene," or the tendency for alcoholism, the craving for alcohol. Because we share DNA, I probably have it, too. I am petrified! I instantly remember a time when she was

drinking nonalcoholic beer, and I tasted it. She was angry and scared for me, thinking that even a taste of the fake stuff would trigger the desire for more. She told me that alcohol almost completely destroyed her. That, when I *do* taste it, *I* might love it, and that might lead to the destruction of all my dreams, too.

By the time I even think to try a drink, I'm terrified, but I still want to just *glimpse* what it does to my body, so I take a sip at a party. I am surprised to find out it's actually kind of gross. It's really confusing to 16-year-old me: I laugh along with people's jokes more and am generally more social than usual. It was an OK feeling—nothing too out of the ordinary. At the same time, all I can think is *DON'T I HAVE THE GENE?????* Yet I get that giggly and lighthearted with my friends *minus* booze. That means I can't *possibly* be a someday alcoholic. Right?

I still don't have an answer. My mom told me the first time she tried alcohol, she didn't like how bitter it was at all. Instead, she enjoyed the feeling of it: the relaxation and eventual loss of control. She was less anxious about interacting socially. She thought that, if it could do that, it didn't matter what it tasted like. She took it to feel better, like medicine.

My mom had depression throughout her life, same as me, but when she was growing up, nobody talked about that stuff. Relief for her was sold in a bottle. She stopped drinking when she started treating her depression. We are now on the same depression medication, but I started two months ago; she didn't start till she was 38. She had my sister a few years prior to that, which made her realize that getting better wasn't a choice but a necessity to keep her loved ones safe. She started going to AA meetings regularly, and gradually stopped drinking altogether.

One thing should be made clear: Alcohol will not *ruin* you, but alcoholism complicates your life and causes you (and

others) harm. Some people can drink to have fun and de-stress and will never feel indebted to it in any way. The evil of the situation is the way a person can be so taken advantage of by its effects and trade everything they are passionate about in its favor. Anyone can contend with addiction: You aren't safe and sound just because your whole family can stand a few drinks. I'm cautious because I don't really know how it affects me yet. If you have alcoholism in your family but still feel comfortable with alcohol, that's fine. If you feel safer swearing off the stuff, do what works for you. It's a very personal choice.

I trust myself and my maturity regarding substance abuse because of the trauma I've seen it wreak, but I am also aware that I could still abuse that responsibility. So, I feel safer in having smaller amounts and figuring out where I stand than drinking as much as I can to decide my limits. Whatever your approach to drinking, it's something you should consider for a long time before you pour a drink. (And when you do that, it should be at the legal drinking age in your country. This sounds rich, coming from somebody who had her first drink at 16, but I want you to be safe and on the RIGHT SIDE OF THE LAW.)

Now, I am 17, writing this: I genuinely have no idea what is the secret trigger, the thing that causes someone to give up their whole lives over wanting to be inebriated. It's heartbreaking to know the destruction that can come of it: how lives can be altered or lost. I think of my mom's cousins and aunts in the cemetery, and I wonder what makes us so different or so similar, and how a complex, strong, and thoughtful person like my mom could be completely controlled by a fucking *liquid*. But she's also overcome it, through immense personal strength and discipline. That gives me hope that, regardless of whether I have the gene, I don't have to let it control me. ☼

Life Skills 401

Your syllabus for total mastery of everything.
By Krista

It's 2015, and we've survived yet another lazy twirl on our planet's axis. We've aged exactly 365 days, and we know *so much more* about life than we did last year! Street smarts? We got 'em. School and jobs and relationships? No sweat. We did it! We're here!

But what's that? You think you could learn even more? Ahhh—you're probably right. Good thing we've updated Rookie's annual list of Life Skills to master in the coming months of this brand-new year— let's get to honing these techniques!

1. BREAKING DOWN A DOOR

Let's say you're babysitting a one-year-old by yourself and it's going really well. After lunch, you notice the trash is full. You lift the bag and quickly pop from the kitchen to the big garbage cans in the garage while keeping one eye on the kid, who is still strapped in her eatin' chair. You struggle a bit to get the trash bag into the bin. When you look up, the door leading to the kitchen is swinging shut. You run over, yelling, "NONONONO," but it closes with a gentle *click*. It's too late. The door is locked! It locks automatically. Your phone is inside. So is the baby. Not only do you not know where any spare keys are, but you need to get inside NOW, because you can't leave a baby alone, even for a very short period. Did you check the front and back doors? Are they locked? OK. Are any neighbors really really nearby? No? OK. Deep breaths.

Here we have an it-could-happen-to-anyone situation in which you might need to break down a door. A fire would be another instance—really, any emergency where a door is separating you or another person from getting to safety is a potential breaking-and-entering situation. Screw the expense of the door: You need to get somewhere NOW, so let's do this.

Is the door made of wood, laminate, or particle board? That is GREAT NEWS for door-breakers. If it's metal, that's less good, but you might still be able to open it if you kick hard enough. Now: Does the door swing away from you when it opens, or toward you? **Away from you is good**: You can probably break the door open. **Toward you is bad**: You won't be able to break the door open, and you need to either figure out another way to get into the house, or run until you find someone who can help you call 911.

If the door swings away from you when it opens, stand a few feet away from the door and brace one of your legs behind you. Pretend it's a tree—that's how firmly you need to plant your back heel to the ground.

Locate where the lock is on the door. That's where the door will most likely break. Put all your strength into your kicking leg, and kick NEXT to the lock as hard as you can with your heel. Don't kick the actual lock—you'll hurt yourself. KICK NEXT TO THE LOCK! Go! Kick it hard! Nothing happened? Do it again, but this time, try kicking directly underneath the doorknob. Where is the door's weakest spot? FIND AND KICK THAT SPOT. You want the lock to break, or the door itself to splinter and break.

Under No Circumstances Should You:
• Try to bust the door open with your shoulder (hello, dislocated shoulder and door that still doesn't open).
• Run at the door at top speed, then try to kick it (you've seen too many martial-arts movies—standing still is way more effective).
• Use your elbow to wham the door open (you will break your elbow, not the door).

If you can't kick the door down after, say, five attempts, abandon this idea and move on to Plans B and C: finding another way into the house (are any windows open?) or locating someone else as fast as you can and calling 911 with their phone.

I hope you never have to use this life skill, but now you know what to do just in case! And obvs don't practice this on the door to your room, 'kay?

2. EATING FOR A WEEK ON $10

Let's hope it doesn't happen (maybe it already has), but it's entirely possible that, at some point, you will be broke. *Really* broke, not like "Haha, I have to stop eating out so much, I'm so poor" broke, but "Oh my god, once my landlord cashes my rent check, I'll have $12 left and payday isn't till next Friday" broke. Broke in a waking-up-in-a-cold-sweat broke. I promise, it happens to the best of us.

Don't worry! If you are temporarily so broke that you are literally worrying about having enough to eat, and you don't have any financial help, and that includes someone to borrow $$$ from or access to a credit card (it is OK to use credit cards to feed yourself, my hungry bunnies), there are ways to streeeeeetch $10 into a week's worth of food. Your menu might be a little boring, but it beats the pants off not eating at all.

First: Stop eating out. No dollar menu at McDonald's, no vending machines, no soda pops, *nothing*. You must make all your food at home to make it last a week, so take your $10 to the grocery store. Do

you have a discount grocery store in your town, or a supermarket known to have lower prices than the others? Go there. No Whole Foods, and (sorry) no organic anything, unless you can find organic produce *majorly* on sale. This is about your *survival*, and your survival for a week on $10 does not include apples that cost $1 each. Wherever you go, bring coupons—you can print them out, find them at the front of some stores, and cut them out of weekly newspaper inserts.

Head to the produce section, and follow the sale stickers like a moth fluttering toward the light: Is there a shelf where slightly bruised or weird-shaped produce is hanging out? Slightly damaged produce is where it's *at*. Nothing nutritionally is wrong with it, but it's often discounted by 50 percent or more. This is a great way to add variety to your about-to-be seriously limited diet.

Even at full price, bananas are usually really cheap, like 69 cents a pound, and they're good, nutritious breakfast food. A pound of bananas will freeze nicely if you want to make smoothies, with, say, a quart of milk or soy that you've found a coupon for. Carrots are also usually really cheap, like 60 to 80 cents a pound. Buy the cheapest potatoes you can: Potatoes usually cost between $1 and $3 for a five-pound bag. A boiled potato is full of vitamin C, potassium, and lots of other trace minerals you need to survive—pop a potato in a pot of water and boil it, then drain, mash, and add anything you can get your hands on to make it as tasty as possible: shredded cheese, butter (if you have these things), salt, and pepper…thank you, apple of the earth!

If you're not vegan, get the cheapest carton of eggs you can find. I know we usually want cage-free and free-range, but not today. Today, we want a dozen eggs for around $1.50. Eggs are little shells full of life-giving protein—they're one of the cheapest ways to get enough of it. Fry them in a pan, scramble them, make an omelet with your discount-shelf veggies—eggs are a nutritious meal at any point in your day.

Now: It's all about beans and rice, baby. Buy a two- or three-pound bag of dried red, pinto, or black beans. They usually cost less than a dollar per pound. Then, get several pounds of rice—a three-pound bag of rice at my local discount supermarket is under $2. At home, soak a pound of beans in a big pot of water overnight—you need to rehydrate them before you cook them into tasty, tender morsels. When you're ready to eat the next day, boil a cup of rice in two cups of water on your stove, drain, and add the beans and any delish spices you might have on hand, like pepper, salt, and/or garlic powder. Cook until the rice is fluffy (about 20 minutes), and hey: You have yourself a complete meal, with plenty of your ingredients left to make it several times over and get you through the week, no problem. It'll be boring, but you won't starve.

Other Super-Cheap Lifesavers to Consider:
- Plain oatmeal in bulk, $1–$3 for a pound.
- Day-old bread, $0–$1 for a loaf. Sometimes, stores will just give it to you if you ask nicely!
- A large brick of generic or store-brand cheddar cheese bought on sale, $2–$2.50.
- Ramen. Although this is a super-salty choice, it *is* really cheap—like 10-cents-a-serving cheap.
- Pasta, $1–$1.50. A one-pound box or package of pasta lasts for several meals, and a package of spaghetti lasts daaaays if you stick to the serving suggestion on the package. That's four to eight servings!
- Two or three cheap cans of tuna, $1 or less each.
- Generic peanut butter bought on sale, $2 or so for an eight-ounce jar.
- Chicken or vegetable bouillon cubes. Use them to make broth, and add your discount-shelf veggies to make soup.

Finally, get creative! Hang out at a less-poor friend's house and, with their blessing, eat all their snacks. Scrounge for free food: Is anyone giving out samples? Is the grocery store offering cubes of cheese on a tray? Take a handful. Is there a bakery near you that gets rid of day-old bread or bagels for almost nothing? Is there a classroom or meeting room near you where they're all having sandwiches or pizza brought in?

There will probably be leftovers! GET THEM. You can do this! You can make it through a super-lean week, and you'll come through with the confidence that you can take care of yourself in a financial emergency.

3. REMOVING SALT STAINS ON BOOTS

Isn't the winter in cold climates beautiful? The fluffy flakes tumbling past your window, the sparkle of ice on the tree branches in the morning…and the inevitable, annual Ruining-of-Your-Shoes Festival, when road salt leaves big white crusty splotches on every pair of leather and fake-leather shoes you own. If you live in the cold, you know: There's nothing you can really do. The salt stains don't come off, and you are stuck with wrecked boots and booties and heels forever.

Or *are* you?

Guess what? I KNOW AN EASY TRICK TO REMOVE IMPOSSIBLE-TO-REMOVE SALT STAINS AND HOLY COW IT'S SO EASY. This works for all types of leather and fake-leather shoes, including suede and pleather, even sneakers.

All You Need:
- One cup of cold water
- One tablespoon (plus a dash more) of regular white vinegar
- A rag or old towel

How to Do It:
1. Pour the water and vinegar in a bowl and stir the mixture with a spoon.
2. Dip the rag into the mixture.
3. Gently rub or buff the salt stains on your shoes until they vanish.
4. Let your shoes air-dry.

Voilà! Perfectly salt-free boots in the dead of winter! Spread the good word and become a hero to your neighbors: I work in a Chicago office with hundreds of people between the ages of 21 and 35, and judging from the sad, salt-encrusted boots on 98 percent of my co-workers, NOBODY KNOWS ABOUT THIS.

4. SILENCING YOUR SNEAKS

Sometimes you need to get out of, or back into, a room in your house, and you need to do that silently. Let's not dwell on why. I'm here to help you, no questions asked. I can't really help you in the moment, so you need to *prepare* to creep around. Let's start with the basics.

A creaky door can be a dead giveaway, so let's fix it! Get a tiny can of WD-40, shake it up, and spray the hinges of the door until they're coated. Wipe away the excess with a paper towel. Spray inside the keyhole on the lock, if the door has one—your key will slide in effortlessly and quietly when you need to go in or out. If you're sneaking in/out and dealing with a screen door that slams, remember that, and eaaaaase it shut.

Got squeaky hardwood floors? Wood floors creak because they've shrunk or expanded on the house's or apartment's foundation, or because they're loose. For no-squeak creeping, walk as close as possible to the edge of the floor, where it meets the walls, even if that means taking the long way around a room. The floorboards are better supported by the house's frame in these places, so they don't squeak. If you've got squeaky stairs, either memorize where the stairs creak and avoid those steps, or walk with your feet on the sides of the stairs, where the stairs are most supported.

Mid-creep, if for some reason you MUST speak to a friend (e.g., to warn them about the squeaky third step), remember what I learned in Girl Scouts: When you whisper, the hissy "S" sound carries the most and is most easily heard, so whisper with a lisp and the sound won't carry. Or, should I say, "Whithper with a lithp"?

All told, here are the three tenets of silent creeping: Plan for it, don't do it too often, and be careful, my babes.

5. CARRYING SOMETHING WITHOUT SPILLING IT

I hope you're sitting down, because I'm about to give you a tiny tip that has actually *changed my damn life*. Yes. It's been that dramatic.

I spill all the things. If you hand me something heavy or sloshy or delicate, I *will* drop it or slosh it. In the past, the rule of thumb for me was simply *Don't hand me something like that, unless you want to see it all over the floor*. A few years ago, I encountered a barista in Seattle who did not know this about me and handed me a giant latte filled all the way to the brim of a heavy ceramic cup, on a matching saucer. She watched as I carefully fixed my eyes to the mug's foamy rim and took my oh-so-careful little steps to the table where I was sitting across the room…and then as the latte sloshed merrily out of the sides of the cup and onto the floor, like a vanilla-scented mini tidal wave of despair. I was so embarrassed—I'd been watching it carefully and going slowly! AUGH, WHY WAS I SO CLUMSY???

The barista laughed, came over with a rag, and helped me mop up. "I'm so sorry," I bleated. "I'll make you another," she said, and walked back behind the counter. "There's actually a trick to not spilling stuff," she said, as she pulled the handle of the espresso machine. "All you do is walk slowly and DON'T LOOK AT THE THING YOU MIGHT SPILL. Look at the place where you want to go instead."

I laughed. Clearly, she had no idea who she was dealing with. She finished making my drink, filled it to the top of the cup on purpose, handed it to me, and said, "OK, try it. Go slow. Look at your target—where you want to set the coffee *down*. DON'T LOOK AT THE COFFEE. Go. Show me."

Like a toddler full of hope, except also clutching a giant cup of caffeine, I fixed my eyes on my table and took slow steps forward. Although it felt so wrong, and I could feel my coffee swaying dangerously…I made it to that table without spilling my drink! This technique works for everything—birthday cakes; pots full of spaghetti water; big heavy crates full of crap! Fix your eyes on where you want to go and don't look at what you're holding, and you'll make it there without incident! This girl changed my whole life in 30 seconds! WHAT THE ACTUAL HELL.

6. NEVER CARRYING A PURSE

I have always hated carrying a purse because I lose it—I set it down somewhere and never pick it up again. Also, I can never find a way to wear one that doesn't (a) fall off my shoulder, (b) separate my boobs weirdly, (c) mess with my outfit, and (d) make me feel so gendered. Don't men have stuff? Like house keys and phones and wallets and lip balm? Why don't more men carry purses?

I'll tell you why: Men, of course, have stuff they need to carry around, but men are also swimming in big, roomy, utilitarian *pockets*. Most pants cut for men have front *and* back pockets, and sometimes their shirts do, too. Men's jackets have pockets on the outside, and often a secret pocket on the inside. On clothing cut for women, pockets are harder to come by, and WAY smaller. Purses exist because clothing cut for female bodies has no storage space. And then purse-carrying women sometimes get shit from non-purse-carrying men for having to carry stuff around with us! CAN WE LIVE?

WHY YES, WE CAN. If you don't want to be bothered with a bag, or are looking to cut down on things you need to carry with you on a night out, YOU HAVE OPTIONS, my love.

Wear tall boots and tuck everything you own into them.

This is my go-to move. Chances are, if I'm wearing tall boots, the sides of them are *stuffed* with my stuff. Inside my boots on an average night out, you'll find: a thin wallet containing my house keys (two keys detached from my main key ring and tucked into the wallet slits), my bus pass, my ID, $20, and a debit card. You'll also find a comb, a skinny tube of lip stain, and sometimes even my phone, depending on how roomy the boots are at the calf.

I find that tall boots that have some sort of "give" to them work best—if the boots are tight and stiff around your calf, this won't work. You need boots with a little wiggle room, so nothing works its way out of the top of the boot. I know this sounds bizarre, but it's not uncomfortable at all—excepting the phone, you barely

notice it! And nothing slips out. I like the feeling of knowing exactly where my ID and debit card are at all times when I'm out. They're touching my leg! I'm freeeeee of straps, bags, and big wallets! Let's go dancing, I have nothing in my hands, and nothing to lose!

Wear your house keys around your neck on a chain.
Or as earrings. Or, you know, dangling from your belly button ring. Whatevs.

Put stuff in your bra.
If you're wearing a bra, you can tuck your money and ID in there, and you're good to go for the night.

Get a cool utility belt or fanny pack and clip it around your hips.
Look, Ma, no hands!

Wear your wallet on your arms.
Love wrist wallets. There are endless non-purse options for stashing your stuff.

7. PEEING STANDING UP

You're at an outdoor concert and you *have* to pee. You can't hold it; you will piss yourself in a few seconds. You make it with zero time to spare to the nearest Port-o-Potty, open the door, and discover a literal shitstorm. This Port-o-Potty can't have been cleaned in a month—there is urine, wadded toilet paper, and worse, all over the floor, rim, and walls. Oh my god, the stench is unbearable. There is nowhere to squat, and *there is no toilet paper*.

No worries, because you're about to master a TRUE LIFE SKILL that will save you in that and plenty of other gross situations. A secret: People with vaginas can totally piss standing up without getting pee all over themselves. All you need to practice it is a shower, lots of patience—it's hard to get it down pat, but completely worth it—and a willingness to touch your parts. Here's how:

Step One: Drink a lot of water, and then, when you *really* need to pee, head to the shower.

Two: Get into the shower and put your feet shoulder-distance apart. Reach down to your labia minora—not the big lips of your vulva, but the little lips surrounding your vagina and urethra (pee hole). Spread your labia minora open with your fingers. If you're going to pee in an unbroken stream, you need to keep the opening to your urethra unobstructed.

Three: Push your hips forward and let 'er rip! Pee as hard as you can in the beginning to start the flow and force it forward into an arc. Continue peeing, using your fingers to adjust how you hold your labia minora, and adjust your stance to get it just right.

Four: As you sense you are running out of pee, push down as hard as you can to stop the flow neatly and with force, instead of drizzling a running-out-of-steam trickle.

Five: Clean yaself. Take your shower as usual.

A sprinkling (yes!) of encouragement: You will probably not get this on the first try, but get back up on the ol' pisshorse. Practice does make perfect, especially if your idea of "perfect" is peeing with impunity and impressing the hell out of your friends *forever*. Eventually, you will be able to do this standing up in a gross bathroom stall, into a urinal when you need to use the one-stall men's bathroom, and outdoors into the bushes. You'll be able to pee off a deck! My god! It's so wonderful!

If you can't (or don't want to) get this down pat, there's always a pee funnel. It's a portable little plastic device that cups your vaginal area and lets you pee standing up, no touching yourself required! Peeing freedom for everybody!

All right, cadets, we've covered a lot of ground this year. You'll be breaking down doors to rescue babies, ditching purses, eatin' cheap, peeing anywhere you want, and creeping around like professional spies in no time! Go forth, Rookie graduates, and CONQUER 2015! ★

The Group

We are it, that is all.
By Erica

Styling by Dario Villanueva.
Lighting by Chelsea Von Peacock.
Thanks to Angel, Bethany, Eira,
and Sadeao for modeling.

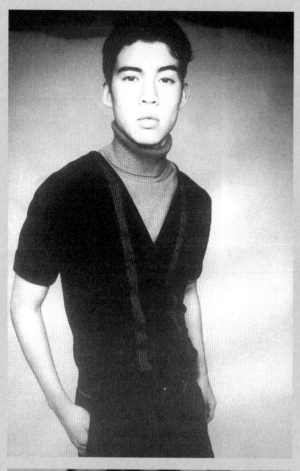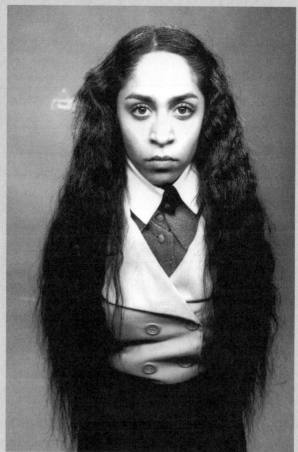
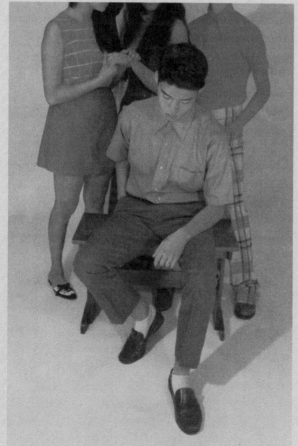

Allied Force

A guide to showing up without getting in the way.
By Jamia. Illustration by Kendra.

Last weekend, I strolled into an Oakland, California, herb shop and saw a sign with a message that stopped me in my tracks: BLACK LIVES MATTER. In only three words, the poster told me that the business owners (who happened to be white) understood the power of using their privilege and their platform, in this case to affirm black people's humanity, and that they could be allies.

Through the Black Lives Matter movement, activists have been calling for an end to police brutality and systemic racism in the United States. The movement formed in response to George Zimmerman's acquittal in Trayvon Martin's 2012 murder, and gained momentum following juries' decisions not to indict the police officers who killed Michael Brown and Eric Garner. As an African-American whose parents lived through segregation and participated in civil disobedience to ensure my access to equal rights under the law, I'm mindful that it's my turn to fight for the right to live without being profiled, targeted, attacked, or discriminated against because of the color of my skin. And while I'm inspired by the profound connection I have with other African-Americans organizing for #BlackLivesMatter, I also know that we can't do it alone. To change politics, culture, and the media, we need white people and other people of color as allies.

I recently asked a close white friend why they hadn't taken a public stand when I'd heard them privately express concerns about police accountability and racism. I said, "I need you to be an ally." The response I got was a sincere question: "I want to, but it seems so big, and I don't know where to start. What do you want me to do?"

After taking a deep breath and explaining that racism is so big, and that it *feels* so big to those of us who have to experience it, I talked them through some guidelines for being an ally. These suggestions apply to almost any situation in which you want to support a cause that does not directly affect you or your identity, and I learned them through my years of being an activist (sometimes, the hard way).

OWN YOUR PRIVILEGE

Before you can be an ally, you have to own and understand your privilege. There are long histories of homophobia, racism, transphobia, colonialism, sizeism, sexism, ableism, Islamophobia, economic injustice, and other injustices in our society. People also receive unearned advantages because of identities that are centered and normalized in the dominant culture: That's privilege. As a woman of color, I experience sexism and racism. I'm also middle class, Christian, cisgender, straight, able-bodied, and an American citizen, all of which come with significant privilege.

A few years ago, a friend tweeted a photo from a shoot she participated in for a plus-size clothing store owned by a young woman of color. I love fashion, so I jumped into the conversation on social media. After complimenting my friend and the store owner on the amazing shoot, I tweeted that I was sad that I couldn't wear any of the clothes, and that I wished they came in my size because they were so beautiful. My friend responded by asking me to think about how many options I have for clothes that curvy women *don't* have because of sizeism and fatphobia. (A lot.) She asked me to think about a time when I'd been in a store and had someone tell me there was nothing in my size. (I couldn't think of one.) She also asked me if I had seen women of my size featured in advertisements. (I have, many times.) With each question, I realized she had a point. I had thin privilege. Plus-size women deserve their own space, and I'm not entitled to it. I was embarrassed, but I understood. I've had the same conversations and frustrations with white friends when they've asked why they can't participate in activities and groups specifically created for people of color. It's another inescapable part of being a good ally—you're going to make mistakes.

BE VULNERABLE

Putting yourself out there as an ally isn't always easy. Being vulnerable is a part of owning your privilege. Expect to be uncomfortable. Be ready and willing to learn, even if it means that you could be called out for not knowing something. If you're called out and it makes you feel upset or humiliated, know you're not the first person to feel that, and you won't be the last. Humans make mistakes. Don't let an error keep you from supporting the causes you care about. Process your feelings with other allies, journal about what you learned and hope to do differently in the future, and make a pledge to yourself to be a better listener and more thoughtful communicator next time. Prepare to apologize when necessary.

LISTEN UP

When a person expresses frustration about oppression that you haven't experienced, it's time to listen. It is unfair to judge the merits of other people's experiences when you haven't walked a lifetime in their shoes. Even if you believe your intentions are good and that you only mean well, derailing conversations or diminishing people's stories does more to advance oppression than dismantle it. One recent example: the ever-present quip in response to #BlackLivesMatter, "But don't all lives matter?" In January 2015, the *New York Times* asked the critical theorist Judith Butler (a white woman) to respond to that very question, and in her response she said, "One reason the chant 'Black lives matter' is so important is that it states the obvious but the obvious has not yet been historically realized." Unlike asking, "But don't all lives matter?" her answer drew attention to the issue at hand without undermining it.

FIND YOUR COMMUNITY

As an ally, you must prioritize the needs of the community you're supporting. If you have to work out your feelings of helplessness, confusion, or shame, and reactions like outrage, fear, or sadness, ask for support from a therapist or other allies—not from the folks who are being marginalized. Working out your guilt or anger on people who are dealing with oppression may hurt more than help.

It may be painful to acknowledge that being born with access to certain social, political, and cultural advantages (like interacting with law enforcement without fearing for your life or the lives of your loved ones) may have sheltered you from certain realities about discrimination, violence, and suffering. Still, focusing on assuaging your own feelings of guilt and shame is less important than working to counter those injustices. Making the world a fairer and safer space for all people is about everyone—and not about you personally.

DON'T TRY TO "SAVE" ANYONE

A quote by the Australian indigenous activist Lilla Watson has been used as a human-rights motto around the world: "If you have come here to help me, you are wasting our time. But if you have come because your liberation is bound up with mine, then let us work together."

Contrary to the messages you'll get from films and books like *The Help*, in which a young white writer exposes racism experienced by black domestic workers, being an ally is not about being a savior—it's about understanding that your freedom is inextricable from the freedom of, or marginalization of, oppressed communities. When I support campaigns for trans or disability rights as an ally, for example, I do it because I know that I'm not free unless we're all free. And instead of assuming I know what's best for communities I'm not a part of, I ask people who are affected by oppression how I can help.

My Christian high school had an archaic policy that required everyone, including non-Christian students, to gather in the chapel each Wednesday to sing Christian hymns. Several Jewish friends approached me, as the co-president of our Black Student Union, to help them negotiate the right to opt out of chapel time if they wanted to. As we strategized about how to change the school's policy, I saw that there was something systemically problematic about the Black Student Union being the only student-run channel through which they could make their demands to the administration. I wanted to help, so I started advocating for them to have their own Jewish students' organization—but my friends' goal wasn't to organize (yet). They had plans for potentially forming their own student group, but they didn't need or necessarily *want* me to drive it. It wasn't my job to jump in front and steer the direction of their organizing. If I had listened and asked what was best for them and the other students involved, I wouldn't have gotten in the way of the people who were actually impacted.

FACE YOUR FEARS

In 1967, during his Massey lectures for the Canadian Broadcasting Corporation, Dr. Martin Luther King Jr. addressed the cost of silence in the face of injustice when he said, "In the end, we will remember not the words of our enemies, but the silence of our friends." Sadly, almost 50 years later, Dr. King's words still resonate. In the weeks since grand juries declined to indict Michael Brown's and Eric Garner's killers, small but mighty gestures of solidarity—like that sign posted in the herb shop—have meant a lot to me when inaction, indifference, and sometimes deafening silence from some of my white friends on social media and beyond have left me wondering, *Whose side are you on?*

If you know, deep down, that you believe in something but are reluctant to speak out about it, ask yourself what you're afraid of and whether it matters more than being true to yourself and your values. Are you afraid of hostility from family members and friends with different beliefs? Or, do you feel like you don't know enough about the facts to take a stand? Weigh those insecurities against the possible consequences of staying silent, then think about what steps you can take to feel supported by like-minded people if you do speak out and face backlash.

SHOW UP

This is an essential part of being a true ally. It means different things, depending on the cause, but if you're offering support in a way that is meaningful and sensitive to the needs of the people affected by the issue at hand, you're showing up. Sometimes that involves volunteering, marching, signing petitions, or making donations. It can also be as spontaneous as listening to a friend process an experience, or calling someone out for making an offensive comment. The key is that you do it when and where you're really needed—and not just when it's convenient for you. One of my favorite recent examples of people showing up for #BlackLivesMatter has been the public protests organized by #Asians4BlackLives. They showed me that other people of color (who are also targeted, though sometimes in different ways) were willing to put themselves on the line to specifically call out anti-black racism.

DO YOUR HOMEWORK

The more informed you are about a movement's history, the more effective you'll be in crafting your messages about why you're involved. It's important to research the history of the causes you're supporting.

Wikipedia's not enough—find out what the movement's key articles and books, speeches, and films have been, and read them, listen to them, and watch them. Then seek out diverse and inclusive media sources to get up to date on current perspectives. I find a lot of the information I'm looking for about different social-justice movements by finding the Twitter feeds of their organizers and supporters.

WATCH YOUR LANGUAGE

Sometimes, damaging and inaccurate messages get reinforced because they are perpetuated in the media or on social media. Use your platform and voice to express and reiterate narratives that help, and don't hurt. Make sure your language is inclusive and inoffensive. Words matter, and it's important that the terms you use aren't harmful. When you witness people using damaging words—like when someone uses transphobic rather than trans-inclusive language—it's often helpful to educate them about the meaning of those words and their history. The idea of "educating" people is tricky, though, and leads to a related point, which is that you should know when to step aside. This may be hard to swallow, but it's crucial advice. I love you, but—this is not about you. I repeat: *It's not about you.* (See also: Don't try to save anyone.)

GIVE CREDIT WHERE CREDIT IS DUE

Cite your sources when you quote people and their contributions to the movement you're participating in, and be sure not to "Columbus" (claiming to discover something that already exists) anyone's work or a movement itself when you talk or write about it publicly. If you're asked to speak on behalf of a movement and there are people who are directly affected who can be in the limelight instead, redirect the query to them so their voices are heard. I often see people tweeting quotes without crediting the people who said them. It may just seem lazy, but it is actually a form of erasure, which cuts out the ideas' originators. This can be especially harmful when it happens to people from marginalized communities, whose histories are often ignored and under-archived. The moral of the story is: Always attribute words or ideas to the person or movement who said them, as much as you can (and if it's online, link to them or tag them, too).

Being an ally might seem intimidating, but it's not. To be powerful allies, we only have to commit ourselves to justice and equality, and open ourselves up to learning (and occasionally making mistakes). It's about uniting with others by being of service and giving the best of ourselves—even if we have to work at it. ⟫

Worst Behavior

On making it through this year.
By Annie

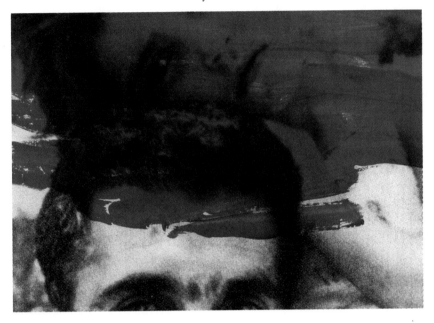

2014.

A year ago, January 2014:

I did a group comics reading that I organized as a debut event for my comic book *Screentests* at Bergen Street Comics in Brooklyn. Someone who worked at Babeland a few doors down gave me a free buttplug—for drawing comics!!! Then I got so excited that I could finally go to a "real Brooklyn queer dance night" that I stayed up later than I knew I could handle. I grew up in New Jersey, and New York still holds an allure for me that I'm embarrassed to admit to. I knew how much a loss of sleep affects my mental health—especially then, when my bipolar disorder still raged full force.

When Sam, April, Sasha, and I got to the club, I realized that as a trans woman, I was as much of a non-entity at this place as at nearly any "radical queer" space. Except for the wonderful Reina Gossett, who co-hosted, I was practically the only one in the room. Trans boys swarmed the club.

These were the same kind of trans boys who I dated back when I identified as a cis fag, and now they looked right through me.

Selfie, drawn in 2012.

I got home to my friend Bev's apartment in Kensington and her perfect cat, Girlcat. I woke up, took the F train to Chinatown, got on the Chinatown bus to Philly, and took the 34 trolley to my house.

I stood on a step stool in the kitchen and grabbed a gin bottle. Its glass neck felt cool. My throat tightened up. I looked around. I knew no one in the house, a punk house, cared if I drank, but I got the feeling that this swig looked sad. I told myself that I was getting away with something by drinking to destroy myself when I knew that this was the worst possible time and way to drink.

I pushed out the memory of being six, 10, 13, and going into the garage to throw out a Diet Vanilla Coke can (I know) onto piles of empty beer and wine bottles that filled two huge recycling bins.

WORST BEHAVIOR
MOTHERFUCKERS NEVER LOVED US

DRAKE   "WORST BEHAVIOR"

2012.

My world ended. That year, I broke up with my boyfriend, went into therapy, recovered memories of being sexually assaulted as a little kid, and started identifying as trans.

Between starting to contextualize the abuse and starting to contextualize my gender, I have trouble parsing out what happened first. I wrote about how they converged in my comic "Body Talk," in *Screentests* (excerpted below).

On New Year's Eve in 2012, John Darnielle of the Mountain Goats tweeted:

⭐ IASMIN OMARATA and 4 others favorited

The Mountain Goats @mountain_goats · 31 Dec 2012
I try to talk to everybody all the time but I have a special word for all my fellow abuse survivors tonight ok

↩   ⤴ 77   ⭐ 159   · · ·

😊 big titty LARPer and 2 others retweeted

The Mountain Goats @mountain_goats · 31 Dec 2012
if you make it to midnight tonight do you understand what that means? TOTAL VICTORY YET AGAIN. AND AGAIN. AND AGAIN.

↩   ⤴ 286   ★ 320   · · ·

🔄 −∞ ← universe → +∞ and 3 others retweeted

The Mountain Goats @mountain_goats · 31 Dec 2012
so here's to us & here's to all of us because I bet this year had its brutal speed bumps for more people than just me but guess what

↩   ⤴ 144   ★ 203   · · ·

🔄 Kaye Blegvad and 3 others retweeted

The Mountain Goats @mountain_goats · 31 Dec 2012
surviving is what we do, and yet again, we did. Thanks to everybody who saw me through this one

↩   ⤴ 192   ★ 250   · · ·

🔄 ShitMuscles2000 and 1 other retweeted

The Mountain Goats @mountain_goats · 31 Dec 2012
And understand this, too: even if you feel like you're barely scraping by, your survival is meaningful to others. To me, for example.

↩   ⤴ 403   ★ 533   · · ·

This echoed the Mountain Goats' song "This Year," in which Darnielle sings verses about being 17, when his stepfather beat him and he tore himself down with booze. Then he gets to the chorus, where he yells that he's gonna get through the year:

IF IT KILLS ME

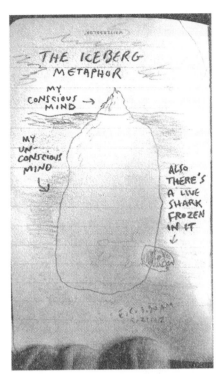

*Drawn at 3:30 AM in May 2012.
I was right!*

2013.

On January 5, 2013, two years and one day ago as I write this, I sent out the email that had been sitting in my drafts folder since Thanksgiving. My therapist had looked over it, and I'd talked about it with friends.

It told my parents that I would have no further contact with either of them because of what had happened to me as a kid. I'd stay in touch with my little sister, the only member of my family I could trust, and she'd inform them that I was alive, basically. I told them that they should give me money, because I suffered from extreme mental disabilities, and because once I started transitioning, I knew it was going to get very difficult for me to find work, even when I would be able to work.

My father emailed me back and, in a line that sounds so corny it now pains me to type it, said that I knew that if my "accusations" were true, it would destroy both his and my mom's lives.

Left to the wolves, but for my silver spoon.

The money kept me under a roof, and for that privilege, I am very grateful.

I thought a lot about God that day, and that January. I remembered how, when I was five years old, I sat in the crying room at the church and thought, "A man can't walk on water."

Everyone in the congregation repeated phrases in unison, robotically, and it scared me.

My suspicion lay way under my skin. My experiences with my parents taught me that the ground could crumble underneath me. Any fucked-up thing could happen at any time. I was dirty. I was stupid. I didn't matter. I was a toy.

When I got my Communion at age 13, I soothed myself by only mouthing the words. I knew I'd get a cheap computer as a Communion gift from my grandpa. I ended up using it to explore porn that confused and scared me but that I felt a compulsion for, for reasons buried deep in my body.

The night of January 5, I walked home toward the sublet I lived in and looked down from the Walnut Street Bridge at the Schuylkill River. I saw an image of my body hitting the surface of the water, made hard by the impact. I turned away from the river and thought of jumping in front of a passing car. I cried and walked straight ahead, my feet hitting the sidewalk and nothing else. I turned from thoughts about hurting others to thoughts about hurting myself. I thought about "This Year." Spoiler alert: I did not kill myself.

2014.

In 2014, by then in that punk house that I still live in, I became obsessed with Drake and the poet Walt Whitman.

I got into Morrissey and the Smiths in high school. Together, Drake, Whitman, and Moz formed a trifecta of creative reactions to hurt and ways of building oneself in opposition to marginalization: Walt and Morrissey against queerphobia and Drake against anti-black racism.

2014 threw me into projects. I made piles of comics, and music with my bands See-Through Girls and Wolf Thistle. I

organized a comics tour and developed more and more confidence in my work. As far as I figured, my name was practically in Elvis lights.

Jane Smiley points out in her book *Thirteen Ways of Looking at the Novel* that what she calls the "literary persona" (that is, the public persona) always has things figured out more than the person who crafts that persona. The "Annie Mok" onstage and on Twitter gets fiery, but for the Annie Mok who burrows in her blankets, goes to therapy, drinks too much coffee, and spends too much money on CDs—that fire can threaten to burn me out.

I need both people, but I believed that I was the person onstage. My inventiveness, my confidence, people sending me nice notes on ask.fm—I learned that these things can't fly me across the rivers of grief that I just have to swim through.

On February 18, 2014, I attended my friend merritt kopas's workshop *Queering Play* at NYU Polytechnic.

I drew a comic about it, "Shadow Manifesto, Part 1" (last page below).

"DIVINE I AM INSIDE AND OUT, AND I MAKE HOLY WHATEVER I TOUCH OR AM TOUCHED FROM;

SLAVE OF GOD

THE SCENT OF THESE ARM PITS IS FINER THAN PRAYER, THE HEAD MORE THAN CHURCHES OR BIBLES OR CREEDS."

FORE HEAD, CHIN, JAWLINE, LITTLE TITS, ALL MINE

FROM "SONG OF MYSELF," WALT WHITMAN, 1855.

The next night, I drew in my diary about all the torn-up ways I got when I started to get close to somebody.

All three parts of "Shadow Manifesto" ended up following the scope of my romantic relationship with merritt, who I was dating at the time. Dating merritt marked the first time I'd really dated another trans woman for more than a couple of dates. I hadn't dated anyone for almost a year at the time, following a fucked-up experience I had in spring 2013.

I FINALLY QUIT LAST SUMMER BECAUSE I SMOKED TO MAKE MYSELF HAVE SEX I DIDN'T WANT.

THE PERSON CHECKED IN WITH ME MULTIPLE TIMES IN A REAL WAY, BUT YOU KNOW WHAT IT FELT LIKE

Besides recent experiences, I'd always had a hard time relating to other women sexually, because of bad, deep, under-the-skin memories getting triggered. "Shadow Manifesto, Part 3" dealt with how the most difficult person to negotiate sexual consent with tended to be me, because I wanted so badly to be immune to the anxiety that came up when I got intimate with someone.

merritt and I dated for only a short time, but it affected me deeply. I told my friend, the artist Sab Meynert, about how freaked out I felt about my feelings, and she said, "Time isn't linear." This jibed with all the ideas I started exploring with "Shadow Manifesto," about art that excited me that dealt with personal modes of perception.

Relating to another trans girl, as a trans girl, helped me feel whole in my body. As Whitman said in a context of closeting and queerphobia, "Divine I am, inside and out."

All the features I listed at the end of "Shadow Manifesto, Part 1" are ones I felt body dysmorphia about. I knew that each could act as a "tell" of my transness in public. I don't need to learn to love my body, but I wanted to at least not actively hate it. I am on some kind of path toward that.

I started going through my Saturn return, a two-year period in a person's astrological chart that shakes up your world and makes you pick up the pieces that work for you, on December 23, 2014.

I ended 2014 as a sober girl, healing in public. I ended 2014 with a question.

(I also ended this year watching a library DVD of the 1942 René Clair comedy *I Married a Witch* starring Veronica Lake. It's on Hulu and it's perfect.)

The question is:

"How do I use my pain to make myself strong but not hardened? How do I soften my heart?

I feel pulled from all directions to look and act in certain ways. Queer scenes, comics scenes, the larger kyriarchal society, my birth family: Each context force-fed me images of how I should be.

Rachel Pollack, a trans woman who's a comics writer, sci-fi novelist, and tarot expert, wrote, "If images have trapped us, then images can free us."

I like seeing artists make new images of themselves, images that integrate multiplicity.

Do I contradict myself? Very well, then, I contradict myself; (I am large, I contain multitudes.)

WALT WHITMAN "SONG OF MYSELF"

164

2·18

SIDNEY LUMET ~~ONCE~~ CALLED MAKING MOVIES—MAKING A QUILT, PANEL BY PANEL.

THINKING OF CROSSING THE WALT WHITMAN, BETWEEN S. PHILLY AND CAMDEN

AND THE WALT WHITMAN PLAZA, A SHORT BIKE RIDE DOWN OREGON AVE. FROM MY FIRST PHILLY HOUSE

MY ROOM W/THE CEILING THAT CRUMBLED THE WEEK I MOVED IN. THE BED WHERE C. WOULD VISIT ME.

From my February–April 2012 daily diary comics project, Bleed-Throughs.

2·19 (WORDS+PANELS)

SOMEONE TRIED TO TAKE ME + BREAK ME ONCE + SO OFTEN I FELT AFRAID I WOULD DO THAT TO SOMEONE ELSE.

PARTICLES FORM A BODY WHICH ONCE CAME TOGETHER IN ANOTHER BODY, BUT I AM NOT HER DAUGHTER.

WHAT DOES 'GOD' LOOK LIKE, SEPARATED FROM IMAGES THAT PRESSED ME

DOWN ON MY CHILDHOOD BED.

On Drake's "All Me," Big Sean runs through all the ways that he can't trust people, and he ends by saying that he's no angel, but:

I am worth it

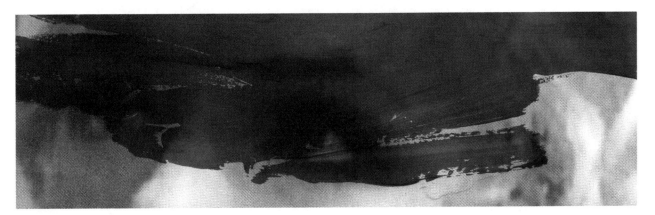

POEM FOR EDGAR

A non-elegy to a beloved uncle.
By Hilton Als. Illustration by Cynthia.

He worked as a short-order cook for most of his life. He rarely slept. He stood five feet eight inches in his stocking feet. Often, he wore black nylon socks. He changed his socks daily, and his white sleeveless T-shirt, but waited until his kitchen whites could be described as something else entirely before changing them. He tried to grow an Afro—it was the times—but his hair only grew out on the sides. He wore green-tinted bifocals and rarely brushed his teeth. He regarded washing as a nuisance, or a waste of time. Time was better spent elsewhere—not on his body, but someone else's: new loves.

He had an unconditionally high regard for women. Those he was attracted to were generally taller than him. He referred to them as *girls*. He never explained why, but wouldn't that make him—perpetually—a boy? He must have amused them.

He had dated my mother when they were teenagers. He'd say: "Marie? The girl of a thousand steps." He never danced. When my mother greeted him, she'd say his name in an exaggerated West Indian accent: "Ed-gare." He enlisted in the army during the Second World War. Then he re-enlisted during the Korean War. When asked why, he said: "I never want to see

here what I saw over there." There were photographs: him wearing fatigues, looking nearsighted in Europe with his buddies; him looking nearsighted in Korea, standing protectively next to women wearing traditional dress.

Sometimes the women were smaller than his sister, Bea, of whom he was particularly protective. She was a hunchback and a dwarf. If you looked at her funny, he shut you down with a look. Once, someone took a photograph of the two of them, the younger brother bent over Bea in an act of benediction. Their mother was critical; self-absorbed; a whiner. He would not hear a word against her. She came to visit her son and his wife every weekend and telephoned him almost daily. He called her "Mama," and no one was allowed to complain about her, because the patience and care he had to exercise to deal with her was greater than any criticism.

After his shifts, he'd drink from six until midnight, or until one or another bar closed. He drank with his wife, who was high-spirited; dramatic; a child of privilege who always wanted to renounce it. He and his wife fought like new lovers their entire time together, over 30 years. To her, he'd say: "You're full of shit and your heart

pumps pee." To her, he'd say: "Oh, blow it out your ass." The invectives they hurled at each other often involved body parts. Later, they'd make love. Their language—harsh, amused—was separate from but equal to their love; their love needed the distance of their language to survive and be; otherwise they would have been too close to it, and maybe they would have smothered it. Their bedroom was a mess. Newspapers, old clothes, crumpled dollar bills, bags of Valium (his wife was a nurse), pocket change. One could also find certain books under his half of the large four-poster bed: Frank Harris's *My Secret Life*, for one. After she died, he'd grow wistful about her, and say: "She was a pretty little brown-skinned girl." She was taller than he was.

When I was on TV once, he said, "Goddamnit!" to the television set. Only he noticed that his nephew was wearing mismatched socks. When I got too sarcastic, he'd say: "Watch your mouth." He asked his nephew where he was going every time he saw him, and his nephew never felt put upon. Care is different from being monitored. Every child knows that.

He loved all sorts of people. Often, his nephew dragged people home to meet him. Later, his nephew realized he was looking to compare the people he brought home to his uncle, his ideal. What he loved about his uncle: his frankness and humor; the thing that attracted him to other boys first, always, was their humor. In looking for connection, he connected to boys who could make him laugh, and who also had what his uncle had because of his sister: a sweet tolerance of difference and horror of vanity. Once, a high school friend visited. She was a singer and liked to have a klieg light on her wherever she stood. She told stories about her family in Kentucky. After she left, he said: "She's OK, but somebody told her she was pretty once." Once, I introduced him to a Dutch lover, who arrived wearing leather. He and the uncle talked about the war. Another time, I invited a lady friend. She had short hair. From behind, the uncle thought it was another boy. When she turned around to greet him, he saw the lipstick and the charm and smiled. Then he said: "Goddamnit!"

When I went to Paris for the first time at 25, he asked if I had been to Pig Alley.

I tried to be clever. "You mean Pigalle! Yes?"

My uncle rubbed his chin and smiled and said: "No, Pig Alley." Years later, the choreographer Karole Armitage performed a duet with the legendary Joseph Lennon. She wore high, high black heels. The show's designer had picked them up in Pigalle and convinced Armitage to wear them in homage to the girls who worked the streets there. My uncle appeared, but in a New York theater context. He was everywhere in his nephew's mind and heart, including worlds his uncle knew nothing about.

He worked until the very end of his life, despite his difficulty breathing. He went to bars. When he died, he was in a taxicab, an oxygen tube in his nose, on his way to visit one of his girlfriends. He was nearly 80. His daughter, who had no heart for such things, asked me to help the undertaker dress him. I purchased a blue tie for him, and a blue shirt. I also put white gloves on him, to comfort the many years of grease burns on his hands. When he died, I scarcely wept. He had lived what he had: his life. ★

DEAR YOU
BY ESTELLE

1. MATHILDE – SCOTT WALKER
2. JESSICA – ADAM GREEN
3. ROGER MILLER – LAKE
4. DOMINIC – RAMONA LISA
5. SWEET JANE – COWBOY JUNKIES
6. GLORIA – LAURA BRANIGAN
7. ANNIE – ELASTICA
8. BILLY – SALLY SELTMANN
9. PRESCILLA – BAT FOR LASHES
10. JOLENE – DOLLY PARTON
11. NATASHA – RUFUS WAINWRIGHT
12. SUZANNE – NINA SIMONE

We Mean What We Say: An Interview With TLC

"Everything we said and did and dressed was true to our hearts."
By Julianne. Illustrations by Alyssa Etoile.

In the early, baby years of the '90s, three ebullient Atlanta teens—Tionne "T-Boz" Watkins, Lisa "Left Eye" Lopes, and Rozonda "Chilli" Thomas—formed one of the most enduring and important girl groups of all time: TLC. They were united by producers and the music industry, but their connection was magical. When TLC put out their first album, *Oooooooohhh… On the TLC Tip,* they changed the scope of music (R&B, rapping, new jack swing), fashion (they're the reason baggy, colorful boy-wear and condom accessories were a thing), and dance. Most important, they advocated that strong women not settle for lesser dates or friends—and they were more about their friends than anything else.

In 2002, Left Eye died in a car accident in Honduras. Since then, T-Boz and Chilli have dedicated much of their lives to her memory, even while they've faced personal obstacles, including T-Boz's lifelong struggle with sickle cell anemia. This month, T-Boz and Chilli started a Kickstarter campaign to support their fifth and final album as TLC, and their mission is the same as ever: to write songs we can live by.

I met TLC earlier this month in a hotel suite in New York City. Chilli was on her phone tweeting her fans, and T-Boz was joking with their manager. Their outfits matched, like they always have: They were wearing the same dark shade of maroon, loose shirts, and baggy, comfortable pants —the chill and so-cool adult versions of those outfits I (and probably millions of others) idolized in their earliest videos. But the reason their music has always been so important is that they've never put on fronts: The second I arrived, they both gave me a hug, and took a seat on either side of me on a gray leather couch, like we'd been BFFs for years. In my mind—maybe yours, too?—we have.

JULIANNE How did you come up with your Kickstarter idea?

T-BOZ Our manager actually came up with it, and we were like, *Oh my god, no way, there's an opportunity to do something that's brand-new, innovative, out the box.* That's something we've always stood for, our whole career. So this is ideal.

And you have always had such a strong relationship with your fans! Beyond the Kickstarter rewards [some include meeting T-Boz and Chilli], how do you think the fans will interact with you?

T-BOZ From reading Twitter, the response is amazing! They're like, "Oh my god, I've waited all my life to do this with you, I'm gonna touch you!" It's so exciting. 'Cause I'm trying to think like, if I was little, and Michael Jackson did this, I'd lose it! I'd probably give my rent money, my car note…[*Laughs*]

CHILLI That's what people are saying! We're like, *No, pay rent, honey!* It's weird because we've never liked to take anything for granted, but it's a relief, because I always stay nervous. We both do. And this is a little bit like, *Whoo-sah!* They are embracing it….It's us.

Have you thought about what the music will sound like?

CHILLI It's a combination of things. It's definitely going to have to come once we're in the studio—that's when everybody's creative juices start to flow. When you're really working like that, you get your best stuff, because you don't have too much time to sit and think about it and this and that. You're excited! But we're definitely not going to stray away from what people like about us, the lyrical content, because there's substance there. I think the reason our music is timeless, like [T-Boz] says a lot, all these years later, is that you can play "What About Your Friends" and every lyric in that song is like, *Man, I can relate to that!*

That's what has resonated with people since you started: You always put forth this confidence, which is inspiring. People have this idea of who you are as self-possessed, strong-ass women. Were there times in your teens, or early 20s, that you didn't feel that way?

CHILLI Growing up, oh my goodness. I was very insecure about my body. Because I was so little! I was like, *Oh my god, I don't have hips! They're not out yet!*

T-BOZ I wore two pairs of pants to be thicker!

CHILLI Yes! And I remember being upset when Janet Jackson's video for "The Pleasure Principle" came out, because I was like, *My body's not gonna be like that!* I remember older people telling me stuff to make me feel good, but at the end of the day, I had to own being a petite person, and I still do to this day. It's internal—it's not just how you look on the outside, it's making sure you're healthy on the inside. With the breasts? I had small breasts, you know what I mean. I didn't put the tissue in [my bra], but I will say this: Back in the day, I heard that if you put butter on the boob-cakes, it'd help them grow, and I did that! Of course, it didn't work. Then when I met [T-Boz and Left Eye], we had so much in common when it came to certain things, and that's why I think my confidence was boosted even more, once I was in [TLC].

T-BOZ The song "Unpretty"—it was actually a personal situation on my behalf.

When I wrote that song, I basically wanted to stand up for how people made me feel in school. I had sickle cell anemia, and I didn't understand the disease I had myself, but people would say to me, "Oh, sickle, you're gonna die." So mean. But this is the thing: I had tough skin, 'cause my mom was amazing. But at the same point, not everybody handled things the way she taught me to, and there were times when I got down. My thing is to give somebody something relatable, like in those lyrics, and to show there is an upside. You can overcome. I was told I wouldn't live past 30, that I would never have kids, and that I'd be disabled my whole life. I'm 44, my daughter's 14, and I've traveled the world in the best group on the planet. So, my thing is, there's always an upside. There's always someone worse off. I tell my daughter: Don't cry. You can cry at home, but if you ignore 'em, they stop every time, 'cause you're not giving them energy. Some people just want any of your energy, good or bad. But you can't give them that.

When you became a group and found your friends, did you gain confidence?

CHILLI For me, it was a combination of things. It was meeting two wonderful girls who kinda almost looked like me. We all had small boobs. As a matter of fact, it was a requirement [to be in TLC] to be short, a certain height. You couldn't be tall, so I was like, *All right!* Like—*What? The way I am is OK, you want me like this?* Man, it was perfect. I think that's why, back then and even today, young girls look up to us, because they relate to us. So all the girls that, for whatever reason, don't want to wear tight clothes—and there's nothing wrong with tight clothes!—but if you don't feel comfortable wearing that, you can look sexy in other ways. And that's what we showed them, you know what I mean? Because that was how we felt. Nothing about us was a faddish anything. Everything we said and did and dressed was true to our hearts, and we meant it, and we stuck by it. And people saw that, and embraced it. The comments that we hear—like when Lady Gaga met [T-Boz], she just about

had a heart attack! You know, because our music touched her life when she was going to school during those awkward moments. T-BOZ I was like, "[Lady Gaga's] looking at me?" And [Lady Gaga] was like, "Y'all changed my life, you don't understand!" She was teary-eyed, and I was like, *OK!* But man, you impact people you had no idea you influenced at all! It's crazy.

Dah Len

You really did revolutionize so much. You showed that you could be a woman in hip-hop and dress sexy and be strong and sing, too, which was so new at that time. And even now: So many teen Tumblrs are totally devoted to you and your style and your music. You're impacting them still.

CHILLI Someone just posted all my baby pics [on Twitter]. I was like, *Where'd you even get these! I don't even have those!* They find stuff now, especially since the movie [*CrazySexyCool: The TLC Story*] came out on VH1 and did so well and broke [ratings] records and everything, like, our concerts are full of like the grandmom, the mom, and the kid. [Recently] this one little girl, five years old, had a TLC birthday party. The Atlanta radio station called me and was like, "You gotta see this little girl!" So I looked at her video, and she [was dressed as] me in the group. And you couldn't call her by her real name, her name was "Rozonda"—not even Chilli, it was Rozonda—so I went and met her. And when she turned around, I felt like I was Santa Claus! She was like, "*Chilli!*" So I invited her to come to rehearsals, 'cause we were getting ready to go to our tour in Australia, and she met [T-Boz] and watched us perform and stuff and it was just—it was amazing. I don't

know if she was excited, but it was exciting to me. Because I know that our legacy is the reason that little girl loves TLC like that at five.

You've always been so internet savvy. [In 1999,] you were one of the first groups to say the word "email" in a pop song—though Britney Spears referenced email on...*Baby One More Time*, which came out one month before *FanMail*, so it's debatable! You've always been relevant and engaged. Even your videos were so next-level—things that you and Aaliyah and Missy Elliott and other young black women were doing, when other people were not.

T-BOZ It's crazy, because we always call it an MTB thing—meaning "meant to be"—but it just naturally happened that way. All of our music was authentic. Everything: We meant it. 'Cause what you see is what you really get in this group. It's not like we were putting on a façade onstage and coming off and acting different! We're the same onstage and off! But *FanMail* was ahead of its time. It's just a part of creativity and evolving and growing. And once you've done something, you have to figure it out and grow and move. The one thing that was hardest for me was *OK, once you've had success, how do you do it again?* We had style, fashion, songs, lyrical content, even down to, like, if I was to go like this [*does the "Waterfalls" dance with her arms and shoulders*], you would know what song [it was from], so our routines even fit the hook. So it was a different combination of things that TLC had for trendsetting.

Before TLC, was being in a group like it part of your "What I wanna be when I grow up" dream?

T-BOZ Since I was seven—same dream. Left side of stage. Baggy clothes. Couldn't see my face. With a mic. Run down to the right side. Same thing. Always. Over and over. And baggy clothes! How scary is that? And I would tell my mom, and she'd be like, "OK," and I'd say, "They're gonna know my

name! I'm gonna be in history, Momma!" She'd be like, "OK, baby."

CHILLI For me, when I was little, I used to grab a brush, anything, pretend it was the mic in front of the mirror, anything. When you're little, you don't know to say, "I'm gonna be a recording artist." You're just like, "I'm gonna be a star!" And that's what I would say forever, and I always had that feeling that maybe it would be a part of my path. But growing up in the South, I thought that I had to live in L.A. or New York, but definitely L.A., so I was like, *How do I get to L.A.?* And then destiny just took over with [record executive] L.A. Reid and LaFace Records coming to Atlanta and putting Atlanta on the map like that. Just the way that every event happened to get here, it was definitely just a meant-to-be situation because I don't know how else you could explain that: I mean, the moment I met [T-Boz and Left Eye]. I was a dancer for Damian Dame for two seconds, another group on LaFace's label, and [LaFace] was gonna have this huge audition to find another member [for TLC], but that got squashed because I guess I was the missing link. And after that it just kept moving nonstop.

T-BOZ Me and Lisa met first, when I was 19.
CHILLI When I got in the group, we were 20 at the time.

Do you remember your first impressions of one another?

CHILLI Yeah! It's funny, because I had a couple of best friends. So I looked at it like *Wow, I'm in this group, this is gonna be amazing.* What developed between us that I didn't even have with my best friends was that experience of sisterhood. I loved them, and I wanted to be a part of it. It was like you instantly have this connection. You know when you meet some people, and you just don't like them? I don't care what they do, what they say, for how long—it's just something about them you don't like. But with [T-Boz and Left Eye], it wasn't like that. I felt attached immediately.
T-BOZ Our arguments were even funny! One time, I remember Lisa called [Chilli] "Pocahontas" [when the Disney movie came out] and she was like, "What!" And I was the instigator, 'cause [Chilli] was so gullible. I was like, "Man, are you really gonna let her say that to you? I mean seriously." It worked.
CHILLI She is an instigator! They got on my nerves so very badly. Both of y'all together!
T-BOZ *We?* Lisa, mostly! Are you serious right now? Oh my god, what I do *together!*
CHILLI You used to hang out all the time. I'd never hang out that much with y'all!
T-BOZ Hey! That was a choice, missy!
CHILLI [*Laughs*] You know what, I didn't, 'cause they were getting into a whole heap of trouble!
T-BOZ She—the one with the curly hair over there—she never wanted to play, or get wet. I'm like, "Well, I mean, all you have to do is scrunch it, Rozonda," and she's like, "I don't like it wet!" So, [Left Eye and I were] like, "Forget her, she don't wanna play!" Yeah, we left you! [*Laughs*] She didn't

wanna have any water fights! So you can't blame us for that, you didn't wanna *play!* We would get kinda rough, and mess up hotels, and get shut out, but they loved us, and they allowed us back! 'Cause I used to be good, too. I mean, [Left Eye and Chilli] would always take their butts out and run around with their pants down. And I would always say, "No! No, no, no!" But the one time they got on my damn nerves, and I actually let [the peer pressure] work and [I ran through the hotel halls with my butt out], the road manager steps out on *my* ass!
CHILLI Literally! On her little booty! He saw the li'l Boz cheeks!
T-BOZ Can you imagine if there had been social media back then? Oh, we would have been everywhere. Like, "TLC kicked out of hotel because of blah blah blah blah blah!"
CHILLI I have to tell you this! Because one time, we were on tour, I think we were on [our first national tour] with MC Hammer. And we were knocking on people's doors and running away and stuff like that in the hallways and so, Lisa—oh my god. You know the ashtrays that had the sand in them? We did something horrible to someone's door, and in the ashtray next door, she put her little Left Eye sign in the sand! Then they came directly to our door, saying, "Well, we saw it in the sand and then saw y'all running!" We still tried to deny it!
T-BOZ Lord, when we toured! We used to take water and throw it down [the studio's] hallway so we could slide on it! We got into so much trouble for messing up that studio, boy!

Pranks must be good for your creativity —or, at least, make being on a huge tour at 20 less boring!

T-BOZ Everybody was either in on it, or would go to their rooms and lock their doors. I'm not lying! They wouldn't even want to ride in the car with us because of the spitball fights! You know, as soon as you'd get your hair done we'd knock on the door and splash you with water! Our hairstylist roomed with us, and she woke up with ice in her face, popcorn in her bed… boy, we were bad! That was fun!

CHILLI We were fearless. What I learned over the years is that as you become older, you get more cautious, and you're not as willing to take those chances anymore. Whereas when you're young—oh my god, you just have nothing to lose. You'd do almost anything! Which is good and bad. You know, it can work out for you sometimes, and sometimes it isn't a good thing. So hopefully you have someone around you who's older, who you can trust, who can help guide you. It takes a village to raise kids, and that's true, because that frontal lobe is not fully developed. And you can make a lot of mistakes in your early 20s—you're not a teenager anymore, you're not an adult, and if you're in school or decide to work or whatever it is, you're not really under the supervision of your parents, and you think you're grown. So you make all these crazy decisions and then you're like, *Oh my god.* And it's funny, because you can tell a 21-, 22-year-old these same things, and they're like, "Mmmm hmmm. I know, I know." Sometimes you have to just experience things.

What do you tell your kids about how to be a human in the world?

T-BOZ I believe that no matter what age they are, all kids deserve a certain amount of respect. But most importantly, I tell my daughter to respect herself and stand up for herself. My thing is, a lot can happen, especially when you're a young female, when you let people run over you, if you're passive. Like, "If you stand for nothing, you'll fall for anything"—well, not in my house. When you stand for something, you're gonna take up for yourself and whatever it is, whatever she wants to do or be, I support it, as long as she has her own morals intact,

her character intact, her integrity, and her self-respect.

How can teenagers find the courage to stand up for themselves?

T-BOZ It's a process at any age! I talk to myself all the time. I think that's a lifetime thing. Everybody feels down. It's emotional, and it's a part of life. And you have to talk to somebody or get it out in some way because if you bottle things up, it's just not good or healthy for anyone!

CHILLI It's just stress, but [when] it turns into poison, it can kill you. I think it's good and healthy to allow yourself to have those moments when, like, you just don't feel like being bothered! You don't have to always be happy-go-lucky, like, "Oh, everything is great," because everything is not always great! And you have your little moment, and then you shake it off and figure out how to change things. Because like [T-Boz] said, it's a lifetime thing that you work on, but that comes in time. Because people are who they are. You have to look at people's characters. That right there is who they really are. If you care enough about yourself to evolve as a person, you have to put yourself in check, like, "OK, I won't do that." But sometimes when you're young you're like, "AAAHHH!" You just go crazy! You don't have to depend on anybody for happiness—you have to make yourself happy. You need to be around like-minded people when it comes to positive things. Not just somebody just like you, but a good-hearted person. That's what you want.

T-BOZ I wanna say this to the young girls, and to the youth, period. Adults should go by this, too: Stop listening to people! Actions show everything! Do not just listen to people. They will *show* you who they are. They could say all kinds of crap, but what's the truth? How are they really acting? How do they treat you?

CHILLI How do they treat the people around them that they care about, you

know? You have to look at everything.

T-BOZ You have to watch people.

CHILLI And when you see it, even if you have that infatuation and little butterflies going on in your stomach, you have got to pay attention to what you're seeing, because those little things that you sweep under the carpet because you're so excited right now? Trust me, it comes back out—and then you really can't stand it. Get out before a feeling starts to kick in and it's harder to leave!

T-BOZ And you know what? Sometimes, when people break up with you, actually, they're doing you a favor. Trust me! If you can get over somebody passing away, and death, you can get over [love].

CHILLI Yep. There are worse things than getting over a breakup. You'll be so OK.

Thank you so much, Chilli and T-Boz.

CHILLI Thank you so much, and thank you to our fans for being so loyal and dedicated to us for so many years, and introducing us to their kids, cousins—all that stuff. We're so fortunate and blessed to have longevity in such a fickle business. It just means a lot, and we mean what we say. ♥

Design by Sonja. Title and playlist lettering by Kate Gavino. Backgrounds and Jane the Virgin, Cassie Ainsworth, and Ugly Betty portraits by Esme. Taylor Swift, Nicki Minaj, and Charli XCX album covers and *We Are the Best!* poster by Seth Bogart. Photo by María Fernanda.

HAPPY VALENTINE'S DAY!

BY THE ROOKIE STAFF

1. SHE BOP – CYNDI LAUPER
2. OOPS (OH MY) – TWEET FEAT. MISSY ELLIOTT
3. BLISTER IN THE SUN – VIOLENT FEMMES
4. BODY OF MY OWN – CHARLI XCX
5. FEELING MYSELF – NICKI MINAJ FEAT. BEYONCÉ
6. TOUCH OF MY HAND – BRITNEY SPEARS
7. DARLING NIKKI – PRINCE
8. KICKS – FKA TWIGS
9. NATIONAL HEALTH – THE KINKS
10. SECRET – MADONNA
11. TOYZ – MISSY ELLIOTT
12. FEELIN' ME RIGHT NOW – KELLY ROWLAND
13. TOUCH MYSELF – T-BOZ

T.S. 1989

NICKI MINAJ
ANACONDA
PARENTAL ADVISORY EXPLICIT CONTENT

CHARLI XCX
SUCKER

A FILM BY LUKAS MOODYSSON
WE ARE THE BEST!
THREE GIRLS VS. THE WORLD

FEBRUARY 2015: ACTING OUT

Hi, Rookies! This month's theme is ACTING OUT. Perhaps a better way of greeting you would've been *screams, stomps, slams bedroom door, scoops up iHome, puts on "Hungry Like the Wolf," ventures back into the world wielding a machete.*

This month is devoted to interruptions, nuisances, and causing a commotion—sometimes for no reason other than celebrating adolescence's angst and freedoms, but sometimes for the good of humanity/sake of your SANITY. The other night I looked at a book of glam rock photography while listening to all my David Bowie records, and it just made me feel so *stupid* for not being more *fearless*. It's not that I sulk around repressing some deep desire to wear glittery eye shadow, but it is very easy to conflate GROWING UP IN THIS CRAZY WORLD with JOINING THE RAT RACE of, um, having low self-esteem? Constantly making compromises and censoring yourself?

I am wary of coming off as obnoxious or opinionated or in possession of any personality whatsoever. I don't want to make other people feel uncomfortable or suffocated or imposed upon. But a full realization of this goal looks like: a chunk of air in a human-shaped outline formed by dust particles. It feels like: sinking into a La-Z-Boy that is not even that comfortable, then slowly folding into its brown flannel butt crack and dispensing the occasional self-deprecating joke until I have vanished completely.

In less butt crack-y words (there's the self-deprecating joke!), here's Eleanor Roosevelt from her 1960 book, *You Learn by Living*:

> The standards by which you live must be your own standards, your own values, your own convictions in regard to what is right and wrong, what is true and false, what is important and what is trivial. When you adopt the standards and the values of someone else or a community or a pressure group, you surrender your own integrity. You become, to the extent of your surrender, less of a human being.

So I am not even talking about urges to wear eye shadow/burst into song/go streaking as much as the tiny concessions we make on the daily: not raising your hand when you really do have something to say; wearing something a little less loud; letting a friend get away with yet another passive-aggressive remark. Not because we would otherwise be causing harm to anyone, but because we are comforted by the security of acting the way we think people want us to act.

The thing is that you are not actually "protecting" other people from anything that would *hurt* them. If someone gets secondhand embarrassment by your non-hurtful acting out, they are probably very insecure themselves and trying to Whac-A-Mole anything that might make them look uncool. And, when you get that worried about how you look to other people, you end up looking at yourself so much that your insecurity is so dominant that you actually become very separate from the people you are trying to connect with (how many times have I stared blankly at someone who is sharing their life with me because I'm running through every possible thought they could be having about my hair?). As Eleanor cautions:

> When one becomes absorbed in himself, in his health, in his personal problems, or in the small details of daily living, he is, at the same time, losing interest in other people; worse, he is losing his ties to life.

DO NOT DIE/BECOME LESS OF A PERSON/VANISH INTO THE BUTT CRACK OF THE LA-Z-BOY. Being comfortable, confident, and visible can be so tricky that it is radical acting out. Even more rewarding than the security of being quiet is the security that you build by listening to your gut and taking risks and eventually knowing in your bones how it actually feels to Be Yourself: no more disconnect between who you wanna be and what you actually reveal to people, but one big Snuggie of selfhood that *cannot be wrong*, so long as it is real.

Love,

Tavi

LIFE IN STYLE

We spent a day with Mexican singer, painter, and performer Zemmoa.
By Zemmoa, as told to Caitlin Donohue. Photos by María Fernanda. Illustrations by Caitlin H.
Styling by Roberto Sánchez. Hair and makeup by Adrián Glez.
Thanks to Andrés Jimenez, aka Mancandy.

I've always been the kind of guy, girl, something, whatever, who loves Halloween. I love Halloween, I love my birthday, I love themed parties. Clothes hold the memories of different times in my life. I don't have a specific color or type of clothes that I always like to wear. It all depends on my feelings. It's feelings that make the clothes memorable. I remember what I was wearing when I had my first kiss, on my birthdays, et cetera.

My parents love me. They worry: for me, for the world, for Mexico, for everything. Parents are always worried. I'm fighting to be free. They say a heart that doesn't see is a heart that doesn't feel, so sometimes I prefer to not put my mother in situations that she doesn't understand or like. I'm doing my career by myself, and I have my connections and support, and then I have my life with my family. It's not a double life, there are just things that we

don't talk about. When I go home I dress the same, just less extravagant. Less fashionable, but still fashion. My style is sexy. Elegant sometimes. A lot of glamour, and a little bit of trash that I can't control. Very Mexican.

I made the song "Ay Mínimo Escribe Un Adiós" because I was very sad over somebody who left me without saying goodbye. I was in bed and I couldn't stand up, I just wanted to sleep forever. I went to my friend, the fashion designer Mancandy, and told him that I wanted to make a music video in my bed, inspired by Madonna's bed scene on the Blond Ambition Tour, and her Jean Paul Gaultier looks.

I wanted to make a video that showed how depressed I was in that moment, but more elegant, more fashionable, more like the fantasy of what I felt. I made that horrible situation into a fantasy and a song, and something that will last for eternity.

Everyone is a character and my character, my expression, my view on life in this moment is Zemmoa. Perhaps I'm not defined, but I'm alive. I have this phrase tattooed on me: *Nadie nos va a vencer*, which in English is "No one is going to defeat us." That's my mantra. I don't know what I am. I have a little of both worlds, but I'm more interested in the women's world. I'm as unique as anybody.

They sometimes say I'm an icon, but that title is a lot of responsibility. It means that perhaps people are repeating my actions, but sometimes I make mistakes and say things that I don't want anyone to repeat! So I don't know. It's an honor, but I have to be humble and stay focused. Life is hard for everybody and we're all fighting.

I love to work in collaboration with others. It is the age of collaboration! I like to be a muse so that designers can express the feeling that I provoke in them: I call it a "love feedback." I have friends in fashion who have been with me, supporting me, and loving me for a long time. There's Roberto Sánchez, who I worked with on the clothes for this photo shoot.

Clothes given to me by my friends who are fashion designers have special meaning. For these photos, Roberto and I chose a skirt given to me by Carlos

Temores, my friend who just passed away. It represents a lot—emotional things, hard things, happy things. That skirt is one of my super skirts. It's a beautiful piece of art. It's also the only one like it in the world, because my friend who made it is now in another place.

Just be you, express you. Don't think too much, don't take things too seriously. Don't gossip, don't lose time—because we lose a lot of time in love and in silly things. Work on you, work on your projects. Have confidence and love for yourself, because your mind is a unique universe, and nobody else has access to that universe. That's why you have the responsibility to do what you have to do, no? You don't have another choice! The only choice is between whether you want to live happy or sad, and if you want to live happy, you have a lot of things to do. Keep dreaming, keep working, and nothing will defeat you. ✳

How to Tell Creepy Dudes to Leave You Alone

No one is allowed to make you feel unsafe.
By Krista

I am an accomplished caller-outer of creepy dudes—the ones who think it's OK to comment on, or even *touch*, my body in crowded public places. Forget roller coasters and skydiving; telling someone who is freaking you out to STOP IT, and loudly, so everyone can hear, is one of the purest adrenaline rushes because you're taking power back from the person scaring you. The first time I called out a creepy dude, I went from fearful, self-blaming, and upset to powerful and confident. I haven't looked back for even a second.

Three years ago, I was on a crowded train, and as it stopped to let people off, the seat next to me opened up. A man squeezed past all the standing people and dropped into the seat. He sprawled casually, opening his legs wide until they touched mine. He was wearing jeans. I had on tights and a skirt. I moved my leg and looked out the window. I could feel him looking at me. I glanced over and wished I hadn't—yup, he was definitely staring. I fumbled for my phone and held it tight in my lap, hunched my head down, and started scrolling through my email.

"How ya doin', sweetie?"

Fuck. He was talking to me. I gave him a tight smile. "Fine," I muttered and went back to my phone, clutching it like a life preserver in the middle of an ocean. Maybe he was the chatty type, and he'd leave me alone if I answered his question. Maybe he was one of those people who think strangers should be friendlier with one another. Maybe he'd get off the train soon.

"Just fine?" he asked. "It's a beautiful day! You're such a pretty girl, and you're just fine?"

Self-blame-y thoughts ran through my head. *I shouldn't have made eye contact, I should have gotten up immediately and moved when his leg touched me, I shouldn't have answered him, I shouldn't have smiled.*

I let a silence pass and then, not looking up from my phone, said, "Yes. Just fine." I used my curt, Mommy-is-very-annoyed-now voice, which was about as confrontational as I used to get with people. He scooted closer. His leg touched mine again. He leaned toward my ear and murmured, "You're a pretty girl. I like tall girls, I like tall girls with a figure, I bet you like wearing skirts with those long legs." Ewwwww. He was talking so softly; no one else seemed to notice! Or if they did, they were staying the heck out of it. I didn't answer and turned my face even more resolutely to the window. I would ignore this asshole. He poked my shoulder playfully.

"Hey," he said. I shrank from his touch, curling myself as small as I could against the wall of the train. He leaned his body over me. He smelled like old beer. "*Hey,*" he said. Still talking softly. Right in my ear. "You don't answer when someone talks to you? Huh? You don't got any manners?"

Oh my god, this was escalating. I was panicking trying to keep it together in front of a large group of strangers on the train. PLEASELETHIMGOAWAY PLEASELETTHISEND. My face was burning red as I tried to ignore him. People always tell you to ignore it when guys do stuff like this, right??? I didn't answer. Didn't look at him. He spoke more quietly still. "Hey, I'm *talking* to you, trying to give you a fucking *compliment*, you're a little *bitch*, you know that? You're a fucking little bitch, ugly and fat, too, you're ugly and fat, you know that, don't you. Bitch."

He kept going like that—hurling a stream of quiet threats and slurs at me—for almost a full minute, which felt like years. I was blocked into my seat, alone on the train but surrounded by people, trying to ignore that his leg was pressing ever harder into mine. And then he put his hand on my leg. And something inside me snapped. I'd had enough. I stood up suddenly, and in the middle of the crowded train, without stopping to think about it, I bellowed at the *top of my voice,* "YOU ARE BEING CREEPY, STOP TOUCHING ME RIGHT NOW."

The train went silent. All eyes were on me and the scary guy. My heart was pounding; it was bizarre—instead of being embarrassed to be making a scene, I felt full of power, and suddenly not alone. There were witnesses. This fucking horrible man was touching me against my will in public, and now *everybody* knew about it. I felt pumped up. I was *furious* and *full of rage*. YOU CANNOT TREAT ME LIKE THAT. A big dude started toward the scary guy, going, "Hey man, hey man, don't be bothering girls like that, c'mon, get away from her." Scary Guy immediately put his hands up in a "I didn't do it, it wasn't me" position and got up to get away from Big Dude lumbering toward him. The train slowed as it approached the next stop. Scary Guy scuttled out of the train without looking back. Shaking, I sat back down. Women all over the train caught my eye and smiled. I felt *spectacular*.

Dudes who are being creepy in public places are not "just being friendly." Nor are they even just expressing sexual attraction. They're trying to assert their own masculinity by acting entitled to your body, and expecting you to receive this invasion as a compliment.

They also know how to be creepy without other people noticing, or at least without other people feeling obligated to get involved. It happens all the time. And it's so, so easy to get away with because they are counting on your social conditioning as a girl, woman, or generally "polite" human to let them get away with being awful. Scary Guy expected that I would be too "nice" to cause a scene.

He picked the wrong person to go too far with. I won't take this shit anymore—I now make a *huge* scene the minute someone tries to be creepy with me in a public place. You can, too! Won't you join me in exposing creeps to the light of day and total public shaming, the actual last thing they want? Won't you hold my hand as we act out in public, doing the exact opposite of what a creep expects a girl to do when he's gross to her?

When a stranger is being inappropriate with you in a public setting:

1. Instead of sitting/standing there and trying to ignore it, immediately get up and/or walk away.

2. As you do, LOUDLY and FIRMLY say: "I DON'T KNOW YOU. STOP TALKING TO ME. YOU ARE BEING DISGUSTING AND MAKING ME UNCOMFORTABLE."

3. Get as far away from him as you can.

There: People just saw that happen. People are now going to be boring holes into that asshole's head. He will be, at the very least, embarrassed, and it's not likely he's going to try something further with you. Think of all the witnesses!

A word of caution: This kind of public shaming is for fairly crowded places only. Other people need to be around to witness the creepy dude's behavior, to apply social pressure to make him feel like a worm, and to help you, if you need it. When you're alone, say, in a deserted public park or any other isolated area, GET AWAY FROM HIM as quickly and safely as possible. If he follows you, be as loud as you can—scream, yell NO!—and call 911 once you've gotten to a safe place, where you can see he isn't near.

It might sound scary to publicly call out creeps, but I promise: It gets easier the more you do it. Try practicing out loud and alone somewhere, like your backyard or room, to help you work up the courage to speak up. You could yell, "GET AWAY FROM ME!," "STOP RUBBING UP AGAINST ME, OH MY GOD, EW," or "YOU DON'T GET TO TOUCH ME, YOU GROSS OLD DUDE." Get *really* loud. It will help make your brain and body more comfortable with the act of actually doing it, which you absolutely can because you are POWERFUL.

You get to be loud, my babes. You get to be angry. You get to fight back. You have a right to be in public without being harassed. No one is allowed to make you feel scared and grossed out because they think they can get away with it—tell them. ◊

FREESTYLE JOYRIDE
BY SUZY X.

1. CARS THAT GO BOOM – L'TRIMM

2. CAN YOU FEEL THE BEAT – LISA LISA & CULT JAM & FULL FORCE

3. POINT OF NO RETURN – EXPOSÉ

4. TWO OF HEARTS – STACEY Q

5. LOOKOUT WEEKEND – DEBBIE DEB

6. FASCINATED – COMPANY B

7. MEETING IN THE LADIES ROOM – KLYMAXX

8. MERCEDES BOY (REMIX) – PEBBLES

9. LET THE MUSIC PLAY – SHANNON

10. TELL IT TO MY HEART – TAYLOR DAYNE

11. DREAMIN' – WILL TO POWER

12. I CAN'T WAIT (POWER MIX) – NU SHOOZ

BOSS OF ME

Rules: See window.
By Rachel

Styling by Emily Beard. Makeup by Kat Krupa-Ringuet. Thanks to Lizzie for modeling.

For Every Sector of Humanity: An Interview With Harlo Holmes

The kickass app developer making life hard for online bullies.
By Hazel. Illustration by Leanna.

Harlo Holmes is a software developer who builds technology for activists, journalists, and human-rights workers. Basically, she figures out how to collect data in ways that help people. One example is the Informa-Cam app, which Harlo created to help us gather more information from smartphone photos—it's super useful for protesters capturing footage that can later be used in court. She's also working on a project called Foxy Doxxing that helps victims of online harassment map connections between their harassers and collect verifiable evidence of their harassment. For Harlo, it's not just the personal that is political: The digital is political, too.

I first heard Harlo speak during a lecture series by the cyberfeminist collective Deep Lab. I wanted to know more about empowering people through coding, so I called her to discuss how she got into computers, how to merge activistism with technology, and how cyberfeminism helps everybody.

HAZEL **Can you explain exactly what you do?**

HARLO HOLMES I'm an independent contractor who does software development in mobile technology, desktop and web software. Basically, everywhere that there's internet, I write software for it.

I work primarily for a collective called The Guardian Project. We write software for human-rights organizations, legal clinics, and press outlets. When people want to make sure the communication at their jobs is private, we advise them how to best do that. We also do a lot of advocacy and training. Half of the time, I'm coding, and the other half, I'm going to conferences to educate people on what different technologies mean, why they're important, and how to use them safely.

When did you realize you wanted to code, or work in technology?

I'd been into computers and programming since I was very young. My mother was a copy editor, and she had a computer in her home office. In the '80s, it was really cool to have a computer in your home. I was obsessed with it! Back then, they were a little harder to use. You had to learn how to direct them to do what you wanted without a mouse or graphics. When my mom realized I liked computers so much, she actually bought me my own!

Computers were always such a big part of my life. In school, BASIC programming was part of our curriculum. I was a huge gamer throughout high school: I was best friends with the school computer guy and we'd set up LAN parties together. I was also really into theater my entire time in school, so theater tech was kind of my gateway drug—like, learning how to program light boards. It was computer programming, but in service of making art and telling stories.

When I graduated from college, my senior thesis was about theater, but in the real world nobody was hiring me to do theater tech. They were paying me to write websites. I shifted gears because it was something I could do. But a lot of what I do now has to do with the critical-theory books I was reading [back then]—about the theory behind software programming and how programming and art come together. I learned that the way that we write code is actually a form of speech that can be political, which I thought was so cool. After that, I went to grad school to study under people who were doing amazing things with code and politics.

There are many different routes a person could go with your app-development skills. It's so cool that you've decided to work for activists and journalists. What made you go in this direction?

I'm a graduate of Oberlin College, a place that incubates people who are super politically aware, and who try to match their intellectual desires to ways of making change in the world. But I've always felt—even prior to Oberlin, because of my upbringing—that you have a duty as a citizen. When you have a particular skill in programming, it's really easy to go down a route that brings you to the highest salary. But there are so many people who don't have that access. Bringing that access to people who don't have it is incredibly rewarding. It's part of my duty.

Where did the inspiration for Obscura-Cam and InformaCam come from?

Working on those two particular apps was the greatest coincidence of my life! I was in grad school at New York University in a class led by a professor named Nathan Freitas that was all about social activism and mobile technology. My background in theater and multimedia made me start to examine the way that photographs, and the metadata in photographs, affect our lives. Occupy Wall Street was happening at the same time, and friends of mine participating in the movement were being arrested without even knowing why! I had the idea that if you created an app that could give extra metadata to footage you'd recorded—that could spell out in an irrefutable way what went on—then, that could help protesters if they were arrested and needed to bring evidence to a judge.

When you say "extra metadata," what do you mean?

When you use Instagram and there's a map of where you took the photos, they get that information from your phone. Instagram puts your GPS into a place in code that embeds it into the photograph. If you think of someone taking a photo or a video at a protest, maybe you also want to add [information] like how the camera was moving or how the person held the camera, because those are indicators you can use to tie the photograph to the person who took it. Bluetooth devices in the area show where you are and who you're around. There are security issues—because sometimes people want to be anonymous, so we try to anonymize that data—but we still want to record it because it has so much to say.

There is a big world of data, or metadata, being collected at large on all of us: our purchases, internet searches, information in our photos, etc. Sometimes, people think of all of this data collection as negative, and it certainly can be. Your work shows that data can also be used for good. Do you feel like most people still think of data collection as harmful?

As devices become more and more integrated into our lives, they're going to collect more data. Not only because people are interested in knowing more about what we're up to, but because that's the way the devices seamlessly talk to each other. There's always going to be some person who figures out how to get access to information about you that you're not comfortable with them having. That's a fact, and it's going to get worse and worse.

However, the question is not about *how* these devices are collecting data, but a few other questions: How are we storing our data? There's a difference between me giving this data to Google, or Facebook, and me keeping this data in my own house. It would be cool if my fridge knew I needed to get more eggs, but Google doesn't need to know my fridge and I are having this conversation. We know that data is being collected, but how should it be stored and shared? That's the intervention you have to make.

On the other side, there are legal interventions [we can make if metadata is abused]. For example, everybody loves the Fitbit app because it's really fun and keeps track of your activity. The problem isn't that Fitbit collects way too much [information] about me. The problem would be if, in the future, your health-insurance rates go up because your Fitbit says you're lazy and not moving around enough! So, you have to make a legal intervention there. It's about knowing what the capabilities are, forecasting how those might be harmful to people, and then suggesting ways to use technology humanely.

Can you tell me a little about Deep Lab and how you got involved with it?

Deep Lab is the brainchild of Addie Wagenknecht, a fabulous multimedia artist based in New York. Addie had the idea of taking the topic of people bullying one another on the internet, putting it in the hands of a group of women from different disciplines, and having them rework it. I don't really know how I got an invitation to join, but she invited me.

I really believe in Deep Lab's mission because it shares my fundamental principle: Code is political. There's a really awesome article from the '80s by a guy named

Langdon Winner called "Do Artifacts Have Politics?" Winner explains how tomatoes in the United States are hard instead of squishy because they've been genetically engineered to handle the bruises a machine will give them when it pulls them [off the vine].

Whoa!

Isn't that wild? The idea that the codes people write and the machines people build have these wild politics baked into them is the force that drives Deep Lab. The fact that the algorithms we encounter are written by one type of person brings up a new question: What kind of software can we make if we change the people who are writing the code? What if those people had different politics?

Deep Lab is a cyberfeminist collective, and I think ideas of cyberfeminism are getting more and more popular as women start to realize how important technology and politics can be to their lives. What does "cyberfeminism" mean to you?

It sounds really corny, but you know that phrase "A rising tide lifts all boats"? The hard battles that feminists and identity activists fight lay the groundwork for everyone else. The benefits of engaging with a feminist practice work for every sector of humanity. Ultimately, it's not about some women-only utopia, but about reworking the theoretical framework around code and making sure all the code you turn out benefits humanity as a whole. We're thinking about how everyone can be represented by the tools that they use, not just the default character.

Your program Foxy Doxxing is still in its earliest stages, but can you explain to our readers what it is, and what drove you to start building it?

It's a software program that analyzes exactly how a group of people might have ganged up on you on Twitter. Really, it's an intelligent robot butler that performs grunt work for you. There are new, interesting studies going on in computer science and statistics about how we can use open data, like Twitter's, in order to suss out people's associations with one another. What I wanted to concern Foxy Doxxing with is what's called sockpuppetry [using a fake identity online to deceive others]. Imagine someone says something horrible about you on Twitter, and that gets retweeted and favorited across the web. It would be useful to analyze that and find out exactly who those antagonistic parties are.

Then, you could say, "There are these assholes on Twitter ganging up on me and

for some reason they're all located in this particular corner of Twitter and they seem to be really active around 4 AM." That's interesting, because the United States has laws against stalking that have to do with people organizing campaigns against you in a digital way. If you're able to produce documentation that shows how organized these people are, that can bolster your case. We're in a time when technology is a little bit faster than the law. If you have to bring a case before local police departments and judges, then you want it to be organized, and to have a dossier to strengthen your case, to get them to understand what's going on.

What advice would you give teen girls and young women who are interested in programming but don't know where to begin?

For teenagers, there are so many supportive organizations where you can be mentored or get involved. Girl Develop It is an awesome group for women to learn Python [a high-level programming language]. Black Girls Code is for girls ages 7 to 17—I'm a volunteer with them, and I see all sorts of girls come in.

You've said that it's easier to get started than to actually stay in this field. What advice would you give to young women for sticking with this line of work?

It can be hard, especially for someone super into politics and activism, because you make a lot more money as an engineer at Facebook or Dropbox or something. I kind of find that soul-crushing. [*Laughs*] I try to stay as far away from their recruiters as possible. My income bracket is a little lower, but it works for me. But there are micro-aggressions. When you show up to a place and you don't necessarily look like the person they're expecting, it makes you feel uncomfortable. You can react to those things however you want: You can swallow it; you can point it out; you can blog about it anonymously, or not. However you respond to those things is up to you. There's literally no wrong way to respond. Just know that it's probably going to happen to you, and when it does, you are absolutely not alone.

I'm 30, and I only just started to meet all these awesome women in this field. They're just as old as I am and they've been programming as long as I have, so, really, it's about amplifying ourselves. Of course, I don't want to knock the gender disparity [in tech], because that is a true problem. But it's really cool to know that, as a kickass lady doing tech, you're not the only one. Get out there and introduce yourself to those people.

THE WALL OF SHAME

IT CALLS TO ME
BY KATE GAVINO

AT THE ASIAN SUPERMARKET, THERE'S SOMETHING CALLED THE WALL OF SHAME.

VIET HOA
INTERNATIONAL FOODS

IT SHOWCASES ALL THE PEOPLE WHO HAVE GOTTEN CAUGHT SHOPLIFTING THERE, POSING WITH THEIR STOLEN ITEMS.

NOTICE
ALL SHOPLIFTERS WILL BE PUBLICLY SHAMED AND PERMANENTLY BANNED FROM THE PREMISES.

FOR SOME REASON, THEY ARE ALL OLD WOMEN.

THE BEST PART IS HOW DEFIANT AND NOT GUILTY THEY LOOK.

MY FAVORITE PICTURE IS OF A WOMAN NAMED NENITA, HOLDING A JAR OF DURIAN JAM.

DURIAN FRUIT IS KNOWN FOR THEIR GODAWFUL SMELL.

SERIOUSLY, THEY SMELL LIKE BUTT.

I KNOW NENITA FROM MY LOLA'S SUNDAY PRAYER GROUP.

ONE DAY I ASKED HER WHY SHE SHOPLIFTED.

"I'M 89 YEARS OLD," SHE SAID. "I CAN GET AWAY WITH ANYTHING. I JUST WANTED TO PROVE IT."

OF COURSE I KNOW STEALING IS WRONG.

SMILE! YOU'RE ON CAMERA

BUT FOR WHATEVER REASON, THE WALL OF SHAME CALLS TO ME.

THE FIRST DAY

I was joining the ranks of fearless women before me, and lip gloss was my way in.

By Devan Diaz

I am the youngest of three siblings. Growing up, I watched as my older sisters reached "girly" adolescent milestones like buying their first lip glosses, hoping for glimpses of my future—even if what I saw in that crystal ball/compact mirror felt unattainable. In the spring of 2002, I was a 10-year-old girl who had been assigned male at birth. I ached with jealousy as one of my sisters slipped into a royal blue prom dress accessorized with butterfly clips and glitter eye shadow. The sight was dreamlike: It all felt unattainable, even though I wanted it so badly. I dreamt of my own prom; I imagined myself wearing the same shades of red that graced my mother's lips. My girlhood was the first thing I knew to be true—although it would be years until my family saw that for themselves.

My life in Tennessee was an exercise in doing the opposite of what I had been taught. Instead of football with the boys, I was fighting with my friends over Beyoncé's spot when we pretended to be Destiny's Child. In this make-believe world, I could embody the strength of songs like "Bootylicious" and "Independent Women." I wanted to feel that way all the time. My transness had no evidentiary support and my body was not an ally, but my girlhood was my foundation—the only thing I was sure of. I maintained my survival through these rare moments of bliss. You could find me wearing my mother's red lipstick while everyone was asleep, taking my dream into my own hands. Seeing my mouth painted the same shade as my mother's connected me to all the women in my family before

me. It allowed me to envision myself joining their ranks. The shyness I felt during daylight hours eluded me when I wore makeup, so I made a nightly habit of it. Resorting to my collection of forgotten cosmetics and perfume samples in secret, I became the courageous telenovela starlets that I watched on TV with my family.

I grew older, and with age came the internet. At 12, I was desperate to locate a virtual home for my feelings. I found it on Myspace, where I discovered girls my age who were also trying to navigate the world. These girls were resilient, burning with desire to be seen. Even though they were pixels on a screen, they had a commitment to living authentically as themselves that I had never encountered in Tennessee.

We helped one another recognize the power of language and beauty, learning the words *gender fluidity* and *transgender*, and googling images of fashion eras. We cut our hair. Bleached it. Cut it again, and bleached it again, making the world see the space we occupied. We shared photos of one another's fashion evolution, and recognized the beauty we all possessed. During the day, hearing words like "abomination" in our communities, where our choices were criticized very vocally, became easier because we could unpack these words online while our families slept. We were, essentially, recreating our lives. For the first time, I found a world I could see myself in.

Androgyny was my gateway into aligning my spirit with my presentation. I eased my way into it by wearing jeans that were just a little too tight, my hair always

just a little too long. I was testing the waters of what it was going to be like to make gender-nonconforming fashion choices in my community. People weren't exactly friendly: I went from seeing the adults I knew as voices of reason, to viewing them as constant threats on identity because of the way they spoke to and policed me. When my peers refused to offer me their friendship, it told me that I was successfully challenging the rigid binary of gender in our school. I found shelter in stores like Hot Topic, where people of all genders were allowed a bit of black eyeliner and glitter.

I had stepped away from the ideas of traditional maleness that had been placed onto my body, but I still hadn't fully revealed myself as a girl. In the eighth grade, my math teacher gave me some advice that I've never forgotten: "The decisions you make now will affect the life you'll have tomorrow." Though she was trying to encourage me to do my math homework, I found her words were more applicable to my decisions about my personal style. I came to the decision that I couldn't experience high school feeling falsified by others' expectations. I knew that they should see me as I had always seen myself.

I had to make a careful entry into womanhood, as my mother's suspicion was rising. She was still under the impression that she had a son when I started sending her hidden signals to the contrary at 13. When I wore clear nail polish at dinner, she was catching sight of her youngest daughter. I came along that year when my

N° 5
CHANEL
PERFUME

mom ushered my 16-year-old sister into young womanhood by presenting her with a blue sapphire necklace before a trip to the Clinique counter, where they chose neutral shades of beige to start her makeup collection. A swipe of shimmery lipstick seemed to provoke awe in my mother: Her daughter was becoming a young woman. I'd always envisioned my induction into femininity in a similar way, and at that moment, I knew I had to be my own maternal figure and give it to myself, just as I had my mother's lipstick.

I may have had my own permission to exist in the world, but funding my decision to be seen as myself proved to be a challenge! Instead of eating school lunch with my weekly allowance of $10, I stowed it away. At school, I distracted myself from my hunger pangs by clipping images from *Teen Vogue*, surrounding myself with vibrant expressions of femininity. I was curating a new image for myself, nourishing myself with hope. On the front of my binder was a smiling Gemma Ward, wearing Marc Jacobs and riding her bicycle in the Australian sun. Being visible in sunshine was something I felt was reserved for everyone else, but I knew my time in the light was near: Five weeks without lunch meant $50 and a visit to the MAC counter.

For as long as I could remember, a visit to the mall meant a glimpse of MAC's anarchistic glamour, which I badly wanted for myself. The artists were their own canvases, with a range of hair colors as extensive as that of their products. They were making their own standards of beauty—and helping me create mine. Their music blared, and the vibrations that had always reached out to me as I passed by with my family created a riotous atmosphere. I was guided by one of the makeup artists who had dyed her hair purple, painted her lips with a shade of periwinkle, and decorated

her face with a nose ring. She introduced me to a world of colors and textures and taught me how to apply lipstick. When this woman brushed the color onto my lips, she conducted the initiation rites I had longed for. I was joining the ranks of fearless women before me, and Pink Lemonade lip gloss was my way in.

I purchased my armor—mascara, pink blush, and blue eyeliner—and got ready to face the world. It was summer break by that point, and I spent it perfecting smoky-eye looks and putting on excesses of blush. As the nights became cooler, I knew that my unveiling was close. Sleep eluded me the night before the first day of school. I felt as though my entire life had been a dress rehearsal, and my big performance was quickly approaching. When the alarm sounded, I braced myself for the day ahead. I crawled out of bed and went over the details I had spent all summer mastering. My mirror was positioned in front of me; along with my reflection, I reminisced about all the times I had imagined this moment as I slowly moved my trembling fingers over my shrine of cosmetics. Next, I had to create an atmosphere, so I pressed play on Joan Jett's "Bad Reputation." I swirled the bristles of my blush brush, took a deep breath, and began.

With an unsteady hand, I covered my eyelid in black with a kohl pencil. My fingers created a haze of smoke on my lids that called on the powers of women like Debbie Harry and Courtney Love. I teased my hair, giving myself an additional two inches of confidence. I took the red lipstick out of my mother's purse and colored outside my natural lip line. Red incites revolution, and today I was Joan of Arc. I summoned the strength of every trans woman who came before me. I adjusted my posture.

The five-inch black heels I ordered online made me feel like every Naomi

Campbell video I had watched on YouTube. Armed with enough perfume to cover a mile radius, I crawled out of my window and rushed myself to the bus stop. At school, I felt as though I was watching the day from a bird's-eye view, and my body was on autopilot. Hallways parted like the Red Sea, and teachers joined in as fellow students yelled slurs. Girls who did not understand our similarities, despite our different experiences, kicked me out of the girls' bathroom. The looks of disgust on the faces surrounding me could be felt even when they turned away.

Being shoved into lockers ruined my perfectly teased hairstyle, but the transcendent ritual of creating it couldn't be taken from me. The flashes of glitter on my nails and smell of my perfume were reminders to myself that I was honoring the dreams I had had from the earliest moments of my childhood. That vindication made it possible to let the insults roll off my shoulders. And? I had anticipated my peers' harsh reactions, but I didn't expect the chain of events that followed. In the weeks after my debut, the dust began to settle, and some of my peers began to rise up. Students of different sexualities and genders came out of hiding. Energy shifted in our school, and the kids who lived in fear stood by me. They told me my act of defiance was their beacon of hope, just as the *Teen Vogue* clippings had been mine. These people became my friends, and together we formed a resistance against our environment, just as my online community had cheered me on in the past. We offered one another protection, and the strength in our numbers could be felt in the entire school. We loved one another publicly, and our friendships continued to flourish long after high school, as did our hard-won lives and identities. My blush had started a revolution. ♇

DON'T HAVE A COW, MAN!

NO APOLOGIES
BY SHRIYA

1. ADD IT UP – VIOLENT FEMMES
2. CHEER IT ON – TOKYO POLICE CLUB
3. SHED – ROOMRUNNER
4. RUBY – THE DOOZIES
5. SHEENA IS A PUNK ROCKER – RAMONES
6. BRICK BY BRICK – ARCTIC MONKEYS
7. KISHI KAISEI – HEARTSREVOLUTION
8. DONE FOR GOOD – SKATERS
9. MAN AND WIFE, THE LATTER (DAMAGED GOODS) – DESAPARECIDOS
10. LET'S MAKE OUT – DOES IT OFFEND YOU, YEAH?
11. SERIOUSLY – SLEEPIES
12. BLACK LAGOON – HOWLER

Green Every Day

Yeah, we rule.
By Allyssa

Styling by Amy Rose. Thanks to Abbie, Alexis, Gillian, Isabella, and Veronike for modeling.

Trust Your Gut: An Interview With Marina and the Diamonds

The singer-songwriter doesn't care about being a "good" musician.
By Brodie. Illustration by Leanna.

Marina Diamandis, the Welsh singer and songwriter also known as Marina and the Diamonds, is the queen of reinvention. She made her pop debut in 2010 with *The Family Jewels* and released the ambitious concept album *Electra Heart* in 2012. It stars a super-glam character of the same name, embodied by Marina, who comments on female pop-culture archetypes (housewives, Hollywood starlets, bad girls, et cetera): "I've lived a lot of different lives, been different people many times," she sings on one of the album's tracks, "Fear and Loathing."

After spending a few years talking about and being *Electra Heart*, Marina put the character behind her, but that doesn't mean we're any closer to knowing the "real" Marina. In an interview with The Huffington Post (March 2013), she said that she "wouldn't want to spoil someone's opinion of [her] by them knowing [her] as a person instead of an artist." We know her because of how she executes her ideas—the things she makes for the world to see and hear.

In April, Marina will release her latest album, *Froot*; last week, I got the chance to chat with her about expressing yourself, playing a character, and sticking to your guns.

BRODIE There was a really high concept behind your last album, *Electra Heart*. What approach did you take to making *Froot*?

MARINA DIAMANDIS I approached it very simply. I didn't really have a conscious plan for what I was going to write or what the album was going to be like. I think I was just really relieved to do things in an uncomplicated way. With *Electra Heart* I still feel very complex [feelings] about it, because there were so many things that I loved about it that were positive, and there were certain things, artistically, that made me realize what I didn't want to do, what kind of artist I didn't want to be. So [making *Froot*] was almost repositioning those realizations.

What were those realizations?

In terms of visuals and the music, [*Electra Heart*] was exactly what I wanted, but I think it was more the fact that it wasn't a true reflection of me. That was something that I was very open about. I wouldn't have bothered to create a character to tell the album through if it had been 100 percent expressive of myself as an artist. That was part of the concept, but I think that was very affecting for me creatively, because it's almost like going around and people thinking you're this one type of artist, when you're actually something completely different.

***Electra Heart* made me think a lot about how, when female artists create characters through which to express themselves, it's often perceived as being fake or phony. As opposed to when men do it, and it's often heralded as being brilliant and mysterious. Did you encounter those ideas while making that album?**

Yeah, for sure. It was something that I encountered, probably because the type of production I had was very much like electropop. I always think it's interesting because people say with *Froot*, "This is your most HONEST album," and I think, *No, they've all been honest!* The lyrics have actually not really changed hugely in their tone since the start, so I think *Electra Heart* was very brutally honest, but I guess because you have these other layers on top of it, people may have not seen that.

Have you ever thought of your stage name as a character itself?

Not really, no! Particularly not now: I feel very chilled out about that aspect of myself at the moment. I don't see a huge separation from Marina and the Diamonds, and Marina. Or, like, being seen with a full face of makeup on, and then not being seen [with makeup]. I think *Electra Heart* made me go the complete opposite way, actually. It's quite a relief to feel like *Yes, I may be an artist, but I'm a normal person. And I like to perform. The end.*

You're not a technically trained musician. Has that ever made you feel like a bit of an outsider, or like you have to work harder to prove yourself?

No, because I don't have an interest in getting better! When I play keyboard, I do it because I need it as a songwriting tool. I'm not a musician who necessarily gets super excited to play a beautiful piano or a beautiful trombone. I don't really connect with music in the way that a more traditional musician would. I've never been geared that way; I'm more geared toward melody, the timbre or tone of a voice, and the lyrics are the number one thing. I've never felt insecure that I, like, can't play the piano properly.

I've heard you talk quite a bit about having synesthesia. How does it manifest itself in your work?

A lot of people think that it's something you experience day-to-day, or is a very strong sensory feeling. But it's not for me; it's more of an added sensitivity to color, so I associate a lot of different colors to musical notes or days of the week. That's how I experience it, but maybe it's different for other people.

As someone who doesn't have it, I think it sounds like a superpower almost!

I know! I think people think it's, like, this amazing thing where rainbows are popping out of your eyeballs! But...no.

Do you get kind of sick of answering questions about it and explaining what it is?

Oh yeah, 100 percent. But if I were you, I'd probably want to ask about it, too.

The visuals for *Electra Heart* were partly inspired by internet stars. Who or what has inspired the concept behind *Froot*?

I've been really obsessed with the idea of using shapes and symbols from nature—like certain flowers and trees and fruits—and representing them in almost a "cyber" way. So that translates more to what I'm going to be doing on stage. But in terms of beauty and styling, I'm kind of taking really classic feminine references and interpreting them in a modern way, via different fabrics and colors. At the moment, I'm really loving pantsuits, so I'm looking at a lot of '70s fashion photography. Essentially, anything that allows you to be feminine but also feel strong.

Do you have specific feminine—or feminist—people you've used as those reference points?

Actually, I think the main one is my mum! I found a load of pictures of her from when she was my age in the '70s, and she just looked incredible! So I've kind of copied her hair and parts of her look. It's very similar to Bianca Jagger's from that time.

Have you ever had to stand your ground and go to bat against anyone trying to control your image or what you make?

I definitely had feelings of that on *Electra Heart*, but at the same time, because I was a bit in denial or trying to make it my own thing and grasp back some creativity, I was like, *Well, this is my responsibility, and it was my choice to take this route!* But if someone keeps persuading or trying to encourage you to do something, I think the only thing you can rely on is your gut feeling or your instinct. If you have to be constantly persuaded, then it probably means that you don't want to do it. Everyone should rely on their instincts, but it's so hard sometimes!

It's hard as well, when you're around that environment every day, to find the space to check in with yourself and remember what your instincts even are.

Yeah, definitely! Especially when you're young and surrounded by individuals who've been in the business a lot longer and are a lot older than you.

You can have a different response to what you'd normally say. It's the most boring advice ever, but you do just need to trust your gut. ⚡

NO WORRIES

Not a single one.
By María Fernanda
Styling by María Rangel. Hair and makeup by Adrián Glez. Thanks to
Alan Balthazar and Ilshakes for modeling. Special thanks to Bianca.

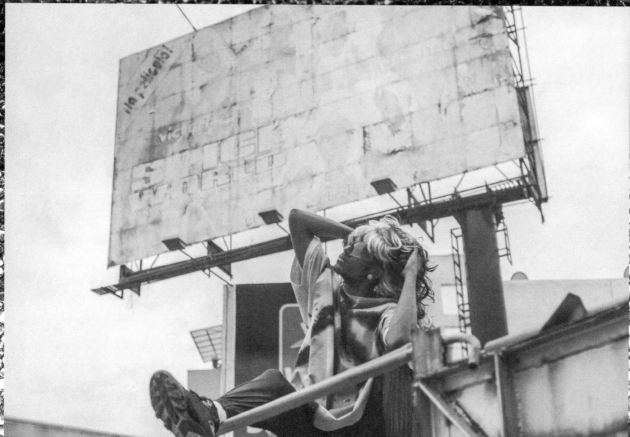

Design by Sonja. Collages by Allyssa. Photos by Tyra. Cutouts by Emma D.

MARCH 2015: **TRUST**

I resent how often I start an Editor's Letter with something along the lines of "Lately, I've been feeling like life is essentially horrible!" I know how silly it sounds—that it conjures images of, like, a bratty sock puppet wearing a tiara; that just because your brain is capable of topping itself with a new thought darker than any of your thoughts prior, it does not mean that this new, dark thought is the most true, just by virtue of its darkest-ness. I know that I feel this every year, and that, each year, I do myself a huge disservice by assuming that whatever I felt in my life before was like Feelings for Babies, produced by Klasky Csupo, sponsored by Juicy Juice; that I am such a dummy for ever having thought that everything I was yet to feel would be basically tolerable.

I want very badly to be good, kind, and "myself" with other people. I worry that "myself" sucks, so I think about everything I'm about to say very hard, and then usually end up not saying anything at all. I get glimpses of what it's like to respond to the world honestly, instead of trying to show people someone I think they will find likable. The former, when I can do it, is rewarding; the latter is safe, but also, as established last month, a form of slowly dying, which sometimes doesn't seem so horrible.

I believe it comes down to trusting yourself—that you won't ruin everything—and trusting the world—that it can be good; that this day won't be painful; that this social interaction won't be the worst. And I don't think you can do a ton of mental maze-running to get there, because that's what draws you out of interacting with what's in front of you; just pay attention as closely as possible to every-thing happening outside your head, and then your head will follow and become occupied with the things that make life worth living: the wonderfulness of the friend you're talking to, the fascination they have with what they're telling you about, how much more there is to learn about the thing they're discussing. Or, if the interaction is genuinely bleak, maybe it's amusing, or something you can write down later or entertain a friend with, or maybe it's just the kind of encounter you accept if you want to be a person in the world. There are worse things than a bleak social interaction, and being a person in the world is too good in too many other ways for uncomfortable social interactions to dictate how you exist. I don't mean to sound reductive, because depression is a lot harder than that, but I hope that my FOMO on life can outweigh my fear of life.

Here are some songs about trusting yourself, not quite POWER ANTHEMS, but sentiments that are sure to turn any bratty sock puppet into an open-hearted, I don't know, hummingbird. Okay, yeah. Yes. Yes.

1. Falling—Haim
2. i—Kendrick Lamar
3. The Ballad of El Goodo—Big Star
4. Everything I Am—Kanye West feat. DJ Premier
5. The Losing End (When You're On)—Neil Young with Crazy Horse
6. Extraordinary Machine—Fiona Apple
7. Control—Janet Jackson
8. Nothin But Time—Cat Power feat. Iggy Pop

love,
Tavi

THE SEX CRYLEBRATION:
PART III

How to relax before, during, and after boning.
By Krista and Lola. Illustration by Esme.

Hello! Fancy seeing you! Come............. here often? It's your old pals, Lola and Krista. You might remember our Sex Crylebrations, Parts I and II, and wonder what else we could talk about, but there's so much more! So much, we couldn't do it alone.

We've invited a group of Rookie contributors to discuss Sex Anxiety. We broke the topic down into four major areas: worrying about sex you're going to have before you have it, worrying about sex because of things that have happened in the past, worrying about your body 'n' mind as you are having sex, and worrying about what your body may (or may not!) be capable of doing.

I. PRE-EMOTIONS (WORRYING, BECAUSE: SEEEX)

Sex can seem wonderful and fun and good-scary, something that can give you delicious butterflies and make you happy! Sex can also feel bad-scary—just thinking about it can cause you stress. Anyone in this li'l circle ever been stomach-churningly anxious before they even tried sex?

LOLA The first time I had sex with a cis girl as an adult, I moved my hand to her golden area in silent terror, like, HOW AM I GOING TO…! ALL THESE FOLDS! when I heard my babely partner apologize: "I have a tampon in right now." A MIRACLE!!!! I was like, "ANOTHER TIME, THEN. Not for me, thanks!" I was completely ready to pretend I was not OK with period sex before I was ready for her to know I might not know what I was doing. But what's so terrible about not knowing Everything About Sex Ever? Even if I wanted to play it Smooth Dr. Sex, I could have just said, "Show me what you want."

TOVA This reminds me of my first time having sex with a girl and feeling very anxious about many things, but most specifically that I wasn't shaved. So when she made a move to my nether regions I whispered, "I'm hairy," and pushed her hand away. We saw each other again after that (I don't know how), and I made sure to eliminate my bush and then MENTIONED IT. She gave me the most confused look, like, Why does it matter? I realized that I was killing the sex-vibe by worrying about my bush, not by having a bush.

NAOMI I wish I wouldn't get freaked out about my pubes!!! Sometimes I don't give a shit about what hair I have and where, but that's usually when I am comfortable with the person I am having sex with. The first time I got naked with someone, I said, "I don't shave my armpits," before I peeled my T-shirt off (I love how we feel like we have to give people a WARNING). He shrugged. He was a teenage cis boy about to see real-life boobs—would he really have been bothered by any hair situation? People can say all they want about their hair "preferences," but nobody is going to refuse sex on the grounds of a bit of hair when they want the person right in front of them—and if they are, they probably aren't worth your time.

KRISTA Body-hair problems! One thing I didn't worry about! I dithered over whether I should have sex with my first cis-male partner for months. I was also battling religious guilt (I had just stopped being active in the Mormon Church), and I had an intense fear that sex would hurt. But, when I finally decided that I wanted this, I got really excited and then also thought for far too long about whether or not I would get blood on his sheets, and would have to buy him new ones. Forget sex bringing us closer together—what if it hurt like crazy and WHAT WAS THE PROTOCOL FOR SHEET-BUYING AFTERWARD?

ANNIE This is getting into trauma, but the idea of what "first sex" is can feel really fucking hard if you either know or think you have been abused in the past. (Memories of trauma can feel hazy and difficult to pin down, and you don't need to know when, how, or by whom harm came to you to know that you've been sexually abused.)

In 2012, I started to identify as trans and came to terms with childhood sexual abuse that I'd repressed for most of my life as a survival mechanism, allll at once. That winter, I dated Z. I only dated them for a few months, but their care, energy, and safe boundaries made me feel like I could let down some of my defenses. For the first time, I felt seen and appreciated as a girl. On our first date, we made out in a park. As we sat on a bench, Z. said, "You're making me want to invite you back to my apartment." I got nervous and I said that I wanted to, but I wasn't sure if I wanted to have sex or anything. They said that they had no intention of pressuring me, and that we could watch *Buffy* and cuddle, or not cuddle, and that I could crash on their couch or in their bed if I wanted to. All my vibes said yes, in large part because Z. made clear their lack of expectations, and because of their open style of communication.

You get to determine your own firsts. The idea of "virginity" is a cult. None of us get to change what happened to us, but we do hold incredible power over our points of view.

Sex can also feel like a first if you had, in the past, approached sex with any number of things that might have been harmful to you, your ability to connect with your body, and/or your ability to know what you really wanted. I never had sex anywhere close to sober for the first few years of my sexually active adulthood, and I put myself in a lot of dumb, potentially dangerous situations. I wasn't nervous the first times I had sex as an adult because I had blasted most feeling out of my body with substances. I had sex with people who I didn't really want to have sex with many, many times, because

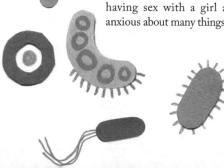

I was addicted to the attention. I wanted that feeling of care, and I didn't know how else to get it.

SO. What do you do when you decide that you wanna let the right one in? You can say you're nervous. No one expects you to be a robot, all cool and unfeeling. The other person is likely nervous, too, because sex makes most everyone shake.

ANNA F. OK, I have something that I don't know 100 percent how to vocalize because I feel weird about it. I am an anxious person, especially about being physically intimate. I was an old lady by the time I lost my virginity, but I had always been sex positive in theory. Like, "Rah rah, rights for sex workers and any wild things consenting adults want to do to one another," and that gave me weird feelings of shame about my inexperience. I knew that line of thinking was wonky, but I would still feel it, like, *Who are you to talk SO MUCH about slut-shaming, you prude-y prude prudella?* Now, I look at Past Anna and think, *Aw, girl, you were being so hard on yourself!*, and recognize the word prude as damaging nonsense, but I am sympathetic to the fact that I had internalized a lot of messed-up approaches to sexuality.

FLASH FORWARD. I can do the sex now. I still have some anxieties, but that has gotten way better by being with people I trust and can joke and be frank with. My problem is…I don't know how to have the sex I want to be having? OK…the sex I'm having is fine. But sometimes I will be watching a Grown-Up Movie (I'm talking about porn) or reading a smutty story, and I will think, *That totally weird freaky thing those characters are doing…seems like something I'd be into.* But every time I approach a position where such a thing is feasible, either I feel goofy, like a little kid trying to imitate what they saw in a movie, or I feel…sleazy, in a self-conscious way, as if I can't get lost in the moment without wondering what my conservative co-workers or the parents of the kids I volunteer with or my late grandmother would think of me if they knew what I was up to. (I know: sexy!!!!)

Again, I recognize that is a loaded thought and if a friend told me they were feeling this way, I'd say, "THERE IS NOTHING WRONG WITH YOU, YOU GLORIOUS PERVERT." But… how do you make the transition from vanilla sex to rocky road, without feeling silly?

ANNIE I'm fairly experienced with light-kink stuff, and it's totally OK to feel silly about these things. I need kink to feel grounded in the idea of "This is play and we're joking around and having fun," and I like to laugh a lot during sex and makeouts, and that can turn some people off.

I've gotten nervous and triggered at least once during every sexual encounter I've had since dealing with abuse stuff, and sometimes the solution is to make things feel very casual. I once walked into this girl's room and she said, "Did nobody warn you that I'm, like, annoyingly into pro wrestling?" I cracked up. We watched WWE on her laptop and made out. It quelled the nervousness that I usually have that goes, Everything Has to Feel Magical and Perfect. Sometimes, it's nice to let makeouts and sex feel not central in my life.

ROSE Laughter is my #1 most important tool in dealing with sex stress. Making out is pretty funny, with all that wrassling and part-palpitating and fluid-exchanging. I giggle a lot when things are getting going, and the best sex I've had is with people who are charmed and/or bewildered by my silliness, or laugh along with me. If someone insists that Serious Business Is Afoot and dislikes my making light of things, I have a harder time opening up about what makes me feel good.

What about when the anxiety is about feeling like you should want to, but don't? For example, your partner is Good and Hot and Nice, but they want to hook up more than you do. Does that make you frigid? OMG, WHY ARE YOU SO BORING WITH YOUR "LOW" SEX DRIVE?

TOVA My therapist has this really smart advice about how, if you're not in the mood and you have sex anyway, you can end up resenting the person or feeling out of your body, like your genitals and legs are these weird masses of flesh that don't belong to you. I think the hard thing about not being in the mood is that it can easily feel personal. But it almost never is! It can be help-ful to talk to your partner about the many factors that make a person not want to have sex. Maybe you're having a bad day, feeling bloated, getting used to medication—anything. Sometimes, I want to just talk with my partner about school, eat ice cream, and cuddle, because that's how I'm feeling.

Lately, I've been dealing with the pressure to have amazing sex with my long-distance partner the night before we say goodbye. The expectations to have sex because it's the last time we'll see each other for a while and for the sex to be memorable make me either overcompensate or completely balk. The most helpful thing has been to tell him what's going on in my head. He was like, "You shouldn't at all feel that way! I just love spending time with you." I feel so much less anxious knowing that he didn't mind what we did, as long as we were together.

KRISTA My anxiety rests in sometimes not wanting to do it as much as my partner does. I often feel like I'm the buzzkill, as if I were a lady in curlers on a sitcom turning off the light and saying, "Not tonight, dear"—like I'm boring, and someone who does not enjoy sex. And THEN I feel really bad about it, and then I try to get myself in the mood, because I "should" be in the mood, and then the sex is really listless/bad (as in OK-I'll-have-sex-but-it's-clear-I'm-not-really-into-it) and my partner can sense it and gets her feelings hurt, and then I burst into tears, ahhhhhhhhh!

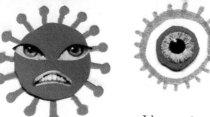

ANNIE It's super important to know that you own your sexual desires or lack thereof. If I get a sense that someone's pressuring me or breaking my boundaries, I bolt and never come back.

What about when your anxiety comes from wanting to do it more than your partner? What if you're battling fears of your partner not being attracted to you, or you're just super horny and wanna dooooo it?

ANNIE That's super real! The worst thing you can do is feel like your partner is the only person who can help out with your needs. Because you are also a sexual partner to yourself—the main one, and the only one who's gonna be able to do what you want all the time.

If this is the case, maybe you can ask—in a way that makes it clear that you're not gonna ask them to do anything that they don't want to do—if the two of you can be sexual in ways that don't involve the kind of sex that you two have been defining as sex. Maybe they don't wanna be sexual at all right now, or maybe they just don't wanna go all the way. You won't know unless you ask.

What if one of you touched yourself and the other one watched? What if you just dry humped? The possibilities are endless.

You can also think about poly or open relationships, where you might be seeing more than one person. That way, you can rely on more than one person when you want some kind of sex. I've been poly for years. Non-monogamy means different things to many people, and mine may look different from yours.

II. THE PAST (WORRYING, BECAUSE: TRAUMA)

The dread of physical/emotional sensation when engaging in consensual sex can come from a history of sexual trauma, but it's not limited to that. Even completely consensual sex acts can bring this on—like, let's say you had sex that hurt, and you're trying it again and can sense yourself holding back in fear of pain. Have you dealt with that?

TOVA I had a bundle of anxieties about sex for the longest time, for a bunch of reasons:

1. I grew up in a super-religious and sexually repressed environment. I had no sex education or understanding of how my body and other people's bodies worked.
2. I worried that having sex would make me a sinner and I didn't know what kind of punishment I would receive for having it.
3. I was sexually assaulted when I was 14, which was my first interaction with a male who wasn't my brothers or cousins. I didn't even know what sex was before I was raped, and therefore associated sex with rape.
4. I was uncomfortable even masturbating and couldn't imagine someone else touching my body.

Getting comfortable with sex was a very long process for me. I am lucky because the first person I dated was extremely kind and patient and never pushed me into having sex. Talking with my therapist, keeping open communication with my partner, and learning about my body made sex seem much less scary. A few times, I felt ready and said, "OK, let's try this!" But when he tried to penetrate me I panicked and screamed or cried. Not just because of past traumas—it also hurt! Finally, we figured out a position I felt comfortable in and made sure everything was properly lubricated. Also, I eliminated all potential triggers. For me, this meant having sex with some light on and seeing my partner's face, but this varies for everyone. I know this sounds really clinical and not fun or sexy, but it was fun. I felt great and confident, not scared.

Even after I was able to do it for the first time, I still had pretty bad flashbacks during sex. One minute, I would be having fun, and the next, I would completely leave my body and shut down. The most helpful things my partner did were PAYING ATTENTION to my reactions and checking in with me: asking if I liked something they were doing, or what I wanted to do, if I wanted to switch positions, etc. Even more important: He stopped when I shut down or seemed disengaged in any way. It took time for me to learn that I could say "stop," and that my feeling comfortable enough to say no built trust between us.

LOLA All sorts of overlapping things contribute to someone's relationship with sex. Some people might feel like, since they "haven't had something happen," like an assault or a bad/painful experience, they "should" have an uncomplicated relationship with sex, but that's not the way it goes. Instead of trying to talk yourself out of your anxieties, give yourself the right to feel those feelings, and know you don't owe anyone an explanation.

TOVA Even being improperly educated about sex can give you reason enough to be afraid. You shouldn't invalidate those feelings.

Talking a lot during foreplay/through sex (especially about sex) has really helped me with sex anxieties. So many of my anxieties take place silently, and talking makes me aware of our bodies. So, when I'm talking about what's happening, I'm actively involved instead of being in my head. Saying the person's name also helps make everything more concrete, by reminding me that I am a person doing things with another person whose name is such and such.

TAVI My friend once said that if you can't talk about sex with your partner, you shouldn't have sex with them!

KRISTA I had an experience years ago where someone didn't listen to my boundaries and ended up making me bleed anally (I had to go to urgent care!), and now, even though I have a loving and totally respectful partner, I have a really hard time trusting that anyone can be careful enough with me and understand how slow I need things to go if we're doing anything back there. Explaining what I need, taking deep breaths, and stopping the instant I feel weird helps me out. I'm working on it. Slooooowly.

STEPHANIE I have a fear of things not feeling quite right emotionally. The first guy I slept with was emotionally abusive, and that also translated into sexual abuse. One day, he wanted me to have sex with him in my friend's garage and she was at home, and I was like, "Dude, no." He got pissed and didn't speak to me for HOURS. He told me that I was rejecting him and if I didn't want to have sex with him that we should break up because it meant I didn't love him.

My interpretation of this was: I said yes once, so I guess this means I have to say yes forever unless I want to break up. So we had sex. I went numb. For the rest of our relationship, this was how sex went. It happened in dirty public bathrooms and other places where I felt super uncomfortable. I went off into my head, like conjugating verbs for my Spanish tests. Twenty years later, I still deal with that detachment. I can't always say what triggers it. Sometimes, it's because I've been writing about him or reading about assault. Sometimes I WANT to have sexytimes, but I'm thinking about work or my cats' vet appointment, and then this thought spiral happens: *Maybe I don't want to have sex now. Shit, what do I do? Do I tell my partner? I don't want to disappoint him. He gets it, and won't be mad. But I'm not sure if I want to stop. I don't want to be in this place again where I'm going through the motions. Oh god that was horrible when I was numb…*and boom, I've frozen up. Fortunately, he knows my whole history. We've had LONG conversations about it, and we have a code for it now: When I start to fall into that spiral, I say, "Hey, I want to just kiss." Looking into his eyes can make me feel connected again sometimes, but sometimes I have to just cuddle. Mostly, I'm cool with that.

ANNIE Whether or not you identify as a survivor of sexual assault, I rec the book *The Survivor's Guide to Sex*. It helped me a lot, though I continue to have hard times in bed. Sex is weird and that's fine. The biggest thing that helps me is to breathe and warmly invite the hard feelings instead of telling myself that I shouldn't have them.

That book recommended something that comes to me again and again: It challenges you to figure out if you have a default setting for sex and push a little against it. If you often break from sex because you feel triggered, it suggests that you gently challenge yourself to push through it. If your default is to have sex all the time when you might not want to, it suggests that you slow down, take a break, or stop.

It's person-to-person, moment-to-moment, day-to-day what you're gonna need. For me, one of my biggest problems has been pushing myself to have sex. Often, I've been with a partner who's checked in with me very compassionately, but I wasn't listening to my needs. There have even been a couple of times when I've pushed myself to do something with a partner who really did check in with me, and I felt like I had been raped.

Even if your sexual experiences feel mostly fraught and you don't know if you're ever going to be able to relax, focus on any little parts of sex that have made you feel lighter, warm, happy. Those moments can show you what it can be like for you. Traces of trauma may always stay in your life, but they won't always cast a giant shadow over everything you are and everything you do.

III. PROBS WITH RECEIVING (WORRYING, BECAUSE: YOUR BOD)

What about body dysphoria, or being dissociated from your body? What about being consumed with worry that you look unattractive?

LOLA One of the most constructive, healing things I've realized is: It's OK to hate your body—even if you hate your body right now, you still deserve sex with the body you have. This doesn't mean you will never learn to love and accept your body, or that it's good to hate your body forever—just that you still deserve to experience pleasure with it as is, in this moment.

KRISTA If I'm worrying I look "bad" naked, or I feel vulnerable about how I look in a particular position, I've brought up my worries to my partner. She always tells me

she was not thinking negative thoughts about me at all—she was thinking the opposite! As in, "You look hot when we're doing it." We are our own worst critics. The body "flaws" that seem glaring to you do not even register to someone who is so into you that they want to do it with you.

ANNA F. A lot of my anxieties stemmed from being much less experienced than everyone else I knew. I was worried I would be a fumbling freak. Finding somebody who I could say that to beforehand—and who could make me laugh about it—was super helpful.

I always left my shirt on when I fooled around with people because I was so self-conscious about my chest. Once, I was hooking up with someone I got along with really well. When I was about to take off my dress I said, completely sincerely, "I need to tell you: My boobs are small." He said, completely deadpan, "I am shocked." We had already been to grope city a few times!! So I took off my dress and my boobs were small and we did all the sex EVEN THOUGH MY BOOBS REMAINED SMALL THE WHOLE TIME. I haven't been that self-conscious about getting naked around other sexual partners since.

TOVA I sometimes feel as though I don't deserve sexual attention. My partner will be going down on or fingering me, and after a while, I get really anxious and stressed out, like, *Maybe they're thinking I'm a selfish lover*, or *They're tired of this*. I used to stop my partner from going down on me, or only let them go down on me if I was doing it at the same time, because otherwise I felt there was some weird debt between us. Now, I think about how I feel when I go down on my partner. It's fun, and sexy, and I love being able to turn them on. I definitely don't feel bored or think they're selfish, and so I have to remember that they feel the same way about performing "sexual favors" for me.

IV. PROBS WITH "CON-SUMMATING" OR WHAT-EVER (WORRYING, BECAUSE: ORGASMS)

Is sex only a race to the finish? What if you're anxious about coming and can't, or you can't make your partner come?

KRISTA People can get hung up on orgasms for very scientific reasons like alien-ing (*I'm worried I'll look like an alien when I come*), twinning (*I should only come when my partner does*), or can't-ing (*I can't come. I don't know why. I just can't*).

TOVA Orgasms can involve a lot of trust and surrendering. Sometimes you lose control over your body when you come, and I find that exhilarating and scary and beautiful to share with someone, which is why I have a harder time letting myself get vulnerable enough to come during casual sex or when I'm first getting to know someone. And then that becomes an anxiety, because they're like, "Why can't I make you come? I am a terrible partner!!" And I'm like, "It takes time. I need to trust you and this has nothing to do with your skills."

NAOMI I've had people say, "I want to make you come," and in my head I am like, *That is a nice sentiment, but do you want to make me come because YOU'LL feel good about it, or because you want to make ME feel good? I can't come just 'cause you want me to.* When anyone says this, I usually ignore them.

ANNIE There's no need for extra pressure or for someone to "prove" that they're a "good" lover! My friend Jetta once said, "There's no such thing as being bad at sex: You're either a good listener or not."

NAOMI You shouldn't worry about coming, because if you're worrying about coming it's not enjoyable anyway—like you're some kind of machine and a certain act should get an immediate response? That's not how it works. Focus on the pleasure—it doesn't matter if you don't come, as long as you have fun. I RARELY orgasm except on my own (or if I've been in a long-term relationship 'cause it takes a while to push my buttons the precise way).

ANNIE Having an orgasm means zero about how good sex is. Lots of people have had orgasms when they've been sexually assaulted. Lots of people (myself included) have had sex they've loved and not orgasmed.

TAVI I once asked a sexual partner why he wasn't coming yet and could I do anything to help and do you need me to run to the store and get you your fave flavor of Capri Sun and DO YOU LIKE ME? He was like, "I like having sex with you. This is not a means to an end. This part is enjoyable to me." Which was a nice lesson in not equating making someone orgasm (or sex in general) with validation.

STEPHANIE I love just kissing my partner so much that we start laughing. Making out is so fun and always reminds me of those first crush/lurrrve feelings I had for him. Getting into that zone where I can feel like I am seeing him naked for the first time, or he's discovering my boobs for the first time,

or whatever turns me on feels really freeing.

It's really important to be PRESENT in whatever you're doing—not, like, tactically moving on to the "next step" or orgasming, but thinking, *That thing that is going on feels sooooooo good.* Once you can get lost in that, you've won. Whether you come or not, you had a really good time!

KRISTA I'm so happy we've had this chat—it's been a rousing (ho ho ho) success! Having a really, really good time during sex is the goal, and it looks like we're well on our way. It's amazing to hear your stories, and I'm happy you felt comfortable enough to share!

LOLA I hope, if you are feeling anxious about anything sexy-related, that you know it's totally normal. I hope hearing other people's experiences eases your worries. Remember to be kind to yourself, and remind yourself that the aim is not to make every experience perfect. The aim is to make each experience as fun and safe and sexxaaaay for you as it can be. 🔦

EX-GIRLFRIENDS

Ashley and I had the guy we both dated in common, but our friendship isn't about him.

By Sandy

I dated a man who was in love with someone else. It was his ex-girlfriend, and they had ended their very tumultuous relationship only a month or two before we met. She was so present for our entire relationship. He always talked about her: the things she did that messed with his head, the distrust on both of their parts, the TV shows they watched that he couldn't enjoy anymore. Mostly, he talked about how he couldn't seriously date anyone because he was so hurt by the breakup. I resented her, this mysterious girl who lived on the other side of the country, this girl who kept me from having a real relationship. I would look at her Twitter, her Instagram—any social media I could find to understand who she was and why she had such a hold on this guy. How she could affect my life and emotional well-being when I'd never met her?

I don't want to talk about that relationship, because this isn't a story about me and him. It's a story about me and her. Her name is Ashley, and she is now one of my closest friends.

I spent so much time and energy thinking about Ashley before we'd ever met. I had been told that she knew who I was, and hated me, by people who like to stir up trouble. Our community of comedians is close-knit and thrives on drama, and I should have recognized that from the start. However, I took their words as the truth. I simultaneously was frightened by her and hated her for petty reasons: She was beautiful and successful, she was all anyone talked about, and, for all I knew, she hated my entire being. But in the back of my head, I thought we'd get along. She was bold and funny. We had mutual friends who sang her praises. I shoved those feelings away because I was trained to hate her. I wanted to hate her! Because if she wasn't a monster, that meant the guy I was dating was. And that was something I refused to believe.

Ashley and I had been pitted against each other. By the guy I was seeing, his friends, anyone who knew both of us. I was the good guy and she was the bad guy, because she was the ex-girlfriend. And all ex-girlfriends are CRAZY!…right?

There are two choices when two girls are pitted against each other without ever having met. They can embrace the drama and hate each other for eternity, or they can meet and decide for themselves whether they like each other. Ashley and I met when a mutual friend threw an impromptu get-together. I had broken up with the guy, and was very depressed about it. I thought of him constantly, and was still occasionally smooching him. Ashley and I spent the first hour eyeing each other across the room. I thought if I came near, she might rip me to shreds. But I also thought, *Maybe we can actually talk.*

As the night wound down and people began to leave, we found ourselves sitting at the same table, separated by a few people. I laughed at a joke she told to offer the first olive branch. We did not make eye contact. Neither of us was sure if the other was still seeing this guy we had shared. My heart was pounding. She told a story of a guy she used to date who didn't treat her well and looked at me. I returned the gaze and said, "Me too."

More people left. I offered, "Should I come sit over there?" Ashley said yes. As I walked over, I was frantically thinking how we'd begin this conversation. Hi, I'm Sandy—*She knows that, you dummy!!* We clearly knew everything about each other. We were both the other woman.

I sat down slowly. She looked me in the eye, put her arm on my arm, and said the most perfect thing: "Sandy, how are you doing." It wasn't a question—she knew exactly how I was doing. She had been through the same tumultuous breakup, and knew that we had to break through the bullshit that had been layered on us. We talked for three hours, nonstop. It felt like the biggest

weight off my shoulders. We blabbed about our mutual experiences, our mutual friends, how wild it was that we had never met. My mind was reeling. Oh, *this girl is a person.* She later texted me, "How weird is it to see my name pop up on your phone?" Her name had always given me the chills, and it now invited comfort.

Meeting Ashley changed my life. What we had in common was this guy, but our friendship isn't about him. It's about two girls who were hurting and found comfort in knowing they weren't alone. It's about how important it is to find someone who understands your pain. And it's about admitting you were wrong for judging someone.

I have a secret that Ashley doesn't know: It wasn't chance that we met that night. I knew that she would be there, and I wanted to meet her so badly, to see if female friendship could overpower the heartbreak I felt. I needed that night as a crutch because there was no way I would ever reach out to her on my own. I was so broken from the recent breakup that I wasn't myself. I'd lost all my confidence and any shred of happiness or excitement. But Ashley restored all that. She knew everything about my situation. She could say, "Hey, you're not alone."

Girls are taught to be jealous of and hate one another from a young age. The term *crazy* is thrown around quicker than a Frisbee. I've learned that when someone is called "crazy," that usually isn't true. I have to judge for myself. Or, not at all.

My friendships have lasted longer than any relationship with a man, and the one I have with Ashley will be strong long after our memory of this guy we shared fades. Because—and I can't stress this enough—it's not about him. It never was.

CALL OF THE WILD

Otherworldly encounters with the outside world.
By Chrissie

Styling by Elvia Carreon. Thanks to Devon Blaser, Elvia Carreon, Addy Davies, Justina Goldbeck, Natascha Greenwalt, Sonia Ionescu, Clara Pathe, and Amanda White for modeling.

Joan Didion wrote that we tell ourselves stories in order to live, but I think we also tell ourselves stories in order to die/kill ourselves slowly. If I don't get up as soon as I wake up, the day is consumed by mental fiction about all the bad things that could happen if I go out, or if I stay here, or if I just have to exist with myself, anywhere, much longer. If I make it out to see a person that night, she is a moving face muted by restaurant noise and glimmers of light and the anticipation of my bursting into tears. I have turned the most innocent froyo outing into a weird TED talk about death. An ironic viewing of *Jupiter Ascending* into a PSA about the meaninglessness of the universe. I was swinging from a tree in a halo of fairylights at the top of a hill in a friend's backyard when it hit me that other people might not know about or at least constantly ponder how everything ends and that I MUST conduct an impromptu doomsday cult recruitment sesh to educate them and make them stay in bed with me; not *in bed* WITH *me* (human connection: gross!), but in their own beds, psychically accompanying me on a nightly basis to the Barnes & Noble midnight release of my brain's biography of my life, titled: *Everything Shitty She Has Ever Done and Everything Shitty That Could Ever Possibly Happen to Her and Things She Will Never Know for Sure (Everything)*. Rookie writer Jenny once asked that if your brain is what tells you when other parts of your body are in pain, how is it reliable in letting you know when *it's* in pain? Despite my knowledge of my own history with mental health, the ability to assign narratives to depression, anxiety, and panic in a way I couldn't with, say, a broken thumb, blows every little obstacle up to epic proportions. Anxiety over anticipating a single conversation becomes screaming and nausea and crying, anticipating all of life's uncertainty. And the memoir's audiobook: "Both Sides Now," the version by Judy Collins.

INCREDIBLY HERB-Y, RIGHT? Also, this is the song that acts as a motif in the Christmas rom-com *Love Actually*, in which Hugh Grant is the prime minister of a real country that people live in? GIMME A COOLER TUNE TO RELATE TO, DEPRESSION. But it's the cheeriness and pace that make it all the more disorienting. Judy's breezy affectation and perfect vibrato are nauseating among the piercing video-game soundtrack, melodramatic black-and-white-movie strings, and marching-band drums. "Both Sides Now" is one of Joni Mitchell's less complex songs, but the nursery-rhyme expression of something so dark is way more upsetting than any kind of nuanced take, and Judy's escalated version doesn't really let you in. It leaves you hanging, fades out, abandons itself. It blasts through the "uncanny valley," where everything is just human enough that you ought to be able to connect, but just unsettling enough that you can't. Jenny said the song reminds her of a scene from *The Tin Drum*, a 1959 book by Günter Grass—and later, a movie—about a boy who decides at age three to stay in his child body forever after witnessing the bitterness and cruelty of adults. The boy visits the circus,

and a member invites him to join them, and the boy responds that he prefers to be "a member of the audience."

I have written this editor's letter so many times—"I can't believe you only get to live in your own body and that *Freaky Friday* isn't real; crazy stuff!"—but this is not the kind of thing that, no matter how basic it is, really stops being upsetting, or, at least, interesting. I did a classroom visit and Q&A last week at the University of Wisconsin and was asked multiple times by readers of Rookie why I write and talk about my mental health so much and I guess I didn't realize that I do, and also never saw it as any sort of statement so much as a natural part of what I feel and think about. Poor mental health should not be mistaken as offering deep insight to the human condition—that's a dangerous story to tell oneself. What I am about to tell you is not the answer to anything, and the answer to my bed-in starts with my doctor, because there are no edgy, artsy ways to feel healthy. But because I would like to leave you with something useful, these are some people I try to view life through when I feel I have seen it from both sides, from every side. This is what I call BE YOUR OWN MOM/ GRANDMA/BFF/ROLE MODEL/BILL MURRAY.

1. BE YOUR OWN MOM came to mind when I listened to the Fleetwood Mac song "Gypsy" for the millionth time and suddenly heard a whole chunk of lyrics that had always gone over my head, about being a "child…enough for me to love."

I try to be my own mom not because I am able to step outside of myself and extend the same unconditional love to myself that a mother does to a child. It's more like realizing that I am still young and developing. We think of ourselves as constantly at the end of something because we are, at all times, older than we have ever been! BE YOUR OWN MOM is like: You are raising a person (you), and you want life to be as easy as possible for her, so maybe do the thing now that will help her most in the future, e.g., it is super easy to indulge negative thinking about someone you're jealous of, but if you're like, YOU'RE RAISING A PERSON AND ALL OF THIS THINKING ADDS UP TO BAD VIBES, you might stop and know that transferring that brainpower to something more productive makes for a happier daughter in the long run.

2. BE YOUR OWN GRANDMA. This is when I get hung up on or victimize myself over a situation that is ultimately catty and temporary, e.g., an acquaintance going on about a stupid pop-culture thing I get deeply invested in and pissed off about because THEIR OPINION IS WRONG! Then I imagine me in my old age being like, "Why did you waste so much time on such fools? Wish that convo about 'Anaconda' wasn't one of my five remaining memories rn!!!" Or I imagine my actual 97-year-old grandma being like, "You want a #TBT? *I'LL* give *you* a #tbt! The

Design by Sonja. Illustration by Brooke Nechvatel.

GREAT DEPRESSION!" And then I zap catty thoughts from my brain as soon as they creep in.

3. BE YOUR OWN BFF. When I feel like I'm *dealing with something* and I have no clue what to do, I think about what I would say if a friend came to me with the same issues, and it's a lot easier to be loving, yet rational. Like, if a friend came to me and was like, "I'm freaking out because life itself is so scary and I can't leave my bed because there is so much sadness in the world and I am so scared of pain," I'd be like, "What've you got to lose! Stop inventing problems! Come out and play!"

4. BE YOUR OWN ROLE MODEL. I am so lucky to have heroes, to have friends I admire, to have found artists whose work or 'tudes I find inspiring. When I'm consumed by mental fiction about a hypothetical—e.g., *I can't tell my partner why I am upset because he'll laugh in my face and then speed away in a monster truck and never come back*—I think about what the kind of person I admire would do. Not anyone specifically, just *the kind of person I would see as heroic.* I often stop myself first, because the self-loathing part of me is like, *But you suck and will never be that anyway,* but then the BFF is like, *Why not just try,* and the grandma is like, *Please don't let me die full of regret,* and then David Bowie is like, *We can be heroes.*

5. BE YOUR OWN BILL MURRAY. Last year's Toronto International Film Festival included a whole day devoted to the work of this fine actor and performance artist. The last question of the interview portion was "How does it feel to be you?"

I think if I'm gonna answer this question, because it is a hard question, I'd like to suggest that we all answer that question right now, while I'm talking. I'll continue—believe me, I won't shut up. I have a microphone. But let's all ask ourselves that question right now. What does it feel like to be you? What does it feel like to be you? It feels good to be you, doesn't it? It feels good because there's one thing that you are—you're the only one that's you, right?

So you're the only one that's you, and, you know, we get confused sometimes—or I do, I think everyone does—you try to compete. You think, *Maybe someone else is, dammit, someone else is trying to be me. Someone else is trying to be me.* But I don't have to armor myself against those people. I don't have to armor myself against that idea. If I can really just relax and feel content in this way and this regard. If I can just feel, just think now: *How much do you weigh?* This is a thing I like to do with myself when I get lost and I get feeling funny. How much do you weigh? Think about how much each person here weighs and try to feel that weight in your seat right now, in your bottom right now. Parts in your feet and parts in your bum. Just try to feel your own weight, in your own seat, in your own feet. OK? So if you can feel that weight in your body, if you can come back into the most personal identification, you know, a very personal identification, which is: *I am. This is me now. Here I am, right now. This is me now.* Then you don't feel like you have to leave, and be over there, or look over there. You don't feel like you have to rush off and be somewhere. There's just a wonderful sense of well-being that begins to circulate up and down, from your top to your bottom, up and down your spine. And you feel something that makes you almost want to smile, that makes you want to feel good, that makes you want to feel like you could embrace yourself. So what's it like to be me? You can ask yourself, *What's it like to be me?* You know, the only way we'll ever know what it's like to be you is if you work your best at being you as often as you can, and keep reminding yourself: *That that's where home is.*

BE YOUR OWN BILL MURRAY really just means…be you. Not *be yourself,* like you have to know who you are and feel super confident in who that is and be ready to conquer the world. Just ready to kind of exist in the world, and let the uncanny valley melt away to a place that is very difficult to navigate, but in which you can absolutely function.

LOVE,
TAVI

Far Away From Me

I was never the girl in that Weezer song.
By Jenny. Photos by Savana.

I used to joke that I peaked in fourth grade when three boys from my class were supposedly going to meet after school and fight over me.

"No big deal," I said to my friends, who went around collecting bets on who would win my love.

In my heart, I knew it would happen again and again. I went to a public school in Queens, New York, where most of the kids who attended were Asian, Latino, or Middle Eastern. Plenty of girls looked like me, and even though none of us looked like we were going to grow up to become any of the women on the covers of magazines or in our favorite TV shows, it didn't matter. Our little world was all we knew, and as far as I knew, I was a *babe* and I was smart and I was funny and I had the best fucking clothes and I could dance like a boss, and I charmed the hell out of everyone who ever met me, and most of all, I *liked* myself. I liked myself immensely, and I couldn't imagine wanting to be anyone else.

Five years later, my family moved to Long Island, and I went to a middle school and then a high school that was attended by predominantly upper-middle-class white kids, and I came out of puberty battered and depressed by the realization that someone like me (aka not a white girl) was rarely included in the examples of female beauty, something I so yearned for—to be a beauty, to be a great beauty. I was convinced that I was hideous, disgusting, and deeply, exceptionally unlovable. That my best shot at love was tricking someone into it or offering them something of inarguable value that would make up for my inferiority, my inherent lesser than-ness.

~ * ~ * ~

I was a pariah in middle school, and when I told the story of how and why that happened, I focused on me as an *individual*, that there was just something about me that the other kids didn't like. I tried not to mention my suspicion that being one of two Asian kids in my entire grade, and the only Asian girl in my class, might have had something to do with it. I tried not to dwell on how my school was segregated as hell, how all the rich white kids just so happened to be the popular ones, and at the bottom of the social hierarchy were the black kids, the Latino kids, the immigrant kids, the kids who came from working-class families, the kids with disabilities, the kids whose bodies did not conform to the thin, able-bodied standard of beauty, the kids whose gender and sexual identities were suspected to be not cis and not heterosexual. The hierarchies at my high school hewed closely to the racist, xenophobic, homophobic, transphobic, classist, hierarchies in society at large, and yet I felt shy about making that connection, afraid whoever was listening to me would think I was another whiner, another self-professed victim who blamed everything on race and gender and structural oppression instead of accepting that maybe it was simply *me*, no other context needed except that I simply sucked. It was far easier to frame my high school experience as just the story of another weird girl who didn't fit in and lived to tell the tale.

And as far as this particular tale goes, I tried to reclaim and reappropriate how much people seemed to hate me by becoming The Ultimate Freak. Becoming The Ultimate Freak put me pretty far from being A Great Beauty, but at least, I told myself, I wasn't totally powerless. At least, I was in control of my own identity. I told my own story, which is something I still fight for in my life—the right and power to name myself before someone names me (or misnames me), to insist on seeing myself first, and to claim the sanctity of my inner world against how I am seen and spoken of and spoken to in the outside world.

So many times I have had to recoil and retreat to the safety of my inner world when someone has asked me, "Are you Chinese or Japanese?" or when someone shouts, "Ni hao! Ni hao! Konichiwa!" at me for six blocks, following me as if entitled to my smile and my gratitude. Or times when someone has insisted, "You hardly even have an accent!" and expected me to receive it as praise. Or times when someone has tried to compliment me by saying, "You're very different from most Chinese people. You don't see much creativity and individualistic thinking coming from the Chinese." Or times when I know I am truly invisible because someone blithely says to me, a Chinese girl, "I would never date a Chinese girl. They're too demanding and superficial and only care about money." Or the time when I endured an entire dinner party with a woman who kept going on and on about how China seemed like a "really scary place," and how the Chinese government was "churning out math and science robots" and all I could think of was how scary *America* was to me as I sat there, silenced by this white woman as she subjected me to monologue after monologue about how *evil* the entire Chinese race was—the kind of fear-mongering rants about yellow peril that felt ripped out of the Chinese Exclusion Act of 1882. And then there are those times when someone has insisted that I was that *other* Asian girl, times when someone has called me by another Asian girl's name and referred to us interchangeably. Time after time, when I have had to remind myself that even though I know how other people see me, I won't submit to seeing myself that way.

Even though it embarrasses me to admit it now, I used to worship the Weezer song "Across the Sea," from their album *Pinkerton*, which I love to this day even though when I listen to it now, it comes across like one big, whiny, humblebraggy, creepy men's-rights activist's anthem. The song is basically about frontman and singer Rivers Cuomo having an Asian fetish, and eroticizing and fantasizing about this Japanese schoolgirl who writes him fan letters from all the way "across the sea" and how he wants to meet her and date her even though it's "wrong" for about a zillion reasons, among them how he doesn't really know anything about her except that she adores him, or how he objectifies and eroticizes and idealizes her as the perfect

dream girl with no other desires in life other than to please and adore him, or how a major power imbalance exists between him, the *adult* rock star, and her, the *teenage* fangirl, and yet when I listened to that song as a teen, it mostly just stirred up this massive yearning for some creepy, delusional, aging rock star dude to fetishize me, to exoticize and idealize me. That, I thought, was my *in*. My only choices, I thought, were to be invisible and ugly or to be exoticized into worthiness.

For girls of color, internalizing the message that we are inherently inferior and ugly and freakish can happen explicitly and it can happen insidiously and it can happen just by repeated exclusion. It can happen when you browse online beauty tutorials only to realize none of these videos and their various tips and tricks work on your monolids or your eye shape or your skin color, and yes, you've seen and you understand the disclaimer that no one size fits all when it comes to beauty, but still, why does the most commonly referred to "size" always seem to not fit the beauty of girls of color? It can happen when you think you'd like to hop on the cotton-candy pastel dyed hair trend only to realize that this is not a trend that is easy to accomplish on dark Asian hair and that to have pastel-pink hair you would literally have to bleach your hair three times and even then it would likely turn dark magenta in a week, and feeling forlorn you scroll through pictures of cute girls with *My Little Pony* hair online and realize almost all these girls are white. In middle school, it happened under the guise of science, when the smartest girl at my school came up to me and told me that she had scientific PROOF that eastern European girls are more beautiful than everyone else. She was, of course, eastern European. Some researchers had conducted a study where the study participants were shown photos of faces from all around the world with all kinds of skin tones and features, and

surprise, surprise, the faces that rated the highest were the ones that conformed to white standards of beauty. I wanted to say that I didn't need a scientific study to tell me that we live in a world that has upheld and continues to uphold the racist belief that white people are better, smarter, more beautiful, more human, more worthy, more complex, more heroic, more inherently good than any other type of person!

Most recently it happened to me when I was in Shanghai visiting my family and decided to pop into an eyeglass store and for the first time in my life, almost every single pair of glasses I tried on fit my face correctly, sat high and comfortably on the bridge of my nose, unlike 99 percent of the glasses I've tried on in the States. *So I'm not a freak*, I thought, *my nose isn't too flat or too oily*. I was just excluded. Again.

So when in high school, I read an interview with Rivers Cuomo in *Addicted to Noise* (December 1996), where he explains (to Clare Kleinedler, the half-Japanese journalist interviewing him) his fascination with half-Japanese girls, I felt my heart leap a thousand acres:

> I suppose that halfway through writing the album, I started to realize or become aware of a pattern in my life that I seem to be having a lot of disastrous encounters with half-Japanese girls. And then it developed into disastrous encounters with Asian girls of all sorts.

Yeah, I suppose it's fair to say that I'm fascinated by Asian girls. [*Grimaces*] For some reason, they're particularly beautiful to me. I don't know why. And when I became aware of that and also the fact that it was the masculine part of myself that I was learning about in these songs, I remembered the story of *Madame Butterfly* and the story of the character Pinkerton in that opera. And I decided to use or refer to that story as a means of unifying the record. And so I kept that in mind as I wrote the second half of the record. Pinkerton is the ultimate character representing male id who goes to Japan as an American sailor and hooks up with this 15-year-old Japanese girl and gets her pregnant and then abandons her. He's thoroughly despicable. [*Long pause*] But I can't deny that there's some of that in me.

I read that and thought: *There are people in this world who prize girls like me more than other girls? How do I get in on this??* In the very back recesses of my brain, I had a general sense that the reason people like Rivers idealize and obsess over Asian girls had a lot to do with the long history and legacy of seeing Asian girls a certain way—submissive, delicate, and mysterious—that went hand in hand with seeing Asian men a certain way—weak, asexual, inscrutable —and all of it went hand in hand with seeing Asian people a certain way—subaltern, perpetually foreign, threatening, devious, strange—and instead of pursuing this history critically and thoughtfully, I waved it off. I didn't want my bubble to burst. Surely, I thought, *there had to be a side to racism that* benefited *me*. I felt my only chance to survive in a world where I was consid-

ered foreign no matter how long I lived in America, where I was considered strange no matter how normal I felt, was to play along. Even if I knew deep down that to try and find love on the basis of being someone's fetish object was damaging, I could still try. *Being the idea of someone I wasn't was better than being no one at all,* I thought.

So I prayed and prayed: PLEASE GOD LET SOME ATTRACTIVE WHITE BOY HAVE AN ASIAN FETISH AND PLEASE LET ME BE HIS TARGET!

~ * ~ * ~

Dear Rookies: Please watch the scholar and activist bell hooks's documentary *Cultural Criticism & Transformation* (1997) so it can change your life already. After I saw it, I felt like the world was the same, but I was now different because I saw differently and understood differently, and most of all, I felt so, so seen.

There's a part where hooks describes how we live in a "white supremacist capitalist patriarchy"—a phrase she uses to evoke the "interlocking systems of domination that define our reality and not to just have one thing [like race or gender]" as the sole lens in which we see the world.

One of the things I've noticed is that the people who benefit the most from living in a white supremacist capitalist patriarchy are always the ones who most adamantly insist it does not exist. The people who have always had the right to tell their own story are usually the first ones to protest when their story is reframed in the context of our white supremacist capitalist patriarchy. The idea that their story, their personal experience, is somehow part of a larger narrative, a larger context, never sits well lives that they are exceptional, whose individuality has never been contested.

As for me, I've been told my whole life that I could be Chinese or Japanese or Korean or Thai or Vietnamese or Oriental or whatever. Who I am has never mattered. I've been told my whole life that I look just like the other billions of Asian women in the world, that it's impossible

and, in fact, unreasonable to expect anyone to tell us apart. My personhood has never been sacred. Sometimes, I'm so used to being powerless, so used to not being seen or heard that I can't relate to people who haven't ever known such powerlessness, who still react hysterically and combatively when the possibility of losing some of their privilege is merely raised.

One way to threaten someone's power is to say, "You think you acted purely on your own free will and individual volition but there are forces larger than you, larger than any individual, that contributed to you being the way you are and doing the things you have done." Or: "Your intentions are not all that matters and good intentions do not absolve you of your complicity in harming others."

The hard part, as bell hooks says, is to remind ourselves of the "interlocking systems of domination"; that the center of all this is not just white folks versus everyone else. That all of this works together—like in the case of marriage (*New York Times*, January 2011.) That there is a reason Asian women are much more likely to marry outside their race than Asian men and are considered to be more "passive" and "deferential," and there's a reason black women are far less likely to marry outside their race than their black male counterparts and are perceived as "masculine," and none of these reasons have anything to do with the actual desirability and worth of any of us and everything to do—back to bell hooks—with this white supremacist capitalist patriarchy.

At a panel discussion last year at New York's New School called "Are You Still a Slave? Liberating the Black Female Body," with bell hooks, the writer and activist Janet Mock, the writer Marci Blackman, and the filmmaker and curator Shola Lynch, the question was raised of what a truly liberatory sexuality would look like in a world where we are constantly contending with the interlocking systems of white supremacy, patriarchy, capitalism, and the legacies of colonialism and imperialism— how do we find, in other words, as writer Junot Díaz said in the *Boston Review* (June 2012), a "decolonial love"? At one point, bell hooks semi-seriously suggested "celibacy" as one way to have a liberatory sexuality, and then joked a few minutes later, "I mean I gotta go home and think about how mentioning celibacy could trouble the waters…" It was such a great moment to witness. I felt like bell hooks was winking at us, as if to say, *Don't worry, I'm doing everything I can to tear down this imperialistic white supremacist capitalist patriarchy, but I'm also getting it back home.*

It was such a needed relief from what can sometimes feel like all heaviness all the time in these discussions of oppression and pain. And it spoke so much to the paralyzing expectations and pressures we put on people of color, especially politically outspoken people of color, to make sure our personal lives and our sex lives do not contradict ANY of our political beliefs. That not only are we supposed to be educating all ignorant people on centuries of interlocking systems of oppression—and in a manner that is calm, nice, articulate, and patient, no less—but we also have to make sure that everyone whose mouths we want to kiss and faces we want to touch faces to has to be thoroughly vetted and pose no difficulty, challenge, or contradiction to our beliefs, otherwise everything we've ever fought for or said is automatically discredited. No big deal. No pressure, right?

~ * ~ * ~

Was I in a decolonized relationship when my boyfriend in college told me that he dates Asian girls because they're "easier to handle"? Was I in possession of a liberated sexuality as a teenager when I would sneak out of my parents' house to spend the night hanging out with older white men who proudly showed me their tattoos of random Chinese characters? Who spent hours talking to me about the *I Ching*, something I had never heard of, and trying to impress me by showing me the Chinese calligraphy they had done even though it triggered bad memories of being forced to attend Chinese school on Sundays? Who kept asking me about the branch of Buddhism my family practiced no

matter how many times I explained to them that we were atheists? Did I find a decolonial love when I dated a guy who would only buy me cute things like candy and stuffed animals because he liked me better that way—cute—and when I started to show other ways that I could sometimes be—opinionated, loud, ungrateful, crude, aggressive, indelicate—he liked me less and eventually broke up with me? Did I exhibit a liberatory sexuality all the times I fake giggled or smiled through clenched teeth when a man told me that, unlike white girls or Latina girls or black girls, Asian girls are just more naturally into pleasing, and on top of that, we tended to have perky breasts and smooth skin?

How could I have loved these men who wanted a living China doll instead of a three-dimensional woman? Instead of me? And yet I did. I loved them. I felt enormous tenderness for them. I confided things to them. I became brave in their presence and because of their presence and in spite of their presence in my life. At times, I even felt seen. In the end, there was nothing liberatory or decolonized about those relationships, but still, there were moments of love that meant something to me. Still, I am not ready to consider celibacy my only option to a liberated, decolonized love.

"Across the Sea" opens with Rivers Cuomo singing about a teenage "girl who live in small city in Japan." Listening to the song now, I realize he's trying to imitate the broken English of the Japanese girl who writes him by omitting the "s" from "live" and the "a" before "small city," unable to imagine that this girl does not likely think in broken English, but more likely exists as someone who thinks and speaks and functions in fluent, grammatically correct Japanese.

When I was an undergraduate, I read the 1992 short-story collection *A Good Scent From a Strange Mountain* by Robert Olen Butler. He was hailed as "the master of the short-story form" by my white male creative-writing teacher whose ideas I challenged constantly. One story in the collection, "Fairy Tale," is told in the first person from the perspective of a naïve Vietnamese prostitute who falls in

love with an American soldier who promises to love her and take her "across the sea" to the U.S. and marry her and give her the good life. Ultimately, he's a shit husband and she divorces him and goes back to being a prostitute but remains optimistic in her advancing years. The story is written in broken English as if this Vietnamese woman would tell her own story in her own head in broken English and not in perfectly fluent Vietnamese. The failure of imagination is on the part of the white male author, Robert Olen Butler, who cannot see this woman the way she would probably see herself, even as he appropriates her voice and what he imagines to be her inner world.

No, my peers and my teacher argued with me, he's just trying to capture how she would have appeared to us, an American, non-Vietnamese-speaking audience. But aren't there also Vietnamese Americans? I shot back. I'm American and I don't see her this way. I was the only person of color in that class and everyone laughed at me, at how uptight I was, at how I always found something to criticize when it came to matters of race. I didn't say anything more on that point, but I did wonder if somewhere there was a book written by a Vietnamese woman who writes from the first-person perspective of an American soldier, and tells his story in broken, embarrassingly bad Vietnamese. Except that story likely would not exist because that white American man likely would only speak a word or two in Vietnamese, if at all. So his story would just be 12 pages of white space. He would be silenced altogether by his illiteracy, his inability to communicate at all in any other language besides English. Imagining that gave me pleasure for a moment, I guess, until I realized that *A Good Scent From a Strange Mountain* won the Pulitzer Prize and was almost universally praised for its depth and insight into the Vietnamese experience. It always takes a white man to make the subaltern finally real. What about a book about the Vietnam War written and told and framed by an actual Vietnamese person? Would that ever win the Pulitzer? Would it even get published to any acclaim?

I guess this is a long way of saying I *have* to speak for myself. I have to tell my story. If I believed that I was who other people imagined me to be, I would be a broken woman speaking in broken English.

I guess this is a long way of saying I was never the girl in that Weezer song. Some people have wanted me to be, and I have gone along with their fantasy of me, but that's all it ever was: someone else's fantasy of a girl.

I want to be clear that this is not a universal condemnation of interracial dating. It doesn't make me or any girl of color a hypocrite for both wishing to be seen as three-dimensional and as our own subject, *and* wanting to date a white boy.

The search for a decolonized love implicates all of us. You can't put a person of color in a world that devalues them at every turn and reminds them constantly of all the privileges and immediate praise heaped on white people for simply being born to a body that passes and reads as white, and then expect people of color to not want the security and immediate validity associated with whiteness. You can't shame and chastise those of us who seek that very security and immediate validity by association, sometimes by romantic association, sometimes by aspiring to and/or conspiring with that whiteness in other ways.

It's true I still hold "Across the Sea" close to me. It's true how I hold it now has changed. It's true I once found that song romantic. I once thought I would only be so lucky to be the girl in the song. It's true I have been described exactly like the delicate stationery that this girl writes the letter on, and there have been times when being described this way has made me genuinely flush with pleasure, and other times, flush with disgust. The more I listened to the song the more I knew I wasn't in it. No one was. The only person present in these songs is the white man imagining all of it. The one who told *SPIN* (November 2010), "I was really touched by the emotion in my voice, especially with the *Pinkerton* songs. It struck me that there's so much sensitivity and pain in my voice."

I still catch myself trying to become the object someone imagines me to be, but then there are other times, when I am free, when I am fluent, when I am unimaginable, that I start to feel like somewhere out there is the decolonized love for me, somewhere out there, there is a love that doesn't let any of us be so lonely. ♥

ARE YOU MY M🌼M?

"adopt me/be my second mom/i think of you as a mother figure you are so epic."
Written by Tavi. Illustrated by Isabel.

I thought up the story for this comic after noticing on social media that people were calling their beloved artist/musician/et cetera "Mom" or "Dad" as a term of endearment. As Lorde explained on her Tumblr, after using the phrase in reference to Kim Kardashian: "Among the youthz ['MOM'] is a compliment; it basically jokingly means 'adopt me/be my second mom/i think of you as a mother figure you are so epic.'"

Isabel and I based the comic, about three teens looking for human connection on their favorite pop stars' Instagram accounts, on the classic children's book *Are You My Mother?*

Super *Natural*

In defense of glamorous makeup.
By Meredith. Illustration by Beth.

Nine hours into a flight from New York City to Sydney, Australia, I started to feel nightmarishly disgusting. I couldn't sleep, so I decided to see what was showing on in-flight TV. That was the day I became *obsessed* with Kim Kardashian.

No matter what sort of chaos is swirling around her family, on *Keeping Up With the Kardashians*, Kim always looks effortlessly flawless. There I was, stuck on a 32-hour flight, completely barefaced for the first time in as long as I could remember and feeling like disheveled, shameful trash, staring at someone so remarkably beautiful that even now, I can't remember the plot of the episodes I watched—I was too busy trying to figure out exactly what combination of genetics and airbrushing led her to look this way.

Kim's face, it turns out, is made up every morning by her "glam squad" of makeup artists. Of *course* her skin is perpetually dewy, her brows on point, eyes bright and wide, jaw contoured. She looks completely "done," but she also looks utterly natural, perfectly herself. The result is that, whether in an invasive paparazzi photo or an Instagram selfie, she's unfuckwithable—from any angle.

Although I don't have a glam squad, I do spend anywhere from 10 minutes to an hour in front of the mirror before leaving the house, meticulously applying product on top of product on top of product. I *never* go without makeup. The idea of going to the market, performing on stage, or seeing someone I'm dating without a full face on is implausible. In a desperate situation, I've been known to make up my face in a gas-station bathroom, or in our tour van's tiny visor mirror. This routine is what it takes to make my face look exactly how I want, so I do it, every day. It's a ritual from which I do not deviate.

People who fall in the feminine range of the gender spectrum are familiar with the pressure to be *pretty*. Everywhere you look, there are advertisements for products to fix your every "flaw," possibly dangerous potions and surgeries to make you thinner or curvier, your skin more even or tanner or lighter, your hair sleek or curly. It's amazing to me that I live in a world with this many products at my disposal specifically designed to help me make my face look exactly how I want. That's what makeup *should* be. If you want purple eyelids, so be it! But there's also pressure governing how much makeup female-identified people use, and the ways we use it.

I learned about that second kind of pressure in the eighth grade. I'd snuck into the bathroom to apply a heavy coat of cranberry-red, almost-black lip gloss that I had bought behind my mom's back, and that my friend Jonell assured me looked totally rad. It was dark and thick and shiny. It made me feel vampish and campy, serious and impenetrable—perfect for English class, where I would read out tortured poetry I'd written about P., a tall, dark, handsome boy, who was also in my class. I was in no way prepared for the peals of laughter that started the second I walked into the classroom. I was used to being stared at because I was tall and zitty, sad and weird, but I don't remember another time that my social punishment felt so immediate or severe. That fucking lipstick might as well have been a felony. Ten minutes into class, I had wiped it all off onto the backs of my hands.

Young women are socialized to understand that makeup is OK, but only in subtle, well-executed ways, so its existence remains invisible. We're supposed to be "naturally pretty," which means not looking like you've spent an hour in front of the mirror, caring about your face. This contradictory demand circulates constantly. A popular meme shows a screencap from a makeup tutorial—an extremely glamorous woman has contoured her face, and wears visible lipliner and long false lashes. The user-added caption reads: "This is why you take her swimming on the first date." Similar memes shame and mock black girls who wear weaves. The implication is that people who choose to modify their appearance with visibly styled hair or makeup are not to be trusted, and that men are justified in feeling deceived, and in trying to learn "the truth" about a woman's appearance.

Then there's the popular "Dear Girls" Tumblr meme, a photoshopped picture of a male model holding up a sign that says, "Dear Girls, don't be insecure. You don't need makeup and nice clothes. You're all fucking beautiful." Though this handsome dude affirming my beauty seemed sweet at first, this meme is an example of flagrant entitlement. *Thank you, sensitive dudes of the internet, for granting me this vacation from makeup!* Maybe that's why the dude in the meme is pictured in outer space—because the idea that "makeup and nice clothes" simply don't matter is *completely illogical* here on planet earth.

Telling women they don't "need" makeup doesn't account for the fact that women are more likely to be judged when we don't wear makeup. While it's illegal to establish gender-specific dress codes, many women have come forward with lawsuits after their employers allegedly fired them for not wearing makeup, or for wearing their hair natural. Trans women who need to "pass" as cis are often accused of "lying" through their appearance, an accusation that can present itself violently, and sometimes fatally.

Navigating gendered norms is crucial to our ability to work and live, and yet the work we put in to meet those norms is as undervalued as women's work in general. Looking at those memes, it seems like makeup is a problem when women appear to be dedicating time to themselves in ways that don't directly benefit men. Getting up early to look "presentable" for work? Required. Spending hours on your face just to go to school, Starbucks, and the gym? Vain, and probably stupid. Apparently, wearing makeup for yourself, because it brings you joy or makes you feel beautiful or happy or creative, is a waste of time.

Last season on *Keeping Up With the Kardashians*, as Kim was entering her eighth month of pregnancy and preparing to give birth, she came under fire from her sisters Kourtney and Khloé for having the glam squad on call for her impending labor. Kim justifies this by saying that the first time she meets her baby daughter, she wants her to think her mother is beautiful—not for the paparazzi that follow her everywhere, not for Kanye, but for her daughter and for herself. Much squabbling ensues. Her sisters and sister-in-law push her to the point where she spends most of the episode, despite being harassed and followed around by the paparazzi, without makeup. She attends prenatal yoga and meditates, eventually conceding that she could stand to be a little less exacting about her beauty regimen, sometimes. And then, when she goes into labor, she gets her damn makeup done and goes to the hospital and has her baby, just like she wanted.

Makeup is important and awesome and magic and powerful, especially when used to augment your happiness and well-being. Everyone should be able to wear or not wear whatever makeup they want, at any time, all the time, without question! It is OK to not let the person you're dating see you without makeup if you're not cool with that, to never listen to anyone who tells you you're wearing "too much" makeup or that you look better without it, and to feel more like yourself or ONLY like yourself when you're totally made up—"natural" or otherwise.

You might be pulling multiple all-nighters studying for the chemistry midterm, working an after-school job you loathe, going through a rough time in your life—hell, you might be going into labor—but at least you can make your face look exactly how you want it to look. It's a question of agency and visibility. Exactly what makeup you wear and how and when is unimportant—the point is, it's *your choice*. Now get out there and face the world. ✿

How to Talk to Your Parents About Transitioning

There's no one "right" way, but here are some ideas.
By Tyler

When you were born, your parent(s) probably had thousands of ideas about what your life would look like. Some of these ideas seem very basic, like your gender and what pronouns to use to refer to you. However, most parents don't assume that their child could be transgender. A lack of awareness and understanding places the onus on you, the child, to come out to your guardian(s), and to educate your families about your experience.

Trans people are often made to feel that we aren't normal, that we're a burden, that changing pronouns and names is "too hard" for the people around us, that we aren't deserving of basic respect or love. Talking to anyone about such a personal subject—especially one that has so many stigmas surrounding it—can be incredibly hard, and guardians can be the most difficult people to start and maintain a dialogue with. Our families are often scared of change, of losing us, of the stereotypes they've grown up with, and sometimes confuse their visions for who they hope we'll become with who we actually are. While we struggle with identity and our place in the world, our guardians struggle with their own fears and emotions. We might want to avoid conversation (and these emotions) at all costs. I understand that, having been through it myself, so I've come up with ways to share your experience with and/or educate your parents about your identity and transgender issues.

Before we jump in: If, during any part of your conversations, things take a turn for the negative, remember that *you are not the problem*. There is absolutely nothing wrong with you. If you need to tune out your parents' emotional reaction to remember that, that is OK. Often, when I've come out to family and close friends, they've made my feelings, my identity, and my transition about themselves. They've felt angry, hurt, betrayed, and even deceived, but your feelings and identity are not about other people, and you do not need to change yourself for the comfort of others—not even the people who raised you. You have the right to your own identity, and you got this!

• When I figured out that I was transgender at 20, I sent my mom a coming-out email from the distance of a university several states away. I knew I wouldn't be able to get the words out face-to-face, or even on the phone—the subject was too personal, too raw, too scary, especially since I rarely talk to my mom about my feelings. But I knew I would need her support (I still depended on her for housing whenever I came home during school breaks), and even though we don't do a lot of feelings-talk, we are still pretty close. Being trans is not something that I could hide from her, nor is it something that I *wanted* to hide, so I had to work up the courage to contact her in the way that felt most comfortable for me. In the email, I explained my feelings, such as the dysphoria I felt as a child that I repressed when I felt pressured to fit in with girls during my teenage years. I also provided definitions for words like *transgender* and listed examples of pronouns so she could better grasp what I was talking about. I included resources like a video of a trans person conducting an interview with his mother, talked about steps I wanted to take in my transition (starting with changing my name), and reassured her that I was taking my time figuring myself out. I ended the email with "It's a long road and we'll see what happens."

• It was easier for me to be open, clear, and patient with my mom via email. Writing gave me more time for reflection and allowed me to be more concise and less reactive to her potential questions and thoughts. A similar approach, even if you live with your parents, is to become pen pals. Write them a letter, decorate it if you want, and leave it in your mailbox. Have them check the mail and request that they write you a letter instead of immediately reacting to what you wrote. Heads up: They may need more time than you expect to process your letter and reply.

• If you prefer a more direct approach and want to have an in-person conversation, think back on other serious talks you've had with your parents, and when/how/under what circumstances they occurred. Were you in the car? (I am wary of having big talks in the car, because I worry about how people's emotional states affect their driving, but some people have great conversations that way.) Were you sitting in your room? Was there a family meeting in the dining room? Were you hanging out by a lake after a game of catch? Think about the circumstances under which your guardians feel most approachable, relaxed, receptive—or at least less busy—and bring it up then.

• My mom and I watched many helpful videos, like the kind I mentioned in my letter, together. We paused every time my mom had a question, or every time I wanted to relay my own experience about the topic. These videos were great dialogue facilitators because they allowed me to broach subjects by pushing the "play" button instead of bringing them up myself (and it really helped to have someone on the screen validating my feelings). It was incredibly useful for my mom and me to see trans people living their lives and talking about everyday things, like shopping and school. Other videos covered topics like hormones, terminology, activism, community—everything under the sun. Pick a topic that you want your loved one to better understand. Gather together on the couch with popcorn, watch from separate rooms and reconvene to discuss, or even watch while video-chatting each other.

• If you are interested in a more creative project, scour the internet for articles and blogs written by trans people. Print out your favorite pieces and make a book or informational pamphlet to give your parent(s). They will have the opportunity to see the time, thought, and dedication you put into both this project and general introspection. Optional: emailing the authors if they seem open to discussion/answering questions/providing resources.

• Does your parent have a hobby, an interest, or a job that you know little about and are interested in (or can fake interest in)? Spend a day learning together. Ask them to teach you something they are passionate about, and in return, teach them about anything trans-related that you want them to know. Create a lesson plan with props (such as index cards, a chalkboard, a PowerPoint presentation), or just talk about what is important to you. Compromise by setting a time limit: The amount of time they spend teaching you is also the amount of time they must spend listening and learning as well.

• Therapy can help facilitate conversation with your parents if you have a knowledgeable and respectful doctor. If you do not know how to find one, contact the nearest LGBTQ resource center and they should have a list of local trans-friendly therapists. If you feel comfortable contacting your doctor or asking a health practitioner whom you know socially or through your family, they should be able to provide you with resources, too. Important note: If you are not out yet and you are a minor, be aware that doctor-patient confidentiality may not stand, and there is a possibility of being outed against your will before you're ready.

• If there *is* an LGBTQ center in or near your area and your parents are willing to take you there, schedule a trip! Check their website to see what meetings or support groups they hold. There are often events for trans youth, parents of trans folks, and parents AND trans youth, in addition to community get-togethers and activities (potlucks, movie nights, field trips).

As always, safety is your number-one priority. If you are unable to come out and/or talk to your parent(s) about being transgender, that is OK—your identity and feelings are always valid, no matter who knows (or doesn't know) about them. Many of the activities on this list can be done on your own, and the internet is a great resource for finding people like yourself to talk to—when all else fails, community is key.

If you are able to talk to your parents in any way, know that everything is a process, and it may take time for them to understand and adjust their language and behavior. But you're making yourself heard, and that's so important and valuable. *You deserve to be loved and respected, and you deserve to be gendered correctly!* I am wishing you lots of luck and love. So much of this is scary, but you're gonna be OK. ♡

GOODBYE, HOUSE

A BITTER, WHINY FAREWELL TO A DEAR OLD HOMEY BY ESME

EARLY THE OTHER MORNING I HAD A STRANGE DREAM

FIRST I SAW THE HALLWAY LEADING TO THE KITCHEN IN MY GRANDPARENTS' HOUSE IN LONDON

WHAT WAS STRANGE ABOUT THE DREAM WAS THAT NOTHING HAPPENED IN IT. IT WAS JUST LIKE I WAS WALKING AROUND, LOOKING AT STUFF. MY GRANDPA'S BIKE WAS LEANING IN ITS USUAL SPOT AGAINST THE WALL.

THEN THE VIEW CONTINUED ON INTO THE KITCHEN, WHERE NOTHING WAS GOING ON EITHER. EVERYTHING WAS VERY STILL AND VERY QUIET, APART FROM THE CLASSICAL MUSIC PLAYING SOFTLY ON RADIO 3... AS USUAL

EVERYTHING WAS EXACTLY AS IT SHOULD BE

I SAW A BUNCH OF STUFF I KNEW AS WELL AS THE BACK OF MY HAND:

THE TILES BY THE STOVE

THE LINOLEUM ON THE FLOOR

SAND- (IRL IT'S KINDA COLORED)

THE BIG FAT BROWN TEAPOT ON THE COUNTER.

AND THEN I WOKE UP WITH A START, SWEATING AND SOBBING.

GASP!!

BUT HOW DO YOU EXPLAIN A NIGHTMARE ABOUT NOTHING HAPPENING IN A HOUSE?

90% ASLEEP

MPH... MBAD DREAM BABY?

DEEP SHUDDERING SIGH

GUESS SO, CAN'T REMEMBER

!!

AS I LAY AWAKE DOING THE DEEP BREATHING EXERCISES I SAW ON THE EPISODE OF 'SNOOKI + J-WOWW' WHERE ROGER & JIONNI GO TO THE ANTENATAL CLASS, I FIGURED OUT THE EXPLANATION: MY SUBCONSCIOUS WAS TORTURING ME, LIKE WHEN YOU DREAM ABOUT AN EX MONTHS AFTER A BREAKUP, JUST WHEN YOU THOUGHT YOUR BROKEN HEART HAD STARTED TO HEAL. I WAS DREAMING OF SOMETHING I LONGED FOR, THAT I HAD TRIED TO FORGET THAT I WAS MISSING. THE HOUSE NO LONGER WAS MINE, AND APART FROM DREAMS LIKE THIS, I WOULD NEVER SEE IT AGAIN.

TECHNICALLY, THERE WAS NO GREAT OR UNEXPECTED TRAGEDY ATTACHED TO THE LOSS OF THE HOUSE. ONCE BOTH MY GRANDPARENTS DIED IT WAS NO LONGER OF ANY PRACTICAL USE TO OUR FAMILY, SO GETTING RID OF IT WAS THE NATURAL AND SENSIBLE THING TO DO. WE ALL KNEW IT WAS GOING TO HAPPEN, BECAUSE THAT'S WHAT HAPPENS WITH HOUSES. THEY'RE JUST HOUSES.

MY PARENTS HAD LIVED HERE WHILE MY GRANDPARENTS WENT ABROAD FOR A YEAR WHEN I WAS 2. ONE OF MY EARLIEST MEMORIES IS OF THE VIEW OF THE STAIRS OVER MY DAD'S SHOULDER AS HE CARRIED ME UP TO BED

(STAIRS, 1992)

MY PARENTS EVEN HAD THEIR WEDDING HERE!

WORE SUNGLASSES THE WHOLE TIME LIKE A DOUCHE

6 MONTHS PREGGO W/: ME!:

(JUST MARRIED, LIVING ROOM, 1990)

MY GRANDPARENTS HAD LIVED HERE SINCE MY DAD WAS 12

(HIS 16TH BIRTHDAY, KITCHEN, 1970)

THEY'D GROWN OLD IN IT

(KITCHEN BALCONY, 1988)

AND MY BROTHER AND COUSINS AND I HAD BASICALLY GROWN UP IN IT

(LIVING ROOM, 1999)

BUT IT WAS STILL JUST A HOUSE, TO BE SOLD

AND BOUGHT AGAIN LIKE ANY OTHER

THE LAST TIME I SAW THE HOUSE WAS JUST BEFORE I LEFT LONDON LAST SUMMER. WE STILL HAD A MONTH LEFT TO VACATE IT. BUT I'D BE BACK IN NYC BY THEN, SO I WAS FEELING A LITTLE MORE SENTIMENTAL THAN EVERYONE ELSE

I WALKED AROUND FOR A WHILE TAKING PHOTOS OF DETAILS I DIDN'T WANT TO FORGET, AND SAYING GOODBYE OUT LOUD TO PARTS OF THE HOUSE I'D REALLY LOVED. I ALSO SMOKED ONE LAST J WITH MY BROTHER AND OUR PARENTS ON THE ROOF OF THE BUILDING, WHICH COULD BE ACCESSED THROUGH A TINY WINDOW IN THE UPSTAIRS HALLWAY AND WAS ONE OF EVERYONE'S FAVORITE THINGS ABOUT THE HOUSE.

IT FELT KINDA RITUALISTIC, BUT ALSO COMPLETELY NORMAL. I KNEW IT WAS THE LAST TIME, BUT I COULDN'T REALLY GET MY HEAD AROUND IT.

IN 'IN SEARCH OF LOST TIME' PROUST SAYS THAT

POETS CLAIM THAT WE RECAPTURE FOR A MOMENT THE SELF THAT WE WERE LONG AGO WHEN WE ENTER SOME HOUSE IN WHICH WE USED TO LIVE IN OUR YOUTH. BUT THESE ARE MOST HAZARDOUS PILGRIMAGES, WHICH END AS OFTEN IN DISAPPOINTMENT AS IN SUCCESS. IT IS IN OURSELVES THAT WE SHOULD SEEK TO FIND THOSE FIXED PLACES, CONTEMPORANEOUS WITH DIFFERENT YEARS.

WELL, NO OFFENSE TO GOOD OLD MARCEL BUT I DON'T KNOW IF I AGREE ENTIRELY WITH THIS IDEA. I'M NO POET, BUT WALKING AROUND THE HOUSE FOR THE LAST TIME, I CERTAINLY FELT LIKE I WAS RECAPTURING MANY OF THE PAST SELVES I'D BEEN IN THESE ROOMS.

HERE I WAS AGE 7, HOME SICK FROM SCHOOL WITH MY GRANDPARENTS WHILE MY PARENTS WERE AT WORK,

AND EVERY AGE AT THE KITCHEN TABLE, WHERE OVER THE COURSE OF THE LAST 23 YEARS I MUST'VE SAT HUNDREDS OF THOUSANDS OF TIMES:

GHOST OF PAST-ME   ME IRL →

AND AGE 9, PEEKING OVER MY G-PA'S SHOULDER WHILE HE WORKED IN HIS STUDIO,

AGE 2, STUFFING MY FACE WITH CAKE AT MY BIRTHDAY PARTY

AGE 8, HAVING A TANTRUM AT MY BROTHER'S BIRTHDAY PARTY

AGE 17, LEARNING HOW TO DRAW FONTS WITH MY GRANDPA

AGE 22, STUFFING MY FACE WITH CAKE AT MY BIRTHDAY DINNER

IF ANYTHING, THE PAST-SELVES WERE TOO MANY. THIS HOUSE WAS LITTERED WITH MEMORY-GHOSTS.

BESIDES, THE ALTERNATIVE OF FINDING THOSE "FIXED PLACES" WITHIN OURSELVES CAN SOMETIMES BE JUST AS "HAZARDOUS" AS PHYSICALLY RETURNING TO THEM. SOMETIMES IT FEELS EVEN WORSE TO HAVE ALL THAT PAST-LIFE ENERGY BUBBLING AWAY IN THE DEPTHS OF YOUR SOUL, JUST WAITING TO BURST OUT AND MAKE A MESS EVERYWHERE. IT'S DIFFICULT TO LIVE WITH THE WEIGHT OF ALL THAT DISPLACED HISTORY!!

FOR INSTANCE, A WHILE AFTER I HAD THE DREAM ABOUT THE HOUSE, I WAS SPACING OUT ON THE SUBWAY—

—WHEN SUDDENLY, WITHOUT WARNING, AND WITH SUCH CLARITY AND SWIFTNESS THAT IT'D MAKE YOUR EYES WATER—

COOL OLD-FASHIONED SOAP RACK THAT I ALWAYS REALLY LIKED

..HUH?

—I WAS 3 YEARS OLD AGAIN, SITTING IN THE BATHTUB IN MY GRAND-PARENTS' HOUSE.

IT HITS ME LIKE A TON O' BRICKS

'OLE WATER-WORKS!

SHORTNESS OF BREATH!

ACK!!

SHOULDERS-A-SHAKIN'!

AND ALL AT ONCE I REMEMBER EVERYTHING, I KNOW AND CAN FEEL EVERYTHING, NOT JUST THE WATER IN THE TUB OR HOW IT WAS TO HAVE YOUR HAIR WASHED WHEN YOU WERE 3 BUT ALSO THE EXACT TONE AND TEMPEATURE OF THE LIGHT COMING IN THROUGH THE WINDOW AND THE CORNFLAKES I'D JUST HAD FOR BREAKFAST WHICH SMELLED OF THE SARDINES MY GRANDPA WAS EATING, NOT TO MENTION THE SOUNDS THE PIPES ARE MAKING AND ALSO THE FEELING OF HAVING A TALL STRONG DAD WITH ALMOST A FULL HEAD OF HAIR STANDING BY TO LIFT ME OUT OF THE BATH AT MY WHIM AND DRY ME OFF LIKE HE ALWAYS DID WITH THE TOWEL OVER MY HEAD, MY HEAD GOING 'OOGY-DA--BOOGEY-DA-BOOGEDA'. I REMEMBER IT ALL LIKE IT WAS YESTERDAY. I REMEMBER IT LIKE IT WAS EARLIER TODAY. IT FEELS LIKE IT'S STILL HAPPENING RIGHT NOW.

BUT IT'S NOT, DUH! AND IT NEVER AGAIN WILL BE! I COULD CHALK MY OBSESSION WITH THIS HOUSE DOWN TO STANDARD NOSTALGIA, BUT THAT WOULD BE A MISDIAGNOSIS—IT'S MORE VISCERAL THAN THAT, AND DARKER. IT'S NOT A LONGING FOR A COZY, FAMILIAR PLACE — IT'S A PERVASIVE, AGGRESSIVE GRIEF, STRONG ENOUGH TO KNOCK THE WIND OUTTA ME, PERTAINING TO THE LOSS OF NOT ONLY A TREASURED MATERIAL ENVIRONMENT BUT AN ENTIRE MODE OF BEING, A COMPLETE SYSTEM OF EXISTENCE. THE HOUSE WAS REPRESENTATIVE OF MY ENTIRE CHILDHOOD, THE NUCLEUS CONNECTING AND SUSTAINING EVERYTHING I HAD COME TO UNDERSTAND ABOUT THE WORLD. ITS ABSENCE MADE CLEAR HOW VERY DEAD THAT WHOLE EXISTENCE, THAT WHOLE UNIVERSE, REALLY WAS. EVERYTHING IS ENTIRELY DIFFERENT NOW. THE HOUSE WAS THE ONLY REMAINING PORTAL TO THAT OLD WORLD. NOW I WAS STUCK HERE.

WAAAHHH

RIGHT IN THE MIDDLE OF THIS HYSTERICAL EPIPHANY FREAK-OUT, MY IPOD STARTED PLAYING JOANNA NEWSOM'S 'THIS SIDE OF THE BLUE' WHICH WAS QUITE FITTING IN A MELO-DRAMATIC WAY BUT ACTUALLY JUST MADE EVERYTHING WORSE.

♪♪ "AND THE REST OF OUR LIVES WILL THESE MOMENTS ACCRUE/ WHEN THE SHAPE OF THEIR GONENESS WILL FLARE UP ANEW/ AND WE DO WHAT WE HAVE TO DO RE-LOO RE-LOO/ WHICH IS ALL YOU CAN DO ON THIS SIDE OF THE BLUE" ♪♪

BUT SO WHAT DO WE ACTUALLY DO RE-LOO RE-LOO?!?! MY SHORT ANSWER: NOTHING, THIS COMIC, MUCH LIKE LIFE ITSELF, HAS ABSOLUTELY NO POINT. I THOUGHT DRAWING IT WOULD BE CATHARTIC AND GIVE ME SOME CLOSURE, BUT GOING THROUGH PHOTOS AND MEMORIES KINDA MADE ME FEEL EVEN MORE ALONE AND DETACHED. I SUPPOSE THE SOLUTION TO A GRIEF LIKE THIS IS TO JUST GET ON WITH STUFF AND HOPE THAT EVENTUALLY THE HYSTERICAL LONGING WILL GIVE WAY TO A SOFTER, CALMER, MORE PLEASANT REMEMBRANCE. IT TAKES TIME TO GET OVER MOURNING THE PAST ENOUGH TO APPRECIATE IT... OR MAYBE THIS FEELING NEVER GOES AWAY, AND WE'RE ALL JUST FUCKED.

I CALLED MY GRANDMA'S BEST FRIEND, WHO IS ALSO ONE OF MY BEST FRIENDS, TO RUN THIS MISERABLE THEORY BY HER:

WELL, I'M TRYNA DRAW THIS COMIC ABOUT E+L'S HOUSE AND HOW SAD IT WAS TO LOSE IT, AND I WANTED IT TO HAVE SOME KIND OF COMFORTING ENDING BUT ALL I CAN REALLY COME UP WITH IS THAT LIFE IS JUST A CURSE WHERE YOU JUST HAVE TO CONSTANTLY SLAVE AWAY UNDER THE CRUSHING MEMORIES OF EVERYTHING YOU'VE EVER LOST, AND ANYTHING YOU LOVE WILL EVENTUALLY JUST DIE AWAY LEAVING YOU TO TRY TO SOME- HOW CARRY ON LIVING WITHOUT IT ALL!!! DO YOU KNOW WHAT I MEAN?!?!?......

YUP. THAT'S ABOUT IT.

SHE'S 87 →

WHEN I EXPRESSED THESE SENTI- MENTS TO MY ROOMIE, SHE SAID,

IDK DUDE YOU'RE OB- VIOUSLY RIGHT... BUT DON'T FORGET ABOUT THE MULTIVERSE. ALL THAT STUFF YOU'RE MISSING STILL EXISTS SOMEWHERE

SO MAYBE THAT'S WHAT PROUST WAS GETTING AT. INSTEAD OF ATTACHING TO ENVIRONMENTS, WHICH ARE SUBJECT TO CHANGE, WE SHOULD CELEBRATE THE MEMORIES...

... AND TRUST THAT IN OUR HEARTS AND MINDS, AND IN OUR HYSTERICAL FREAKOUTS AND THE DUMB COMICS WE DRAW, AND IN THE MULTIVERSE, THEY WILL CONTINUE TO EXIST.

... AND TRY TO PRESERVE THEM HOWEVER WE CAN... (MY NATURAL INSTINCT AS I LEFT THE HOUSE FOR THE FINAL TIME WAS TO DO THIS:)

OOOOH-KAY, LAST SELFIE IN THE ELEVATOR, YOU GUYS!!

OH FOR HEAVEN'S SAKE, ESMERELDA WHAT DOES THAT EVEN MEAN?!

JUST TAKE IT AND LET'S GO

YOU GUYS WANNA GO GET CHEESE BURGERS OR SOMETHING?

GOODBYE, HOUSE. THANK YOU FOR EVERYTHING. I WILL LOVE YOU FOR EVER.

EMPATHY, IN EXCESS

"Hardening my heart" against my abuser was not only OK, but necessary.
By Jenny

I have lived my whole life swearing there's no truth more complete than Walt Whitman's parenthetical line in the poem "Song of Myself": "I am large, I contain multitudes." I believe we are capable of anything—that anyone can be driven to do extreme harm; that anyone could be moved to radiate extreme love. I believe a person could switch from open-hearted tenderness to cruelty. I believe in nuance. I believe in contradiction. I believe in mistakes, and giving people the space, and the right, to make them.

But I believe in abuse, too. Clear-cut abuse. I believe that sometimes nuance is unhelpful in abusive situations, especially when it involves telling yourself that your abuser can "sometimes be kind and loving," especially when your faith in someone's multitudes keeps you in an abusive relationship instead of getting the hell out. I believe that trying to love some-one who consistently hurts, and erases, and destroys you can turn you into an empty shell of *nothing*. These beliefs have been harder-earned.

"You're an idealist," my best friend said two years ago, after I told him about my growing suspicion that I was in an abusive relationship.

"It's not fair to say I'm the victim and he's the abuser. Sometimes the shit I do to him is straight-up evil. Sometimes I think *he's* the victim and *I'm* the abuser. It's complicated."

"Of course it is," he said. "No victim is 'perfectly innocent' if you dig deep enough into their lives. And it *shouldn't matter*. Victims of abuse shouldn't have to prove

they're perfect angels. Some situations require that you smash your idealism away and—at least for the time being—see things in black and white. No shade. Yeah, in an ideal world, forgiveness is infinite, and so is compassion. Yeah, in an ideal world, we can get into the full contradictions and complexities of someone who is a victim of abuse without it being a way to dismiss and undermine that person. But you can't operate under those ideals right now. He's abusing you and you need to end it and get out. Full stop."

"No," I said. "It's more complicated than that."

"Full end stop," he repeated.

Whenever I was hurt, Scott (not his real name) was *more* hurt. Whenever I was tired, he was *more* tired. If I told him that he was making me sad, or that our relationship wasn't working, or that he perhaps needed help and that that help was beyond what I could provide, he diverted the conversation from whatever I had been saying to one about how much he was suffering. He was frequently at EMERGENCY levels of pain. "I'm really not OK," he would say. "You have no idea what I've been through the past few days," he would say.

He was never OK. He was never not *going through some shit*. He was always on the verge of a physical collapse, whether it was because he hadn't slept in 28 hours, or because he hadn't eaten all day—even though he had an extremely high metab-olism that required him to eat every two or three hours, or else he would become disoriented, weak, and unable to function, and despite being this way his entire life,

he never carried trail mix or nuts or energy bars or any kind of snack with him. And when he was hungry and tired (he was always hungry and tired), he would take it out on me.

His constant distress gave me heart palpitations and omnipresent anxiety, especially whenever we neared the three-hour mark without his having eaten. Since he was so often without food whenever we were together, I began to suspect that he *wanted* me to feel burdened and panicked about his hunger. "Please," I begged him. "Please start carrying around trail mix or nuts or energy bars. I love you, but I need you to try to help yourself."

He promised, but never did. For every unkept promise, there were so many extremely complicated and difficult-to-follow reasons he could not keep them. In the case of why he could not possibly carry around ANY snacks with him EVER, he simply didn't like trail mix and other such energy-giving snacks! He wanted *real* meals, like a burrito or a plate of hot food, or, at the very least, a sandwich, and as he was explaining all this, he looked at me as if he had been persecuted and mistreated his whole life by people who didn't understand that he merely needed six daily hot meals carefully curated for variety, and prepared for him by someone other than himself. Because I was wading eyeballs-deep in the seas of his nonstop mindfuckery, I felt ashamed that I had ever tried to make him feel like a burden and resolved to be a more compassionate girlfriend.

After all, he had been *so devoted* to me in the beginning. He was wildly, declaratively *in love* with me from the moment we met. Within the first 24 hours of our courtship, he was sending texts and emails to his friends about how head-over-heels in love he was for me, how I made him feel like a GOD, how I was the end-all and be-all of ALL. He made little books and posters filled with writing and love letters about what a genius I was, filled with little things I had said that made me feel like he was listening *so intently* to everything I ever said to him. One night, I mentioned summer in New York was hellish without an air conditioner, and a day later, he returned from an eight-hour quest to buy me an air conditioner that led him all the way to Massachusetts and back. He neglected his schoolwork and all of his other responsibilities—financial, social, familial, etc.—for me. It was as if he didn't care about anyone or anything but me, which is, of course, really unhealthy.

At one point, overwhelmed by how quickly things were happening, I asked him how he could possibly love me after only knowing me for a week. And wasn't he sort of in love with someone else a week before he met me? Wasn't that partly the reason he moved to New York, for this other girl? But he insisted that I was just that amazing. That I made him forget about his previous crush. That I crushed all his previous crushes.

Part of why people stay in abusive relationships is because, *in the beginning*, your abuser might be the most devoted, loving, kind, patient, caring person you've ever met. They might make you feel like you are the sun, the moon, and the stars. Mine certainly did, and he did it at a time when I was lonely and vulnerable. Instead of being creeped out by how quickly he became obsessed with me and his aggressive pursuit of me, I was flattered. He found me at a time when I felt like I was nothing and I was no one, and here was someone telling me that I was everything and I was the only one. So I believed him.

I became codependent. I relied on him, even though he was increasingly more and more unreliable. He started subtly blaming me for all his problems—like how he was doing poorly in school because he

had spent all day driving to Massachusetts to buy me the air conditioner I never asked for (and when I asked him why he had to drive to another state to get it when there were plenty of air conditioners within a 10-mile radius of where we lived, he was evasive and distracted). Or like how I was causing him to have bad mental-health flare-ups because he was stressed that I didn't love him as much as he loved me, which, in effect, put pressure on me to commit to him and say "I love you" way before I was ready. He flooded me with gifts and love letters that were cute at first, but became increasingly burdensome: Not only did this leave me with no space to think and be alone, but his "gifts" to me were always fraught with how much time and effort he had to sacrifice to make me happy—even though I never asked for these things, even though I explicitly told him to take care of himself first and to give me some space.

I thought he was going to be my savior, my hero. Instead, he was my parasite. He literally took my words and put them in his own poems. He had few ideas of his own, and instead co-opted mine while convincing me that I couldn't succeed as a poet without him. He bombarded me with constant proclamations of what a genius I was, telling me how his poems were full of "tributes" to me, that he incorporated my words because I was his muse, and these were his love poems…dedicated…*to me*! The more he did this, the less flattered I felt, and the more overwhelmed and terrified I became. I needed space desperately. I needed him to stop telling every single person he met all about me. I needed him to stop publicly proclaiming his love for me.

I finally told him, after several weeks of him ignoring my request to slow things down, that he was suffocating me and I needed space—time and space—away from him, and in response, he banged his head against the wall. "Ow, ow, ow," he said. "It really hurts."

"That's it," I said. "You're scaring me now. I have to go."

"No," he shouted and swung his arm against the bedpost and cried out in pain again.

"I think it's broken," he cried. "I have

to go to the hospital. I need you to drive me to the hospital."

"Your arm is fine," I said. I slammed my own arm against the wall and pointed to it. "Oh, look, I broke my arm, too." I slammed the other arm. "Both my arms are broken, see?"

"It's really broken, Jenny. I'm sorry you hurt your arm, too, but I might actually need a cast."

"Then let's call 911 and have them send an ambulance and the hospital can get you x-rayed."

"Hey," he said, "actually, I think my arm is fine. It's just bruised."

I hung up the phone, but I said I still needed to leave. I wanted to stay at a friend's house nearby to clear my head, be alone, and think things through, which triggered another meltdown that culminated in Scott sobbing, "I'm really not well. I need help. I'm serious, Jenny. I think I'm having a breakdown. I need you to take me to the hospital."

"Fine," I said. "I'll drive us to the hospital." But when we got in the car, I collapsed with my arms wrapped around the steering wheel. "I can't do this," I said. "I will call 911 if you really need to be hospitalized, but I can't be the one to take you."

"It's OK," he said. "I feel good now. I promise. Let me take care of you."

"OK. Thank you," I said, as if he had done me a favor that I should only be so lucky to have been granted.

Incidents like this happened again and again. As the frequency of his emergencies increased, I suggested the possibility of seeking outside help—basically, relying on someone other than me. I suggested he start seeing a therapist regularly. I programmed his parents' numbers into my phone so I could call them when he was headed to a bad, self-harming place. I told him if things got really bad and I didn't feel capable of helping him, I would call 911. But whenever I pulled out my phone to call for help, he immediately changed his tune. Whatever problem he had been using to manipulate and confuse me—instantly cured! He did everything in his power to make sure we were always alone: Isolating me made it easier for him to refute all my memories of what had happened later on, so that I started to think I was actually going crazy. That he was the calm, reasonable one, and I was the psychopath, freaking out over things that never happened, misremembering incidents and flipping the story: that it was really me who was the terrorizer, and him who was terrorized.

"I never said my arm was broken," he claimed in subsequent fights. "You were the one slamming your arm against the chair on purpose. You were the one who said you needed to go to the hospital. You admitted to me that you only said those things to make me feel bad. Remember?"

But the way I remembered it was that as soon as I started dialing 911 on my phone, his broken arm magically healed.

"I've become this weak, pathetic, needy, deluded person," I said to my friends one night, after hiding everything that had been going on for months and months. "I've literally become that girl I used to pity. The one who keeps making excuse after excuse for her shitty boyfriend who isn't even very clever or smart or good at anything, but somehow he's a mastermind at manipulating her and getting her to keep giving him more and more chances to ruin her life."

While I was with Scott, I cut myself off from everyone who cared about me. I stopped seeing my friends and replying to their texts and emails and phone calls. When they asked me how things were going with Scott, I said, "It's complicated. I don't feel like getting into it." Every time I thought I had reached my breaking point, he drew me back in. Every time we discussed breaking up, he threatened suicide, flooding me with texts and emails and voicemails about how he couldn't go on, how I was the only one he could turn to now. Before we started formally dating, I told him that I didn't want to be in a monogamous relationship and would only consider dating someone who accepted that and embraced that and was on the same page—someone who could be open and honest and communicative and unafraid.

"I can be that person," he promised me. "You make me capable of anything."

But somehow, Scott had the uncanny ability to time all of his breakdowns and suicidal thoughts to the exact nights when I had plans to see other people. When I told him that he didn't seem like someone who could deal with being in an open relationship and perhaps it was not such a great idea to keep dating, he became despondent, self-destructive, and suicidal.

So I picked up his calls. I replied to his emails and chats. I didn't sleep for days. I found new white hairs on my head constantly. I frequently woke up in the middle of the night, panicked at the thought that Scott might be emailing and texting me and leaving me voicemails *at that very moment*. I told myself that I had limits, that I had been in relationships before, and I always knew when to get out.

There would be a sign, I told myself. There would be an obvious sign.

Scott knew how to explain away "signs," though. "I'm the king of coincidences," he said to me when we first met. "Really, it's uncanny how many coincidences I'm a part of." Like the time I wouldn't go with him to the bodega around the corner from his house to get a sandwich after an extremely exhausting late-night fight, and when he came back half an hour later shaking and crying, I ignored him, knowing his pattern too well by then. When he saw that I was unmoved by his tears, he broke down in front of me and said, "I was robbed! At knifepoint!"

I took him in my arms. After all, he had nearly died…AGAIN! AT EXACTLY THE MOMENT WHEN I WANTED TO LEAVE HIM!

This mugging was a "coincidence" in another way, too: Scott said that his attacker was the same guy who had tried to steal his phone one month earlier. The same guy who had come up behind Scott at one in the morning when he was on the phone with me while going back and forth between his apartment and the laundromat. We were in the middle of a tense argument when his voice dropped out just as I started to say I needed space to breathe and time alone. When he came back to the phone, he told me that some "big Latino dude" had slapped his phone right out of his

hand. Scott pleaded with the guy to take his money instead, which, incidentally was *my money*, as Scott had, earlier that day, offered to take my clothes to a consignment store and sell them for me.

"I'm sorry I lost your money," he said. "I was just so scared that I wouldn't be able to finish our conversation. I was terrified I wouldn't be able to tell you how much I love you."

I felt so bad for him that I told him to forget about the money, even though it was quite a bit of money, and decided that it wasn't a good time to ask for space, as he was so clearly shaken and in need of comfort. After all…*he did it for me*. He gave away my money so that I wouldn't think he was mad at me and had abruptly hung up on me. *It was because of me.*

Now was not the time, I told myself, *to hold grudges, to be cold, to be concerned with what I needed*, which was to be alone, which was to get the hell out of the relationship.

For the same reasons, I didn't question this second mugging, in which, Scott said, the guy HAD successfully made off with his phone. I had to spring into action. I had to calm him down. I suggested that we get into Scott's car instead of standing exposed on the sidewalk. Once we got into the car, I tried calling Scott's phone as a last-ditch attempt to perhaps negotiate a deal and get it back from the guy who stole it.

As the call was being patched through on my end, I heard the faint sounds of Scott's ringtone from somewhere inside the car.

My immediate reaction: "Oh my god. YOUR ATTACKER IS HIDING IN THE CAR WITH US!"

And then: "Oh. Wait a second…"

And then, Scott: "OK, don't be mad, but…I lied."

It turned out he had stashed his phone in the trunk of his car and was planning on lying to his parents about the stolen phone and having them wire him 700 dollars to buy a new one. Instead of using it to buy a phone, he would use that money on me to win me back. He ALSO admitted he wanted me to see how wrong it was for me to not have accompanied him to the store. That it was dangerous out there, that I was wrong to be so stubborn, that I could have gotten hurt, that he could have gotten hurt, that I should have gone with him instead of sitting alone on his stoop.

If, at this point, you are wondering why I didn't break up with him then and there, I'm wondering the same thing. I think I was in shock. I think I couldn't even process how supremely fucked up this was, and worst of all, that this was no more fucked up than anything else he ever did to me, only this time he got caught.

"I'm not mad," I said. "Don't worry. I'm just glad you weren't hurt."

My friends told me I had to GET OUT and never look back. I wanted to so badly. I agreed with everything they said, but I couldn't act on it.

Instead, I reported everything my friends advised me to do back to Scott.

"Everyone tells me you're toxic for me and we shouldn't be together."

"My friends tell me the same thing about you," he said.

"I think you are mentally unwell and need to get professional help."

"We're both mentally ill. I'd like for us to help each other, but I don't know if that's possible anymore."

"You're abusive to me, and I won't take it anymore."

"You're abusive to me, and you've even admitted so, and my friends think I'm crazy to even continue to speak to you."

His fragility was his weapon. His helplessness was his weapon. His attempts to mirror whatever I said about him back onto me were his weapons, and all of it worked. When he told me that I was abusive, I took it to heart. When he told me all his friends thought I was cruel to him, I agonized over it for weeks and weeks.

After all, I was no angel. I've hurt so many people in my life. I've been unforgivably, disgustingly selfish. I've been cruel. I've been manipulative. I've used my own pain to guilt someone into staying with me or feeling sorry for me or capitulating to me. I was no angel. Not even close. How could I say I was victimized when I was capable of behaving monstrously, too?

When I told Scott about my fears that I was not a good person, he seized on them. Later, he used what I told him in a moment of vulnerability and openness against me: When I tried to tell him that he was being cruel to me, he responded, "But you yourself have said that you have a history of being abusive to others. You yourself said you have acted in deplorable ways."

Later, much, much, much later, maybe even as later as this very moment that I am writing this essay and reprocessing all these memories, I noticed something. I noticed that whenever I was being hard on myself, whenever I was being unsparing and unforgiving of my flaws, my mistakes, whenever I started talking about my fears that I was letting myself off too easily, he sort of listened with a distracted look in his eyes, but what he never, ever did was reciprocate with similar candor and self-reflection. He seemed unwilling to list his own flaws, to look deeply at the ugly parts of himself. In almost everything he ever told me about himself—he was the victim. The hapless center of all these coincidences. He was always innocent.

When I was in sixth grade, I read the original Hans Christian Andersen version of "The Little Mermaid"—the one that doesn't end happily ever after. The one where the little mermaid gives up her entire life and family and everything she's ever known to be a human woman to try to win the love of a shipwrecked prince she saved. She goes to a sea witch, who tells the little mermaid that if she really wants to be a human woman, then she must cut off her tongue, become mute in exchange for human legs, and endure the stabbing pain of sharp swords with every step she takes. As if that isn't enough, once the little mermaid becomes a mortal human woman, she can never go back to being a mermaid. She can never see her family and loved ones ever again. *On top of all that*, if the prince she loves so much does not love her back and marries someone else, then the little mermaid would die and become sea foam. So, naturally, the little mermaid takes the offer and goes up to the human world, mute and stabbed. She's taken in by

the prince, who, frankly, seems as dumb as a bag of bricks. He does not realize that she's the one who saved him, and treats her like a little sister.

"She's the ultimate abused woman," I theorized to my friends in college. "She lets the prince treat her like she's just a funny object. She watches the person who she is literally dying to be loved by love and court someone else, and treat her like an afterthought. She cuts ties with her family to be with someone who doesn't even know her. Her sisters cut off their beautiful mermaid hair and barter it with the witch to try to save the little mermaid from turning into foam. The sisters tell the little mermaid that if she stabs the prince and his bride-to-be before sunrise, then she can go back to the sea and reunite with her mermaid family. But she is so deeply inside the abuse at this point, so isolated and alienated from her loved ones, that she would rather die herself than hurt the man who has never done anything for her except cause her anguish and pain. As the sun is about to come up, the little mermaid stands over the prince and his bride-to-be with a dagger in her hand, but she can't do it. He's too innocent. He doesn't deserve it."

After our relationship ended, I thought the noble, virtuous thing to do was to keep a vow of silence (lest someone accuse me of being a drama-stirring, shit-talking, spurned ex-girlfriend) and not out him as an abuser, or humiliate him, or shame him publicly. I felt that I was being a good person by extending empathy to him. I wanted to think of him as helpless rather than malicious. Mentally ill and untreated, rather than intentionally, calculatingly unkind and cruel. This way of thinking also helped me to see myself as less of a victim and more of a magnanimous soul capable of loving and forgiving anyone—as someone who saw the world with way too much nuance to ever think of another person as a monster.

After all, you can't be a victim if you're a bitch sometimes. You can't be a victim if you're a brat sometimes. You can't be a victim if you're selfish sometimes. You can't be a victim if you are a bully sometimes. You can't be a victim if you are conniving sometimes. You can't be a victim if you are calculating sometimes. But the truth is you can be anything, you can be worse than all of those things, and still be a victim who deserved better.

I couldn't be a victim because I didn't want to see myself that way. Because I wanted to see myself as too smart and too strong and too capable and too *good* to be a victim. But to be free from him, I *had* to think of him as a monster—the minute I started feeling sorry for him and making excuses for him, trying to see his side of things, was when I would become susceptible to his manipulations again.

Our relationship ended in stages, and in the most predictable way—over an argument about racism. Scott was a self-professed progressive when it came to issues of feminism and racial justice. He said that, unlike his ex-girlfriends, I had the right ideas about patriarchy and racism, ideas that closely aligned with his own. ("Thanks, man!" I should have said. "I'm glad my views on racism and feminism are almost as good as yours.") When I finally summoned up the courage to be vulnerable enough to open up to him about my experiences with racism and misogyny in the poetry community, he became furious and defensive.

"Are you calling me a racist?" he said, even though I hadn't called him anything, and was only talking about myself and my life and my trauma. Once he invoked the dreaded concept of white fragility,* which always manages to trump black and brown pain, the conversation was over. He wasn't interested in hearing about my experiences with racism. He was interested in talking about how despicable it was that I could even imply that he was anything but 100 percent NOT A RACIST.

---

*A concept defined by the scholar Robin DiAngelo in *The International Journal of Critical Pedagogy* Volume 3, No. 3 (2011) as "a state in which even a minimum amount of racial stress becomes intolerable, triggering a range of defensive moves. These moves include the outward display of emotions such as anger, fear, and guilt, and behaviors such as argumentation, silence, and leaving the stress-inducing situation."

Two weeks later, even though we hadn't officially broken up, he was in love with another girl, someone whom, he said, "I could see marrying one day." He had depleted me as a resource and moved on swiftly. When that relationship ended, he moved on to another person, and then another. That was when I realized that my silence wasn't noble or virtuous, and my feeling sorry for him and worrying about him, even after I decided he was an abuser, only enabled him to target other girls and do to them what he did to me, and that made me sick.

After we broke up, I lurked in online forums for people who were getting out of similar emotionally abusive relationships. I read a lot of posts that were something to the extent of: You have to harden your heart. Even if he says he is going to commit suicide. EVEN IF HE COMMITS SUICIDE, you can't look back and blame yourself for any of it. The only way someone like that can change is if they hit rock bottom, run out of resources, and realize no one will enable them anymore. When they reach that point, they will either end their lives or finally seek help.

I remember crying at my computer, thinking, *So who is supposed to love someone like that? Doesn't that kind of thinking imply that there are some people who can't or shouldn't be loved? Are we supposed to abandon them? And how can I accept a world where that is true?*

The thing about getting out of an emotionally abusive relationship that does not leave any physical traces is that it feels like it should be no big deal. That it's wrong to compare the trauma of emotional abuse to the trauma of physical abuse. That it's downright insulting to suggest what I went through is at all comparable to what survivors of physical partner violence have experienced. But it's all connected. Emotional violence may occur with a physical component, but physical violence never exists without an emotional component. For a while, I became obsessed with Nicole Brown Simpson, the murdered wife of O.J. Simpson. I read the letter she wrote to him, which was released during his trial, over and over (it is, of course, really heart-

breaking and maybe triggering to read—please don't continue if you think it'll be hurtful to you). Other than the constant violence he inflicted on her, what disturbed me the most was how she still seemed to be struggling to see things from his perspective, to offer him compassion, even though he treated her like she was less than human. At one point, after describing the time she genuinely feared for her life, she writes:

> I just don't see how our stories compare—I was so bad because I wore sweats & left shoes around & didn't keep a perfect house or comb my hair the way you liked it—or had dinner ready at the precise moment you walked through the door or that I just plain got on your nerves sometimes.
>
> I just don't see how that compares to infidelity, wife beating, verbal abuse—I just don't think everybody goes through this....

The uncertainty in her tone when she says, "I just don't think everybody goes through this" scared me because I recognized that tone. That was the tone of the voice in my head that kept saying, "I don't think this is normal, but what if it is?"

Last year, when TMZ revealed a video of the football player Ray Rice punching his now-wife, Janay Palmer Rice, in the elevator of an Atlantic City hotel and then dragging her unconscious body out to the lobby, I had to step away from social media, knowing that in the aftermath of something so bleak, so obviously clear-cut, there would be many who would rationalize and excuse the actions of a man caught on videotape punching his wife, that there would be many who would spend more time interrogating the abused wife for going back to her husband than they would interrogating a culture that does not unilaterally condemn violence against women and survivors of domestic abuse.

In an interview with Matt Lauer on the *Today* show in December 2014, Janay tearfully describes how her husband was *terrified* after he knocked her unconscious. "I asked him after I saw [the elevator video],

'Why did you just leave me there like that?' He said he was terrified. He was in such shock that this had just happened and he didn't know how to function at that point. And then, you know, obviously by that time hotel security is there, the police are there."

I can't pretend to know what kind of tears she was shedding, but I suspected a part of her was shedding tears for Ray, for what he had to go through. How the 200-pound guy who punched his not-200-pound partner was the terrified one. I thought about Nicole Simpson writing to O.J. that even though he beat her so badly, she was sorry for not wanting to go on many trips after they married. I thought about all the times a guy has derailed a conversation about rape and sexual assault against women by talking about how *offended* and *hurt* he was by the suggestion that all men are rapists. I thought of all the times a conversation initiated by a person of color about racism is derailed by white tears and white fragility, derailed by a white person talking about how hard it was for them to have to endure being called racist, instead of how hard it was for the person of color to endure racism.

I know this seems like a stretch. I'm not making a clean one-to-one comparison, but I *am* trying to connect some dots. I'm trying to think through the world we are in. I know there are many who will be offended by what I'm suggesting. But think about it…the kind of person who tells a broken, traumatized person, "Do you even know how hard things are for me?" is absolutely connected to the kind of person who interrupts a person of color recounting their experience of racism to say, "Are you calling me a racist?" And then, there are those people who don't even have to say anything at all, because they are so powerful, and so used to abusing others, so ensconced in their privilege, that their feelings, their well-being, and their needs automatically matter more than the people they have erased and overtaken.

My heart goes out to anyone who has protected, made excuses for, or genuinely loved their abuser. I was that person, and I don't want to be ever again. I also don't fault anyone who doesn't want to see themselves as a victim, who doesn't want to see their abuser as an abuser, and who wants to believe in a world where every single person is deserving of love, compassion, and forgiveness. Because I *still* believe in the largeness of every individual! I believe in the capacity to change. I believe in forgiveness and redemption. But after my experience with Scott, I believe in limits, too. Sometimes, to save yourself, you have to save your multitudes. ☙

Dueling Duets
BY ESTELLE

1. LOVE ME HARDER
   Ariana Grande and the Weeknd

2. DON'T GO BREAKING MY HEART
   Elton John and Kiki Dee

3. YOU'RE THE ONE THAT I WANT
   Olivia Newton John and John Travolta

4. JACKSON
   Johnny Cash and June Carter Cash

5. JUST GIVE ME A REASON
   Pink feat. Nate Ruess

6. WHERE THE WILD ROSES GROW
   Nick Cave and the Bad Seeds feat. Kylie Minogue

7. WHAT ABOUT THE BABY
   Wyclef Jean feat. Mary J. Blige

8. THIS MESS WE'RE IN
   PJ Harvey feat. Thom Yorke

Field *Day*

We make the flowers grow.
By Amanda Leigh Smith

Styling and modeling by Bridget Donegan.
Hair and makeup by Clarity Mettler. Clothing provided by Milk Money.

EYES ON ME

Sometimes I like attention from strangers.
By Naomi. Illustration by Beth.

I wasn't used to getting attention as a teenager. I was mostly stuck in my head, where it was hard to decipher what was reality and what wasn't: I spent as much time composing scenarios using my imagination as I did having actual interactions. Long solitary walks were my main exposure to the outside world. I felt quite plain, without much of an identity except through the books I read. I felt more of a connection with them than people.

When I began to mature and look like a woman rather than a child, men started to glance when I walked to and from park benches. Depending on my mood, this reaction to my appearance could frustrate or delight me. I couldn't predict how it would make me feel, whether I'd be ready for it. How was it possible to enjoy something and dread it so simultaneously? I felt partly uncomfortable with this newfound attention, especially if the men were significantly older, or when they spoke to me, and partly that I finally had confirmation of my existence. It added to my sense of *being*: feeling I had a physical presence rather than being some kind of detached spirit, floating within the confines of my room. Being physically noticed was a break from my mind.

I encountered a piece by the artist Barbara Kruger around my loner-time: a black-and-white stone profile of a woman bordered by red, with the words "Your gaze hits the side of my face" emblazoned down one side. I interpreted it to mean the physical feeling you get when you are conscious of someone looking at you. I had an investment in romance: A lot of my daydreaming had to do with another human loving me in a way they wouldn't love anyone else. I thought that what I was searching for, ultimately, was the romantic gaze. I printed out the Barbara Kruger quote and stuck it on my wall because I thought it represented that kind of ultimate affection, like in *Before Sunrise*, when Julie Delpy's character, Celine, says, "I like to feel his eyes on me when I look away."

I was desperate to be noticed. It seemed like such a romantic gesture—to turn someone looking at you into a physical manifestation of interest, admiration, or longing. The times I tallied a guy from the boys' school across the road lingering over my appearance held significance for me—the possibility of the unknown, the romance I hadn't experienced yet. When the majority of the time you feel lonely, being noticed can be just a *Someone is looking at me…wow* feeling. It made me spark with excitement, but it never lasted long enough to pacify me completely—so I reached for that feeling again and again, and went for more and more walks.

It wasn't until I was older that I realized my favorite Kruger piece could be interpreted a very different way. I decided it was more likely that it expressed the violation and violence that women are subjected to as objects of the male gaze. The male gaze is perpetuated throughout culture and assumes all consumers are straight men who want to be able to look at the female body in a mostly sexual way, making her an object rather than a fellow human being. An object has no feelings or emotions, which makes looking a supposedly harmless or guiltless activity. Laura Mulvey wrote about how film often displays the woman as a sexual object in the 1975 essay "Visual Pleasure and Narrative Cinema," enabling the male gaze to "[project] its phantasy on to the female figure." This made total sense to me and explained the odd feeling I had when I was glued to the music channel as a young girl and noticed that, sometimes, the men were fully clothed and singing, whereas the women were lesser-clothed background decoration. But it couldn't be all bad if the women chose to be there, right?

In John Berger's *Ways of Seeing*, published in 1972, he examines the tradition of objectifying women in European art. What is most striking about this history is the sheer number of nude women, painted solely for men's pleasure:

> Men look at women. Women watch themselves being looked at. This determines not only most relations between men and women but also the relation of women to themselves. […] She turns herself into an object—and most particularly an object of vision: a sight.

In some ways, women were painted so they could be owned. Before the internet or magazines, the paintings were framed and hung on the walls of nobility as a highbrow form of porn. These nude women were silent and immovable, formed into being by the eyes of men. But could anyone criticize this objectification if it was expressed in such pretty, flattering artistic depictions? Like a so-called compliment on the street that some men say we should be grateful for, when the intentions behind street harassment are usually to intimidate.

I don't have much control over being seen, only how I am seen. Even if I don't have the will or energy to do anything to my appearance, and just roll out of bed, I am aware that I may still be looked at. I have experienced both sides: being unnoticeable versus being "an object of vision: a sight"—I experience it still now, going to buy milk in my PJs versus making an effort. Neither side is particularly enviable: You are either ignored or painted into a perfect fallacy.

But, sometimes, I don't find admiration from strangers intimidating or intrusive. It is possible, I believe, to be admired without being objectified. The unspoken chemistry with a person my age, sitting across from me on the train, the sneaky glances and the sense that you both know that you are both intrigued is perfectly acceptable, consensual, and exciting. But in a world so static with the consequences of men holding power over women in almost every situation, it can be such a fine line. I have so often experienced some sort of male-led interaction in the street and laughed at it, wondering with my friends later, "Was that OK?" Once, on a cold walk home from my friend's in the dark, there were a couple of guys heading away from a pub, and one began to pee on a wall. I smirked as I walked past and he said, "Sorry! You would be able to see it if it wasn't so cold," and then waved goodbye as he crossed the road. I laughed. But later I wondered again, "Was that OK?" When does a compliment become harassment and when does being noticed become dangerous? There are no explicit rules to what is acceptable. That I laughed in this instance, that I didn't feel threatened, makes it seem all right, but another person could have felt deeply uncomfortable.

As validating as it felt to receive more attention, it wasn't as romantic as I'd hoped—sometimes, I *did* feel threatened. I became a talking object to men who felt like they had a right to my body—to grab my waist in a club or force me into a hug. Once while jogging along the canal path, I was shocked by a slap on my leggings-clad arse by boys cycling past. I fought the raging desire to throw their pathetic little bikes in the water, and walked home completely dejected. There was an imbalance between me and any male who dared to wolf-whistle. It felt menacing: I knew the physical strength of many men as compared with mine would make it hard to fight if I needed to (although this is obviously not the case for all girls, who are capable of being as strong as, if not stronger than, guys). This part of our cultural consciousness makes me writhe with anger: It's 2015, and men still act like women owe them attention, a response, or even ownership of their body.

The way I view my body and persona fluctuates depending on my mood. Sometimes I see it as a collection of mechanical functions, making sure I breathe, my heart beats, I digest my food and produce antibodies. Sometimes I view it as a collection of body parts only: my sizable breasts, skinny hips, and long limbs. Sometimes I love to watch myself, and so I don't mind if others enjoy it, too. If I am in the mood to be looked at and no one complies, I get annoyed. But I also want to be seen as an autonomous being, someone with a sizable intellect, with passions and pleasures. If I am just being passed on the street, it's pretty much impossible to dwell on my internal life. So a glance is sufficient; a glance can make me feel powerful. But "to feel his eyes on me when I look away" isn't what I look to for fulfillment anymore—I want the way I look not to be all there is, but to signify what lies beneath. ★

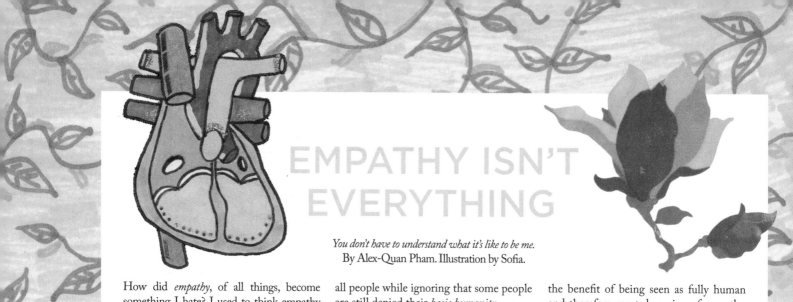

EMPATHY ISN'T EVERYTHING

You don't have to understand what it's like to be me.
By Alex-Quan Pham. Illustration by Sofia.

How did *empathy*, of all things, become something I hate? I used to think empathy was the all-purpose cleaner for social ills. I thought that if I could just muster up enough compassion and care for others, I could solve any conflict. Empathy was first defined for me in class, where teachers brought it up as a way to resolve disputes between students. I was supposed to use empathy not only to understand my classmates, but also to connect with the overwhelmingly white protagonists in the novels I'd been assigned to read at home. Empathy seemed like the easy fix: If we could understand one another, conflict wouldn't exist and oppression would evaporate.

Over the past few months, I've had empathy thrown at me on social media and in offline conversations, not as an extended hand of love but as a silencing tactic. I've heard a billion variations of the same tired message: I'll make my case against a straight cis white man with toxic opinions about trans people, and the people watching the conversation unfold will tell me, "Maybe he was just brought up this way, you really can't blame him." Why can't I understand that white men are only human? That they are flawed, like all people, and that they deserve patience and kindness? Why can't I give him some of that universal empathy—everyone deserves empathy, right?

In an ideal world, everyone would have equal access to empathy, but empathy, like equality, is one of those utopian values that operate within systems that reward some people at the expense of others. We can't talk about empathy without talking about how systems of oppression influence who gets empathy and who doesn't. And we can't demand that empathy be given to

all people while ignoring that some people are still denied their *basic humanity*.

The world works in ways that make it much easier for white people to receive praise, mercy, and other forms of generosity. This shows up in the ways that white people (and non-black people of color who sometimes have access to white resources) have their freedom spared and their humanity preserved, even when they commit terrible crimes. Crimes committed by white people are seen as isolated incidents, despite the fact that white people make up most of the leadership of corporations that commit large-scale violence on marginalized communities[1] through environmental pollution[2], imprisonment[3], and outright murder[4]. The majority of school shootings are perpetrated by white men[5], but we have yet to see white communities being policed as if whiteness is criminal by default. When white or white-passing people commit terrible crimes, they are treated with empathy by mainstream media, which searches for reasons to "understand" what went wrong with the shooter as a kid. Proximity to whiteness, and other privileged identities, means access to empathy, even when you've committed the most heinous acts of violence.

The emotional lives of white people, whether expressed through music, film, or otherwise, are treated gently and polished often. White people have, in other words,

1. *Fortune*, "Microsoft's new CEO: One Minority in a Sea of White," February 2014.
2. *The Guardian*, "Call Climate Change What It Is: Violence," April 2014.
3. *Fusion*, "Shadow Prisons," February 2015.
4. Lisa Bloom, *Suspicion Nation*, 2014.
5. *Political Research*, "Mass Shooters Have a Gender and a Race," June 2014.

the benefit of being seen as fully human and therefore most deserving of empathy. I still cannot forget how angry I was after seeing international leaders march hand in hand after the *Charlie Hebdo* shooting when there was not nearly the same performance of support and solidarity during the #BlackLivesMatter movement. This was the most glaring example of why #BlackLivesMatter was necessary and how the humanity of black people was being deliberately denied. And when I posted a comment about this on social media, a white man scorned me for not having enough empathy for those slain in France.

For those living in the margins, empathy arrives—in crumbs—only when someone finds a way to attach a marginal issue to privileged people. To make feminism appeal to men, women call themselves "sisters, daughters, mothers, and aunts" of men, rather than people who are under attack by patriarchy. They are forced to ask, "What if she was your mother?" rather than "Why can't you see her as her own person and acknowledge her pain on her own terms?" The women, and their experiences, become an afterthought. Their voices are only heard when they can prove that feminism will help men, too. They are displaced from the center of their own fight.

The same goes for representation in films. Marginal narratives like those of trans people are stolen and glued to Jared Leto in *Dallas Buyers Club* or Eddie Redmayne in the upcoming *The Danish Girl*. Our pain draws empathy only when people can avoid confronting our bodies and seeing us for everything we are. We only appeal to audiences when we fit the script of helpless trans people needing to be saved or when our narratives are plastered on an actor *deemed more human*. We are forced to cater to "relatability" because if the privileged can't relate to us, we may as well not exist at all. Our pain draws empathy when we are disembodied and made invisible.

As a brown-skinned, queer, and trans Asian millennial, I find empathy is often out of my reach. When I voice concerns about being a person of color at a predominantly white college, white students criticize my tone instead of addressing my concern. When I demand that trans roles in movies be given to trans people, I am dismissed as asking for too much.

I used to blame myself when people neglected to give me the empathy they offered others. I thought that maybe it *was* my tone, or that I was too assertive, or that it was just me. But as my support system of people of color grew, I learned to recognize my worth. I understood how growing up in a culture where white people were the only people I saw being celebrated, where straight people were the only possible role models, and where trans people were topics of discussion only as corpses rather than as people, had made me so used to being erased. Without even realizing it, I prioritized others with more privilege than me, and began to erase myself, too. I would sweat to make myself as physically small as possible in public spaces, so that others could expand and fill the world with their presence. I'd become quiet in political spaces, out of habit, to let them voice all of their biases without pushback. I had become used to my ideas and experiences being painted as invalid, imaginary, hysterical, and exaggerated.

My community of people of color showed me that if I mirrored the lack of empathy with which society treated me, I would continue to hurt myself, and talk about myself with more hatred than love. It has taken me 19 years of life to realize that I *do* deserve respect, that I *do* get to narrate my life and my body and my history. I learned to take care of myself. But the burden should not be on me to shift my thinking; it is the responsibility of those with more power—on this uneven playing field—to call for an empathy that falls in line with justice.

I don't want to know if you can understand what it's like to be me. I want to know that you will give me the due respect despite your inability to understand.

If you can only empathize with me when I fit a prepackaged narrative about queer and trans people of color, or when my narrative is filtered through a white male body, please keep your empathy away from me.

My presence is enough. My body is enough. My voice is enough. ♥

HOW TO STRUCTURE YOUR DAYS IF YOU'RE DEPRESSED

Or even if you just need a little order.
By Ragini

My daily structure—waking up early, showering, attending school—came undone with my mother's death and my subsequent free fall into depression. I lived in several apartments, all of which devolved into health hazards at alarming speed. My ex named my toenails "dragon claws," and my fiancé christened them talons the first time we met. I went for a good seven years without brushing my teeth. (That's one of the things we don't speak of.) But everyone loves a good turnaround story, right? Fast-forward to now, and I still surprise myself with my spotless apartment (and teeth), marveling at my general togetherness. How I came to be this person is a long story riddled with mental illness, apathy, and the occasional intestinal parasite—this, however, is not that story. This is a guide to how YOU can coax yourself out of formlessness and put together a routine.

For most people, a routine comes prepackaged with family, school, and work, living as part of that larger machine that runs them through the day in efficient harmony across time zones and cultures. This guide has ideas for those who slip the cogs for more reasons than I can list: dysfunctional families, psychological difficulties, or simply a need to function without the clutter and clamor of constant social navigation. Sometimes, an isolated life isn't just a comfort—it's a necessity. But the finest strength of isolation is also its greatest drawback: the rolling vistas of empty time you're saddled with. Since we're so used to having that time structured for us, doing away with the rigging can plunge you into a free-falling free-for-all. Bedtime becomes a distant memory, meals are potato chips and convenience-store sandwiches, work is the hillock of books you don't even have to try and ignore anymore…in fact, hillocks are everywhere you look: hillocks of laundry, dishes, candy wrappers, and that unscalable mountain of apathy under whose shadows you lie, day upon day. But you can start somewhere, even if you feel that everything is fucked and there's no hope left, you can start with that desolation and *still* get better.

Cherish your isolation: It has given you the space to survive. It is in that space that you'll craft your life. I was in my final year of high school when I dropped out and realized that none of my friends had time for me unless I was there to match my steps with theirs. I floundered in their slipstream for most of my 20s before accepting that I had to unmake that world, and make a life for myself. Because that's what you do, whether you're homeschooled, chronically sick, or just prefer solitude: You make a life for *yourself*.

~ * ~ * ~

Here's where you might be right now. You *really* have work to do, but you'd just rather…not. Mornings feel like such dead ends, productivity-wise, that they start unraveling the day from under you until evening takes you unawares. Reuse and repeat the next day, and before you know it, a week, a month, a decade is gone. Well, here's what's amazing about the human mind: Once you've managed to get a routine chugging along, it will run on autopilot if you just provide the spark.

Structuring your life is like exercising a little-used muscle: You can't expect it to function at full potential from day one. That, I feel, is the biggest mistake people make when they try to create a routine, or the one I made, at the very least. Armed with visions of turning over a new leaf, a brand-new improved Ragini 2.0, I'd overwhelm myself with a barrage of tasks from the get-go and run out of steam shortly afterward. It took me a very long time to understand that it's simply not possible to wake up one morning with a fully kitted-out to-do list and have it all ticked off by the end of the day. Think of running, or playing an instrument, or horseback riding—any skill that requires practice to develop. You wouldn't walk in through the doors and expect to ace a marathon, have a platinum album, or be a world-renowned jockey, would you? If we don't place such absurd expectations on our bodies, why burden our minds that way? I like to think of building a routine as a juggler's performance. The act begins with a single object tossed in the air, and then another, and one more till there's a full set of pieces up in the air in an expert dance of unhurried motion. That's what a routine is. And that's what you're aiming for.

Begin by charting out things that you actually enjoy doing. Not as a list, if you don't feel up to it: Just run them over in your mind and pick one. Be it reading, writing, video games, sports, art, crafts—

spend a tiny bit of time on your Thing every day. This is actually the hardest step if you're struggling with your mental health, because it can be so difficult to remember anything being enjoyable. Try to think of something you used to enjoy, something you might objectively, remotely remember enjoying, and schedule five minutes for it every day. Just five minutes till you can slip out of wakefulness and back into bed again, and you'll end the day knowing that you accomplished A Thing. That's a good feeling. Once you find yourself devoting time to your one enjoyable activity with fair regularity, take it up a bit. Add five more minutes. Add 15. Then add another enjoyable thing. Work up to your routine instead of letting it work you to exhaustion and defeat.

My day starts with making the bed, and I've discovered that if I can complete this one task, the rest follow with barely a complaint. This is the principle of Might As Well. I made the bed, so might as well do the dishes, and shower, and take some blog photos, and get back to that bit of writing. Might As Well is the queen of forces: Never underestimate its power, for it is singular in its capacity to motivate while maintaining the lowest of low-key profiles—you get stuff done practically without noticing. You got out of bed, so you might as well have a productive day.

Micromanagement can lend Might As Well an entire helping arm. Breaking things down is useful not just because it creates tiny units to deal with at a time—it also gives your brain a recognizable pattern it can step into unthinkingly. Any thinking you save on is energy saved, which potentially leads to that pinnacle of efficiency: multi-tasking.

Let us take a moment to consider my dishes. If I sound a tad obsessed with my dishes, it is merely because my understanding of micromanagement began with them. For the longest time, dishes stayed in the sink, wherefrom they were unearthed at times of great need. They were a tower of intimidation and filth I dared not rouse. Except, one day, I realized I could break that tower down to cutlery, plates, and pans, and I haven't been scared of them

since. I can do dishes in my sleep now because my hands have a body memory of them. My hands take over the housework, unassisted by my mind, which is then free tosolder this piece into being, for instance!

Since we're on the theme of housework: A messy and cluttered environment is a difficult place to breed positivity and motivation, and junk has a way of multiplying almost overnight. If you're starting off with a room, apartment, or house that needs "unfucking," the website Unfuck Your Habitat is an invaluable resource that breaks down every step of the process to digestible bits.

Break down everything you can. Vanquish the dragons by reducing them to a sheepish lot of puppeteers in a painted canvas skin. Break down your coursework, your study schedule, your exam prep, your self-care. Break down emails, cleaning, socializing, unopened bills. Break down essays and term papers most of all because nothing works as well as having your sections in place before you fill them in. I was one of those people who'd tackle papers the night before the deadline in one panicked rush and later come down with the flu in exhaustion. A lack of confidence in my academic ability contributed a great deal to this, but it was also the idea of a gargantuan block of text I was somehow expected to author. And then came my master's dissertation: a 20,000-word monsterpiece I had to submit for my degree. I spent a good few supervisor meetings moaning to my professor how it could never be done before she put me under strict instructions to take on a single section of a single chapter at a time and submit the finished work before going on to the next. I started taking notes while I was reading, eventually on my phone because sitting at the laptop was significantly more mental strain than I could handle. *All you have to do is read*, I told myself, *read and take notes*. It was the barest minimum, and its magic was that I'd have the bones of my chapter neatly laid out by the time I'd done my reading. Collating and editing and the actual grunt work of writing was ever so painless after that because I always had my structure to look to—even in my worst bouts of anxiety, that structure of notes steadfastly propped me up. I ended up getting my degree, contrary to all expectations, most of all mine. So scribble, jot, highlight, and transcribe with a vengeance for your coursework and papers; it's the best advice I've received in my five years of academic training. Even though I came late to it, good advice is like Easy Cheese—it never spoils.

What with the process of tricking your hindbrain through repetitive micromanagement while you scramble for the wherewithal to keep up, forming a routine isn't easy. The tedium of doing chores may hit you when you least expect it, slump days will follow, and then you'll find yourself in a low-level fugue wondering why. Why are you taking this on when you could just melt, flee, or disappear, a memory soon forgotten?

Being functional is an excellent motivation, but it isn't *aspirational* in the sense of glamour or prestige. And without aspiration, without dreams decked out in all their ridiculous pomp, the fugue beckons toward a vegetative stillness. There's a reason aspiration sells the way it does, despite our collective agreement that it's all smoke and mirrors anyway. Aspiration fuels our dreams, and dreams, even the least practical of the lot, pull you out of the fugue. You know the secret ambition you keep squirreled away and only scrape the dust off to examine and adore when no one's watching? Make that your motivation, because it's precious to you. It will seem laughably far off at first, and ridiculous for the longest time after that, but when you make that impossible dream your motivation, you begin to navigate the ponderous trail toward it. I grew up in a dysfunctional family so my dreams were always of home and love, yet I felt singularly ill equipped for them. How could I possibly care for another when I couldn't even look after myself, a blundering, crashing, and particularly grimy Wile E. Coyote of hygiene? I started small, with a daily shower at first, and then aided by micromanagement and Might As Well, went on to housework, social contact, blogging, learning a language, and, finally, writing. I looked inward to the microcosm as, unbeknownst to my faculties, it transformed into a reflection of the universe

I'd only hoped for. I didn't even realize as the changes stacked up and slotted in that the maps they plotted marked my dream of a home, family, and farm. I was just trying to be functional as I gazed at that distant constellation every night, and frankly, I'm still astonished.

After all that musing on the nature of aspiration, it's a bit anticlimactic to have to come crashing down to the packed earth of time and energy management again, but these are the foundations that build up to our stars. A routine is of no use if it can't help you efficiently manage your time and energy, and since your energy levels will vary based on their inscrutable whims, your routine has to be flexible to your limitations and needs: All days aren't made the same. Some days, you might feel full of energy. On others, it could be a serious task to drag yourself out of bed. I always make the most of my high-energy days by fitting in more tasks than usual so that I'm not lost in a sea of deadlines and emails when I crash later on.

It's crucially important to not be hard on yourself, even, or especially when, you can't accomplish what you'd set out to do, or anything at all. If you, like me, have low self-esteem, beating yourself up is the most immediate response to failure. It's because of how your brain is wired, as any therapist would tell you: Self-flagellation has literally been wired into your neural pathways, and deliberately reminding yourself of this is the first step toward ceasing that internal violence. Rewiring brains is a long process, as is finding trust in yourself. I still beat myself up terribly, but I also try to give myself a chance to disprove that cruel voice inside. There's only one me, and the one me just has one life. If I don't give myself a chance to fix things, who will?

It might sound aphoristic to say that "tomorrow is another day," but it's the one motto that convinces me that I'm not a lost cause when I'm buried under the covers in yesterday's pajamas with takeout. Remind yourself that this structure you're trying to create is absolutely novel to your brain and body, and that time and practice are key to developing any skill.

When I see things going well, I tend

to pile on too much at once and then crash. Moving backward a bit is helpful because it puts my brain back in a place it's familiar and comfortable with, and then I can think of moving forward again. I don't handle change very well; most people with anxiety don't. The idea is to introduce everything gradually and take time familiarizing yourself with them. If you find that you're skipping out on your goals several days in a row, take things down a notch. Go back to an earlier version of your routine that was easier to handle. I'm going to use a cringeworthy metaphor here, but you know how your computer tries to do a system reboot after a disk failure? That's exactly what you do after a routine failure.

A routine isn't a set of commandments that you have to follow to the letter or be damned to perdition, so don't be afraid of switching things up every so often. You might discover better systems of organization, find that you tend to work better in short bursts than longer stretches, or realize that your concentration is at peak levels in the middle of the night because background noise really gets to you. Remember the juggler who can juggle any number of things any which way because they are practiced, sure, and confident that they will not fail. Eventually, your routine will have a core set of tasks that won't need any fine-tuning. Use those tasks as your anchor and launch yourself into newer, stranger, more exciting things: a new skill, unexplored branches of knowledge, fascinating new people! Your boring chores will be your safe space by then, the space where you sit back, dig your heels in, and unpick all the sights and sounds of the world as your autopilot quietly whirs on. And that, to me at least, is the greatest comfort.

A bit of patience and some kindness toward, and trust in yourself go very far in sketching the bones of a structure you can fill in, embellish, upcycle, and renew until your routine reaches beyond the everyday and holds you up to face your dreams. If your dreams exist to give you a purpose, your daily routine is a microcosm of that purpose. And there is nothing quotidian about that. ♕

Dear Zayn

We just want to say thank you.
By Brodie, Tewsdey Erickson-Million, James Lyons, D'Arcy Carden, Syar S. Alia, Ruchi Gupta. Illustration by Leanna.

Zayn FREAKING Malik,

Thank you so much for the nearly five years you spent in One Direction. Thank you for your seemingly effortless high notes and riffs. Thank you for making bold hair and wardrobe choices. Thank you for making Louis, Liam, Harry, and Niall happy. Thank you for making fans happy. Thank you for getting out of bed so early all those years ago to help set this incredible band and fandom into motion. And lastly, thank you for leaving a piece of your soul in each remaining member of One Direction. I can see it burning in them. Good things are coming for the boys, for you, and for all of us who love you guys so much. Peace and love as we all embark on this exciting next step —

♥Tewsdey

Zayn,

Thank you for leaving, for showing us that it's okay — and possible — to put your self first even with a whole world of expectation on you to do the opposite. Thanks for taking care of yourself & thereby taking care of your talent. I'm so excited for your next work.

Thank you for One Direction. I'm so grateful for the work & energy & hours you gave to the music & touring & being famous, to create something that uplifts me and inspires my creativity. Thank you for sharing so much, so bravely.

♡

---

thank you, zayn, for the music, the love, the way you taught me about friendship & self-care & the potential for forever.

sending you and your boys all the love in this new phase. we will find a way through the dark ♡♡♡♡

SYAR 2015

Dear Zayn

A thank-you letter to YOU could take up the pages of a book... but it would make me too sad so i'm gonna keep it short.

Thank you. Heres the deal... i was sad, so super sad for a little bit in my life... and then i discovered you guys and i started to get happy again.

I felt like i discovered the best little secret the world ever had. And YOU were the secrety-est secret of all. I really felt like i SAW you. So funny — deeply funny — endlessly sweet and just COOL. The ultimate coolest.

I'm glad you are taking care of YOU now. that has always been my #1 wish for you guys. I am so proud of you... and oh my goodness i have so much love for you.

♡ D'Arcy

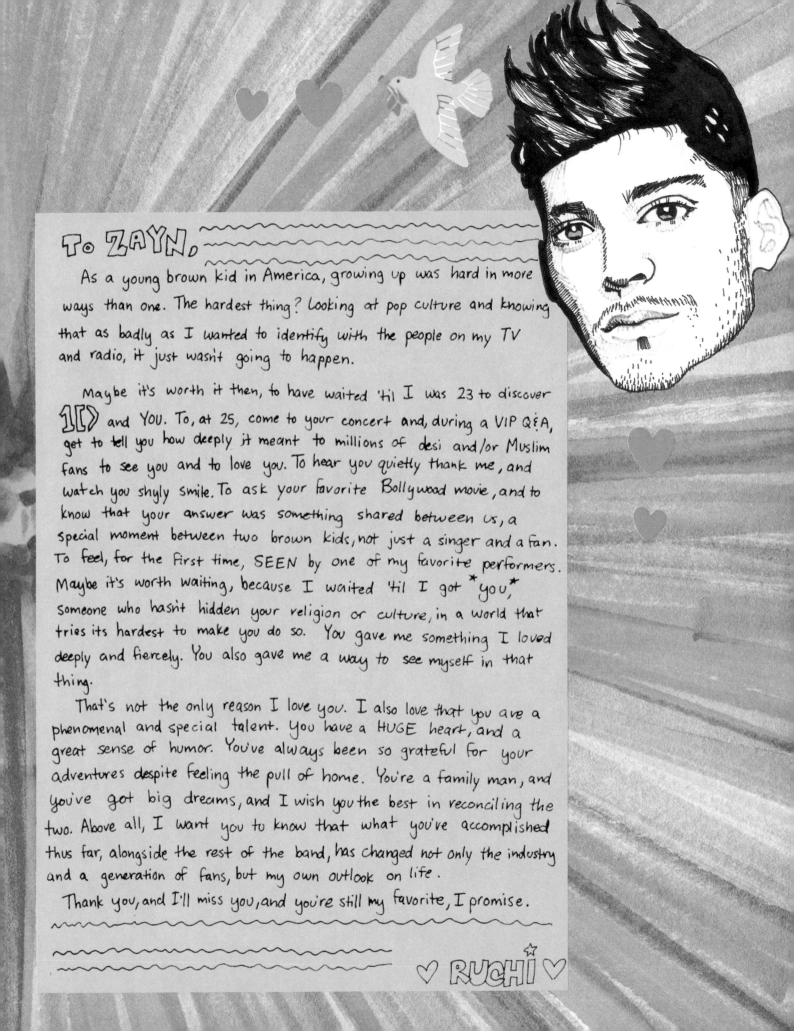

TO ZAYN,

As a young brown kid in America, growing up was hard in more ways than one. The hardest thing? Looking at pop culture and knowing that as badly as I wanted to identify with the people on my TV and radio, it just wasn't going to happen.

Maybe it's worth it then, to have waited 'til I was 23 to discover 1D and YOU. To, at 25, come to your concert and, during a VIP Q&A, get to tell you how deeply it meant to millions of desi and/or Muslim fans to see you and to love you. To hear you quietly thank me, and watch you shyly smile. To ask your favorite Bollywood movie, and to know that your answer was something shared between us, a special moment between two brown kids, not just a singer and a fan. To feel, for the first time, SEEN by one of my favorite performers. Maybe it's worth waiting, because I waited 'til I got *you,* someone who hasn't hidden your religion or culture, in a world that tries its hardest to make you do so. You gave me something I loved deeply and fiercely. You also gave me a way to see myself in that thing.

That's not the only reason I love you. I also love that you are a phenomenal and special talent. You have a HUGE heart, and a great sense of humor. You've always been so grateful for your adventures despite feeling the pull of home. You're a family man, and you've got big dreams, and I wish you the best in reconciling the two. Above all, I want you to know that what you've accomplished thus far, alongside the rest of the band, has changed not only the industry and a generation of fans, but my own outlook on life.

Thank you, and I'll miss you, and you're still my favorite, I promise.

♡ **RUCHI** ♡

MAY 2015: FORCE OF NATURE

May's theme is FORCE OF NATURE, and thank you to Maggie for thinking of it and to Eleanor for providing ideas that were a starting point for fleshing it out! This is a month when the idea of being part of something larger than yourself meets the idea of self-love; when the comfort of being unimportant to the universe can make you feel like a powerful little force of nature yourself. Think/feel tiny stars in a vast sky and anthemic lullabies and, like I said when we were all brainstorming, "This month isn't really HIPPIE so much as it's like POWERFUL NATURE GODDESS FLOATING THROUGH A CONFETTI SKY CELEBRATING HERSELF AND HER SISTERS." (You know that reference? That reference to that thing that doesn't exist?) Here is another bad idea I had for this month that nobody wanted to make but which I will not allow to perish in the bowels of my outbox:

"IN DEFENSE OF NOT CARING ABOUT CUTE PICTURES OF ANIMALS." This is a formal request for a comic/taxonomy of total sociopaths who LOVED animals and it DIDN'T MEAN SHIT or maybe even meant they were dissociated from human sympathy, e.g., the *Sopranos* pilot where Tony kills people mercilessly and then cries because the ducks in his backyard pool flew away!!!!!

If you or someone you know would like to assuage my guilt over my chronic immunity toward panda .gifs, please get in touch.

LOVE
-TAVI

HERO STATUS: MEDUSA

I wish someone had told me when I was 13 that it was OK to be a monster.
By Hazel. Illustration by Kelly.

I read Virginia Despentes' *King Kong Theory*, a book written in celebration of female "ugliness," in 2013, the same year I was devouring classical Western mythology through writers like Ovid. At the same time, Rookie writer Arabelle was building and blogging what she called "girl monster methodology," an exploration in terrifying beauty and opting for vulnerability and monstrosity over classical prettiness. It was the year I found women who were writing about and representing what I was always looking for: in King Kong girls, in monster methodology, and in Medusa.

The Greek myth of Medusa goes thusly: She was a beautiful woman who garnered many suitors, but after she was raped by Poseidon in Athena's sacred temple, Athena cursed Medusa with snakes for hair. The legend asserts that she was so horrific-looking, men turned to stone when they looked at her. Medusa, for me, began to represent the double-edged sword I've been faced with when I try to understand beauty. When she was gorgeous and sexually desirable, it only led her to be cursed with an ugliness so terrible it killed men in her path. She represented how female beauty can only exist in the strictest of ways, and when it fails, ugliness, and therefore monstrosity, is the inevitable outcome.

I'm not sure what kind of girl I am. I wish I could say I knew for sure—that I could put a name to my feelings like Despentes and Arabelle have. But for the entirety of my teen years, I sincerely thought one thing: I was not a pretty girl. I was sure I was definitely ugly. And while I possess what is, by mainstream standards, a celebrated body (white, thin, cis), the moment I grew out of childhood I became someone whose existence was deemed unacceptable by an influx of seemingly invisible standards. I failed to make the smallest marks: I felt like my hair was wrong; my face was always over-flushed in embarrassment; boys didn't kiss me, and when they did, they had kissed everyone; girls didn't want to be me.

In reality, my conviction of my ugliness wasn't unusual. I was a teenager poking my way around my body, sex, and beauty, all of which is almost aggressively normal, but somehow my failures to be traditionally pretty and desirable made me feel grotesque. The truth is that every girl has some Ugly in her. It's because we're constantly taught *not* to be. If a girl is acceptable by the standards of the world (and largely of men) she isn't Ugly, and so it manifests in the corners of our minds and our hearts. The ugliness of Ugly Girls ends up as an umbrella for everything we're not supposed to be: loud, messy, clingy, smart, queer, unshaven, fat, etc. "I think monsters trump the binary of smart and pretty and instead adopt power as the ultimate make-over," said Durga Chew-Bose on '90s teen movies for *Cléo Journal* (December 2014). "Maybe I'm just living in a post Nicki [Minaj] 'Monster'-verse era where I think it's important to fully inhabit all of our many contradictions and missteps, and if doing so, we as women become so-called monsters, why not?"

I wish someone had told me when I was 13 that it was OK to be a monster, because the truth is, you're going to feel like one a little bit, some more than others. And everyone will tell you you're not one, or that you're bound to be pretty eventually. But what I wanted was for someone to tell me not just that I was fine just the way I was, but that there was something more to attain than prettiness. That the other end of the spectrum, ugliness, could be a source of strength, a way to turn the men who could merely objectify me into stone simply by existing in a way that didn't meet their sexual expectations. "I am writing therefore as a woman incapable of attracting male attention, satisfying male desire, or being satisfied with a place in the shade," wrote Despentes of her ugliness. "It's from here that I write, as an unattractive but ambitious woman, drawn to money I make myself, drawn to power, the power to do and to say no, drawn to the city rather than the home, excited by experience and not content with just hearing about it from others."

I can't tell anyone, especially people with bodies maligned in ways that mine will never be, to reject sexiness and embrace ugliness. But for me, I love this ever-growing space. I needed Arabelle's monsters and the King Kong girls and Courtney Love screaming, "Is she ugly?" over and over on "Pretty on the Inside," like a war cry. It's not a place of self-love and it's not a place of self-hate—it's between the two. It's basking in the feeling of being perceived as a monster. It's a celebration of all of your unruly parts, the parts you keep untamed, the parts you don't have figured out. If anything, it's an attempt to escape the scale of fuckability that you're automatically placed on as a young woman. As the novelist and art historian Umberto Eco wrote in his book *On Ugliness*, beauty follows predictable models, and so is not only limited, but limiting. Luckily, there's another way to see the world—and be seen by it: "Ugliness is infinite, like God." ⚡

IT'S NOT ABOUT YOU

Sometimes a conversation just doesn't need your input.
By Akilah Hughes

When I was four years old, my mother bought me and my sister black Barbie dolls. We rejected them outright because "they weren't the dolls from the commercial." We didn't think they were good enough, and certainly not as good as the blond, white Barbies our friends had. We weren't born thinking that way. But since the age of four—*before I could read*—I knew that blackness was considered less-than and *different*.

During the incredibly successful #BlackOutDay of March 6, black people posted selfies on social media to promote community and the acceptance of features less visible in popular media. It was an uplifting day meant to remind black people, "You're beautiful." Some white people took offense. It wasn't long after #BlackOutDay trended worldwide on Twitter that #WhiteOutDay appeared.

#BlackOutDay did not claim that non-black people are immune to body-image issues or don't face societal pressures. But, without fail, any time a historically oppressed group asserts their equality by boldly denying inferiority, some member of the unoppressed majority takes it personally. When oppressed groups take the initiative to lift themselves up, it is not an invitation to victimize yourself. Would you go to a toddler's birthday party and kick over their cake to announce that you, too, have birthdays? No.

If we examine the magazine aisle of any store or any TV channel, the images we see most are overwhelmingly of white people, *all the time*. Sure, a handful of popular shows feature diverse casts, and black people do appear on magazine covers, but let's be honest about the harsh reality. It is highly unusual for features more commonly possessed by people of African descent to be considered beautiful.

Popularized by psychologists Kenneth and Mamie Clark in 1939, the "doll test" showed that the way we see ourselves is largely dictated by the world around us. A child is presented with a white doll and a black doll and is asked to associate characteristics with each one. White students mainly associated the black dolls with negative

traits. Shockingly, black students did, too.

Growing up in Florence, Kentucky, one of America's least diverse places, I constantly struggled to look a way that I just don't. People made fun of my skin color, my hair texture (even as I tried to assimilate to their straight hairstyles), the size of my butt and lips. It's shocking to see how positive a reaction certain white celebrities get for possessing those features, while they are shamed when they appear on my own face and body.

My story is not unique. Our society has loads of unlearning to do when it comes to racist and damaging stereotypes. Racism is more than hurt feelings; it affects how the gatekeepers of the world—employers, educators, coaches, landlords, the entire infrastructure—see and treat me. There are huge privileges in passing as white in a world that values lighter skin above other shades. Seeing people who look like you in media not only affects the way you see yourself, but also the way others see you.

I get that it may feel like an affront that black people are spending a day telling one another that they are beautiful and worthy and interesting and deep and lovable, but imagine the other 364 days a year that we face major barriers to mainstream acceptance because we are black.

A knee-jerk reaction is: "But *I THINK BLACK PEOPLE ARE BEAUTIFUL!*" or "I've played with black dolls, I watch *Scandal*, and I am not a racist! So why do you need a special/separate day?"

It's not about you.

It's a hard lesson to learn—that the struggles of black people, gay people, trans people, poor people, disabled people might be different from yours. I learned this myself a few years ago, after reading a Tumblr post where the writer joked about disliking heterosexual relationships. I was taken aback. I considered myself an ally of LGBTQ+ communities, and found anti-marriage laws lamentably archaic. Still, I couldn't believe that people with different sexual orientations were making light of me, a straight person. *My life isn't*

perfect! I am not rich and I am Black! How dare you make a joke at my expense?

I talked to a friend of mine, an out lesbian who is very involved in our local gay community. I was taking the post personally. I think I even said (shudder), "If a straight person said the same thing about gay relationships, that'd be homophobic!"

Yeah, it would be *hella homophobic*! And homophobia is a *real problem*, whereas being straight isn't. I have the advantages of being straight in a world that overwhelmingly supports straight marriage and spousal rights and overwhelmingly denies personhood to anyone with a different sexual orientation or who identifies as a gender outside of the one they were assigned at birth. Homophobia is a problem with tangible consequences; someone joking about straight people isn't.

My friend was smart and patient. She asked, "Did you lose anything when they lifted themselves up?" The world hadn't changed. I wasn't somehow disadvantaged because queer people asserted their right to exist. I didn't lose my right to marry, or suddenly have slurs hurled at me about my sexual orientation.

Realizing that their gay pride didn't take away from or negate my lived experience helped me grow up so much. I saw the other side of the argument and *they were right*. While I don't condone making fun of anyone, I certainly do not think it makes sense to equate my personal situation with the history of oppression that anyone who isn't heterosexual carries on their shoulders.

It wasn't about me.

Since that conversation, I've learned to *listen* before I take offense at movements about which I'm not educated. It isn't always easy to stop the instinct to be defensive, but it is necessary if things are ever going to get better. After hearing the other side, ask yourself if anyone loses rights or status when that group gains theirs. It's important to remember that sweeping progress benefits us all, so let others do what they must to finally achieve equality. ◊

Let's Do This For Real: An Interview with Alessia Cara

"Young people are really standing up, and I hope I can be one of them."
By Julianne. Illustration by Kelly.

Alessia Cara's first single, "Here," is about something almost everyone can relate to: being the shy person at a party where you don't feel comfortable. "I would rather be at home [...] by myself," she sings. It's kind of a miracle, in that it's a pop song about being a total loner in a landscape of pop songs that seem to have the aggressive goal of getting you to participate in the soirée. Listening to it feels like a kind of permission: *Hey, girl, if you think this place sucks, then go ahead, skedaddle on home. Being alone is sometimes the best thing for you.*

The 18-year-old singer/songwriter is gearing up to be everywhere, but only recently built up her own confidence, having once felt as shy about performing as she did being at parties. She bolstered her self-assurance by posting YouTube videos and taking drama classes at her Brampton, Ontario, high school, where she graduated last year. After taking a gap year before college to work on her music, Cara found herself in the middle of a whirlwind: She was discovered on YouTube and soon swept up by Tab Nkhereanye, the music exec who signed her to Def Jam, which will drop her album this year.

I spoke with Cara about being on the cusp of stardom, overcoming shyness, and supporting other young women.

JULIANNE How does it feel to have a record deal?

ALESSIA CARA It's obviously amazing, but in my situation, it feels like a dream, like I don't feel like I'm actually doing this, you know? Everything is happening so quickly.

Did you just graduate high school?

Last year—I would have just finished my first year of university by now.

Did you choose not to go so you could work on your music?

The thing is, in my school, you have to apply to colleges—that's part of the graduation process. I applied to programs I thought I would like, because at the time my family was encouraging me to have a plan B. Doing music professionally was not a thing they thought I could do full-time. I ended up getting scholarships and was about to [go to university], but something told me not to do it. I don't know, I felt like it wasn't right for me, and I had to explore that side of my music and my passion. So I said, "Let me take a year off so I can see." And in that year, I got signed! So it worked out!

That's such a hard thing, to trust yourself and know that you should follow your dream. How did you listen to yourself?

It's something that I always knew I would be 100 percent happy doing, and I knew that if I were to do anything else, I'd be settling. I thought, *It can't hurt; people take a year off all the time.* I took a chance. School will always be there, you know?

True. When did you first know you wanted to pursue music?

I don't remember a specific time. I remember singing all the time—it was something I've done since I was two or three years old. Some of my cousins and aunts and uncles sing or dance, but my parents don't really sing. I did choir one year in elementary school, but I didn't take any music courses in high school. I took a lot of drama, so I did a lot of performance in that way, but I didn't take any music classes, which is weird. It was something I always used to do as a hobby, but I was really shy to do it in front of people at first. I used to think it was so scary, so I would do it on my own. As I took drama, I really started loving the performance side, so I thought, *OK, let's do this for real.*

You were shy before? How did you break out of it?

[By] being pushed by my teacher, and by my friends who knew I could do it. They played a huge part; the reaction I was getting from people [made me feel] like *OK, I can do this. I guess they like me! I guess I'm good at it!*

How do you write your songs—in a journal?

Sometimes, yeah! When I did this album, I did most of it in a studio. We go in, and I let everything out at the studio. But I'll write things in a journal, and then go back and remember how I was feeling and write things out on my guitar. For my first album, I wanted not only to talk about my own experiences, but to really make an album for everyone. I want at least one song to resonate with every person. I have a lot of talk about body image for women, self-acceptance for everyone—accepting that you might be weird or you might be a little uncool but you could still be cool if you find your own space. There's a lot of empowering stuff, some vulnerable stuff.

That's awesome about the empowerment stuff. It always seems like there's someone or something out there that wants to bring us down.

With me, it wasn't even other people. A lot of the stuff growing up, it was internal. I always thought that I wasn't good enough, even if other people may not have felt that way. Getting confidence from the people around you who love you and care for you—that kind of reminds you, *You're not an idiot! You're not stupid! You're not uncool!*

It's one of those fundamental things about growing up that's so hard, finding your confidence. Did music help you get there?

It really did! Before, I always felt like I was average at everything, and I wasn't good at anything—that I faded into the background. I wasn't popular, I was a regular kid. I felt like I didn't have anything that made me *me*, or separated me from anyone else. When I started singing in front of people and seeing the reaction I was getting, it really made me confident, like *This is something that I'm really good at. This is my thing.*

How has your family reacted to you being signed, and was there more pressure because you knew they were watching you?

My mom's and my dad's reactions were very different. When I first sang for my mom, she started to cry and was like, "This is what you're meant to do!" She was so into the whole idea. Of course, the mom side of her wanted me to be safe with a backup plan, but she also wanted me to do this. I knew I had

her support. My dad was like, "No, this is not a career for you!" He was very strict, you know, it's like a strict Italian family. But then he started traveling with me. He's still traveling with me everywhere, pretty much, and I think he's beginning to see how real this is. He opened up to the idea, and he's supporting me more and more. It's really cool to see that he gets it now. I felt the pressure, and it kind of sucked at first to have my family telling me, "It's not a job," but in the back of my mind, I knew I would get it.

Just listening to your voice, I'm like, *Yeah, you should be doing this*. It makes sense! Good job! What about your friends? You're probably traveling a lot.

It's good to have those friends where you maybe don't see them for months, but then you see them again and it's like nothing ever changed.

Totally. Who is your best friend?

I have two best friends. One is like my other half. We've known each other since we were 10, and we're like the same person. And then my other friend I've known since ninth grade. She was my first friend that I made in high school. They're the two people I go to for everything.

What do they think about all this, getting signed and everything?

They were telling me that I was gonna do this before I even knew. And not just them. My other friends, people from school, acquaintances, would come up to me and say it. They supported me way more than I ever did in my head. It's such a confidence boost, to have your peers tell you that you're good at something. It's cool!

I guess it's a weird time to ask you about your hopes for the future, since you're at the beginning of your career. But: What are your hopes for the future?

Besides putting out my album, becoming better at performing and singing, I wanna be really, really good at everything, including

writing—everything. [I want to] make great albums in the future, and I want people to look forward to my albums as bodies of work, as [being] whole, instead of just a number-one single. I would love to do all those fancy awards shows and typical artist stuff, and to help people out, meet new people, and learn as much as I can. With my album, I wanted to represent youth, and to represent me.

Do you think we're in a time when smart young people are being heard more?

Especially in the music industry, there is a big shift where young people have a voice now. You see people like Lorde or Raury—anyone young and doing it right now—and we're really starting to show our faces and prove that young people have a voice, and we actually make sense, and we have important things to say, too. I love the shift that's happening in entertainment, and in life in general. Young people are really standing up, and I hope I can be one of them. Not only in this industry, but in life, it's so hard to be a girl, and to feel like you might not have a say or the rights that other people have. The only thing we can do is support other girls and be happy for them. Don't be mean to girls who really like what they're doing and who like themselves, because it's so hard to like yourself. Be happy for them! ☽

STARS IN MY EYES

So bright we've gotta wear shades. By Rachel
Styling by Emily Beard. Hair by Tomomi Roppongi.
Makeup by Isobel Kennedy. Thanks to Vanessa Omoregie for modeling.

HOW TO MAKE FAKE-FUR SANDALS

So flossy. By Rian

Maybe I've been watching too many episodes of *Lizzie McGuire*, but lately I've been so taken by fashion of the early 2000s. I'm ready for the revival of blue tinted sunglasses and Skechers. If you've been feeling those looks, too, you can easily turn boring old shoes into glam fuzzy sandals that would be especially cute for prom. I'll show you how!

WHAT YOU'LL NEED:

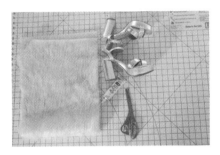

- Paper
- Pen or pencil
- Scissors/shears
- Fake-fur fabric in the color of your choice
- Pair of high-heeled shoes or sandals you don't mind gluing fur to
- Strong glue
- Blow dryer (optional)

STEP ONE

Line an edge of your paper up with the top edge of the sandal's strap, and wrap the paper from one side of the sole over the full length of the strap. With the paper, you're going to be making a pattern that will give you a rough estimate of the top of the sandal's shape and length.

TWO

Use your pen or pencil to make marks on the paper that correspond to the top and bottom edges of each side of the shoe, starting and ending at both sides of the sole, then draw lines that connect those marks.

Tip: It's better to make the pattern a little too big and size it down later than to make it too small!

THREE

Cut out your pattern.

FOUR

Place your pattern on the fake-fur fabric and cut around its perimeter, then do it again. You'll end up with two pieces.

FIVE

Place a fur piece over the straps of one shoe. It should line up with the soles on both sides—if it's too long, cut it down until it's the right size. Now repeat the same step on the other shoe. (Optional: Blow-dry the fur to make it stand up all fuzzy and ridiculous!)

SIX

Fold over the short sides of one fake-fur piece an inch and glue them down; then fold over one of the long sides a half-inch and glue it down, too. Repeat the same steps on the other piece. (You're about to use a lot of glue, so make sure you're in a well-ventilated area.)

SEVEN

Apply glue all over the straps of both shoes.

EIGHT

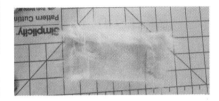

Carefully place one piece of fur over your first sandal so that it lines up with the straps, and then firmly press it into place. Repeat with the other piece on your other shoe.

Don't they look SO CUTE?! Resist the urge to try them on for a couple of hours, so the glue can dry completely—then you're done and ready for fun! ✿

Something to read While Debating whether or not to Call your Ex

Because almost anything else is a better idea than doing that right now. By Tavi

Maybe you broke up with them. Maybe they broke up with you. Maybe it was circumstantial, maybe it can only be summarized by the title of Denise Richards's reality show (*It's Complicated*), maybe you need to down a few glasses of Manischewitz before even *going* there.

Due to whatever love-pickle your thunderous heart got itself into, there is a person in your life with whom you should not be speaking, but at this *very* moment *right now*, there is nothing you want more than to call them. Check all that apply:

1. You're crying and screaming, and contact with this person seems like the only remedy (until you have to say goodbye again).
2. You're terrifyingly numb and need this person's attention to bring you back to life (until you have to say goodbye again).
3. There is a gaping hole in your heart where the love used to be, and you can fill it a little by hearing their voice (until you have to say goodbye again).
4. You messed up so bad and you need another chance to explain and you cannot live knowing that this person won't forgive you (even though they've made it clear they won't).
5. They messed up so bad and showed no remorse and you will not be satisfied until they fully understand the extent of their sociopathy (even though they've made it clear they won't).
6. Et cetera infinity because IT'S ALL SO LAYERED; wow @ this crazy "thing" called "*Love*"!

The common factor in these scenarios is that getting in touch will alleviate your suffering temporarily while worsening it in the long run. But how can it be that you "shouldn't" talk to this person if your feelings so badly want to? Not to reduce your feelings to a *Bill Nye* episode, but you are still physiologically attached to this person as if they were a DRUG. According to a study conducted at the Einstein College of Medicine, MRI scans of people going through breakups are comparable to those of people overcoming cocaine addiction,* making relapsing very real. Terrifying!! Time will be your best friend as your body slowly forgets your ex, and reasoning will be your greatest resource in transitioning the pain from physiological to emotional to almost purely intellectual. Here are some questions to ask yourself before getting in touch:

1. How will it feel to hang up?
2. If they were a jerk to you: Do you want to give them the satisfaction of knowing this is troubling you? The opposite of love isn't hate, it's indifference!
3. If you were a jerk to them: Would it hurt or anger them to hear from you? Is giving them space a greater gesture of respect?
4. Are you hungry, dehydrated, or tired? Breakups suck no matter what, but like *everything in life*, they suck even harder if you are not hitting the base level of Maslow's hierarchy of needs.
5. Did you smoke weed or drink today or yesterday? Weed and alcohol are depressants and fertilize the pain they might temporarily distract you from. Know that this is where some of your sads are coming from, even though heartbreak is an obvious explanation.

Look: It would be unnatural to pretend a person you used to exchange fluids with suddenly doesn't exist, and sometimes being all "NEVER AGAIN" mythologizes your ex till they occupy an oppressive place in your mind, making the idea of calling them suddenly so unimaginable that it *must* be cathartic. The cold-turkey extreme demands to be combated by an equal extreme, and then not only do you give in and have to go through the pain of another goodbye, but you feel EXTRA shitty because YOU SAID YOU WOULDN'T AND NOW YOU DID AND THAT IS JUST SO *CLASSIC YOU*—this suddenly represents all of your self-worth as you were trying so hard to be strong.

The most productive question is if there is anything else you can do *right now*. If so, do that thing, and whatever else you need to do *for yourself*, and you might find that your desire for contact has lessened. Instead of making any declarations, take it one day, or even one hour, at a time: Can you get ready in the morning without sending a text? You did it! Can you commute without any communication? Done! Keep focusing on what's in front of you, and you'll start to appreciate whatever you're doing way more, and that's one baby step toward Life After Heartbreak.

PLOT TWIST: I am writing the advice I need. I begin fruitless arguments knowing that I'm prying open any sense of closure, and I have to go down every road to see the dead ends for myself. It doesn't matter how much I thought I knew that ex-people don't suddenly go, "Wow, you have located the hole in my argument! My logic *is* flawed, and now my gut will change its mind and my heart's brain will decide to love you. You are *so* good at debate. Are you in Model UN? Let me guess—you represent the country of France, because you, too, speak the language of love, and resemble Kim in her and Kanye's *Vogue* spread, and because you're just so, gosh, idk, *lovable!!!*"

Eventually, these attempts dwindle from in-person fights to long phone calls to essay emails to petty texts to Snapchats of dog shit to nothing. I guess the only way out is through. But I don't think you should have to, like, *earn* that relief by *exhausting* yourself, you know? It's possible I took the doctor in *Louie* too seriously when he said: "The bad part is when you forget her […] so enjoy the heartbreak while you can, for godsakes."

Right now, taking care of yourself means not making time or space for what is over. This is not a betrayal of the love you once had or the person you now miss, and that person probably does not want you to be in pain. (If they do, all the more reason to become your own hero and leave 'em in the dust.) Self-care is not anti-love; it will actually serve the love you'll have in the future. Self-care can never *backfire*, like, *Oh no, I took too-good care of myself and now I'm closed off from the world and living in a giant shoe with passive woodland creatures.*

---

* "Reward, Addiction, and Emotion Regulation Systems Associated With Rejection in Love," *Journal of Neurophysiology*, May 2010.

Self-care becomes self-respect, and when insecurity is at a minimum and your walls can come down, THAT'S when you are the most open to the world and capable of loving. That is when the connection you find will be its most true, and more valuable than whatever's on the other end of this phone call.

I leave you with a few notes I took after seeing the singer Joy Williams live:

1. She talked about how many changes took place in her life in a condensed period and how, in the face of a challenge, you can either break down or break open.
2. Her voice is a force of nature and she exudes the kind of confidence born out of necessity.
3. At times of heartbreak I feel torn between (a) being a Girl and stopping myself from self-care because it feels at odds with the relationship I am mourning and the person I was then, because I don't want to harden, because it was nice to have someone chase my butt; and (b) being a Man and moving on and wearing asexualized clothing and detaching emotionally under the guise of "strength." Joy finished the show with the song "Woman (Oh Mama)," and I felt like being capable of love is not counter-productive to strength and vice versa, and how good it is to be in this place because it means that something new can unfold.
4. At the end of the show, I saw a text from Lola: "There's a fixed essential part of my being that only comes alive in the place where romancé ends." ♥

Creative Solutions

How to get your brain going in all kinds of artistic directions.   By Anna F.

During my first day of high school, my English teacher had everybody share a couple of facts about themselves. The first girl said, "I hate math." The teacher responded, "That's OK. I find people who hate math tend to do well with English."

This was news to me. Math and English had always been my favorite subjects. I found numbers and logic problems to be reassuring, almost soothing. My teacher probably said that to make my math-averse classmate feel better, but it added to my mini-identity crisis that had begun the year before, when my application to the writing program at an arts high school was rejected for not being "creative" enough. I had this romantic belief that I was *born* to be a writer, but pop psychology seemed to tell me that people who tend to be more logical and analytical are doomed to a life of being unimaginative bores.

I am 25 now, and I work full-time as a freelance writer, and my favorite things to publish are creative humor pieces. I don't think I was born to be a writer, but I don't think anyone is really born to be anything. Creativity is a skill that can be learned and strengthened.

1. RETHINK THE WHOLE IDEA OF "CREATIVITY"

Recognize that creativity is not limited to the arts.
Being a creative person doesn't mean you have to be an artist living La Vie Bohème in Paris. No matter what you want to be when you grow up, it is a helpful skill to be able to make something out of nothing, or to approach topics from unpredictable angles. I am currently reading *The Joy of X* by Steven Strogatz, and it's all about how some of the most essential mathematical formulas were developed by people who stretched their brain powers like Silly Putty to work out solutions. A lot of the math that I learned in high school—like the Pythagorean theorem or the value of pi—was discovered by people who looked at regular triangles and were able to think outside the box (or the "regular hexahedron," if you will—just some geometry humor for you!!).

I think a lot about Rookie writer Hazel's interview with the astrophysicist Neil deGrasse Tyson (July 2012)—specifically:

In the history of science, there are three kinds of discoveries you can make. One of them is what you expected to be there—confirming your understanding of nature. Another one is, you *don't* find what you expect to be there, so you have to go back and rethink everything. And sometimes, when you're forced to go back and rethink things, you end up making discoveries you had not previously anticipated.

Science, obviously, involves a lot of analyzing and adhering to rules, but it also involves constantly restructuring the way you think about the world and finding new ways to approach old matter to better understand it.

This is true for other careers, too! Last September, I interviewed Allis Markham, a taxidermist at a natural history museum, for The Hairpin. Markham's job combines sculpture, craft, and biology. She spoke of styles unique to iconic taxidermists that she admires, and says about her work, "If you look at a Venn diagram of science and art, taxidermy is where they meet." Different skills and interests don't have to be mutually exclusive. When science and math work together with art, magic happens.

Recognize that being analytical can fuel creativity.
The arts are *filled* with math geeks, from Leonardo da Vinci to the creators of *Futurama*. Even if you are the type of person who is constantly falling asleep during your first-period calculus, how neat is it that this language of numbers permeates lauded works of fine art?

I am constantly deconstructing what I like and finding new methods that work for me as a writer. A lot of my stronger humor pieces follow a pattern. This doesn't mean that I recycle the same jokes, but when I brainstorm

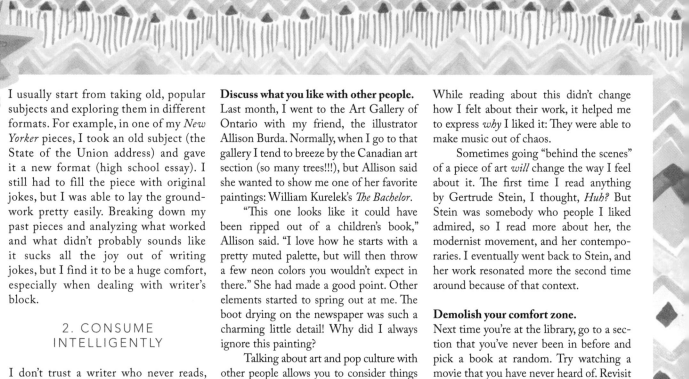

I usually start from taking old, popular subjects and exploring them in different formats. For example, in one of my *New Yorker* pieces, I took an old subject (the State of the Union address) and gave it a new format (high school essay). I still had to fill the piece with original jokes, but I was able to lay the groundwork pretty easily. Breaking down my past pieces and analyzing what worked and what didn't probably sounds like it sucks all the joy out of writing jokes, but I find it to be a huge comfort, especially when dealing with writer's block.

2. CONSUME INTELLIGENTLY

I don't trust a writer who never reads, and I can't imagine being a musician who never listens to music, or an actor who never watches movies or plays. There is a world of art that can inspire, challenge, and otherwise provoke your own work, especially if you engage with it thoughtfully and critically.

Question why you like what you like (or why you don't).
This may sound like a boring habit, but it helps me appreciate both "highbrow" and "lowbrow" art more and identify what I respond to and want to incorporate into my work. My mom once asked me why I am obsessed with old episodes of *The Simpsons* when I had seen each one a million times. I realized it was because it's a show that combines different types of humor, both wacky slapstick and subtle satire, so that it can be enjoyed both when you're tired and don't want to think too hard, *and* when you want to pay attention to every little joke. I would like to write jokes that combine all of these elements!

Don't worry about what you're *supposed* to like or dislike, but instead what you react to on a gut level. You don't have to like the books you're assigned in English class or the movies that win Oscars every year, but it might be helpful to question *why* you respond the way that you do to these things.

Discuss what you like with other people.
Last month, I went to the Art Gallery of Ontario with my friend, the illustrator Allison Burda. Normally, when I go to that gallery I tend to breeze by the Canadian art section (so many trees!!!), but Allison said she wanted to show me one of her favorite paintings: William Kurelek's *The Bachelor*.

"This one looks like it could have been ripped out of a children's book," Allison said. "I love how he starts with a pretty muted palette, but will then throw a few neon colors you wouldn't expect in there." She had made a good point. Other elements started to spring out at me. The boot drying on the newspaper was such a charming little detail! Why did I always ignore this painting?

Talking about art and pop culture with other people allows you to consider things that you might have otherwise ignored. Because Allison is a visual artist, she made me appreciate a painting that I've walked by countless times. Sometimes I'll talk to other friends who have read the same books I have, but had completely different interpretations. My friends and I will argue about a movie that one of us loved but the other hated, forcing ourselves to identify exactly what we did or didn't like!

What's that, you say? Your friends aren't interested in talking about those types of things? Allow me to introduce you to a little invention called THE INTERNET. On my Tumblr dashboard right now, I can find an in-depth discussion on the merits of One Direction fandom, and high-quality screencaps of an old art film, right next to each other. It's the perfect place to indulge in what you already love *and* discover new obsessions.

Read lots, and read *about* lots.
The first time I listened to Sonic Youth, I thought, *I like how they sound like how I'm feeling*, but I couldn't express myself beyond that. (Born to be a writer, right?)

So I read about Sonic Youth. I learned about the context in which the band formed (on the tail end of New York's no-wave scene, which was all about creating art without defined rules) and how they created their sounds (on their first album, they included a recording of a power drill).

While reading about this didn't change how I felt about their work, it helped me to express *why* I liked it: They were able to make music out of chaos.

Sometimes going "behind the scenes" of a piece of art *will* change the way I feel about it. The first time I read anything by Gertrude Stein, I thought, *Huh?* But Stein was somebody who people I liked admired, so I read more about her, the modernist movement, and her contemporaries. I eventually went back to Stein, and her work resonated more the second time around because of that context.

Demolish your comfort zone.
Next time you're at the library, go to a section that you've never been in before and pick a book at random. Try watching a movie that you have never heard of. Revisit an album you hate, and see if you still feel the same way. Look outside the realm of traditional "art" for inspiration and pay attention to what you see in nature. Go for a walk in a new neighborhood. Strike up a conversation with your lab partner and find out the kinds of things they're into. Inspiration is literally everywhere, as long as you keep your eyes peeled and your mind open.

3. MAKE STUFF

Keep a notebook (or something like one).
I never go anywhere without a notebook and pen. Most of what I write in my notebooks would be unintelligible to anyone else: scraps of overheard conversation on the bus, unusual things I've seen that day, moments I liked in movies, titles for unwritten books. Ninety-nine percent of what I record I never use again, but this exercise is twofold: It gets me paying attention to things that I wouldn't otherwise notice, and the one percent of the time I capture something brilliant, it leads to some of my best ideas.

Notebooks work best for me, but Tavi uses notecards because, she says, "They're noncommittal and smaller!" Rookie writer Lola has a similar system with index cards. Haley Mlotek, who runs the website The Hairpin, swears by the app Evernote because it's accessible on multiple devices. And if you have an iPhone, it comes with a built-in Notes app that can connect with your email. If you're more of a visual person, make a password-protected Tumblr to store your inspiration photos. Play around with different systems and figure out what works best for you!

Put limits on yourself.

This might sound counterintuitive, but the more restrictions I put on my work, the more I am inspired to create.

Rookie's monthly themes are a good example. At the beginning of every month, the editors send contributors a detailed email with guidance, including topics to explore, references to consider, vibes to embody, and a host of visual inspiration for the illustrators and photographers. These are incredibly helpful when it comes to pitching ideas, because instead of thinking, *I need to think of a good idea*, I think, *I need a good idea that fits with this month's theme*. Brainstorming becomes way less overwhelming when I have a jumping-off point.

I love children's books for this reason. Generally, kids' books cater to a short attention span, and the stories are simple and age appropriate. A lot of crappy kids' books are out there, sure, but when they're done right they can be hilarious or creepy in a way that adult books rarely can. I'm a huge fan of Jon Klassen's adorably terrifying picture books *I Want My Hat Back* and *This Is Not My Hat*.

Try to make something with an arbitrary rule: Describe your day using only five-letter words, or paint a picture without using the color red.

Collaborate!

When I was in school, I hated group projects. Usually, the groups were assigned by the teacher, and I would end up with people whom I never saw eye to eye with. I often got totally frustrated with them for not recognizing my *obvious* brilliance and ugh, couldn't the teacher *see* what I had to put up with??

First of all, my past self needed to stop taking that fifth-grade geography project so seriously. Secondly, working with other people can be filed under the "Demolish your comfort zone" and "Put limits on

yourself" lessons I mentioned above. Being able to adapt and incorporate other people's ideas into your own can be very useful!

Working with a team can also make you more accountable and inspire better results. Since most Rookie posts include an original illustration, I'm more motivated to stay on schedule and try to make sure I hand in my drafts before their deadline so the illustrators have time to work on them. When you know somebody else's name will be on the final product next to yours, you want to put out your best work possible.

Plus, when you're creating stuff for fun, you can pick your collaborators. Real life is not school!!! Other people can give you feedback, provide ideas, ET CETERA. Like, a sweater taxonomy from *Rookie Yearbook One*: Tavi came up with the original idea/format, then I came up with a list of jokes for each sweater and sent them to her, then she built on the jokes that she liked, then Cynthia illustrated it, and the end result is PRETTY ADORABLE.

Don't force your ideas.

Things evolve and change. That's OK! Sometimes you will start a project with an idea of where you want it to go, and it will end up in a totally different direction. Sometimes an editor or collaborator will make a suggestion that wouldn't be your first choice, but ultimately makes sense for the project. Sometimes, you will put a project aside for a few weeks, come back to it, and have a new perspective. There are paragraphs that I've written and loved but ended up cutting because they didn't work with the larger piece I was writing—and later incorporated into other essays.

It took John Green 12 years, after having the idea for *The Fault in Our Stars*, to actually start writing the book, and even then it went through dramatic rewrites. Of the editing process, he told the *New York Times* (April 2015): "Whenever I get a letter from [editor Julie Strauss-Gabel], I go through this mourning process. The first day, I rage all day. The second day, the tears set in, and I say she's right, and I'm a terrible writer. The third day, I say I'm not a terrible writer, but I can't write this book. The fourth day, I get to work."

Likewise, learn when you need to take a physical break. If you're sitting in front of your computer screen for hours and nothing is coming, it might be time to go for a walk or do any of the things from the "Consume intelligently" section. That said, sometimes the most important thing to do is to make something, even if you don't already have an idea.

Make something every day.

The biggest secret to being creative is to create things. That sounds like a paradox, but not everything you make will be brilliant, and that's OK! Sometimes you just need to get started.

When I begin writing a piece, I try not to think too hard about whether it's good or not—I just get the words out. Eventually, I will stumble onto an idea that I want to develop further, and even then I will go through multiple drafts and edits. There are many, many things I've written that will never see the light of day. There are pieces I've published on Rookie that would be unrecognizable if I showed you my first draft.

Above all: Don't be self-conscious about "getting it done" when you start on a new idea!

There's a line, most often attributed to the humorist Dorothy Parker: "I hate writing, I love having written." Some days, I totally understand, but most of the time, I really like writing as an act in and of itself. Setting goals for a finished project is great and good and wonderful, but if "getting it done" is the only thing you're focused on, you are missing out on some of the best parts of being creative.

There's a moment a lot of creative people speak of, when they refer to being in the zone. Do you ever have that experience—when you're working on something you love, and it seems like the rest of the world dissolves and nothing matters except for what is happening right in front of you? You might feel at peace, or maybe it comes to you as a complete adrenaline rush. That feeling, however it comes to you, is a *great* reason to get out of bed in the morning and make something. ✎

Your Creative Energies Must Be Released: An Interview With Sana Amanat

"Comics can be and should be for everyone." By Marie. Illustration by Kelly.

Sana Amanat is doing groundbreaking things at Marvel Comics. As a comic-book editor, she helped create the character Kamala Khan, aka Ms. Marvel—Marvel's first American Muslim teen character to have her own series. Sana also worked on *Ultimate Comics: Spider-Man*, featuring Miles Morales, a black Latino Spider-Man.

Growing up as a Pakistani-American Muslim kid in New Jersey, Sana remembers feeling different from her peers. She found solace in watching the *X-Men* series, because she identified with the mutants' struggles and experiences.

MARIE You're now Marvel's Director of Content and Character Development, and you still work as an editor. What do you do?

SANA AMANAT I'll continue to serve as an editor in a smaller capacity on books like *Ms. Marvel* and *Daredevil*. An expansion on that will be developing content and projects geared toward our emerging audiences, and evaluating what content would connect with that particular readership.

The larger role will be focusing on the franchises that we're developing across our divisions, and making sure those divisions—publishing, TV, animation, films, games—are coordinating with the larger vision.

In your TEDxTeen talk, you mention that *X-Men* was one of the first comics that you loved as a kid, and you connected to the characters because they were different and misunderstood. Did you identify with a specific character?

It's always hard to nail down one specific character—so many have resonated with me in different ways. However, I loved Rogue. She is wisecracking but vulnerable, and despite how difficult things become for her, she remains strong and determined. I could connect with that—the doubt, the uncertainty, but the desire to always find a laugh somewhere. Also, I want to give a special shout to Storm, because, well, STORM.

Were there other comics that you felt a kinship with as a teenager?

Archie Comics! That's where my love of comics started. It's about a group of friends who are silly and lovable amid their teenage drama. I still love those kinds of stories and try to imbue things I work on with that sensibility.

When did you realize you wanted to work in comics?

I never realized you could be a comic-book editor if you chose to be! I had daydreamed about the idea, but always thought it was implausible. Fortunately, I knew I had a love for publishing and I interned at a few magazines, eventually getting a job with *Time* magazine out of college. From there, I took on a few different jobs, all publishing-focused.

When an opportunity arose at an indie comics company, I jumped at it. That was where I got my real start, getting trained by a fantastic former Marvel editor, MacKenzie Cadenhead, who gave me the necessary skills to craft stories. I met some wonderful people at Marvel, eventually getting me to where I am today!

If our readers wanted to make their own comics, how should they start?

Dive all in! Web comics' presence has increased significantly in the last few years because there are so many talented creators with unique voices. So if you have a story, put it together and post it!

Start with the pitch. What do you want the story to be about? Who do you want it to resonate with? Grabbing onto the central metaphor—the main pitch for the story—is the ground floor of storytelling. From there you add the other elements: main characters, environment, conflict. If you're a writer, find an artist to work with, and vice versa. Don't wait, your creative energies must be released!

What are some challenges you've faced as a woman and a person of color in a male-dominated industry?

Doubt. Doubt from others, doubt in myself. The problem with working in an industry where you are very much perceived as the minority is that there may be some people who don't believe in your capabilities, or your understanding of the medium. I was an outsider in every way. Physically, sure. But I also didn't grow up with the same sort of history with comics that many in the industry had. There was this perception that comics had to be told one way, for a specific kind of reader—and that created a lot of doubt on my part because I never felt like I could measure up to others' standards. But after a while, and with some great supporters here at Marvel, I realized I *shouldn't*. Comics lend themselves to inclusion and diversity. They can be and should be for everyone, and that's why with every book we work on, we hope that message comes across.

You co-created Ms. Marvel, the first teen American Muslim superhero with her own monthly series. Can you talk about people's responses to the character?

The larger idea resonated with a wide audience—not just Muslims, or women, but anyone who championed the idea of diversity in comics and the media at large. We also had a lot of expectations, with some people thinking that I would address all issues affecting Muslims, and others so excited about the concept that the story itself was getting lost. I did have a few people saying it was a PR gimmick, or that we were pushing the "Muslim agenda," but I hoped once they read the comic they'd change their mind. When you do something like this, negative reactions will always surface. People are afraid of what they don't know, and angry when you try to change what they've treasured for so long. But to that I'll say we aren't trying to take anything away, just trying to show how wonderful these characters can be in a slightly different light.

How do you see the future for women and people of color in the industry?

I see them being bigger power players in companies like Marvel. Marvel has always supported a push for diverse voices on all sides of the business, and that has come across in particular in the past few years. As both our stories and creators become more diverse, I expect that to become industry standard. Let's get to a point where we don't need to have the conversation anymore, where we can be supportive yet challenging of one another, to create the best, most exciting, most inspiring stories we can. ⚡

How to Wear Flowers in Your Hair

You'll look as fresh as a daisy.   By Rian

This is a simple DIY for quickly dressing up your hair with fresh flowers, which I recommend for prom, a graduation party, or any time you want to feel like a nature goddess/woodland fairy/garden nymph. The style will hold the flowers securely in place but is easy enough to undo if the blooms get droopy.

WHAT YOU'LL NEED:

- The flowers of your dreams, freshly picked or purchased in a bouquet
- Bobby pins (optional)

STEP ONE

Near your center part (or wherever you want to place your flowers), separate a roughly two-inch section of hair. I started with hair that was freshly washed, conditioned, and blown out on my blow dryer's hottest setting. Clean hair is optional, but for this style it helps to avoid oils, serums, or slippery products.

TWO

Separate the section of hair into three strands.

THREE

Braid the three strands, starting from your hairline and stopping when you have about two to three inches of braided hair. Pull the braid tight to your head (this will be the cradle for your flowers!), and leave the pieces at the braid's end loose.

FOUR

Break off a flower with some stem attached.

FIVE

Slide the flower stem-first into the braid's center root.

SIX

Adjust the stem so that it is covered by the braid or by loose hair behind the braid. If the stem still pokes through, or if your hair doesn't securely hold the flower in place or stay braided on its own, you can discreetly bobby-pin the stem, or make another braid over it.

Repeat the same steps on any other part of your head where you want to tuck a cluster of flowers. Congratulations: You look as fresh as a daisy!

THE HOPE FOR CONNECTION: AN INTERVIEW WITH GENEVIEVE LIU

A 16-year-old who created something beautiful after losing her dad. By Lena. Illustration by Kelly.

Genevieve Liu is a 16-year-old high school sophomore from Chicago, Illinois, where she lives with her mom and younger brother and sister. Last year, she founded Surviving Life After a Parent Dies (SLAP'D) to give teenagers who are grieving the loss of a parent, or both parents, a place to talk to one another, and to provide them with resources and professional support. SLAP'D came about when Genevieve was 13 and processing her own grief over the death of her dad, Dr. Donald Liu, who drowned saving two boys in Lake Michigan in 2012.

LENA Let's talk about when you started working on SLAP'D.

GENEVIEVE LIU A little over six months after my dad died, I knew that I wanted to do something for teens [who were also grieving for their parents]. Even though I had an incredible community in Chicago, I still felt very alone, and like no one really understood. I had friends who were my everything, but I felt like I couldn't relate to them very well anymore. I felt like I couldn't reach out to my siblings, because they were still trying to figure things out. Talking to the guidance counselor was awkward and awful. The people who were most helpful were teens who were in a similar situation. So that's the concept—the hope for connection, and to foster a sense of community. It started as *Let's make a blog*. But then it evolved into something a lot more interactive—more of a community and an online resource.

How did you find other teens to talk to?

There was this girl named Isabel. In fifth grade, the teacher announced that Isabel had lost her mom. I remember that Isabel left the room, and I cried. The entire class was crying. It wasn't that I could understand her situation, but I could sense the gravity, and I knew that

her life was never going to be the same. Fast-forward three years. Isabel's and my paths never really crossed. She was way cooler than I was—I was more on the quiet side. My mom, after my dad died, got Isabel and me in the same room. I was talking to her about random things, like what happens when my mom wants to date other people? What is it like going to family events? We weren't talking about profound things, but I really, for the first time, felt like I had the—she helped me make a connection that I needed to move forward. That's where the idea for SLAP'D was really born. The two of us started writing articles about parent loss. We started talking about and planning a website. Isabel and I were really a team. We don't work together anymore because she doesn't go to my school, but that was how it began—with us talking. We didn't know what was going to happen, but we knew that other teens in our situation deserved something similar to the empowerment we felt by talking about our experiences.

Before you and Isabel talked, how did you deal with your grief?

Before my dad died, my strength was in writing. After my dad died, I wrote about my experiences. For a long time, I wrote to him. After a while, I couldn't really bring myself to do that all the time. It took so much emotion, and it was very mentally draining.

Once you and Isabel had the idea for SLAP'D, what were the steps?

I was a technologically challenged 13-year-old. It shocked a lot of people that I said, "I want to start a website, potentially for millions of teens."

The thing is, websites at SLAP'D's level of [*laughs*] fanciness? They're incredibly expensive. We estimated that SLAP'D would have been in the range of 35 to 50

grand to build. My family could never dream of paying that. That meant that we needed a *lot* of pro bono work. I pitched six or seven web-development companies and found Elite Research. I love them because they saw the potential in the idea when I was a 13-year-old. They decided to code it, and they did it pro bono at the time. We're still working with them.

How did you find the other people who helped get the site off the ground?

We've tried to harness the strength of my entire community. Currently, we work through the University of Chicago's Polsky Center for Entrepreneurship and Innovation, where they focus on social innovation. I have a mentor there, and everyone at the center has helped me figure out what SLAP'D is going to become, who should be involved, and the long-term vision. I also created a board of directors early on, and they've guided me and given me the confidence I needed to self-promote and talk to people. The greatest support I have, without a question, is my mom. She's not just my hero, but also totally my best friend. She is a surgeon by training, but she works in her own nonprofit-y organization for early childhood language development. She really believed in me and supported me emotionally and financially through it.

When the site was getting started, what was your day like? Go to school, come home, then work on the site for hours?

Yes! That was pretty much it. Now there's a group of people working on the website, but there was a period when it was just me. It was scary. I knew I could always ask my mom for help, but…I don't know how to put this super eloquently, but the best medicine, or the best empowerment, for my grief was purpose. I found purpose in just looking at these other teens, and I felt like nothing could stop me. Obviously, it was still difficult in the day-to-day, but it was exciting to have something to look forward to and fight for.

Now, things have changed a lot for me with school. But this is what I wanted to do. I come home, I write articles. I have a calendar in my phone that I check constantly—I learned how to do conference calls when I was 13. It's like being a mini-businesswoman.

What are some resources you want to make available through SLAP'D?

Communities are woefully unprepared to help teens who have lost a parent, or both parents, and it's very difficult to move forward—emotionally, financially—in a positive way. The site offers peer support [through forums], but we also offer links to professional support. We've found through data, as well as talking to teens through SLAP'D focus groups, that teenagers are often unaware of the professional resources that are available, or that they're not ready to ask for them. Through SLAP'D, we're trying—I stress *trying*, because this is how we're moving forward—to create a portal for teens to get the resources they need. We're also looking forward to having SLAP'D offer scholarships for teens who have lost a parent, through organizations that are already doing these things.

One really interesting thing on the site so far is the Tributes section. How did that come together?

You know how I was writing about my dad, and to my dad, on the daily? That was helpful then, and still is, looking back—remembering these moments that I might have forgotten otherwise. As a teenager, I love class and I have so much going on that I sometimes forget to reflect on certain moments. SLAP'D is a place for teens to memorialize their parents, in a way that's comfortable and familiar to them on the internet, you know? That's how the tributes came about. I have an aunt who's always on Pinterest, and we make fun of her for it, but I realized that not only is the site addictive, but it's also a brilliant way to easily share information. The tributes are pinboards where people can memorialize their parents, through music, or writing, or whatever they need. It's one of the most highly trafficked parts of the website.

That's beautiful. Now that you've built this community, what do you see as your role at SLAP'D in the future?

That's a question I'm still figuring out, because it's constantly changing. There's a lot more to do on the website now, and I definitely play more of a supervisory role, but it ranges based on what's needed. I'm making SLAP'D sound like it's completely established—and that's not true. The heart is established, but it's always moving and changing. Right now, we're trying to scale to reach even more teens in need.

When I get wrapped up in, like, the politics of the team or different opportunities that may not be going super well I go back on the site as a user. That I find very empowering.

Are your sister and brother now old enough to use SLAP'D?

Yeah! My sister and brother are the coolest kids ever. My sister's 10, and my brother's 13. My brother's using the website, but my sister's not yet. They've both been incredibly supportive about it.

Outside of SLAP'D, what is your teen life like?

It feels a lot is moving really quickly, and then I also sometimes feel like a really lazy person! Extracurricularly, my passion outside of SLAP'D is Model UN. I recently got elected to our executive board, which has been a dream of mine since I was a freshman. I've always loved painting and drawing and writing. Also, my boyfriend is a filmmaker, and we make art together. It's a really nice escape. I have a great group of friends. I can't even begin to explain to you—I don't think I could have done any of this without them. We all have our own lives; the school that we go to is intense. Yesterday I had a really hard day. There are just some days when I really miss my dad. It was a little overwhelming, but my friends swarmed me.

You created something that you needed when it didn't exist. Now that it does, what are you getting out of it?

People ask me whether the experience has been healing, or whether it's made me grow as a person, and the answer's yes and no. I've grown because I've learned to be a leader, and I've learned to be passionate in my beliefs. Honestly, middle school was rough. In high school, I feel like I found my niche, and I knew what I wanted to do. And that brings great peace of mind. My dad was my best friend. That sounds clichéd, but no one understood me like my dad, and it's so hard to think about. The truth is that when I give lectures and talk about SLAP'D, it almost feels like I'm not internalizing it—like I'm not accepting the fact that I'm a person who lost a parent. So I don't know if this is my own way of healing—in many ways, you can never really accept it, and I feel like in some ways I've blocked it out. But I think I've found a way to at least move forward, without really moving on.

I still have to grow. People think I have the answers, or they're like, "You're so strong." And sometimes I feel like I'm not. But this community makes me strong, knowing there are other people out there, and that there are people around me. In middle school, I didn't know who I was. I always stayed close to my family and didn't branch out much. One of the things I've learned from this experience is that some people who you think are going to be there for you really aren't. But some people amaze and surprise you. I'm lucky to be able to surround myself with people I adore, and it's mutual. That's something you have to learn early on, after losing a parent, and I was lucky in that respect. It might sound weird to put it that way, but it's true. ✧

WE FOLLOWED THE SUN

Our month-long road trip through the western U.S.
By Chrissie, Eleanor, and Rachel Hardwick

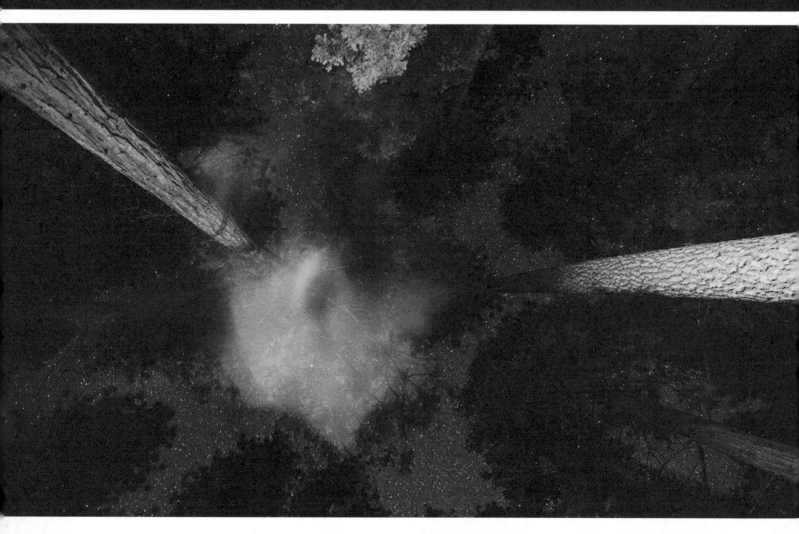

EXISTENTIAL CRISIS WEEK!!!

SPEND SOME ALONE TIME IN YOUR ROOM. MAYBE FOR A FEW HOURS. OR LESS.

GO TO SCHOOL FIVE DAYS OF THE WEEK. HAVE TESTING FOR TWO DAYS.

ONLY LISTEN TO SONIC YOUTH'S "WASHING MACHINE" FOR TWO DAYS STRAIGHT.

RIDE YOUR BIKE AROUND YOUR NEIGHBORHOOD (PREFERABLY AROUND SUNSET) WHILE LISTENING TO ARCADE FIRE AND MAC DEMARCO.

SPEND WHATEVER FREE TIME YOU HAVE *doodling*.

APRIL

☑ CUT YOUR HAIR
☐ GO SEE THAT BAND YOU'VE REALLY BEEN WANTING TO SEE

BRIANA + BREANNA
(me)

April 25th, 2015

this was supposed to be a r...

It is my fifteenth birthday today, but I do... IS TIME A SOCIAL CONSTRUCT?? Anyway, h... to go out later to watch Scream IN TH... suddenly craving Umami Burger truffle fries

IN 35 MM
TWO BY WES CRAV...
SCREAM
& SCREAM 2

FRIDAY!

SOFIA
AMANDA
LULA

CHERRY glazerr!

#GALSQUAD

Finally scored some INDIE CRED when I fell down and cut my shin on the stage. This was also my fifth time seeing them.

me in the process of blinking in a photo that is on the NYLON website

Perhaps the most fun I've ever had in my LIFE. (so far)

274

Title lettering and illustrated diary entries by Briana.

ROOKIE REGULARS

Hark! All the writing that was never tied to any monthly theme! Since the very beginning of the site, we've asked a handful of teenagers to keep a weekly diary, so here are a selection of written and illustrated entries from those who kept it up for Rookie's fourth year. Thanks to Briana, Britney, Marah, Ananda, Lilly, Simone, and Alyson for letting us into your heads and hearts, and to the graduated diary-keepers: Caitlin, Dylan, Katherine, Minna, Naomi, and Ry. Following diaries, we have answers from our contributors to questions from our readers, regarding life, love, homeschooling, broken hearts, and what to do if you can't pinpoint what your "passion" is. Proceed!

Love,

DEAR DIARY

Sanctioned snooping into the lives of real teens.

: BRITNEY :

June 11, 2014

She makes me want to be less destructive. She makes me want to be a different kind of person, one whose main quality is not uncontrollable impulsivity. I want to be someone who says the right things and can carry on long conversations without trying to cover up my awkwardness with jokes. It's really hard sometimes to remember that she likes me, especially when I am holding a microscope over my worst features.

She is my favorite person, someone I can lie down with in a field and listen to Beck and laugh and talk about anything. I feel like talking about how much I like her is the opposite of what I should be doing here, for some reason, but it would be harder to write about my week without mentioning her.

It feels so odd, after years of devout pessimism, to fall for someone who completely overturns my dark worldview. It feels a little uncomfortable, that sudden change, but I wouldn't want it any other way. Nothing is perfect, but everything is better.

June 18

It feels funny to come to this diary today with too much to say, because usually I'm fumbling for words to string together, straining to think of something that happened that people might actually be interested in reading about. But I'm writing this on Sunday night, and the past three days have been three of the most important days of my life! There are parts of what happened that I still cannot fully comprehend, and other parts I can't share for several reasons, but let me tell you, it has all been life-changing.

I had my first kiss. It happened quickly in a subway, as do so many milestones when you are a New York City teenager. All that I could think about on the Q train back to Brooklyn was how it felt as though her lips had imprinted themselves on mine. And yet, everything that happened the next day made me temporarily forget all about the kiss. (I'm back to not being able to stop thinking about it, though: replaying it in my mind, trying to remember each small detail that I held on to in the hours immediately afterward.)

Let's backtrack for a second. On Thursday, my best friend and I saw Mac DeMarco play in Brooklyn. I had never seen him live before. Then we unexpectedly ran into him at a festival two days later and even got to meet him (for a split second). It felt totally random and weirdly significant at the same time. He's been in my life a lot lately.

Friday night, I went to my very first sleepover. It was Friday the 13th and there was a full moon, so my friends and I decided to pull out the Ouija board for the first time. (So many firsts!) We talked to more than 20 spirits over the course of the night (and into the wee hours of the morning). At one point, we decorated the board with a bunch of Nirvana albums, including *In Utero* and *Nevermind*, and the next spirit we contacted said they were a fetus who had died in a miscarriage. Here, from my notes, is what they said to us through the Ouija board:

> hello
> 0-R7-BORN 0
> seventh child—miscarriage—1980
> mother R.Z.
> 7 [There was a circle around this number.]

Too much happened after that. There were some spirits who contacted us that I can't talk about. Other ones included an old college classmate of my best friend's father who had died the day before and a seven-year-old who had died in the Holocaust (they said they "HATE MUESELINI" [*sic*]). It all felt very eventful, and I was glad I hadn't done it back in 2012, when I first talked about wanting to try it. I wouldn't have been ready for it then. I am now.

I feel heavy. Thinking about going outside tomorrow feels like a threat to my well-being, but so does staying inside. My soul feels very reliant on being anxious and not knowing how to phrase anything and being worried and revisiting old thoughts without learning from them. All I can do is go over past things: the Ouija notes from Friday night, conversations, things I've written. I am afraid of not caring enough. I am afraid of being someone who doesn't care enough, who forgets about other people's cares and lives. I have seen too much of that kind of callousness in these past few days.

September 3

I broke up with her. It just wasn't working out. I try to convince myself that it was for the best while I'm standing on the train, thinking about us holding each other after the freshman formal, or at 2:33 in the morning, trying not to cry as I remember being in her arms at a punk music festival by the sea.

Everyone talks about how hard it is for the person being broken up with, but no one has ever mentioned to me how it is to be on the other side. No one explains how to build a barrier against the onslaught of memories of better times. No one tells you how to be sure you made the right choice and not try to back out of it.

November 12

I see my mom every few days when I go to visit her at the hospital, but I don't really remember what it is like to have a mother. She looks nothing like she used to, sounds nothing like she used to. It is hard to believe that this is the same woman who once spent almost all of her time worrying about me. I look in her eyes and see nothing but utter confusion, an unfamiliarity, which scares me. I don't know what to do, but even more than usual, to a "real-world" degree that extends to foreign subjects like the fate of a human life other than my own, and bills, and being absolutely alone emotionally, perhaps more than I was before. I hate this more than anything. I can't handle it.

December 3

1. The worst words I have ever heard in my entire life: "Britney, your mother passed away." I don't think I have to elaborate on the fact that out of every single thing anyone has ever said to me, those hit me the hardest—a sudden blow that knocked out my knees and birthed a dull ache that spread across my body in seconds.

2. I can't remember the last time I came home and my mother was in motion, walking around, cooking, poking her head around the corner to say hi and to watch me take my shoes off—knowing that I would come over to her and hug her. I can't remember opening the door and seeing her smile or hearing her tell me that I was home early. I can't remember the full effect of feeling her smile land on me.

3. I couldn't even hold it together on Thanksgiving. I don't know what I'll do on her birthday (December 12), on Christmas, on the 16th birthday that I was supposed to spend with her. I feel the weight of a thousand future moments that we will never share together, and I try not to cave in on myself. I try not to think about the fact that there are more than a thousand that we will never have together, because the idea of just one is hurtful enough.

4. Everyone tells me, "You will get better but you will always feel sad." This is not comforting, as you might imagine. All I've learned is that there is too much loss in the world, and that I am destined to always carry this sadness around like a ball and chain that will exist even when I am happy.

5. I am jealous of Past Me, the one whose worries were limited to staying up late and homework. I am jealous of all of my friends who can go home to their parents and talk about them with an air of carelessness, who don't have to worry that the apartment they grew up in will be gone in less than a month or who their new legal guardian will be because there is no one they are content with. I am jealous of my friends who are hanging out and going on dates and don't have to bury their best friend, the one person they could safely say they loved more than anything or anyone else.

6. I'm afraid of death, and I have been for years. Every time I think the words *The next time I see my mom, I will be dead,* I get incredibly terrified, and I should probably go see someone about it because this one sentence repeats in my mind daily. (Another thing: What if for some reason I don't see my mom after I die? What if I do something stupid in life and ruin all chances of that? Why should I even have to think about this? I shouldn't.)

7. There are so many things I should say but I can't. I don't know anymore! I really don't know! I don't know!

December 24

I find it funny that all of this is happening, and yet I am simultaneously falling more and more in love with the girl I've mentioned countless times before. She is one of the very few solid reasons that I am happy to be alive, and I mention her every week, but that is because I can never fully stress how amazing she is and how strongly I feel about her in one entry. Even writing about her now makes me smile, despite myself. Besides my mom, she is probably the only person that I have loved unconditionally. It's so strange to think about, but in the best way possible. She reminds me of something that my mother wrote about me, when I was younger: "I love her more than anything else."

January 14, 2015

"My chronic feelings of emptiness and boredom came from the fact that I was living a life based on my incapacities, which were numerous."
—Susanna Kaysen,
Girl, Interrupted, 1993

The loudness is what terrifies me the most about the situation. As soon as the lights shut off and images flash on the screen, it crashes down on me, a wave of sound drowning me. I come out of the fetal position that I contorted my body into on a plush chair in the very back corner of the theater and look around frantically, trying to see if anyone else realizes that it is too loud in the room, that someone needs to tell whoever is in control to turn it down, but unsurprisingly, I am alone in my shock. Everyone else seems fine as they continue either talking to whoever came with them to see the movie or eating, their eyes fixated on the flashing pictures as their hands move mechanically to their waiting, open mouths. The room is small. I am in proximity to everyone here and yet I still feel a strong absence of human contact. The girl who was supposed to see this with me did not show up and I am all alone and it is now that I realize that I have not been to a movie theater since what seems like ages ago, on July 8, with my mother for my birthday. There are tears in my eyes as the trailers play, and I can't tell if it's because she's not there or because the girl isn't there, and then I decide that it could be both, but it doesn't matter. There is a severe feeling of unwantedness that gnaws at my chest as I try to assimilate to the actions of the other people in the room and watch the screen quietly, letting its strong glow pull me in.

After the movie ends, I am eating lunch when the girl tells me that she was late but is still in the area if I want to meet up. I'm not surprised; I tell her that I'm going home and walk to the F train, an action that feels unfamiliar even though I did it every day up until recently. I am a professional out of practice. The train has not arrived, so I stand on the platform, waiting for a few minutes, when suddenly, something inside my mind switches. I don't know what it is, and the only two things I can liken it to are a cloud of murkiness and depersonalization, although the second comparison is severely flawed. It feels a lot like depersonalization in the sense that I am no longer in my body and am watching from the outside, but I still know it's me. It's more comparable to when you're in a dream, and you can see everything that is happening to you from a bird's-eye view. I hear the train coming and see its familiar lights on the dirty tiled wall of the subway, and I walk toward the edge of the platform. It feels normal, like I am walking down the street, and then, when I am about to step off, I snap out of it and pull my body back, shaking. This is what causes me to look up "involuntary suicide attempt" later on (the search yielded no real results but I'm sure it's happened to at least a few other people). I am scared when I realize what I am doing and I am scared later on, thinking and writing about the experience, because I don't understand it at all. I think my life is, in layman's terms, pretty much garbage, but not enough for me to actually want to kill myself. Even when I think about it, it is still a passing thought, nothing that I would ever actually want to do, so it terrifies me that this happened, and it makes me incredibly uneasy to think that my body, for a few minutes, was able to control my mind.

When I get home, I tell the girl about what happened, with great hesitation (but of course, the need for release overrules the wariness). She tells me that I will get better. Someone insists that I will get better at least once a week, tells me with an almost convincing smile that soon my life will be great and that my mind will be stable and I may even be happy. It's almost like a game; I tell someone about my life and they tell me not to worry and I say OK and they believe that I am taking their words into account. It's a trope. I still tell it to myself every day, though, and mentally make very short lists of things to look forward to (warm weather, being put on the antidepressants that I've needed for years), and hope that in a few months I won't have to constantly remind myself of reasons I should feel good about life, or feel untethered, floating in a sea of my emotions, spilling how I feel to anyone who will listen. I miss not feeling either empty or full of a toxic mix of anger and sadness.

February 11
Nighttime is a chamber of reflection—a fact that I no longer take comfort in. I am always too afraid to sleep; even when I do, I wake up every few hours, jolted by my own mind. The wind shrieks outside my new room every night, and closing my eyes with the lights off racks my body with anxiety: I constantly think that I hear something, or see something in the corner. I get four hours of sleep at most. I am a shell of a shell of my former self.

February 18
I despise how my face looks so much that it literally makes me hate my life. Out of everything that has happened to me, I find it funny in the saddest of ways that this is what hurts me the most. I don't like bringing it up or telling others because I feel like I am exposing the most vulnerable part of me to them, and I hate having visible weak spots, but it is something that presses on my mind to no end. It's the one thing that I feel completely hopeless about, and that makes me feel furious and sad and all sorts of other negative things that I'd rather not be feeling, especially now.

I don't like wanting to punch my reflection the way that at least one angsty teen protagonist has done in some movie. I don't like feeling the most dreadful jealousy when people come up to my friends and me and tell them how beautiful they are while I idle in the background, feeling like I did in middle school when I tried to keep a straight face as people told me how ugly I was. I pass by windows and try not to cry when I see my face looking back at me.

It has only gotten worse and worse as I've gotten older and not blossomed into the beautiful young lady that everyone has led me to believe I'd become. In fact, I didn't even become cool enough to compensate for my looks. I'm just…here. I hate it, and to a certain extent, I hate me.

March 18
I. My hair smells like the clay that stained my fingers with its scent in art class when I was younger. I think of you.

II. I listen to "Cherub Rock" by the Smashing Pumpkins and it makes me think of freshman year. For the first time in a while, I feel it, like, REALLY feel it. When I watched the video for it before school last year in the living room of my old apartment, I thought my heart would burst out of my chest.

III. It is warm out, to my surprise. I am wearing your brown flannel. I know I will have to give it back later, but it was enough to smell you as I slept.

IV. I wish we could go to Enchantments together today. I cried every day of September after we broke up. I had night terrors for a week. I'm not kidding when I say I think you're a witch, an absolute enchantress. Your grip on me refuses to falter, and that makes me incredibly overjoyed.

March 25
I. You are the seraph in the corner of my eye, always.

II. I don't want to be a lonely soul. I bleed from the inside. It is the spring equinox yet winter still bears down on the city outside my frosted window.

III. The metal of your braces is beautiful. "ANGEL" is embroidered on my chest in white. I cling to small details; they keep me grounded.

IV. I think about making a blood pact with you. I have *Natural Born Killers* on the brain. It reminds me of how morbid I used to be. What happened? I can't tell if I've been dulled or reformed.

V. I ask you if we can go to a forest when it is warm. In my mind, we exist separate from the world, the way everything else that I love comes to exist. I don't understand certain parts of my life anymore so this is one thing that I can keep sacred, that won't confuse me and won't burden me. I feel free with you.

April 1

1. When I was in the tub, through a Xanax- and Ambien-induced haze, I came across two brothers on a path; Cain and Abel, perhaps? Shrouded by death, they tell me to go back, go back, not yet. I sink deeper, and the burning sensation of the water flooding my body propels me forward, leaving me gasping in the middle of the bath, shaking and fragile.

2. I realize that all I do now is compile my thoughts through lists. I've become less interested in focusing on a single moment and more involved in stringing together the pieces of my life each day, each week. It brings me comfort.

3. I've met a Pisces who does not have my Cancerian moodiness and understands the feeling of being unable to get out of bed for school, and hating Prozac, and existing within a void, and constantly searching for people who can understand you—who are willing to listen no matter how abnormal your feelings and thoughts may seem.

4. A task to complete as soon as possible: Clean out my room, create space for an altar, surround myself with figurines and pictures and symbols that make me feel completely comfortable and safe, that let my internal world imprint on my external environment.

5. One of my best friends and I make a pact to spend the summer after senior year in the Midwest. We believe that we share a past life that nobody else understands when we try to explain it to them. We've met just once in person, and yet we seem to share a soul.

6. There are scratches and open wounds all over my body; they are unintentional. I seem to attack myself during my sleep. My restless subconscious takes out my issues on my flesh.

7. I think of my mother every single day but I am happy. Memories no longer consume me to the point of immobility. For once, I feel whole, or almost whole. Things are getting better; I can say this with absolute assurance.

April 8

I. I listen to Teen Suicide, and Sonic Youth's "Bull in the Heather" on repeat, whether I am walking the dogs or staring out of my window, crying, hoping the release of my tears will somehow soothe the aching in my chest. "Cherub Rock" reminds me of the Pisces. I blanket myself in songs that call him to mind even though I know how dangerous that is. Music has always provided me with solace; now, it's making me more confused than ever. Attaching songs to people is dangerous, I realize, and yet I still do it. I never learn. My mother used to tell me that. "You never learn, Britney," she'd say disapprovingly. She was right, in a sense.

II. My anxiety levels have gone down. I do not have panic attacks. I do not shake on public transit and dissociate on the way to school. Yet I worry about the future, about things not working out the way I want them to, so much that it's consumed me. I wear a coat of apprehension throughout everything. People tell me to focus on myself and I can't. I can't, I can't, I can't.

III. I've morphed so much in the space of a few months—internally and externally—that it's incredible. I can't even begin to sum it all up but I wish I could because there have been so many significant changes. I never thought that I'd be at this point. I never thought that any of this would happen to me. "It's like we're in a movie," the Pisces said when he came over.

IV. The Pisces tells me to look at him. Our staring contests have become a quick ritual. His eyes change from green to the color of the ocean. He tells me that my eyes are black. It would be best if I stopped thinking about him.

V. I've become less relatable. I don't know how that makes me feel.

VI. I am my own hell.

May 6

Inpatient was my very own *Girl, Interrupted;* I didn't realize it until halfway through my stay. There was no girl hoarding chicken carcasses the way Susanna Kaysen told me there would be. Instead, there was a girl with paranoid schizophrenia in the room next to me—she would laugh to herself, had a table all to herself during our group sessions, and punched at least one person in the ward a week. There was a 17-year-old convinced that she was going to hell, who had a bar through the tip of her tongue and ROSEMARY tattooed in giant letters on her arm. She was the first person I saw when the intake nurse wheeled me into the unit in the dead of night; she was standing in the doorway of her room, grinning deliriously. Her smile carved itself into my brain for the rest of the night, until I woke up bathed in daylight to the presence of 10 or so doctors at the foot of my bed.

I have no intention of filling up this entry with all the details of my stay. I made friends. I filled page after page of my diary with surprising introspection, and how intensely I missed the Pisces (to whom I wrote a letter, addressed to "the Pisces with blue eyes and fragile skin," with the words "MY HEART IS ON ITS DEATHBED" at the top of the page). I stayed up for two days talking to my second roommate—the first was a schizophrenic girl who snored—our hours-long discussions not stopped by the nurses making night rounds, or by the interruption of sunrise. The paranoid-schizophrenic girl followed me to my room when I was packing up, screaming about how she should've been the one being discharged, until a nurse restrained her. I cried when I left. I have not felt the same since.

This diary entry does my stay absolutely no justice. It does my feelings no justice, it does my thoughts no justice. I wish I could list all the people I met, all the experiences I had with them, the small quirks of the ward that simultaneously pissed me off and made me feel like I was in the right place. I miss sitting around a table with all the other kids on medication and comparing our shaking hands. I miss the endless card games. Most of all, I miss how safe I felt. I feel so vulnerable out here, in the real world, and it worsens every day. I have no motivation. My future seems more like impending doom than something to look forward to.

Today on the train, I saw a boy with long brown hair who reminded me of myself so much. It was the way his eyes looked, their blueness tinged with an unmistakable sadness, the way he kept glancing at himself in the window and then letting out soft sighs of frustration. He was so beautiful to me. He reminded me of one of the thoughts I had on my first day of inpatient, when I lay for hours underneath borrowed sheets: *I want to be with someone who can recognize what I'm feeling by looking into my eyes, who is sensitive and interesting and actually makes me think.* It's funny how a stranger can bring about a sudden rush of forgotten emotions; I think it mainly has to do with my Cancerian nature, to project so much onto people I don't or barely know. Everything I think about now, I somehow manage to connect it to something that has happened in the past week at the hospital, and I hate it. I'm sick of being the type of person who holds on to things so strongly, because, in the end, the result tends to be great pain.

I'm tired. ⚡

{MARAH}*

June 11, 2014
Tomorrow my dreams will come true. I will bid my family farewell, leave my hometown, and head to Damascus, the capital of Syria, to sit for my high school final exams.

---

*Marah is a pen name created to protect this contributor's identity. Marah's diaries were produced in collaboration with Syria Deeply (syriadeeply.org), a digital news outlet covering the Syrian crisis. They were translated from the Arabic by Mais Istanbelli.

I'm happy and scared at the same time. The fear is overwhelming! I will have to go through two checkpoints, where I will be searched and asked for my identification papers. Supposing I'm able to pass safely through the checkpoints, the next step will be to go to the home of my relatives, with whom I'll be staying. How will life be with them? I don't know them super well, and this will be my first time staying at their house. Will I feel comfortable?

I'm currently studying as much as I can. But the harsh living conditions and regular power outages don't always allow me to study well.

I often wonder if I will be able to fulfill my bigger dreams, and whether I am worthy of them. My mother's happiness hinges on my success. She has worked herself to the bone to get me to where I am today. She smiles at me, but I know she's even more confused and scared than I am. I will miss hearing her voice.

What if I don't make it back? What if I never see my siblings—two sisters and a little brother—again? I am not ready to face the possibility of losing them. I'm a bundle of nerves.

For the first time in the two months since I started this diary, I'm writing it with a shaky hand and teary eyes.

June 18
Everything in this new world is unfamiliar. So many of the people I have known and loved are now gone, and I'm alone, struggling to find my way. My father, my grandfather, and my grandmother were snatched away. I remember my favorite uncle—I looked forward so fervently to his visits. He was hit by a mortar shell and died. I miss him.

My extended family used to gather at our house. That was before the war. Everyone's gone; our city looks like a ghost town. Both of my aunts fled as soon as the bombing started—one now lives in Egypt, the other in Turkey. Most of my uncles managed to make their way to Libya. Another one went to Lebanon. The last one is still here. We were once a family, but we've splintered into so many fragments that it would be impossible to reassemble

us into a whole.

I often call my cousin, who used to be my confidante, and my friend Hanin. I'm attached to the phone—it is my salvation from the darkness that shrouds my city. But hearing people's voices doesn't satisfy my yearning to see them in front of me. And the phone can't put me in touch with those who are gone forever.

Those who have stuck around here are permanently scarred. My uncle is present, but distant. My friends are so consumed with their own sadness that it's hard to reach them anymore—we've lost our closeness. I am terribly lonely. I fluctuate between love for everyone and hatred for the ones who left to lead better lives elsewhere. It hurts to think about the latter group—they remind me of my past, the grand life that I loved, that I still love, but that is painful to remember.

June 25
I had my first encounter with love at the age of 15. I was walking to school when I suddenly got the sense that I was being followed. I turned around and saw a boy who used to live near my house. He was tall, dark, and handsome, with big eyes. He was dressed beautifully. He wasn't like any of the other guys I had seen around.

It took him a while to gather the courage to approach me, but one day he came up to me at school and asked if he might have five minutes of my time. He told me he liked me and wanted to be friends. I wanted to get to know him, too, but in that moment I got shy and said no. He looked crestfallen, but accepted my answer.

That night, in bed, I couldn't believe what I'd done. I wondered if I'd lost my chance forever, or if he'd talk to me again. Next time I wouldn't be so nervous.

The very next day, that boy called me on my cell. After that, we talked on the phone often, but in school, we ignored each other. We didn't want people to realize what we were beginning to: that our friendship was becoming our first love.

When Syria's war began three years ago, the boy decided to fight with the opposition. Before he left our city, he asked me to meet him at the library. There, he

told me he'd be gone for two months of training. I cried a lot. His hand reached for my face and settled on my cheek. Our first physical contact! I blushed.

I didn't hear from him for two months. I was a teenager in love in a time of conflict; I was scared for him and yearned for him. Then he returned and we met once again at the library. We ran to each other and grabbed hands. He wanted to hug me, but I refused—I am from a conservative family and was brought up with strong religious values that prevented me from being physically affectionate with him in public.

We sat in the library for a long time, talking about our present and our future. He said he was going to fight on the front lines in the morning. I begged him not to go, but he had made up his mind.

I got the news the next day that he had been killed. At first, I couldn't believe it. I cried so much I thought I would die. My mother, who knew nothing of our romance, could tell something was wrong. I finally told her the whole story, regardless of how she would react. (She was not angry with me.) I couldn't forgive myself for refusing to hug him the day before. That night I had a dream that he and I were together, walking in the rain.

It's now been two years since my first love died. Don't mock me, but my broken heart tells me that I will meet him again.

July 30

He is a handsome man in his 50s, with a white face, green eyes, and a gray stripe through his hair. He is well educated. He has never been married. He is an old friend of my late father. He even resembles him, inside and out. He lives far away, in Sweden. We call him Uncle Amjad.

He offered to send money to help my family. I said if he tried, I'd just send it back. He praised my mother for the way she's raising us. He said my father was lucky to have had her as a wife.

Then he asked me to marry him. He told me I'd be his spoiled princess. He said he'd make all my dreams come true.

I'm seriously considering it. He could be my savior, the man who could put me

on a magic carpet and carry me from a land of despair to a world where wishes and ambitions stand a chance of being fulfilled. I would move to Sweden, where I could study and have a good life, and Uncle Amjad would take care of me and treat me like a princess. It sounds so much better than staying in Syria, a country that is falling apart.

I told my mother about it. She was furious. And then she calmed down and explained to me how dangerous it would be for me to accept his offer.

"He is 30 years older than you," she said. "You won't be able to understand him. He won't understand you, either. This is not right for you—try to find your own way. You're still young. Please, don't waste yourself like that. You'll regret it. Marriage is not about relying on someone else completely; it is about sharing. Such a relationship will never be balanced. He would just be like a financier for your ambitions, instead of being a life partner."

I always trust my mother, no matter what. So for now, my notions of Uncle Amjad have been dashed. But would it really be so bad to marry him? How much worse could that life, as Uncle Amjad's wife, be than what I'm going through now? It seems like it would be a much more peaceful existence, with no problems and no pain. Is it wrong of me to want it? I need your advice, please.

October 15

Not long ago, I was shrouded in darkness. Then I saw a light at the end of the tunnel: I passed my government exams and graduated from high school. My heart skipped a beat, my emotions ran wild, I felt like my joy was too great to be contained by the world itself. I had a new lease on life!

Now, I embark on a new journey: I have left al-Ghouta, my war-besieged hometown, and enrolled at a university in Damascus, our capital, to continue my education. I feel like a new person, on the threshold of a new life, after having weathered so much suffering. I will open the door to this next phase with strong arms and a steady heart. I will try my best to live up to this dream that for so long

seemed impossible to attain. In spite of the rigid educational system here, which dictates what you can and can't study according to your grades, I will find a way to study a subject I love.

I called my mother in al-Ghouta to tell her the news. Her trembling voice revealed her happiness as she congratulated me. She asked me to share the story of my success with my two sisters. They had left al-Ghouta a month earlier and moved in with our great-uncle in al-Tal, an area far from the capital. My mother stayed behind, as leaving the city requires a lot of money and even more paperwork, neither of which she has finished putting together. I heeded my mother's advice and went to pay my sisters a visit, crossing many checkpoints on the way. We spent a happy, joyous evening together—the kind of night I haven't had in way too long.

But it seems all our fun had angered the fates, because the next morning al-Tal was hit by heavy shelling. The city went on lockdown; no one was allowed to leave. I spent two days locked up in my great-uncle's house, filled with a terror that has become all too familiar to me. It's unbelievable how this quiet city turned into a battleground the moment I arrived!

I wonder why we are denied joy. I don't know what happened or what will happen, but I know that I am stronger than I used to be, and I will overcome all obstacles to live in a new world—one I will create for myself.

October 22

I remember my father every day. I miss him and I wish he were still here. I wish he could share my joy at finally going to college. I decided to enroll at the pharmacology institution in Damascus, which was a dream he always had for me. Today, I made his wish come true, and he is not around to bless my success.

I will study here for two years, then I will do two more at a specialized pharmacology college. After I finish, I plan to open a medical laboratory of my own. My classes start next week. I'm so happy about this new phase of my life that I am starting to see a glimpse of hope; I feel that a whole different life is ahead of me.

Life is vast with open doors, but my mind always tempers my joy with a fear of disappointment and frustration. At my age, you might imagine that I'd be an adventurous, wild teenager with some handsome guy in my life, but I'm not like that. The pain of war forced me to get over all that. It turned me into a very serious girl. I don't trust fate anymore; it keeps taking happiness away from me. I have reached a point when my motto has become: After the rain, there is always a flood, and after the calmness of the sea, there is always a storm of waves.

I'm not weak. I know my goals and I'm going after them, but I'm a human being, not a stone. And I question where my place is in all of this. Am I going to be worthy of the future?

October 29

Something happened to me that may have changed the course of my life. I saw a little child with one leg, walking and leaning on a stick, and then he suddenly fell to the ground and smashed his nose. Although his father was next to him, I ran to him and held his hand to help him up. His father told me that they came from one of the damaged areas in my country. The child had lost his leg as a result of being hit by missile fragments, and they came here to Damascus to seek treatment, after a lot of paperwork and bitter struggles. I came back home with so many thoughts troubling my mind. I pictured the disabled children and young people in every street in my hometown. I felt their pain and suffering, and then there was this weird feeling of missing my town and its people. I miss it and long for it, even after I went through all the trouble to run away from it. Sometimes I feel my soul seeking its ambition, and sometimes I feel very weak and vulnerable, worn out by pain and devoid of feelings toward those I love… that's if I still can feel love!

And for the first time I've started asking myself: What have I done to my town, to my people? What is my duty now that I have become aware of and responsible for my country?

I spent the whole night sleepless, and I kept seeing those images in al-Ghouta, like a constant film of suffering repeated over and over, and then a crazy idea that I had never thought of before hit me. The idea was to leave my field of study and move from pharmacology to learning about prosthetic limbs and physical treatment, because my country and its people are in extreme need for people working in this field.

I told my mother, and she encouraged me to quit pharmacology, as she knows I only went for it to fulfill my father's wish. I wish I could study prosthetics abroad—it would enable me to fulfill my duty to my people. Maybe if I do this, my soul will be at peace, and it may calm the restless chaos and constant worries inside me.

November 12

I had my first day at the prosthetics institution where I now attend university. For a special session, a professor asked us to observe the amputation of a leg—those who could bear the sight of it. I was among those who volunteered to watch the amputation. The doctor positioned the leg before us. My hands and legs were shaking and my heart was beating too fast. I blacked out, although I looked awake. The whole procedure happened, but it's as though I didn't see any of it—I don't remember how it was done, although I was standing right there with my eyes open.

My body was there, but my mind and senses were far away, like the scattered body parts and blood in my war-torn town. I suddenly remembered my friend who disappeared, and my father, whose limbs were scattered, and the many disabled people in my hometown. Despite my desperate need to reveal my pain, I held back. I went home to my bed, where I'm used to drowning myself with tears of hurt and anger. I left my hometown hoping to forget all the injustices and horrors I went through, but it seems impossible to let go.

The funny yet sad part of the story is that the other students revered me for witnessing the amputation. I thought and thought, and I still don't have a logical explanation for what happened.

The doctor praised me for hanging in

there and not stepping back, too. He told me that, with time, I will get used to it. But the truth is, I don't want to ever get used to it. I fear that I might have chosen the wrong field of study, because it requires a strong and healthy heart.

December 3

Great news! A wonderful surprise! I was finally going to see my mother again. It had been seven months since I last saw her, and she called us to say she was arriving the next day. We almost danced to the news. My sisters and I stayed up waiting for my mother's return and for our lives to resume. My youngest sister turned into a little chatterbox. My middle sister pushed her books away and cried with joy.

The next day, we skipped school and stayed home waiting for her arrival. We shared an overwhelming happiness and excitement. Then the phone rang: There had been problems and our mother wasn't going to make it. What's worse: She didn't mention a date on which she could visit us. Our disappointment was insurmountable.

The pain and disappointment left my youngest sister ill. My middle sister turned to her books again and stopped talking to anyone. My aunt with whom we're staying made fun of us, not knowing what we're going through. She doesn't understand that our mother is all we have left of our family. We lost our family, our community, and our city. Only my mother is capable of gluing us back together. Seeing our own mother has become a far-fetched dream, maybe even an impossible dream. Cold people, robbed rights, and slumbering people and states. Will we be able to find ourselves?

A robot is an emotionless entity, commanded by chips and wiring. That's what humans here have become, led by interests and money and robbed of their humanity. I feel bitter pain when I discover the ugliness of people, especially in those I love. I'm talking about my aunt with whom we're staying. She stirred up problems between us and used hurtful words. I did not respond, as I was brought up to respect my elders. I took my sisters to our room to avoid further confrontations, but my aunt was relentless. I decided I wanted to move out with my sisters and rent our own place, but my mother opposed my decision. She said she's scared for us and that she's being respectful of the traditions in our city. It isn't allowed for three girls our age to live on their own. What would we do if the security situation deteriorated? Our city was completely destroyed, its people displaced, but its traditions are still firmly rooted. How strange!

My mother asks us to be strong, but if we dare make our own decisions or take an independent step, she stops us. I'm so tired. That I'm the eldest of my siblings means I am responsible for them. I often have to encourage and comfort them, assuming the role of our mother. I miss fighting with my sisters. Our silly fights used to add flavor to our days, but my relationship with my sisters has grown stronger. We learn new lessons and have new experiences, but when will these lessons stop being hard and painful? I'm bored of all this. I don't know what to do. What kills me is the silence. Must I find a bottomless pit and scream into it like they do in the movies? I hate silence, and there will come a time when I will erupt like a volcano, not to destroy but to rectify what's gone astray.

January 14, 2015
Our hearts and feelings can swing like a pendulum, as I discovered in a recent adventure. I was invited to my friend's wedding, and I accepted the invitation because they insisted (in addition to a tiny feeling I had that I wanted to go). I was scared and hesitant because I had completely forgotten wedding and party traditions, as they have vanished in my city. Weddings in my town are now only held inside people's homes, and most marriages are arranged without a wedding or a celebration in fear of earlier raids and recent bombings. Anyway, all these matters are trivial when there's chemistry and harmony between the couple.

I prepared myself for the party, and if you only knew how much trouble I went through, because I found myself unable to use the hair dryer that had been lying there for three years. In the end, I did my best to look like the other girls. I walked into the hall with my friends, and it was very exciting, lights everywhere and loud songs echoing all around, and there were women and girls moving around elegant tables, all beautifully dressed with the finest hairstyles, exchanging polite smiles. The bride looked like a queen in her white dress with her friends and relatives around her like her maids, a charming scene that I hadn't seen in four years. I didn't even think it existed in this new world. I was staring at everything as if I were a Neanderthal looking through a window to the 21st century, because those years of pain, agony, and deprivation of all joy are not to be underestimated.

I was attracted by the sight of the girls dancing gracefully and skillfully. I was invited to dance with the bride, but I refused because I didn't know how to dance anymore. I used to be one of the best when I was a teenager, when all I cared about was having fun and going wild.

The truth is, I wished I could dance madly and be myself again for a few moments, but I only stood there and watched, not wanting to be made fun of.

In the middle of the party they announced the arrival of the groom, who had just come from the men's party to take his bride. There was a special song for his entrance, and the bride moved to meet him after she covered her face with her veil. The groom came and lifted her veil and kissed her cheek. In that moment a weird feeling touched the female inside me. My heart moved, and I watched how they put the rings on each other's fingers and kissed and danced like two little birds, unaware of the crowd around them.

The camera was following them, and a big screen was showing pictures of them as children and teenagers, and of their engagement and wedding. Then the groom gave a little speech thanking the bride for agreeing to marry him, and she did the same, and then she threw the bouquet of roses and the girls rushed to catch it, each of them hoping to be the next bride.

Finally, the groom took his bride away in a decorated fancy car, and the party was over and I went home with images of the wedding in my mind. When I put my head on my pillow, tears started pouring down my face. I'm not sure why! Is it because I was feeling sad about my hometown and what happened to it, and the difference between here and there? This wedding allowed joy to sneak into my heart and shake it, and revived my sense of femininity after its long slumber. It provoked my desire to be a bride, and I started to imagine how that would be against my will.

But I wonder if it's possible for me to come out of this crisis as a normal girl willing to love, marry, and have a family. I have no interest in men anymore, so how can I ever fall in love and become a lover?! And if I ever do, I don't think it would be a successful story, because the crisis ruined all beautiful things inside me in a way that they cannot be mended. Most important, there isn't a single person in the world that I can trust; thus, I cannot fall in love with anyone. Life keeps swinging us between dreams and wishes, pain and hope, and eventually what happens to us is only what's destined to happen, so I only hope the unknown will be more merciful and gentle to me. I only hope.

January 21
I would like to start this diary entry with a moment of silence for the victims of the crisis in Syria, which has seen hideous death and pain. We have lost too many, and we would drown in tears if we were to count them all.

The last four years have been odd beyond imagination. No one could have predicted these strange years of sad Syrian history, as the whole world watched passively, and just waited for what was coming next, with its arms folded.

Now it's a new year, and we don't know what's in store for us. We cannot predict it, because the balance of life is disrupted. Smiling faces in the street, traditional Christmas cookies, the delightful Christmas trees full of bells: All these things used to symbolize happiness, and perhaps these symbols could be restored. I feel very sad about Santa Claus, who turned from being a symbol of hope and goodness into a symbol of horror, and the gifts of Christmas Eve were bombs raining on children's beds, taking their lives and killing their innocent childish dreams. I'm sorry for the redness of Santa's outfit, as it became a symbol of all the bloodshed.

When I was a little girl, New Year's Eve was a very special occasion. I used to wait for Santa Claus to put a gift under my pillow. It's not our Eid to celebrate, but my mom seized joy wherever it was, and she always brought some of it home. I used to look forward to this day, as we used to go to the al-Hamidiyah market to watch Santa Claus stand at the gate giving out candies and balloons. At the end of the market, Umayyad Mosque stood tall and proud, and on its right was the Goldsmiths' market, which used to be bustling with Jewish people. Close to that was the area of Bab Touma, where Christians mostly lived. There was also the Sayyidah Ruqayya Mosque, which is a shrine for the Shiites. All the shops in the market celebrated, and this gave the impression that Eid was for everyone, and you could feel the harmony among people of different religions to the extent that you couldn't tell the difference between them. We've always shared their joys, and they've shared ours. We respected their religions, and they respected ours. I remember going back home filled with happiness with a Santa hat on my head, thinking thoughts of peace and love. This night was also my father's birthday, so my mom made sweets and we all sat together and filled the place with laughter in the wonderful candlelight.

What distorted our religion with all the killing and horrors? What drew a red line between it and other religions? Sectarianism was spread among us, although we're all humans and all living in Syria. We were born to build on this earth, not defile it. Everything around us has changed, or maybe it's us who changed. We love what we hated, and maybe hate what we loved, to the extent that we forgot what we once clung to, and our principles are gone.

With the beginning of 2015, let's allow ourselves to reflect on the old days. Let's take a look at the past four years and wonder, *Were we winning or losing?* Our losses are limitless, we lost the lives of many, a lot of us are physically or psychologically disabled, our youth lost their dreams, our children lost their smiles. We live a life without hope, our days have no future, there is disintegration, dispersion, and homelessness. The most precious thing we lost was our humanity and our self-respect, for we will realize that we've been fighting one another only when it's too late, when Syria sinks in great pain and with deep wounds, and Syrians have lost their dignity and their lives.

I will do what I used to do when I was little: I will close my eyes and wish for a new year in which the lost humanity will find its way back to being human. Let's all clean our hearts and minds to find peace, and to live a decent life.

Will my wish for this year come true? Or will it remain only a dream?

February 11

Through the darkness of the night appears the moon; from a thorny plant emerges a delicious fruit; beautiful flowers break through rocks and stones. That's how life is, with all its pain and ugliness. It also gives you hope to lift you up and bring you strength. In spite of all the difficulties I'm facing, success finds its way to me, giving me sweet pleasure and pushing me to be optimistic about life.

I passed my educational training in the specialized camp for prosthetics, and I managed to make and install a prosthesis all by myself. I scored third in my class. I was hoping for better results, but it's OK for a beginner like me. My participation in this camp was of great benefit for me, as it was practical to what I'm studying. After two months, there will be a course in my field of study held by the Ministry of Health. But to register, you have to pay a certain amount of money. Honestly, I felt embarrassed to ask for the money from my mother when I know that she barely has enough to manage our lives, so I had to work.

For the first time in my life, I have a job, and I will get paid for my own work. It's been two weeks in the job now; I feel exhausted because I go out in the morning to my college and as soon as I finish my lectures I run to my job, which is at a big company that sells electrical devices. My job is to explain the features of the devices to customers.

The thing that bothers me about this job is that I have to smile and accept whatever customers say without making any comment. The owner of the business is a kind man. He reminds me of my grandfather with his kindness, and I like and respect him. I am excited to have this experience, in spite of its disadvantages, as it will provide me with the money I need without asking my mother, who hasn't yet found a job here.

Life in the capital is not as easy as I thought it would be. Sometimes I blame myself and feel responsible for encouraging my family to come here. I was unaware of the costs here, such as rent, study expenses, and other expenditures. For example, a week ago, I got hepatitis. We spent a lot of money on doctors, tests, and medicines. It made my mother very worried that the infection would spread to my sisters and brother, and she did her best to avoid that. I always fear her strength will weaken and she will lose her smile, which is the secret to our life.

My 11-year-old brother, Muhammad, no longer settles for little after seeing the difference between here and home. He's also become aggressive. He has lost his ability to communicate with others, especially adults. He has become bad tempered, unwilling to listen to what my mother tells him, and his reaction to everything is always to attack. My mother is very worried about him, and she's trying her best to correct his behavior, especially now that he's in the beginning of his teenage years.

As for my 16-year-old sister, Lana, she's adapting fast. My mother fears for her in this messy new atmosphere, where it's easy to slip and make mistakes. As for the middle one, Maya, who is 17, she's preparing to graduate from high school. It's aching my mother's heart that she hasn't been able to provide her with tutors or a good school. Maya clings to her books, dreaming of a great future.

Is it the place that changed us, or is it our financial situation that's affecting us? In spite of all this, I feel that a great event is ahead of us. It could be a golden job opportunity for my mom, or a chance for my family to travel, or…I don't know, but something inside me is giving me hope. Tragedies can break glass, but they make iron harder, and I won't be easily broken, ever.

March 4

I was brought up as a rose is tended to in a loving environment, one that's given fresh water and nurtured by a gentle breeze. It left in me the senses of youth and tranquility, which, until now, I thought would always be present. I didn't know that the world around me was filled with ugliness.

I experienced the same strange feelings as when my father died, when relatives turned into strangers, and when friends turned into enemies. My mother argued with me about this realization, convincing me, once again, that every person has their own set of circumstances and reasons that would explain their situation, excuse their actions, and relieve them of any guilt or blame.

But then I saw the ugliness with my own eyes. My city was filled with bad people who had lost their humanity, who didn't care about a child going hungry or being cold, and who didn't care that the blood of innocent people was being shed as they blindly followed their greed for wealth.

I left my city in search of a better and purer world. Unfortunately, I have only encountered the worst here. Everywhere I turn, I see degenerate people whose lack of morals and deceit I've never been accustomed to tolerating or accepting. They are a different breed. For a minute, I thought they might belong to a different planet. This was particularly true in university, where one can find all kinds of people. I found myself making up excuses for everyone, silencing what I believe in, and not knowing how to get myself back on the right track.

I soon started a new job—the one I told you about—which allowed me to meet different kinds of people. One customer was an arrogant, ignorant man with no manners. On his second visit, he tried to harass me in such a lowly fashion that I couldn't help slapping him out of rage. The store manager held me accountable; he only cared for the reputation of the store, and the customer was a man of means. I

insisted that I wasn't in the wrong. That alone would have cost me my job if it weren't for the company owner, a lovely old man who intervened and put an end to the situation with a few wise words.

After the customer left, the old man pointed out that I shouldn't repeat what I did, and that I must learn to control my anger. He said power lies in the ability to exercise self-restraint, and asked that I be stronger and wiser to face the city life that was very different from the quiet countryside where I came from.

I returned home, my mind racing. Am I meant to become a monster fighting in a jungle full of predators, or am I meant to give up my principles and go with this overpowering tide that's pulling me elsewhere?

I asked my mother to explain what the required change was, and she told me the story of the falcon. When a falcon turns 40, either it chooses to succumb to death or it decides to go through a painful transformation where it breaks its claws and beak, and plucks its old feathers that had been hindering its flight. My mother explained the amount of pain and hardship the falcon must go through to allow itself to live on for another 30 years. It was only then that I realized that one must change on the journey of self-improvement. I will do my best to change for the better, and when I am where I want to be, I will work on eradicating all of the misconceptions out there. Only then I won't be marginalized and weak, but I will be stronger thanks to the positive transformation I went through. ♆

ANANDA

July 16, 2014

The night was quiet and the sky was dark. Heavy clouds slowly made their way through the atmosphere. I crawled into bed, my stomach full of cake and my head with the wish I made when I blew out the candles. I was slowly drifting off to a peaceful slumber when my phone buzzed.

"Hello?" I whispered. There was heavy breathing on the other end. "Jess, you there?"

"Ananda." I could tell from her voice that she was crying.

"Jessica, what's wrong?"

"I don't know what to do, Ananda. There's blood." I clutched my phone tighter.

"What do you mean?" I asked, even though I knew exactly what she meant. I just didn't want to be right.

"I didn't want to be here anymore."

"Jessica, where are you?" I said, trying to sound calm.

"Home," she whispered.

"Ten minutes," I said.

"Ten minutes," she repeated, sounding unsure.

I threw off my duvet, slipped on my trainers, and grabbed my bag. It was 1:27 AM. My parents were asleep—I could hear my dad snoring. I tiptoed down the stairs, pulled on my coat—this was back in January—and slipped out the door.

I closed my eyes and shivered. A storm was coming, I could feel it. I walked as fast as I could to Jessica's house and was about to knock on her front door when something made me try the doorknob first. The door was unlocked.

The house was dark, but I could see light coming from her room upstairs. I stood outside her bedroom door for a few beats, bracing myself for what I might find inside.

I've known Jessica since the beginning, when cartoons were cool and my dad was Superman and her laughter was real. I knew her before school, before Facebook, before social hierarchies, before this kind of pain even seemed possible.

Gingerly, I pressed my hand to the door, and it creaked open. Jessica was sitting on the floor next to her bed, tears streaming down her face, fists clenched at her chest. I knelt down and took her hands in mine. I saw the cuts on her arms and had to look away to stop myself from crying.

"Open your hands," I said. She was holding a small blade. The idea that this tiny little thing could cause so much damage astonished me. I put it in my bag.

"It's going to be OK," I said. I stood up, grabbed her hand, and led her to the bathroom, where we washed her arms. I found a tin of anti-infective cream in the cupboard and dabbed that on. I thought about all the times I'd asked Jessica about similar scratches on her arms and been satisfied when she said, "Oh, it was just the cat." How could I have been so naïve?

Hours later, I snuck back into my house, up the stairs, stopping on the landing. I could still hear my dad's snoring. I got into bed and heard thunder, a few drops of rain. The storm had arrived.

October 29

You know when you desperately fancy someone and it's just utterly amazing and you think you're feeling these feelings you've never felt before, but at the same time you want it to end because it's actually kind of painful? You're in this weird state where you wish the torture would end, but you also don't know what you would do with your day if you didn't have this one person to obsess over. As soon as I'm not crushing on and obsessing over someone, I feel kind of bored and empty. Can you relate? Because that's where I'm at now.

Some people jump from one intense relationship to the next without taking a breath; I do the same thing without actually ever being in a relationship. And now that I'm not in a state of fixation, what am I meant to fixate on? Because schoolwork isn't an option, let's face it.

It's probably not healthy that I can't be content unless I'm discontented about someone else. But I'm not healthy anyway, so oops.

April 29, 2015

Sometimes, you need to remind yourself that you were the one who carried you through the heartache, through the bad days and the worse days. You are the one who sits on the shower floor, and picks yourself up. You are the one who cries yourself to sleep, and turns around to smile at your loved ones. You are the one who takes care of your body, who feeds it, who clothes it, who tucks it into bed, and you should be proud of that. Having the strength to take care of yourself when everyone around you is trying to mess you

up, ignores you, or is simply busy taking care of themselves—that is the strongest thing in the universe.

You need to remind yourself that you are important and that everything you do is an achievement. If all you do today is take a shower, then good for you, you are clean. If all you do is get out of bed, then good for you, that's awesome. If all you did was sleep, then good for you, at least you're well rested. ◬

LILLY

July 16, 2014

I went to the swimming pool twice this week. The first time, things went downhill from the moment my friend peered across the concrete and asked, "Is that your ex?" Followed by "I didn't know she was a lifeguard." Exactly the person I didn't want watching me closely as I tried to swim and enjoy myself. I felt childish, too big and too small for my skin all at once, and ended up lying on my towel for most of the time, trying to forget my self-consciousness in the heat of the sun.

The second time, I came with a group. If my ex was there, I didn't know it; my friends and I were too busy running around, racing one another down the slides and testing which ones were faster or slower and flattening our bodies to speed ourselves up. When we all had our fill of laughter and chlorinated water, we sat on the grass and ate cake and got bug bites and it was perfect.

October 8

A reminder to myself: Time is relentless.

When my legs are dragging and I feel like I can't take another step, the clock still ticks. While I fidget in the last class of the day, thinking of all the homework I'll have when I get home, time goes on. When I toss and turn in bed, unable to sleep, or when I'm anxious and I lean against a wall to feel its solidity, I must remind myself that every single moment will pass.

In moments of anxiety or pain or despair, it's not easy to think clearly. It feels like I can't think loud enough to drown out

everything else in my head. I don't need to be told to "take deep breaths," or "just calm down." I'm already telling myself that, shouting it to myself in my mind, desperate to be heard above the commotion. All I need to know in moments like that is that those moments will end. I can keep good ones in my memories and find solace in the fact that the bad ones will fade eventually.

May 13, 2015

It's that time of year again when everything seems like it's in free fall, spiraling toward the end of the school year and the false allure of yet another lazy summer. Those nothing-filled days of seasons past will be a little more elusive this year. I'm seeking out summer jobs—a teenage rite of passage—and volunteering opportunities. If I can work out my schedule for next school year in time, I could take an intensive Portuguese class at the local university come fall semester, and I'll need to prep for that. I'm going to finally put in my hours behind the wheel and try to get my driver's license. I'm going to fully rehabilitate my ankle and spend my mornings readying myself for my next competitive season, especially if that comes at the end of this year rather than the spring of next.

My English course this semester is on the coming-of-age novel, so in class we've been talking about the entire concept of "coming of age" and how we each perceive it. One of the hottest debates, predictably, is whether coming-of-age can be described in a single moment, or even a series of moments, or whether it's a subtler shift that takes place over time, best viewed in hindsight. I'm not sure what my stance on the matter is. I feel like I've had a lot of experiences—with many more ahead—that could be viewed as coming-of-age moments. But I still don't feel like it's happened. I don't feel like I've come of age. I'm chasing all these loose ends this summer like maybe I'm hoping one of them will lead me to some definitive future and I'll be slapped in the face with a sense of maturity and adulthood.

There are things that only my journals and Spotify playlists know. I think they might know me better than I do myself. ◉

· SIMONE ·

April 1, 2015

I still have no idea where I want to go, or what I want to study. I love films, and I've always thought I'd end up a film major at film school. But the genuine intellectual stimulation I experienced from a weekend like this tells me to exert my passion in something practical, like politics, or business, or law. While writing this entry, I'm also exploring the college software my guidance counselor gave me access to last week, and listening to an early demo of the Beatles' "Across the Universe." They feel contradictory in conjunction. If I decide where I want to go, I can begin to plan my future "perfectly," so I can go on to live the "perfect" life. But John keeps reminding me that it doesn't matter. At all. The universe is so big, and nothing I can or will do matters in relation to it. So, should I still put all this time and effort into making the right decision for myself, even if there's no point?

April 22

There is one thing that always makes me cry. This weekend, I got to witness it.

There's a girl in the sixth grade on the track team I volunteer as a coach for. The entire team is girls of middle-school age, and each week the coaches bring up a topic to discuss as a group before we run. Bullying, gossip, puberty, fun life things. This week, the topic was body image. All was going relatively well, then one girl raised her hand to share an experience from dance class. She said her dance teacher had called her fat, so she tried not to eat for the following two days. She said in that moment, she'd wished she was anorexic. I, and everyone else, knew that it wasn't just in that moment.

There's this weird age between child-hood and adolescence when kids are devel-oping adolescent insecurities but still speak with the openness of children. I felt like I knew too much. She tried to hide it, but her vulnerability was so apparent. I told her

anorexia is not a diet, or an exhibition of self-control, that it's an illness that could kill her, and most definitely alter her life forever. I don't know if she believed me. I don't know how long it'll take for her to see herself, young and growing, as more than an object to be perfected. She is so bright, and inquisitive, and a great runner. It took all my will not to hug her and cry then and there. (I postponed the crying until I went to bed that evening.)

I remember the first time someone called me ugly at school. I was in second grade. I remember wishing I could be a size smaller in Abercrombie Kids, and feeling ashamed when I had to start wearing women's sizes. The first time I weighed in over 100 pounds at the doctor's office my dad congratulated me, and I went to the bathroom and cried.

I've grown to accept myself for who I am, and I know that I am more than a weight, or a clothing size, or my makeup quality on any given day. But I'm still uncomfortable with how I look, and most people around me are, too. I can barely remember the brief time when we weren't.

I just want that poor girl to care about herself as much as I do. ⛸

◇ ◇ ◇ ◇
◇ ALYSON ◇
◇ ◇ ◇

April 1, 2015

We are driving home from Arizona. It has taken me 16 years to get used to vacations at my grandparents' home. There is one trip, probably my first trip, that I can remember being happy. It's like a GIF of a memory—my parents parking up front and four-year-old me, wearing a long pink dress covered in berries, running up to an endless house I'd only ever heard about. Inside, I was immediately hooked by the (mostly defunct) sitting room—soft and white—which appeared to be a portal, or to be cupped by an invisible hand that preserved its timeless aura and ancient fragrance. It still has a bit of the same effect on me; not all of the mysticism has gone.

I can generalize about my attitude toward our trips from ages six to 12. Feeling displaced and depressed about being there, I would go behind the desk in my uncle's old bedroom (where I would usually reside) and cry or read, or both simultaneously. My grandparents did—and do—everything they could to make our stays amazing. However, coming back from a game, restaurant, theme park, or mall, I could never shake the subtle paralysis that pushed me into this mental pit and prevented me from climbing out to enjoy everything that everyone else seemed to have no problem enjoying.

This is the first time that I can remember—in a couple years short of a decade—that I have been able to enjoy the enjoyable, to almost my fullest capacity. Mentally, I was Claritin-clear, and I lived the best I could while I could keep it up. Oh, what a relief it was.

May 13

I wonder when I passed the point of no return. The point where bodies become something more than a vessel; the point where they no longer have to just keep you alive, they also have to contradict that function by being something they were never meant to be.

It's funny how I can recognize this, yet still try, endlessly, to morph into the mythological creature that people somehow find realistic. It's realistic for some people, to be the definition of "well proportioned," but not for me. Just like how being me, in all of my "unproportionality," isn't realistic for some people. They smile at you, praise you for your achievements, but it is all in vain, because if my hips are two inches "too big," then what does it matter?

The confusion, which has been in my mind for years, is a lot like a bruise. Should I try to change myself even more, or finally live in harmony with the body that has carried me so far? But I know that it is not my body that is the problem, it is my head. Somehow, that makes me feel less bad.

It's incredible that after all the hate we bury our bodies in, they haven't just up and left already. 🌱

JUST WONDERING

Non-expert advice from your biggest fans.
By the Rookie staff

I have been homeschooled for my whole life until this year. I'm halfway through 12th grade in a public school. Whenever I leave the house, my parents are in constant contact. They are always asking if I'm OK, where I am, etc. I'm not doing anything wrong, but I hate the feeling of being monitored constantly, and I don't want to worry about them. Sometimes I just don't want to tell them what I'm doing, you know? How do I help make my parents more comfortable with the idea of me leaving the house without telling them exactly where I'll be and how long I'll be gone?—Mishka, 18

I feel this in my SOUL. I've been in public school for quite a few years now after growing up homeschooled. My parents can be worriers by nature, reminding me to be careful on my five-minute bike ride to a friend's or telling me not to shower until one of them gets home in case I fall and hit my head. When I started attending my current high school, which gives students a lot of freedom on the local university campus, they asked me to text them every time I left the building and again when I was back. (And my mother reads everything I write for Rookie, regardless of subject matter. She's probably reading this now. Hi, Mom!)

I don't know how homeschooling worked for your family—if you had a sit-down-and-study kind of environment that mimicked an actual classroom, or a system that left you with a lot more freedom, or maybe something in between. But if it was something like the first case, where your parents might have been in close contact with you for most of the day, it does make sense that they might be a little overprotective now that their baby is making her own way in the world! I get called out sometimes for UNDERsharing with my family, so you could try what I do: If you see your parent(s) in the morning before

school, briefly talk them through the day you have ahead of you. It doesn't have to be anything special or heartfelt, but reminding them of your plans ahead of time could reduce some of the checkups. Even just an "I'm studying with Lucy at the library after school and I'll be home around 5 PM" can make a big difference. Over time, I was able to change that to something more like "I might go out on campus today, but I'll text you if I need anything." In my experience, providing my family with a semi-frequent flow of information has mostly stopped them from requesting a constant one.

Of course, some parents just cannot be stopped, because they love you and you are their baby and they are Safety Parents™, which is what my fam jokingly call themselves when they realize that they are being a bit intrusive. Are you planning to go to college away from home next year? If that's on your radar, maybe bringing it up with your parents could help you indirectly gauge how they view your burgeoning independence. We all gotta get out there eventually. Good luck, good talks, good travels!—Lilly

My best friend (the most wonderful person in the entire world) is going through her first breakup. I'm fairly certain it was an emotionally manipulative/abusive relationship, and it kills me to hear her talk about how she's broken. As someone who doesn't have any firsthand experience with relationships, I find it hard to convince her that she's worth more than what this guy thinks of her and that she shouldn't give him the power to make her feel that way. What do I do? —Liz, 17, Los Angeles

You DO have firsthand knowledge of relationships, Liz! You've had them all your life, even if they haven't been romantic like your best friend's (I'm going to call her

Tina) was. You are someone's best friend. That is a sacred duty, and you are the best person for Tina to forge ahead through this harsh realm beside.

Tina is in a tight spot, but she has to get out of it herself. You can't flip her insecurities like a coin or glue her heart back together like a ceramic cup. You can't grab her gently by her half of a best-friend necklace and shake it, yelling, "IF YOU'RE GONNA ASSIGN YOUR SELF-WORTH TO ANYONE BESIDES YOURSELF, WHY NOT ME, YOUR BEST FRIEND, LIZ!!!!" until she sees herself the way you see her: the most wonderful person in the entire world.

You can't do anything but focus on communicating one glowing thing to Tina: "Even if you don't think you got this, you got this. And until you know you got this, I got you." Doing nothing may sound easy, but it is hard as hell. Watching someone that you scream-it-on-every-street-corner cherish go through emotional agony that you can't fix and can't make go away can get tiring REALLY FAST. It won't help Tina if you allow her sadness to take over your feelings, too.

Only Tina can, or should, change her mind about how she feels about herself. Build that. Don't try to convince her that she's not "broken"—even though you have your mind perfectly right about how she's worth more than how her ex values her, she needs someone to support her where she's at, not tell her that her opinions are invalid. Instead, try telling her that while she thinks she's not good enough, you don't see it that way. Tell her what you told me—that to you, she is the most wonderful person in the entire world—and tell her everything that helped her earn that title, and why she's so loved by you and, I'm sure, so many other people in her life.

ALONE again

Talk about the things she's done and how they've affected you. Let her know in your eyes, she matters. A lot.

You also write that from the outside, Tina's relationship looked like it had some abusive characteristics. That completely sucks and I wouldn't be surprised, considering how invalidated Tina sounds in your letter. Just like before, even with your suspicions, you can't tell her she was in an abusive relationship, but you can be there for her when and if she figures it out herself. This is not about what you want for Tina, this is about what Tina wants for Tina: The more you focus on that boundary, the easier it will be to support her.—Lola

My friends are all feminists, but I'm not. I'm all for equality of the sexes, but I don't think women are superior to men or that 99 percent of men are jerks. Unlike my friends, I can enjoy a Nicki Minaj video without talking about how it's "super anti-feminist" or whatever. As a result, my friends constantly yell at me about how I'm wrong. I don't want to fight with them anymore. I wish they would respect my opinion the way I respect theirs. What can I do to get them to stop trying to change my mind?—Clara, 15, Belgium

My idea of feminism is about equality for all sexes; it's not about shaming girls and women for their opinions. Given how judgmental your friends are being, I can totally understand why you wouldn't want to identify as a feminist! Believing in the equality of all genders is actually the only thing that's necessary to be a feminist. Not judging other people, not reading a specific number of books, not thinking all men are evil jerks, not even calling yourself a feminist—just believing that all people deserve the same rights and respect, regardless of gender.

When a person is learning about feminism, one of the things they might see is people on social media being publicly shamed for saying the "wrong" thing, not taking their beliefs far enough, not knowing enough on a specific topic, or choosing to focus on other aspects of their beings and/or life than gender and its related politics. It's important to me, as a feminist, to support all women, regardless of their backgrounds, beliefs, identities, and experiences.

There's nothing "anti-feminist" about a Nicki Minaj video. Nicki Minaj's feminism might not look like your friends' feminism, but it's unfair of them to tell you you can't love and/or be empowered by Nicki. A simple googling of "Nicki Minaj feminist" brings up tons of articles that could be fascinating for all of you!

You've got a few options for dealing with this. You can ask your friends questions that challenge their opinions, like: "If feminism means supporting women, why are you being so harsh on Nicki?" But if you're uncomfortable doing that, or you just don't feel like getting into it with them anymore, you have every right to change the subject—talk about the things that DO inspire you. What I would honestly advise, though, is spending more time with people who support you and don't yell at you when you disagree with them. Your friends are not changing your mind; they're making you feel like crap. They need to stop telling you what to do and be respectful of your thoughts and feelings. You could even argue that what they're doing now—disrespecting your intellect and making you feel awful for having your own convictions—is what's "super anti-feminist."—Meredith

I recently applied early decision to a competitive college. Since I sent in my application, I keep hearing about everyone else in my grade who applied to that school, and it's giving me tons of anxiety, especially since a lot of them are friends of mine. By now, word has gotten out about who applied where, so if I am rejected, I'll not only have to congratulate people who got what I wanted, but everyone will know. I really want to stop freaking out about this. Help!—Isabel, 17, Connecticut

I'm not going to spend this answer telling you how hard getting into college is OR that, yes, if you're rejected, you can transfer in later, because I suspect you know these things. Instead, I'm going to ask you to not freak out about your classmates knowing about what your decision was.

OK, let's assume, for a second, that you get rejected. First: Please erase any worries from your brain that you have about people knowing you were rejected. Are you worried that people will think you didn't try hard enough? Or didn't have good grades? Or weren't the prototype the school wanted for their class? Everyone is going to get rejected from some schools. Many people get rejected from their dream schools, which is why they're called "dream schools," unfortunately. So, if you get rejected, what does it say about you? Pretty much nothing: It says that this is a school that rejects a lot of people, for hundreds of reasons, and it's not a reflection on you as a person.

It seems like you care a lot about what your peers will think or say and the school environment you'll have to deal with post-(imaginary!) rejection. And that makes sense! When you're a senior in high school during this time of year, there's SO MUCH EMPHASIS on where you're going to school or if you're going at all, and, OMG, what does that say about your future!!! AGAIN: It really doesn't say much. Kids will get into college. Some won't. Some will go and decide to transfer. Some will definitely drop out. You might not ever speak to any of these people again after high school. The days after the decisions are made public and people are congratulating one another, there will be a lot of mourning, too, and both the congratulating AND the mourning will end quickly. Then everyone is off to the same place: the future. And in a year—literally—when you're at college, you will LOL about how much you cared about the college-application circus, because you'll be living a whole new life.

Yes, you should probably congratulate the people who did get in, but you're also allowed your own personal venting time. But I don't think you should freak out. It is OK if people know if you're rejected, because I can assure you with all my heart that nobody will care or think less of you. I got rejected from my dream school early decision and posted about it on Facebook. It was fine! A lot of my friends got rejected from their dream schools, too. In short: Don't freak out. It's OK if you get rejected and people know about it, because rejection is the norm—and because your future is not your college decision.—Hazel

I have a crush on my friend. A couple of minor physical things have happened between us, but he doesn't go to my school, so I usually have to wait months to see him again. Meanwhile, I'm losing my mind! We talk on Facebook regularly, but he hasn't made any moves toward becoming a couple. I can't stop thinking about him. Do you think it's worth pursuing a relationship with him if it's making me so crazy? —M

I know all too well the mind-melting crush fever of which you speak, and it seems to me that the easiest, swiftest, and most honest way to break this delirium is simply to TELL THE TRUTH about the burning fire of your heart 'n' loins! If you have something to say, sing it from the rooftops! Declaring your love to a crush is way less hysterically terrifying and impossible-seeming in theory than in practice, and if not pursuing a relationship with him is what's driving you so crazy, it might be time to make your move. It doesn't have to be a big move—just something to steer your friendship in a more romantic direction.

It's quite possible that your crush is reciprocal, based on your history and sustained friendship (especially as it's lasted in spite of the different-schools thing). Even if it's not, at least you'll know, and be able to move on to someone worthier of your devotion. (I was always surprised at how easily I shrugged off crushes I'd been OBSESSED with once it came to light that they didn't feel quite as passionately as I did.) Pursuing a relationship with him, telling him how you feel, or just suggesting you go to the movies next weekend, will probably exorcise a few of the crush-demons clogging up your neurons and give you some clarity.

OR: Here's some entirely conflicting advice! While I believe that being honest and true to yourself are the basic answers to any problem, ever, it's occurred to me lately that it never hurt anyone to bide their time a bit to process their feelings. I wonder if some of the times I was led by my EMO-TIONS when it came to boys (by speaking my mind/declaring my love/keying their car), I should have shaddup and waited to see what else was going to happen. Time is a crusher's nemesis—math class becomes an entire lifetime as you watch the clock's

hands tick toward the hour that you can finally see your crush again—but it can also be an excellent tool for figuring out your feelings for someone and theirs for you.

What's the rush? Are your thoughts of him taking over your life and brain to the extent that you NEED to find out IMMEDIATELY how he feels about you or you will ABSOLUTELY lose your mind? Or can you stand to do the Facebook-chat thing for a little longer? What you're living through currently is the crush buildup; for all you know, you're already on a slow-moving trajectory to Smooch City.

Be brave like a bear (saying how you feel), but sly like a fox (deciding when to say it). I know that no matter what you choose to do, you're gonna kill it (even if you've decided to chill it). —Esme

I've been very stressed out lately. My parents tell me that I should study more so I can get into a decent college, but, honestly, I just don't want to do that. I hate studying enough as it is. I can't imagine spending at least four more years preparing myself for a job I will probably hate, as well. The worst part is, I'm only good at studying. It's not like I have any other talents or interests to fall back on. The small number of things I'm good at, I hate, but I don't like anything else, either. I've tried everything—music, art, writing, sewing—but there's nothing I feel passion toward. What should I do?—Rose, 16, Denver

Hey, Rose Parade. I know it seems like you NEED TO FIGURE IT ALL OUT RIGHT NOW or else consign yourself to a dullard's existence in, like, the office from *The Office* for the rest of forever, or else just be broke or something—whatever way, involved in a boring life populated with boring people and it's all boring forever-bore. Let's do away with the constant freakout over the imminent monotony of eternity, because it's fucking up your life right now. Studying is already punishment enough without a thick layer of self-pressure on top. Part of the reason you're lodged tight in this hatred of every single talent or interest you could pursue is because you're not actually doing it. You're watching yourself doing it, going, WHAT DOES THIS MEAN FOR MY FUTURE? and

then becoming disappointed and disillusioned when nothing magically reveals itself as 100 PERCENT DEFINITELY YOUR LIFE'S CALLING—THIS IS IT: YOUR RAISIN D'EXIST-O.

Why does future-you get to (with any luck) be happy, but present-day-you has to suffer? Why don't you start with being kind to yourself right now?…she said beatifically, as though it were that easy! (It's especially not easy when you're depressed. Are you? That is also worth checking into, because if you are, contending with that will be a big part of dispelling this churning dissatisfaction with the complete offerings of human life.) Those facile-sounding questions, though, are sadly valid. How to begin the alternate beginning is the hard part. (Also, how to talk about this without sounding like a Dr. Phil self-help moron is the hard part. We just have to be earnest for one second to get through this; I'm sorry. IT'S ONLY FOR THE WELL-BEING OF YOUR FUTURE, no big deal!) It has a lot to do with putting an end to asking, "Am I good at this?" or, "Do I like this?" and instead doing things because they occur to you, or because you want to test them out, and seeing how that goes.

Recently, I committed myself to PAY-ING ATTENTION TO THE ACTION I AM DOING AS I DO IT. This is expressed in events major and minor: forcing myself to watch the mascara wand as I jostle it along my eyelashes, dissolving inside a Rothko at the museum while I lean into the shoulder of the person I love, writing a shopping list for my grandmother, all of it. I try not to expect anything of anything, or of me, and it happens, and I love it better. Keep your eyes sharp and your head focused out, instead of in. When you stop dissecting everything you go through in the world like it has the potential to augur who you are and what you do, you'll begin to respond to the things around you honestly. You'll join yourself within whatever action you're up to—you will conjure yourself by forgetting, instead of needlessly second-guessing, yourself, my vault of Rose gold. Then you can self-examine about how it went and felt and whether you liked it at the end of the day, in your bed, where you're resting after really and truly having done something without fixating on some hypothesized test result. Again: You are already studying enough.

Music, art, writing, and sewing are all hunky-dory, but I find that I need them all, plus more, to build this kind of scaffolding in me that ensures I don't lean too heavily on one support beam and then watch it snap like Jaws's toothpick after I've expected it to provide the sole foundation for my existence. (Well, except sewing. I embroidered some cursive on the back of a denim vest last summer and my boyfriend, cruising by, asked, "What does that say? 'BRUISE COFFIN'?" I had meant it to say "HEART ANIMAL," basically the opposite tonal concept. Sewing was not at risk of being tasked with providing the sole foundation for my existence after that.) I am not like you, in that I have always known I wanted to write, which sounds like one of those irritating self-mythologizing things writers say to evince that they're really writers, but it's true: This is the prime way I know to feel good in or make sense of the world. STILL, even that lifelong certainty is fallible, and it doesn't exist in a vacuum. In each period of my life, much of which has been spent, ratio-wise, as a teenager, when I have found myself thrashing inside some net of my own misery, it's because I am not insulating the writing thing with other things, or because I'm spending too long on one thing, period (a job; a relationship; school).

This is even truer when the sole concern of my life is my life. A really good way to stop thinking about YOU so much—to not worry if you're right, if you're wrong, if you should NEVER HAVE EVEN TRIED TO PICK UP SEWING IN THE FIRST PLACE, UGH—is to do things for other people. (Especially ones you don't know, since that strips away the value differential of "I did this person a favor, and now they owe me!!" that some of us feel from time to time.) Yes, actually—definitely help strangers, because that will thrust you into a moving planet, and you will be interacting with all kinds of people, doing valid, necessary work in places like soup kitchens or after-school tutoring programs or libraries or food pantries. Another charming, cruising-for-a-bruising-type self-analysis that I'm gonna offer up right now, in addition to always understanding the deep and irrepressible truth that, as…I believe it was Chaucer who said, in his private correspondences, "Wrytying—the pen, the page, the pissant pyrsonalyty—is, like, totylly my raisin d'exist-o": Helping out at the community dinner in my neighborhood once a week was one of the most crucial aspects of ripping myself apart from a voluble, ever-present despair I listened to a lot last year. I ferried boxes of milk and yogurt from the basement despite having linguini biceps. I scarfed down kielbasa and onions offered to me by Elena, the RAD old lady who runs the show. I learned to cut up a tray of spaghetti so you can portion it onto plates with a pair of tongs in a flash (shout-out to Elena, again). I assessed oozing trash cans in the kitchen—how to get them to stop oozing?

It's far easier to get out of your own way—to PAY ATTENTION—when you're working because you've chosen to spend your time working—not because you have to—and you have discrete, tangible tasks in front of you to complete, and you're doing them to the end of boosting up someone or something else. One by-product of this is that you see how you react to the world, and you can use that experimentation to help others as you help yourself: Even if you hate it, it will not have been a waste of time, like nearly everything else is. Also? See everything as a waste of time, and it simultaneously levels the playing field when you decide to apply the framework of that mindset the other way around: Everything becomes a miracle just as readily. (So definitely tell your parents college is a waste of time/miracle and that's why you're not doing it, is what I'm saying here. They will definitely see and understand your unassailably pristine logic and not immediately try to send you to WEED REHAB. Advice answer over; I think I nailed this one?)

The only way to make a permanent mistake right now is to do nothing. Keep doing things, especially if they're not IDEALLY TAILORED to you—at least you will know more about the world that way, and then, if you hate it, you can avoid it in the future! Also? The same applies to studying, which really isn't so bad. I'm obviously biased, but reading stuff you wouldn't choose for yourself is a way of seeing the world before you can see the world with your own (focused, attentive) eyes. You hate it, and I hated it, and now I find myself doing it on my own all the time, for nothing, because it unlocks the hell-crypt of my head and reminds me that I exist among a million contexts, and also one prodigious, all-encompassing one. Sorry I'm telling you to study—soon, you never have to again if you don't want to—and also, please don't tell anyone I said I liked it. I've got enough problems maintaining my tuff persona as it is (see: "writing a shopping list for my grandmother," for cripes' sake).

Square up with the reality that you're going to have to do some shit you hate in this life, and that it will galvanize you and make you want to do more, and better. Your question is a manifestation of this. It's fine if you don't want to go to college, but make sure you do SOMETHING. Work at places that don't matter to you or do; write a play or don't; join the Peace Corps (you will be traveling the globe AND doing good works AND, I guarantee, very much out of your head) or AmeriCorps, or just skip around the country or wherever while farming via WWOOF-USA, or volunteer at home; fall in love eight hundred times or none; embroider a denim vest poorly or well.

It's boring to only care about yourself. I hate everything and see it as a waste of time when I do, but if I vary my brain and life and include service in it…IT'S MIRACLE TIME, MY DUDE, MAKE A WISH OR TWELVE ON THE AVALANCHE OF SHOOTING STARS THAT IS THAT SELFSAME EVERYTHING I ABHORRED A SECOND AGO. You have options—try to see that as an impeccable stroke of luck (I often think of this Chris Ware quote, from a Rookie interview in November 2012: "Being able to say, 'I don't know what to do with my life' is an incredible privilege that 99 percent of the rest of the world will never enjoy"), instead of letting indecision stifle you. Love you lots. I hope you figure it out and also stop trying so hard to figure it out, Roseadocious.—Amy Rose ✦

Artwork by Kendra

EXTRA-SPECIAL, NO-PIXEL YEARBOOK FOUR EXCLUSIVES

Everything you've seen thus far has existed on our website in some form (just not as huggable; NO OFFENSE, WORLD WIDE WEB). Everything you are *about* to see is brand-new and exists only in this book! Rashida Jones wrote about the survival tools that got her through high school, and Maxine Crump did the only thing one could do to elevate such a treasure by illustrating it. Willow Smith composed a handful of motivational phrases, and Hattie made them into some very motivating posters. We asked Devonté Hynes of Blood Orange, Ezra Koenig of Vampire Weekend, and Lorde to trace their work back to its artistic influences, and Lucy, Sofia, and Isabel translated it all into maps by which we will now navigate the world. Online, Rookie runs a monthly Friend Crush where we interview two best-friend readers about each other; for the book, we asked some of our most beloved artists to do the same. More of our heroes also gave or conducted interviews, and we have plenty of cut-out DIYs that you can find the directions to on the back of the sticker sheet at the very end of the book. Prepare to decorate your bedroom with a bunch of cute stuff, including A BEDROOM DIORAMA. Now, *bon appetit!* (She said as she morphed into a middle-aged dad showing off the new recipe he just got from the side of the Annie's Mac and Cheese box.)

Love,

TAVI

P.S. Let it be known that Ariana Grande did her and Tyler's interview while on a treadmill like a high-power business woman with shoulder pads; the first mental image I get is the headless assistant from *Powerpuff Girls*. In addition, Tyler wrote "How to Talk to Your Parents About Transitioning" on page 223, so: POWER COUPLE.

FRIEND CRUSH:
AMANDLA STENBERG AND KIERNAN SHIPKA

Founding members of the Brunchin' Crew on acting, fashion, and always having each other's backs.
By Tavi. Illustrations by María Inés.

TAVI Do you two talk about acting? When I did a Sister Crush last year with Elle and Dakota Fanning, they said they don't talk about acting at all. They don't talk about the process, or the industry stuff. Do you talk about that?

AMANDLA STENBERG We usually don't. We'll talk about films that we like, and directors that we like together, because we kind of have similar tastes, just because that's not what our friendship is built on. It's built on being in this weird world together and going to these events and navigating that.

Do you mean the world is weird or the film industry?

Weird acting world. There are often competitive vibes between young women in this world. Our relationship is very much not that.

Did you feel that competitiveness was something you had been taught, and you had to unlearn it?

I think you have to unlearn that competitiveness. That's something that you're taught in the world, in general, not just the acting industry. Girls are supposed to compete against each other, whether it's accomplishments or looks or for guys. It's all pretty dumb. Girls support each other, actually. It's what human beings do. I think definitely, growing up, I heard messages like "Oh, you can't become friends with other girl actors, because they're going to stab you in the back or they have other motives or they're auditioning for the same roles, therefore you can't support each other." I think that is very silly.

How did you guys meet?

It's actually a pretty funny story. Kiernan and I originally met on the set of a Lunchables commercial, when we were about eight.

How old are you and how old is she?

I'm 16, and she's 15. We both completely forgot about it. We met each other again several years later at a Women in Film party. We just clicked instantaneously, because I thought her style was really cool. She was so chill and knew a lot about film and was just classy, as always. Then, it wasn't until months later that she sent me an email of all these pictures of us when we were little in the Lunchables commercial, and it was all these funny pictures of us doing, like, a *Golden Girls* pose and throwing up peace signs and doing gangster poses. They're really cute.

We started going to brunch together, and we exchanged numbers. She's the coolest. The only reason why I know any good Los Angeles restaurants is because Kiernan has taken me there. She knows all the waiters and the owner. They're like best friends. So, going out to eat with her is especially fun, because she introduces you to everyone.

The world is like her sitcom coffee shop.

I often refer to her as the queen of L.A. She always denies it when I say that, but it is very much true.

You said she looked super stylish, but you both have really distinct styles. Do you go shopping together a lot?

Yeah, we go to thrift stores all the time. It's so bizarre: Kiernan will invite me to something I'm not invited to, I'll invite her to something she's not invited to, and we always end up color coordinating, even though we don't text each other what we're wearing. It's so weird. There was this one event and everything was perfectly color coordinated. I was wearing a blue skirt, and she had this dress that was yellow and blue, and I had on yellow heels. It was perfect. Everyone kept commenting on it all night.

That's magical. Do you ever pick stuff out for each other?

We'll text each other pictures of stuff we like from runways and stuff. A lot of our relationship is having common interests in fashion and movies, but also, she's one of the most supportive people I know. I have shows with my band a lot, and she comes to every single gig. Through her, I've met an entire group of friends who are really, really cool. After my gigs, we all go to Kiernan's house and go swimming and play games. It's the best.

I've never had friends like this before. They're incredible people. Of course they are—they're Kiernan's friends!

In what ways are you most alike and most opposite?

We're most alike in terms of our appreciation of film and art and our similar tastes. We're most opposite in how we meet other people, because I go to school, and she doesn't. Kiernan is actually done with school, because she did an online program. I think the way Kiernan approaches the world is very much from the viewpoint of an adult, whereas I go to high school, and I still approach the world from a teen standpoint.

What makes her stand out from other people in your life?

Kiernan is so very wise. Whenever I'm dealing with dumb boys and grades, it's like she comes from this otherworldly perspective where she's like, "Don't worry, your career is going to be OK, and boys are stupid, and you're above them." She's so above boys. When she has a relationship, it's going to be with the most incredible person ever, because they have to be up to Kiernan's standards. She's the most elegant lady ever.

There are probably like two people in the world who should be allowed to go on a date with her. It's going to have to be a prince. Just Prince, actually.

Exactly. Perfect.

Do you have nicknames for each other?

I call her Kiki. I also sometimes call her Nan, because I think it's really funny. She'll call me Man Man, occasionally. In her phone, I think I'm Ruby.

What can I ask her that will make her laugh?

You can ask her about Coachella or Tino or Brunchin' Crew—that's how we refer to the two of us. We have a schedule.

~~~~~~~~~~~~~~~~~~~

TAVI **So, Amandla had a few things I could bring up to make you laugh. The first was Coachella. What happened?**

KIERNAN SHIPKA Coachella's such a major festival. You don't quite know what you're getting into, because it's hyped up. It was super overwhelming at first, but we ended up having a really, really fun time. We shared a really small room with a large number of people, all really good friends of ours. We got to see Lorde perform, and we got to go backstage. That was super surreal. And spending time in a car with friends is also making memories, and listening to good music.

Who else did you see?

We got to see Blood Orange, which was awesome. Neutral Milk Hotel was really good. They have the cutest fans, too. We saw a couple of bands that we didn't even know that well, which were super fun.

Can you think of any music you showed her or that she showed you?

She likes Cherry Glazerr and Girlpool a lot. She's also such a great violinist, and she's in a band. She's really, really an incredible singer and violinist. It's cool to see her up on stage, performing.

She also said to ask about Tino.

Tino, oh my god. OK, so when I was younger—maybe six or seven—I had a doll phase. My parents got me two. Tina, she's the lady, but Tino is this mannequin head, basically, that I used to do makeup on. It's so creepy. I forgot about him. He was in the basement, and about a year ago, my friends found him, and it's this weird mannequin head with sparkly eyelids. They've named him. They've gotten him an Instagram. Now he's kind of become a fan favorite. It's all mental, but when you look at this mannequin head, it looks like he's expressing emotion.

Amandla also said that you send each other pictures of runway and other clothing items. How would you describe her style?

She pulls off a backpack better than anyone I know, for sure. She mixes patterns really well, which is something that I love about her style. Even when it's something simple, she really makes it sing. I think she does really cool makeup, too. She always has a fun lip. Her hair is just incredible.

Do you remember your impression of her when you met again at 13?

I remember shaking hands with her and meeting her really briefly at an event. I knew who she was and stuff. It was right when *The Hunger Games* was coming out, and I knew other people from the cast. Then, a couple of months later, I was at an event, and I was hanging out with another person who knew her, and then we all bonded and stuck together the whole night. It was at a Women in Film event. It was nice to have a crew of girls to hang with at the party. That's when we really started chatting and bonding, and after that, started hanging out. We're each other's dates at a lot of different events and social things. We always have each other's backs. I feel that I can lean on her and also have fun.

What makes Amandla stand out to you?

She has a really good sense of self. She's very smart, and she knows what she wants. She's a really artistic and creative person, and has a lot of wisdom.

Do you have nicknames for each other?

She calls me Kiki a lot. I was at her birthday party, and her friend called her Amands, and I stole that. But, besides that, her name is so good. Amandla! 🎁

ALWAYS LISTEN TO YOURSELF:
AN INTERVIEW WITH JAZZ JENNINGS

The author and trans youth activist discusses finding your happiness, high school, and mermaid tails.
By Hunter. Illustration by Mithsuca Berry.

At 14, Jazz Jennings is an accomplished children's book author, a transgender activist making waves in the LGBTQ community, and a master maker of silicone mermaid tails. On top of navigating her life as a young transgender woman, making her way from middle school to high school, and starring in her family's upcoming reality TV show, she is touching the lives of many people, and helping change the world's definition of gender identity and self-expression.

HUNTER **Your age [14] seems to come with a very fresh perspective. How does it feel being a part of a LGBTQ activism community that's mostly older people?**

JAZZ JENNINGS Being a part of a community where a lot of the people are more experienced and have already gone through what I'm going through right now is very helpful, because they're like my mentors and can guide me on a path where I can find the kind of love and acceptance and support that can really help me with my journey. It's a great community, and everyone is so loving and accepting and unique. Everyone's just incredible.

As your profile has grown, has the amount of support or bullying changed?

The more well-known you are, you're going to receive more hate, but you're also going to receive more acceptance in the end. As I've shared my story and continued to put myself out there, I've [met] a lot of people who admire me and look up to me, and I really appreciate that. I just want my message to live on. There are going to be people who disagree with my message and therefore are gonna spread hate and disagree with everything I'm saying. So yeah, of course I receive more negative remarks, but it also comes with more positive [comments].

You and your family will soon be featured on your own reality TV show! Can you tell us how everything came together?

We were approached by the production company, who thought our family was pretty interesting, and that people should see who we are, get to know us, and realize that we're just a normal family. So the company made a little promo video and sent it to the network [TLC], who responded, saying that they wanted to create a show about our family! Things just kind of moved from there. The experience has been very fun. It makes life a little more interesting—sometimes a little overwhelming and stressful, but in the end I know it's going to make a difference and help so many people.

This show is a huge opportunity for trans visibility to grow. Who are you hoping your show will reach?

Of course, I want it to reach other transgender kids or individuals like me who are struggling with finding themselves and being true to who they are. But I also want it to go beyond that, I want it to reach everyone. Everyone who doesn't understand what it means to be transgender, or people who don't accept trans individuals, or even people who admire being transgender and want to watch my story. So I hope it reaches many different kinds of people and, in the end, makes everyone feel like we should treat each other equally and we should all love and accept one another.

Was it hard adjusting to having cameras all of a sudden documenting your personal life?

It's a little strange, but since I've done so much media stuff in the past, I've just gotten used to it. When we first started I had to open up a little bit more, but by the end I started acting crazy and being more myself. So yeah, it was definitely an adjustment, but also fun!

You're starting high school this year. Are you looking forward to anything specifically? Anything you're nervous about?

I'm excited and nervous; it's bittersweet. I'm excited because I finally get to feel a bit older—some people say kids get more mature and that high school is so much better than middle school, because middle school just kind of sucks. I also get to stay with my friends since we'll be at the same school. But I'm nervous because things could get harder; maybe people won't accept me, you know? I'll have to wait and see what happens.

As you've continued to transition physically, have you felt your identity change?

I've always wanted to have a female body, but it wasn't always for the judgment of myself, but judgment from other people; like, if female adults have boobs, then I want boobs as well. So I guess the physical transition does help me build confidence and feel like it's *my* body. My body gets to transition with my soul as I become a woman—I've always been a woman, but as I fully appear as a woman.

If I don't have a female body when I get older, I'll probably receive some harsh criticism. I kind of just want things to be easy and for people to stop being annoying. [*Laughs*] The reason I transitioned physically is because I want other people to know that I'm female, but I have always known I'm female.

How do you respond to people who ask personal questions about your sex/gender? For example, being a trans person, I've had complete strangers ask me about my private parts.

People are always curious what's between the legs because most people think that whatever is below the waist is what defines you. But that's not true. What defines you is what's between your ears, not what's between your legs. People have to understand that a person is a person for who they are on the inside and how their brain works. It annoys me when people ask about my private parts and whatever's "down there." It's none of their business. They wouldn't go up to a cisgender person and be like, "So, do you have a vagina?" That's not how it works. We should be treated the same, and equal, because we *are* the same.

Your video in the Clean & Clear campaign was amazing! How did it feel knowing that you would be making waves in the beauty industry?

I never thought it was going to be as huge as it was! So many people watched the video and it made a difference. I'm glad that I was able to make an impact by having fun and being myself—just being the real me. It was a very fun campaign all about girls finding the courage to be their true selves, and I'm so glad I could participate, because I live by that.

The campaign's message seems very true to what you're all about.

[*Laughs*] Yeah, BE WHO YOU ARE.

Have you had any experiences with a fan that you would like to share?

Yeah! I've had so many experiences it's hard to pick out one, but a lot of the time I'll be talking to people online and they'll say something like I'm their inspiration, and then we'll meet in real life and become friends! It's really cool. We'll talk and start hanging out—I'm with some of my friends right now who I first met on the internet.

That's awesome!!

I also received a message from a kid who said he was about to walk into a street full of cars, but then he thought about my message and what I live by and decided to continue living. If he could be himself, then he could find happiness. That's another story that always sticks with me as something so powerful and strong, and a reason to keep sharing my story.

Wow. You basically saved a life.

When we first started all of this, we knew we wanted to make a difference, but we never knew that we would actually be saving lives. Once you do something like that, it's like, *I can't stop now, I have to continue to give my message to people.*

It's incredible what a simple message like that can do for people. On a lighter topic, your silicone mermaid tails look fantastic! Could you see yourself taking your designs somewhere in the future?

I love making the mermaid tails but recently I've been so busy, I haven't had much time for them. It's kind of a hobby that I do in my free time, but I really do enjoy making them. Maybe someday I will invest in some sort of mermaid tail company. [*Laughs*]

Last year, you published your book *I Am Jazz*. Why did you decide to create a children's book?

To me, children only understand what people tell them—like, if the parents are religious, the child is most likely religious, too. The people around kids heavily influence them. I'm hoping the book helps kids to be open and accepting. It clearly exemplifies being transgender as something that's OK; it's OK to be yourself and to be different. They're gonna think, "It's fine if she's transgender; it's cool because Jazz said it's cool." Or, maybe for transgender kids who are struggling to find something that they can relate to, the book can help them know that they're not alone. These kids are the minds of the future and the upcoming generation, and if they have the right ideas about acceptance and love, they continue to spread the legacy.

Now that you're getting older, you probably have more independence. What do you and your friends do for fun?

We're always being goofy, 'cause we're girls and we like to have fun! This summer I'll definitely be hanging out with friends, playing outside. My friends and I want to start flipping—like backflips and stuff—we want to get into that more. We used to be able to do them! And mermaid tails: I'll be making them with some friends who want to help out.

Nice! Do you have any advice for young people out there who may be questioning their gender identity and are trying to understand this part of themselves?

My main message has always been to stay true to who you are on the inside. Follow your heart, follow what *you* think about yourself, don't listen to what people might try to sculpt into your brain, because only you know who you are, only you know what you want to become. Always listen to yourself; find your own passion.

I love that! That's something that can apply to everyone! While there has been much progress made in campaigning for trans rights/recognition, the world can only move so fast. What do you hope to see change in your lifetime?

Although this might be impossible, I wish for a day when all people could be treated as equals. I want society to accept people, no matter if they're strange. Love people for who they are on the inside. No one's perfect, the world isn't perfect, so things won't ever be this perfect, but if we could somehow achieve a more utopian society, even if we didn't get there, but tried and worked to be better people and make a difference, then that's good enough for me. I'd look at the world and smile. I always say I want to leave this world a better place than when I arrived, and I live by that. I'm going to pursue that by continuing to share my story, continuing to make a difference. Not just for LGBTQ and the trans community, but for all people! All people deserve to be treated the same no matter who they are.

What do you hope to be doing in 10 years?

I'm just trying to go with the flow. But I love to do so many things, I'll probably follow many different paths. In the end, I just want to continue helping people and finding my happiness. Continuing to make a difference! ⍦

BRAIN MAP

BY DEV HYNES!

illustrated by Lucy

ROCKY HORROR!

I WAS MAYBE NINE YEARS OLD WHEN I FIRST SAW THIS... TOO YOUNG? WHO KNOWS... I KNOW THAT I ATTEMPTED SONGS FROM IT AT AN EARLY SHOW-AND-TELL AT MY PRIMARY SCHOOL.

HAIR

... OUR THE SECOND MUSICAL ON THIS LIST?
This is the one musical I know all the words to... am I the second... OK, the fifth!? Anyway, I discovered this when I was 18 and would go back to it every couple of years, digging deeper each time, acting out scenes in my bedroom.

ERIC CANTONA

In another life, I might be playing professional soccer. This is the tale that many a musician has blurted out before; I'm not claiming I would be crushing it in that field. But soccer was my main passion as a child; I played the cello and piano, but football was my love. I played for maybe four different teams all through my childhood in London, and I loved Cantona — French, erratic (and now an acclaimed actor?!?!). I had his number 7 jersey, even though he was essentially before my time (Beckham would later swoop in and claim that number). You could get budget DVDs of old seasons, so I would watch them on loop and try to imitate them in the park.

ONE OF MY FAVORITE FILMS. I SAW IT THE FIRST YEAR I MOVED TO NYC, AROUND 2007 OR 2008. I WAS SPENDING A LOT OF TIME IN SOHO, AND I LOVED HOW THE STREETS ARE DEPICTED IN THIS FILM. ALONG WITH "THE KING OF COMEDY", THESE ARE MY TWO FAVORITE SCORSESE MOVIES.

After Hours

OCTAVIA ST LAURENT

I saw "Paris is Burning" when I was 18, and it influenced and changed my life forever. The interviews with Octavia throughout her life, which I intensely kept up with, gave me all the support and comfort I needed in trying to deal with past bullying, based on my race and sexuality. My first Blood Orange album was dedicated to her.

When I was 13 I was obsessed with this band. I worshipped Paul Draper, the singer. I covered one of their SONGS for my last album— I was at a party and that song entered my mind, so I ran to the bedroom and recorded a version. I'm not sure what awakened that musical love that had lain dormant for so long.

MANSUN

DETERMINATION — AND IDEA-WISE — I DON'T KNOW IF HE CAN BE TOPPED. HIS INFLUENCE HAS BEEN THROUGHOUT MY LIFE IN SO MANY WAYS, FROM BEING VERY YOUNG LISTENING TO ADAM ANT IN LONDON, TO DISCOVERING "BUFFALO GALS", TO THE WORK WITH HOUSE OF XTRAVAGANZA FOR "DEEP IN VOGUE," TO ONE OF MY FAVORITE ALBUMS, "FANS", WHERE HE MIXES PUCCINI OPERAS WITH BREAKBEATS AND SYNTHS. NO ONE COULD SHUT DOWN HIS IDEAS, BECAUSE HE JUST DID WHAT HE WANTED TO DO, AND HOW HE WANTED TO SEE IT. I'VE TAKEN THAT VERY DEEPLY TO HEART. I'VE ALWAYS SAID THAT AS LONG AS YOU PLEASE YOURSELF IN ART YOU CANNOT FAIL, BECAUSE REALLY, WHAT ELSE IS THERE IN CREATION? ONCE YOU'VE MADE YOURSELF HAPPY, YOU CAN SHARE THAT WITH THE WORLD, AND HOPEFULLY THEY CAN TAKE THAT JOY WITH THEM, TOO.

MALCOLM McLAREN

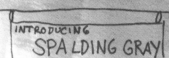

INTRODUCING
SPALDING GRAY

I was around 19 when I heard "Another Thought". It changed everything for me. Also, cello being my first instrument, I always neglected it, and he made me fall in love with it again in a whole new way. Once I saw all the different types of music he was making, that really spurred me on to pursue everything I wanted to do and explore musically, with zero shame.

ARTHUR RUSSELL

I DON'T KNOW HOW I DISCOVERED HIM. IT MIGHT HAVE BEEN THROUGH THE MUPPETS. SERIOUSLY, I THINK MONSTERPIECE THEATER DID "MONSTER IN A BOX" AND I LOOKED IT UP. I SAW IT ONLINE WHEN I WAS 19 OR 20. I'VE READ EVERY PIECE THERE IS TO DO WITH GRAY. MOVING TO NYC WHEN I WAS 21, HIS WORDS BECAME LIKE A BEST FRIEND TO ME, MIRRORING MY ANXIETIES, SUCH A FRIENDLY VOICE. REALLY CHANGED THE WAY I VIEWED WORDS.

JAMES BALDWIN

This is a late influence. I decided recently to read only interviews with him, and read bits of his novels over the years, but in recent his interviews are striking [...] with me. From him [...] back into my past, [...] the picture that has been pa[...] me, and re-appropriate it in[...] something positive.

DEVONTE

299

FRIEND CRUSH:
EMMA ROBERTS AND SARAH PAULSON

The American Horror Story *actors and pals on big laughs, age gaps, and working together.*
By Julianne. Illustrations by Alyssa Etoile.

EMMA ROBERTS I'm so excited to do this.

JULIANNE I'm such a fan of all of your work. How did you first meet Sarah?

My boyfriend Evan [Peters] is on *American Horror Story* with her, and I went to the premiere of Season 2 with him and I remember seeing this blond girl just cracking up—running around the party, friends with everyone, making everyone laugh—and then she came over to me and was like, "Hi!" and hugged me like she'd known me forever. We took a picture together and a couple of my friends saw [it] and were like, "You guys look like you're BFFs." I was like, "We're not, but I'm kind of obsessed with her."

How did she reach out and say that she wanted to be friends?

Season 3 of *AHS* was shot in New Orleans. Everyone was kind of uprooted, and it was like, "Let's all hang out together" and we swapped numbers. We were kind of attached at the hip. And she's just so funny. She does the craziest impressions. In *AHS* there's some pretty dark material, and she'll be walking around set, making a really funny ugly face and pinching my ass before giving an award-worthy performance. I'm like, "You were just grabbing my butt and now you're crying your eyes out and doing the most beautiful scene I've ever seen."

Does working together bring you closer?

I love working with people that I'm friends with, especially when you're working somewhere fun.

We got to work together in New Orleans, and we went out one Halloween with everyone. All of a sudden this girl comes up to Gabby Sidibe and glitter-bombs her. I remember Sarah just being the protector, like, "Whoa, whoa, whoa, what is going on?" It was hilarious. She totally had our backs.

It's so cool to be around women like that, because sometimes you feel intimidated or out of place. Especially coming onto *Coven* for the third season, she'd already been on it since Season 1, and she made me feel so confident. I was so nervous my first episode, and she talked me through it. We didn't even know each other but I was like, *I need to call her, I need her to calm me down*. I'd ask her [for feedback] on set because I trust her so much.

Sometimes I overthink things and I'll be really critical, and she always makes me feel better. The first time we went to the Golden Globes was two years ago. I was really nervous. She gives me a sip of her cocktail and is like, "It's all good. You look gorgeous." I was like, "Oh my god, Reese Witherspoon is standing over there." She's like, "I know her. Do you wanna meet her?" I was like, no, no, no I can't. She grabbed me out of my chair and was like, "Hi, this is my friend Emma, you have to meet her, she's amazing." I remember thinking, I don't know a lot of people that would be like, 'Oh my god, you're a fan? Come here.' And pull you out of your chair and make you say hi. You need a friend like that, instead of someone that's gonna overthink it with you.

I noticed that she tweeted about a book that you recommended to her, *The Children Act*.

I'm always reading on set and she'll be like, "What are you reading?" Whenever I go to sets I'm always pushing books on everyone. And they'll be like, "I finished it in one day." I'm like, "Trust me, I'm a book guru." I have a problem though. I keep buying them before I can finish them; I've become

a book hoarder.

What are you reading right now?

I'm reading the new Anjelica Huston memoir, *Watch Me*, which I love. Being an actress and living in LA, the way she talks about that scene from back in the day, it's so interesting. It makes me nostalgic for that time, even though I wasn't alive. I wish I had been. My favorite book ever—well, one of them—is *Blue Nights* by Joan Didion. I read it in one plane ride, and was crying at the end. It's heartbreaking, but it's beautiful.

Does the age gap impact your friendship with Sarah?

She makes me feel like an equal. There are people you meet and they automatically feel like you're younger than them, like they have their "real" friends and you're their "little" friend. And sometimes you get excluded from things because of age, but she would always be like, "'Emma, are you coming?" And that was really nice.

She sounds like the best friend ever.

I know! We were having dinner one time and we were literally talking over each other because we had so much to say. And I looked at her and was like, "By the way, how old are you?" And she's like, "Ahahaha! Yeah, right." I said, "No, really, how old are you?" And she was like, "Older than you!" We'd been shooting the shit for an hour or two, and it dawned on me that we weren't the same age. I can tell her anything and she'll never be like, "Well, when you grow up, you'll feel this way." She'll say, "Oh yeah, I dealt with that the other day." If I had to describe her in one word, she's just real. Even people I've known for like 10 years sometimes do something and [I'm] like, "What? That's not who you are." Sarah's the same person all the time. Every time I see her, whether it's at the

Golden Globes or on Sunday or on set, it's always the same Sarah.

〰〰〰〰〰〰〰〰〰〰

JULIANNE **What is your memory of meeting Emma?**

SARAH PAULSON It was before we worked together, at the Season 2 premiere of *American Horror Story: Asylum*. I was so excited to watch the episode for the first time, but I was secretly equally excited to meet Evan's girlfriend. I'd always admired her and thought she was extremely chic and beautiful. But back then I only knew her via the on-set rumor that Evan was going out with the dynamic, sparkly Emma Roberts. I just loved her way. She was so sort of gamine and unafraid to take risks both in her career and fashion choices. So Evan was just a vehicle to get me into Emma Roberts's hemisphere.

The thing you notice about Emma right away is this totally infectious giggle that comes out in kind of a cannon-ball. And it's not the most dainty laugh, which is so great, cause she's very tiny, like, I don't know what, a small poodle? When this sound comes out of her being, it comes from the tip of her toes. The whole room kind of shook. And I thought, "Oh, she looks like a little girl but really she's a badass lady, with a ferocious laugh!" And then we worked together, and it was a whole other level of obsession. Her performance as Madison Montgomery was a revelation. On the page, I thought it was going to be a very specific kind of one-note thing, but she brought so many layers and a dynamic, fully realized three-dimensional character. And to not make her [character] just a typical catty bitch, you know? It was incredibly nuanced. She's a bit of a mystery, that one. She's a very surprising creature.

She essentially said, 'The first thing I noticed about Sarah was her laugh.'

That just goes to show that there's a similar level of healthy narcissism going on, where we both like the sound of a big laugh because we both have one, and so we admire it in one another and we're trying to give each other support.

When did you start to bond?

We had an *American Horror Story* ice cream social. The producers had gathered everyone together on one of the sound stages and we were meeting some of our crew, and her name tag said "I'M EMMA!" It was probably a little bit unnerving to come onto a show where Evan was everybody's love. And here comes Emma and she's this new presence in the world. I have to imagine that would be a little bit daunting.

You kind of want to pick her up and strap her into a Baby Bjorn and carry her around. You want to protect her, celebrate her, show her off. Like a perfect new baby pony. But a pony with a tremendous amount of gravitas. She's a very serious girl. She reads more books than anybody I know. She's a voracious reader. She was the new kid on the block, but I think she's the person that a lot of people become instant best friends with, because she's incredibly accessible and warm and present and curious, and asking a million questions about you. She doesn't ever try to play it too cool for school. She's a big doofus-maroofus.

Being in this public industry, do you find that having a friend who can understand your experience is comforting?

It's the rarest thing in the world to find somebody that you recognize as a member of your own tribe, you know? Especially in this industry, it's something you really wanna hold on to. Because it can be very isolating. You pick up and move from Los Angeles and find yourself in New Orleans, which is a wonderful city, but it's not your home. So Emma and I were like, "You're a member! This is gonna be good."

When you're in a work situation where most of your coworkers are really powerful, strong women, does that add depth to your friendship?

When you're working on something that requires a certain focus and commitment, it's inspiring to have other people that pull that out of you even more. Working on *Coven*, we were totally surrounded by an incredibly powerful group of women. Some had Academy Awards…so it was a constant learning experience. I kept pinching myself going, "I can't believe I get to be around all these people who are

so at the top of their game, and I get to steal everything they've done and pass it off as my own." I would watch Emma, and she's incredibly authentic in front of the camera. She's not full of shit. That's the only kind of acting I admire, people that don't tell lies—on camera or on stage or anywhere where they might be performing. Whatever she's feeling, you can see under the surface of her skin and in her eyes. She has that in spades. I had a harder time later in the season, when [my character] Cordelia was always mad at Madison [Emma's character]. When you care about someone offscreen, it can illuminate things about scenes that maybe weren't even there. A close relationship can permeate your work. I hope we get to do more of it, because it's a really delicious thing to work with people you love and that inspire you.

This is so heartwarming.

Emma Roberts is a topic near and dear to my heart. You'd probably pass out from boredom by the time I was done extolling the virtues of Emma Roberts. I had a birthday brunch in New Orleans and she worked until like 4 in the morning the night before. And there she was, bright-eyed and bushy-tailed at my brunch. With a present. She takes care of her own. To have that so young is an incredible gift that will only get richer and richer as she gets older. 👻

WILD DISCO

Singer-songwriter Charli XCX shares her wardrobe's greatest hits.
By Charli XCX. Illustrations by María Inés.

I'm most definitely going through a zebra phase at the moment. My stylist, Lisa Katnic, and I created these outfits together. We were inspired by disco and Debbie Harry. I wanted these outfits to be sassy. I always want my shows to be wild, so I need to be wild, too. I like to make the audience sweat and I like to sweat, too—it's not a good show unless that happens. And it feels good to do that in these outfits. I like how there's such a rock-and-roll element to these clothes, but also a real Barbie feel to it, too. Everything's so dramatic. My favorite piece is the choker, which really sparkles in the lights. I also love the flares. I have been doing all my most serious meetings in them recently, because I feel like it freaks people out just the right amount, and I think that's nice.

These are my plastic angel wings that my band and I wear on stage. They are super cute and tacky at the same time. We found them in a Halloween store in Los Angeles. I call my fans the angels, Charli's Angels.

This is one of my favorite outfits ever to wear. It takes, like, two seconds to put on and it hugs in all the right places. I feel like Barbarella when I wear this outfit, which honestly is one of the best ways to feel, I think. I think when a playsuit is done well, it can be the best best best thing ever!

This lilac dress is something Lisa found in a costume house. She showed it to me and I fell in love with it straightaway. The material falls like water and there's something so goddess-like about its shape, but it's disco, too. It reminds me of Amanda Lear! I like wearing it without a bra, 'cause I always think nipples look cool through material, and particularly cool through this material!

This is just a simple T-shirt, but I love the writing. I have another one that says, HANDLE WITH CARE, which I wore in a hip-hop video I shot recently, and then also one that says, BORED OF BEING BORED, which I keep wearing in all my meetings with record-label execs and it seems to make them a bit frustrated, which I like. I really like bitchy, simple T-shirts. They are very key to my wardrobe and remind me of bands like the Donnas, who have always been a style inspiration to me. 𝝅

STEPS TO SONIC VICTORY

The mixtape pro on honing those lines.
By DeJ Loaf, as told to Julianne. Illustration by María Inés.

1. CHOOSE YOUR TOOL

I used to write on paper in high school, but now I like all my notes in my phone, because I have it with me everywhere and I like to write however I feel.

2. RIDE OUT WRITER'S BLOCK (IT'S OK, THE WORDS WILL COME)

If I can't write, I just stop, because I feel like if I force it, it's not gonna be good. I like things to be natural, so if I couldn't get it yesterday, I just try again today, you know what I mean? It's easy to get it going—life's so crazy. But that's why you have to feel [the song] before anyone else can. Don't fake it. Just be natural. A couple of shots of Hennessy may help me, but I don't know if that's something for the younger girls [*laughs*].

My main advice is, let it come to you. No matter how long it takes, even if it takes a couple of days, when it finally comes out, it's gonna be great.

3. KEEP YOUR SONGS ON LOOP

I try to stay away from [listening to other songs for inspiration]. It's not even that I don't wanna listen, I just don't have time. I'm not really inspired by a lot of music nowadays. When I was younger I used to, for a while, like Jay Z. But these days I'm more into listening to my own song over and over, trying to figure out what I can do to make it better.

4. GET YOUR FEELINGS OUT

Writing lyrics can be just like keeping a diary. I feel that anytime I write a song, I am expressing how I feel, getting things off my chest, as long as I've been rapping. As emotions go, it's a release. It's definitely helped me, and then later you can look back and go, "Yeah, that happened!"

5. DO YOU

Stay true to yourself. Don't get lost in trying to be like anyone but yourself. You're you for a reason. You are your own unique style. Don't look at it like "Oh, I have to be like this person," or make songs just because this is the wave right now. Stick to your guns! Write about your life. That's interesting, and it will last longer than any music that's fabricated.

Be yourself and you'll last longer; the fabricators are here today, gone tomorrow.

BRAIN MAP

EZRA KOENIG

The Vampire Weekend front man on what's permeated his psyche over the years.
Illustrated by Sofia

1 - The Fifth Element - I was 13 when I first saw it and for at least six months it was "my favorite movie of all time." It got me thinking about "world-building" in art and now every detail (the dialogue, the music, the clothing by Jean Paul Gaultier) combines to form a greater whole. Late '90s cosmopolitan trip-hop glamour will always have a special place in my heart.

2 - Picnic at Hanging Rock - I watched this in college and was very moved (and weirded out) by it. It's a beautiful quiet movie. It made me think about "time" in a way I never had before, and a line of dialogue from the film inspired the song "Hannah Hunt." I probably saw [the movie] when we were starting to make the first album but I wasn't ready to explore those ideas in depth until our third album. Some things just need longer to gestate. Also, when we first played Melbourne, me and [bassist] Baio went there with the promoter and climbed the rocks!

3 - The opening lines of the Bell Jar - The Bell Jar is such a classic, beloved and be-hated book. I have lots of feelings about it, but whenever I think about it, I think about the opening lines. Summer in New York, feeling disconnected, a vague sense of horror at the headlines, the drama of the weather. [Sylvia Plath] describes a very familiar feeling and setting. She helped me pinpoint a feeling I wanted to write about too.

4 - "The Red Wheelbarrow" by William Carlos Williams - In college I had to front a lot like I cared about poetry. As an english major, you have to spend a lot of time closely examining poems and poets you might not care about. This poem is such a classic, it almost feels corny to rep it, but it's one of the only poems that ever moved me like music. I don't know if I was just feeling emo but I remember staring at it and feeling like I finally got it. It unlocked a wave of emotion in me. Minimalism and simplicity can be a shortcut to making something "cool," but I love when something feels cool, deep, and emotional at the same time. The [poem] about eating the plums is tight and funny but this one hit me harder. Also, WCW is from New Jersey.

⁵New Jersey - Suburban New Jersey is so dense and strange. I was born in Manhattan and my whole family is from New York, so I was raised to feel like I was living in exile in New Jersey. I'm glad I live in the city now but I'll never hate on New Jersey. It's an intense mix of beautiful/ugly, natural/polluted, old/new. I think that's why it's inspired a bit more great art than your average suburban area. The Sopranos, Bruce Springsteen, etc. Also, it's kinda nice to be from a place people hate on, makes you work harder.

⁶Mexico City - Vampire Weekend spent a week there when we were working on our second album, Contra. We recorded "Cousins" at a studio around the corner from Frida Kahlo's old house. If I'm keeping it real, [Mexico City is] probably the coolest city in North America.

⁷Elvis Costello - Sometimes, I listen to demos I made in high school and college and I'm singing in the worst voice. It's like this barely pubescent, American, Elvis Costello impression. It makes my skin crawl hearing it, but I guess it shows how much he meant to me. The early Elvis Costello aesthetic was smart and punky. Definitely an inspiration. I loved more hard core music too, but Elvis Costello seemed like someone I could emulate without embarrassing myself (which is not to say that I didn't embarrass myself by emulating him many times).

ELVIS COSTELLO

⁸Chromeo - When I was a freshman in college, I went to a concert at the Bowery Ballroom. The opening band was two guys playing electro-funk. At one point, the singer picked up a fake phone and pretended his girlfriend was calling him. He said, "Baby, I can't talk—I'm playing a show!" I was very fascinated. Little did I know, I would become close friends with those dudes. Chromeo gave me a model of a "band" very different from the rock bands in NYC at the time. Postmodern, irreverent, not beholden to rock and roll. Very important to the way I think about music.

CHROMEO

⁹Raj Haldar, aka Lushlife - Raj was a senior in high school when I was a freshman. He was a real mentor to me. He schooled me on hip-hop, Indian music, the Smiths. We'd drive around in his Honda Accord listening to Midnight Marauders over and over again. I shudder to think about how I might have turned out if I'd never met him.

Talking and debating music has been an important part of my life since I met Raj. I know people say you should "let the music do the talking," and I mostly do that when it comes to my career, BUT in my personal life, I love to theorize, argue, and brainstorm with friends about music. These days, Raj raps under the name Lushlife.

10-Andrei Padlowski - Andrei was another important friend I met in high school. He once made me a mixtape that was all Japanese music on one side and all Icelandic music on the other. I still have it. He turned me on to a lot of "cool" music, but really the music he liked seemed cool to me because he was cool. Know what I mean?♦

SENSITIVE AND POWERFUL:
AN INTERVIEW WITH DONNA TARTT

The author of The Goldfinch *and* The Secret History *discusses writing and personal style with Florence + the Machine's driving force.*
By Florence Welch. Illustrations by Mithsuca Berry.

FLORENCE WELCH **The male characters in your books are so convincing in their "maleness" (or at least as far as I can gather from a female perspective).**

DONNA TARTT I'm glad if they're convincing—I think that any novelist, if he or she is any good, needs to be able to write from the point of view of the opposite sex (and also from the points of view of people who are much older or younger, and from all kinds of different backgrounds).

Do you feel more comfortable writing for male characters?

Honestly, I don't think about my characters in terms of gender—it's more about what's best for the story I'm writing, and these were the characters who were right for *The Goldfinch*. But, that said: The speaking voice of Theo, my narrator, is not a million miles from my own.

I often feel there is a conflict between the masculine and feminine sides of myself during performing and songwriting.

A conflict? Or an interesting balance? I think to be a good performer (or good writer, or good artist of any kind, actually) you need a kind of synthesis between dreaminess and fantasy on the one hand, and straightforward hard work. The very best artists, in any field, are both warm and cold, sensitive and powerful, cerebral and emotional. Sometimes people speak of those polarities in terms of masculine-feminine, which is part of the picture, sure—but it's actually much more complicated than that, I think. At any rate: I think there's no question that a good artist has to be able to work in a whole lot of different ranges.

Do you think of yourself as a tomboy, perhaps?

In some ways, yes…a tomboy without the team sports, I'd say. When I was a child I was sort of a daredevil—a tree-climber and roof-climber—and I loved animals, and I loved to draw, and more than anything I loved to read. Certainly, I didn't like to play with dolls—but on the other hand, I would do almost anything to get out of games and athletics at school. I think most artists have an element of androgyny in their characters, which is perhaps part of what makes them artists in the first place.

You dress wonderfully. Are you interested in clothes?

Yes, very interested in clothes. Always have been.

Do you like presenting an idea of yourself to others by what you wear? Or do you think it's superficial?

It's not so much about presenting an idea—it's more that I wear what I like and somehow it all fits together. I've always had very strong ideas about my clothes—when I was little, my favorite shoes were red patent leather; I wore as many lockets and charm bracelets as I was allowed to and/or could get away with; but as far as actual clothes went, I strongly rejected anything girly or frilly and always went either for boys' clothes or for what I thought of as "orphan dresses"—that is to say, plainly cut dresses in the darkest, drabbest colors I could find, like gray and dark brown. When I was about five or six I remember begging my grandmother, who was an excellent seamstress, to make me a black dress—"Certainly not!"

At any rate, I think my love of clothes has at least partly to do with my love of detail. Lots of writers have been clotheshorses and dandies—Proust, Oscar Wilde, Baudelaire, Colette all come to mind… even Emily Dickinson in her white muslin dresses or Ivy Compton-Burnett with her diamond brooches and severe Victorian black. Poring through racks of vintage clothes or obsessing over just the right shade of sky-blue or violet satin for the lining of a black jacket stems from exactly the same impulse that makes me tinker happily with a sentence all afternoon, changing adjectives and moving clauses around until it's just right. Then, too: I so enjoy looking at *other people's clothes* that it seems only proper to take a little care with my own. As Isabella Blow so famously said: "My style icon is anyone who makes a bloody effort."

Do you have those antique roses that smell of raspberries that Henry grows in *The Secret History*? Or did you research to find weird, unusual ones to suit him?

I *did* have that Reine des Violettes rose, growing in a pot, but sadly it died during a cold winter a couple of winters ago—I'll have to buy myself a new one. It's a beautiful, decadent old rose, a deep purplish-fuchsia color with petals that tend to curl and go black at the edges as it fades. Whenever I'm anywhere near a botanical garden during rose season, I'll always go and smell the rarities, as so many antique roses have undertones of other scents—lemon, oranges, honey, myrrh. Anyway: I grow a lot of old roses myself now, but when I wrote that part of *The Secret History*, I was living in a tiny New York apartment and longing for a garden, and I gave Henry a rose that I wanted myself.

I was incredibly moved by the passage at the end of *The Goldfinch* about how we are inherently ourselves, for better or worse, unable to change who we are, or whom we love. Do you feel that writing helps you to define how you feel about the world? Love? Relationships? And somehow understand yourself/them better?

Absolutely.

Are the characters' revelations your revelations, too?

Sometimes! I find that a book is never very good if you've figured the whole thing out in advance. As Robert Frost said [in his 1939 essay, "The Figure a Poem Makes"]: "No surprise for the writer, no surprise for the reader."

I hope this hasn't taken up too much of your time. I really am such a huge fan, and I hope we can meet face-to-face someday.

I hope so, too!

And please get in touch if you ever want to come to a show, or if you're in London and want to go for tea.

I will. I don't know if you are ever in New York, but if you are, give me a call—I'd love to meet you for tea (and, maybe take you to the flea market if you want to go!). Thank you for doing this—and thank you, of course, for your music. And yes, much love to you right back. 🖋

FRIEND CRUSH:
SHAMIR AND CHLOE CHAIDEZ

How two singers met on Twitter and bonded over Cheetos.
By Gabby. Illustrations by Alyssa Etoile.

GABBY **How did you two meet?**

SHAMIR I saw her band Kitten open up for Paramore back in 2013, a little bit before I graduated high school. I remember being blown away. Me and my best friend went to go see her instead of going to prom. We've been obsessed with Kitten ever since and then last spring she tweeted at me and was like, "Oh, I love your music, blah blah blah," and I was like, "Are you kidding me? I love *your* music." And we ended up becoming roommates and best friends.

Your dreams were coming true!

It's still weird to me that we're, like, super close. I'm roommates with one of my favorite pop stars.

When did you guys go from good friends to best friends?

Literally the first night we hung out we felt like best friends. I remember it so vividly.

Can you describe a moment when she was really there for you?

There are so many! Probably the support and help that she's given with the band I manage. They're up-and-coming, and really young, and she let them open for her in the town that they're from. Any time I need help with them or need advice, she's so supportive.

What makes her stand out from other people in your life?

She's so freaking talented. I have a few musician friends back home in Vegas, but she's kind of the only musician who pushed me. We push each other. When we were living together we were singing around the house and writing songs, asking: "Does this song sound good?" It was such a beautiful experience to live with and know a musician who's your age, but who is also more advanced, so they push you.

What ways are you most alike and most opposite?

We're so freaking alike it's kinda ridiculous. We're both messy people, but we know we're eventually gonna clean up. The apartment will look a hot mess for a week, but then one of us is gonna take initiative. The thing that makes us completely opposite is the cooking thing. I did all of the cooking, but along the way she did learn a few things that I was very proud of.

So you like cooking and she doesn't?

It's not that she doesn't like cooking…she's just not that good at it.

What was her biggest cooking disaster?

One time while she was making breakfast, she kept cutting herself. I was like, "Chloe, do you not know how to use a knife? This is ridiculous, you've cut yourself twice in making one breakfast."

What do you think is the biggest change in your relationship since you first met?

I moved back to the West Coast and it became a long-distance thing. But we still see each other in between. We're both in California right now, so we're gonna have dinner tonight. Whenever we're together, it's like nothing has changed.

〰〰〰〰〰〰〰〰〰〰〰

GABBY **How did you and Shamir meet?**

CHLOE CHAIDEZ We met on Twitter, kind of. I saw his track. I think he got best music on Pitchfork, like, a year ago. And I remember seeing that he was 19 and crazy awesome and he looked like, *Wow, that's a fucking star right there*. And he's 19! So I tweeted him and was like, "Shoutout to other 19-year-olds making music." And he tweeted me back in a matter of seconds like, "Oh my god, Kitten,

I saw you open for Paramore in Las Vegas a couple of months ago!" And I was like, Oh shit! So we were immediately fans of each other because of that. I think we were both surprised that we knew of each other. And then we just kept in contact through the next six months until I went to New York. Shamir was like, "Come meet me! I live at this punk DIY venue." I got there and I fell in love with the venue and the place. And he was like, "My roommate's moving out next month, you should move in with me." And I did, and I just never left New York.

Do you feel like there was a time you went from good friends to best friends?

There was always this connection, because of our age and the music we're making. And being front people, as douchey as that sounds. That will always connect us. And being singers, songwriters. And when we moved in together, we realized we both liked Hot Cheetos. It was just little things that bonded us immediately.

Can you describe a moment when he was really there for you?

There are many! He's always been there during my venting of my love problems. Or nonexistent-love problems. Any time I wanted to bitch about my many love affairs, he was always the one to listen, and, you know, not everyone can handle that.

What's something amazing about Shamir that makes him stand out from other people in your life?

He's so genuine and authentic in what he does. Nothing about him is contrived. He just is what he is. That kind of real realness bonded us. I love Brooklyn to death, but you get a lot of people from different places kind of wearing this uniform, too cool for school, afraid to admit they like certain things. Shamir and I are able to cut through the bullshit and laugh about it.

In what ways do you feel like you're most alike and most opposite?

We're both messy, which worked out splendidly because we never got upset with each other. We're both fairly social *and* antisocial. Like, when we want to be social we'll definitely feed that desire, but when we don't, we like to be alone and work on our music. And he's a big cook and I don't cook.

What's the most elaborate meal he's made?

He makes cow tongue! Lengua. It's so good! He made it for me when I first moved in. He marinated it for three days. Of course, I picked at it for the three days. I hope he doesn't know that. It's delicious. He makes homemade taquitos, too. He's a really good cook. Oh, I know one way we differ! He likes some really questionable pop music.

Can you give us a hint?

I'll put it this way, it's so questionable people don't even know. They're not even known names. But he'll argue that it's brilliant and his favorite thing ever. That's what I love about him. He doesn't care!

What has been the biggest change in your relationship since you first met?

When I first met him, I was like, "Oh, show me your music." And he played me "On the Regular" on his phone. And I was like, "This is gonna be the best music blah blah blah." And now, to see that the song has like a million views…not that that's changed our relationship, but I think it's almost bonding to go through that with someone.

Yeah, you've seen him when he…started from the bottom.

I hate to, like, Drake it out, but you know, "started from the bottom, now [you] here!" It's like watching a flower grow. It's beautiful! And I saw the whole thing! He's my little flower. All grown and gonna be huge. Also, just being in New York together. We always joke about how we want to pitch a show to the E! network, like *Chloe and Shamir Take New York*.

Do you have nicknames for each other, and where do they come from?

Oh yeah, Little Bae! I don't even know where it came from. When I have a deep affection for someone I call them "Little Bae." It just comes out. It could be a dog. It could be my aunt. It could be, like, someone who I met at a party and got drunk with who I really love. I'm like, "Oh, you're the littlest bae!" Littlest Bae is what I call Shamir. ♥

AN ADOLESCENCE SURVIVAL GUIDE: FROM AN 80's/90's TEEN TO HER MODERN COUNTERPART

Funny person, Parks and Recreation star, and sensitive teen on making it through puberty.

BY RASHIDA JONES

I grew up without a cellphone. I had an Apple IIc+ desktop computer, which I primarily used for its word processor. At the time, it was NOT considered cool to own a computer. Kids with computers were considered geeks. I feel lucky to have grown up in that time but I certainly understand the pressures of not feeling good enough, pretty enough, cool enough... I was an emotional and sensitive teenager and spent a lot of time being boy-crazy. The point is, I don't think I was that different from you. Here are a few words of advice to survive the teen years:

> well, isn't that special!

Figure out what you're good at and get better at it. When I was a kid, my parents would let me stay up late to watch *Saturday Night Live*. At my 13th birthday, I made everyone stop dancing so I could do an impression of the Church Lady. I'm not sure any of my friends were too happy about this but my love of comedy reigned supreme then and now.

Find the song that makes you cry the most and then lock yourself in a room for a couple hours and just... cry. It feels good, and it's good for you. Maybe even write a journal entry. In high school, my pick was "In your Eyes" by Peter Gabriel. (EPIC.)

> I WANT TO TOUCH THE LIGHT, THE HEAT I SEE IN YOUR EYES

Remember that teenage boys are SIMPLE. (Well, all boys, really.) They may seem like they're thinking deeply about your shared future, but they're usually just thinking about food or sports or boobs. Probably just boobs.

Be present. Live your life for you and THEN maybe share it with the world. No one will remember what you posted on Instagram 20 years from now. But YOU will remember the memory that made you think it was important to post.

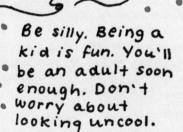

Be silly. Being a kid is fun. You'll be an adult soon enough. Don't worry about looking uncool.

Make fashion and hair mistakes. A lot of them. This is the time to do it. Take chances.

I LOOK GOOOOOD!

ALWAYS have snacks. Being hungry makes you emotional, and therefore make bad decisions.

we're all pretty bizarre. Some of us are just better at hiding it, that's all.

Watch all of John Hughes's movies. And then memorize important lines from them. There are so many that still apply to everyday life. One of my favorites is from *Ferris Bueller's Day Off*: "Life moves pretty fast. If you don't stop and look around once in a while, you could miss it." ◆

ILLUSTRATED BY MAXINE CRUMP!

REVELING IN THE EXTRAORDINARY:
AN INTERVIEW WITH TRACEE ELLIS ROSS

The Black-ish *star on how to be magnificent.*   By Jamia. Illustration by Mithsuca Berry.

As a producer, model, comedian, fashion writer, and video blogger, Tracee Ellis Ross is a pop-culture polymath. The *Black-ish* and former *Girlfriends* star possesses stellar comedic timing, trendsetting style, and a whole lot of wisdom.

JAMIA **My friend and I are longtime *Girlfriends* fans. We were talking about how you're like a modern Lucille Ball with your comedic courage.**

TRACEE ELLIS ROSS Thank you! I'll take that. For me, comedy is about telling the truth. *Trying* to be funny doesn't work. I have always been silly and joyful. I express things physically. I'm always doing some weird dance or movement, or turning something into a song. It seems to work with what I do, thank goodness. Otherwise, I'd be in a straitjacket somewhere.

You have a really distinct sense of style. How would you describe your aesthetic?

Ooh, that's a good one. Tell me yours to give me an idea of what you're asking.

[*Laughs*] I'd describe mine as '60s inspired, Parisian bougie with a Saudi Arabian twist.

[*Laughs*] I can see you just by hearing that. My friends are better at describing my style than I am. How do you describe mine?

I'm all over your Instagram, so I can do this! You're classically chic, but flamboyantly sophisticated and elegantly sporty.

Sometimes, I need to talk myself into wearing pants that have a zipper. I get dressed up for a living, "for camera," either while shooting or for a red carpet, so I love comfort in my personal life…[but] always with some flair. I don't mind if there's a little sporty [quality] in how I dress. I love feeling elegant, glamorous, and comfortable, combined in one. I love statement pieces, I love simple and complicated.

I work out with a matte red lip; I'll wear a tuxedo jacket with sweatpants. [I've worn] a satin evening gown with Birken-stocks with a cardigan sweater. But I have a strong sense of appropriateness about environments I'm in. When you go to the White House there's a way to dress; when you go to a red carpet there's a way to dress.

How has hip-hop influenced your style? I'm thinking about your TMURDA persona and videos.

The style of hip-hop is rich, bold, and in your face! So much of that inspires me. In the '90s, I had doorknocker earrings made with my name on them. I loved Neneh Cherry, and Mary J. Blige during the *411* era.

I've always loved sneakers and the influence of street style in general. When I was working in fashion at *New York* Magazine, I pitched a story about how the street was influencing the runway.

I love high-end glamour but there's nothing better than how it gets translated on the street. The street has style and life in it. Fashion has fantasy. Some things that are in fashion don't work on me. The skinny jean. The low-rise jean…[or] do you mean "a quarter of my ass" jeans? Forget muffin top, it was like a champagne glass. I runneth over. That's how I discovered the pencil skirt.

Preach! I've always felt that the skinny jean was invented to troll black girls worldwide.

Because of my body type and my curves, my sexuality is expressed better when I'm more demure. I have an ass. I have a waist. I never felt like I needed to hide it. High-waisted jeans have always worked on me. I look great in a wide-leg trouser. There's nothing more elegant than a pencil skirt. I've always loved tank tops and my collarbones. I like working with my body type.

Since we're talking about fashion and culture, I want to ask you about your thoughts on cultural appropriation in fashion. It's something we've had a lot of conversations about at Rookie.

We would all be remiss if we didn't consider the historical context of things—where they come from, and the importance of how different cultures have always expressed themselves through beauty and style. And how that beauty and style is often marginalized when in its authentic form, but celebrated when it's adopted by white culture.

It's not that anyone shouldn't borrow, enjoy, or try on anything, but if you do it without knowing the historical context, the culture of beauty, and how different races have been marginalized throughout this journey, then I think that is ignorance.

There also must be room for people to make missteps. There are always things we won't know unless we make mistakes. But the mistake is the opportunity. In our culture we seem to vilify people to the point where there is no space to learn. We need to be mindful about not vilifying in a way that a person, organization, or institution becomes so wronged that a learning experience cannot occur. It's also not to say people shouldn't take responsibility. Personal responsibility is a must.

What frightens me most is when people have no idea that what they have said is offensive because they are so busy defending themselves. We have to remember that there is a place where we all will say or do things that are ignorant. We are humans. We all have blind spots. I know I have a ton. I try my best to be compassionate about this kind of stuff. I really want to be the type of person who can hear things, reflect on them, and then continue to be teachable.

At Rookie, we have a style feature we call "Secret Style Icon." Do you have any style icons?

I don't think any of my style icons are a secret, but some of them aren't people who are in the public eye. My friend's mom is one of my style icons. She's an artist and a ceramicist, and she embodies style. Not just clothing. The way she navigates the world is stylish.

My own style started as armor and a way that I protected myself. It has evolved as a way that I express myself. So, I respond well to bold personas, women and humans who are fully embodying their own spirit—even if it isn't the way I would dress, even if it is totally contrary to who I am. I'm inspired by the flair and sensuality of Josephine Baker, the bubbly charisma of Audrey Hepburn, and the power of Katharine Hepburn. The swirl of those three is the inspiration for how I attempt to navigate the world stylishly.

Have you ever heard of shine theory? Feminists and pals Aminatou Sow and Ann Friedman coined the phrase.

What?! I totally just got covered in chills. Tell me more.

It's about how women should collaborate instead of compete with one another. If your friend shines, you do, too.

That theory is one of my underlying intentions. One of the reasons I started my website is for a like-minded community to use the internet as an opportunity to support each other, rather than tear each other down. It's so fun dancing in curiosity with each other and reveling in the extraordinary, and in the absolute ordinary, that we are.

How do you revel in the beauty of the ordinary?

My mom used to say something like "There's no such thing as being bored. Only boring people get bored." There's always something to be excited about, just like there's always something to be grateful for. It's a choice to move that way and it's not always easy.

I came up with a sort of mantra with my mom. "May the space between where I am and where I want to be inspire me." My mom helped me come up with the "inspire me" part. Often the space between is what frightens me.

I want to know more about how to be inspired by "the space between."

How do you make sense between where you are and where you want to be? The gratitude and curiosity is how we hold on to that beautiful joy that makes [us able to experience] the ordinary as the extraordinary.

I did grow up in an extraordinary family. We experienced an extraordinary life, as a result. I traveled the world by an early age, Andy Warhol painted me, I went to wonderful schools, and I met presidents…but within that was family, dinnertime, and connection.

I thrive on routine and the basics: walking my dog, doing my dishes. I think it's easy to confuse ordinary with [boring]. Boredom comes when we don't feel challenged. We're left doing things that leave us feeling unfulfilled. I encourage people (and myself) to find space to do something that is an expression of joy for ourselves. These experiences turn our lives into joyous mixed bags. There are good days and bad days…there are bad years.

That reminds me of this sweet, old love letter that I found at my parents' house. My dad wrote my mom a letter about how they have had good years and bad years, but she is the only one he'd want to be in the foxhole with forever.

That's a beautiful testament about love and self-love. I've heard many people say they learned to love themselves through their partners or kids. I do not have either. But, I have learned how to love myself by how I treat myself, how I talk to myself, and by building a community of love around me. They say self-esteem comes from esteemable acts. You cannot feel your way into a new feeling, but you can act your way into one. ACTION and BEHAVIOR. I have days that I'm at odds with myself, months, sometimes. But I choose to stay with myself no matter what, and to treat myself kindly and lovingly. And if I am falling short, someone close to me is hopefully able to love me when I can't love myself.

Speaking of loving yourself, I'm kind of a fanatic about natural hair. I have locs, and I have a clear bias about this subject. Let's talk natural hair.

[*Laughs*] Yes! I'm with you! Let's talk about it.

You have worn your hair natural throughout your career. Have you ever felt that it has affected how or whether you were cast for roles?

I have no idea. I never noticed. Learning how to navigate my natural hair texture in a world where not a lot of people had my texture, or my mom's texture, required a lot of trial and error. I didn't have a ton of girlfriends with my texture. I was navigating it pretty much on my own.

Being an athlete and trying to figure out my hair was quite a journey. When I was a model my hair was just beaten up. So, by the time I started acting, I became my hair's advocate because I had worked so hard to get it healthy.

My journey to self-acceptance had a lot to do with my journey with my hair. I've always been like, "Put a wig on me or blow my hair out, but this is my hair." All my acting jobs have opted to use my hair.

I'm not anti-weave but I've never worn one. I'm pro self-love and self-acceptance. I tell young women and girls to look for how they feel the most beautiful, and to keep in mind that there is an overt and unconscious culture that has a limited view of what beauty is.

One would be remiss to ignore the historic context about how women of color are made to feel about our natural or authentic beauty. My advice is not to listen to anyone who thinks that there is one rule that applies to [everybody]. At the end of the day, you are with you. At the end of your life, it's you who gets to go back and say if you lived for you or for someone else. I know it takes a shit ton of courage. I have a community of wonderful wild horses and extraordinary women who give me courage to keep leaping into myself, into the furthest reaches of who I am. 🐎

FRIEND CRUSH:

HAYLEY WILLIAMS AND JOY WILLIAMS

The Paramore frontwoman and Civil Wars vocalist on the power of singing your own stories.
By Brittany. Illustrations by María Inés.

BRITTANY **How did you and Joy meet?**

HAYLEY WILLIAMS I think I was 12. My mom and I moved to Nashville to try and get away from my hometown in Mississippi. She was going through some stuff in her marriage. One of my closest friends had moved up here, so we came up to stay with them. We started going to this church right outside of Nashville, and I guess Joy must've gone there, because we met her one of the first weeks we were there. Joy used to sing a lot of Jesus and gospel music, and just had this incredible voice even when she was super, super young. I think she was maybe 18 when I met her. I was already a fan. So when I met her, my mind was absolutely blown that she wanted to talk to me and hang out with me. You know, because I was so inspired by her. And she had no ego. She didn't act like she was better than anyone, even though in my mind, she was this incredible, talented, wonderful person.

So we started hanging out kind of often. She would come over to see my mom and me, and hang out. She would listen to me sing songs on the piano, or we would talk about life and boys and all that stuff. It was cool, because it was like having an older sister. I've always been the oldest sister.

When did you go from good friends to best friends?

It's been a long journey, because she and I went our separate ways for a while just by accident. I joined Paramore at 13. And life started moving at super speed.

Later, when I was 19, I was hanging out with Taylor Swift and she was like, "I love this band the Civil Wars." And I was like, "Oh yeah, I've heard of that band." And I went home and downloaded their EP and loved it. I was like, "Ah, this is so beautiful!" And I had no idea it was Joy, for probably a couple of weeks. And then, when I realized it was her, it was like [rediscovering] someone you've known for a very long time. Like, *Why are you here? How are you here?* I reached out and was like, "Oh my god! The Civil Wars is so amazing. I had no idea that was you, and I'm so excited for you."

We slowly started talking more and more. Then the middle of last year, we asked her to do a duet with us. We've always sort of checked in with each other. And now, we're at the point where I just feel we're, like, soul sisters, you know?

What was it like to hear the Civil Wars and watch Joy become successful with that?

It kind of felt like a long time coming. When she was singing Christian or gospel music as a young teenager, you could already tell. Her voice was insane. Her range was crazy. She grew up on a lot of singers who really sing. It's like an art form. It's not just singing a melody. That's why I loved her voice so much and that's why I was so excited to meet her, because I was like, "I like to sing like this too." I like my voice to sound strong and I like to do these big sweeping notes.

Then I found the Civil Wars stuff she was writing and singing…I think it's always interesting when you have a vocalist who grows up focusing on their vocals and then they learn to write for themselves—the lyrics and the way they move the melody around for their voice—it usually changes how they sing. It changed how I sing a lot. When I was singing other people's songs, as a kid growing up in church, those weren't my stories so much. But now Joy is singing her own stories and there's such depth. She can sing anything in the entire world, but when she sings her own stories, there's so much power you can't deny it.

What makes Joy stand out from the other people in your life?

She's so calming to be around. She's very strong and she has a lot of opinions, but you don't ever feel like you have to shield yourself from her words. She's one of the most honest people I've ever known. But also, she's so graceful about it. I've gotten to watch her grow up, too. I've seen her in her marriage. I've seen her have a child. I've seen her navigate different eras of her musical career. And now she's starting a brand-new career with a solo album that's so insanely good.

In what ways are you most alike?

We do everything with a lot of conviction. But we also don't think that we're the best. We feel like we are on this journey to constantly get better and be better. To me, it isn't a comfortable place, because every day, I'm in a mindset of *OK, what can I be doing better to do this?*

And in what ways are you opposite?

She moves with a lot of grace. I feel like I stumble around a lot. I don't feel graceful at all. Because she's just a handful of years older than me, I'm always hoping, "Ah, in six years, I hope I'm like Joy." I don't feel like I will be, 'cause I feel like the clumsiest person, both emotionally and physically. But you know, we can aspire to greatness.

Do you two ever write songs together?

Yeah. The first time that we ever really sang together was for our duet that came out last fall called "Hate to See Your Heart Break." It was so amazing because Paramore's never done any collaborations, really. The thing that worked about it is that Joy and I both grew up listening to a lot of divas, like Whitney Houston, Patti LaBelle, Mariah Carey…really poppy music with a lot of vocal aerobics or acrobatics. But we ended up singing different styles of music. For the Civil Wars, Joy did a lot of that Americana sound that was dark. And I ended up singing aggressive songs and pop songs with Paramore. But none of it really sounds like what we grew up listening to.

It was so amazing to share that duet with another singer who understands little inflections…she's such a smart singer. She puts so much taste into what she does. When I was harmonizing with her, I would follow those little things. So, if you really pay attention, you can hear where her style is sitting right on top and I'm following that. And then the moments where she's harmonizing to my melody, you can hear how she's following my little subtleties. So it was amazing to share that moment as friends, but even more, I think, as singers who really understand singing together. We don't get to just sing with other women all the time. I wish I did it more, because I feel like that experience was so good for me as a singer. I learned a lot and felt like it showcased something in both of us we haven't been able to show for a while.

Do you ever talk about business-related stuff, or give advice? Or is it very separate, like when you two are together you don't really think about work?

No, it totally all overlaps. We've grown up in the music business together. She saw me as a person before she ever knew me as the girl who's in Paramore. And I knew her as a completely different artist than she is today. So we kind of have always gone to each other for advice. While she's been working on this record, I've been so lucky to hear songs take shape. She sent me a picture she did for her photo shoot for the album package. It's so beautiful—it's stunning. I was like, "Oh my god, this is my friend Joy who is literally about to take over her area of music and it's going to be so powerful and it's going to mean so much."

So it's been cool for me to watch because we are friends and because it's not like we have to run every single thing by each other to do what we do and do it well. But it's nice when you have someone who trusts you. It's not weird to talk about music. It's just part of who each of us is.

〰〰〰〰〰〰〰〰

BRITTANY **What was your impression of Hayley when you met?**

JOY WILLIAMS Hayley was in junior high when we met, and I wasn't much older. I remember she had this spark even then. She had this bounce in her step always. She had determination. Bangs, bright clothes, an obsession with 'N Sync. I can still remember her pounding away on her red keyboard in her bedroom, eyes closed, singing me a new song she'd just written.

Hayley told me that hearing the Civil Wars' EP helped you rekindle your friendship. How did it feel to reunite with her?

Getting back in touch after a few years of us both touring and going through our own whirlwinds on the road was a gift. It's not like we had a falling-out or anything like that—it was just schedules, and life in general, that got in the way. But I was always keeping an eye on the tours, the songs—and looking back, she was doing the same. When we were able to reconnect, it was like sitting down with someone I'd

never really been out of step with. That's when you know you've found a dear friend—when you can pick right up where you left off.

What makes Hayley stand out from the other people in your life?

Hayley has an amazing blend of badassery and total humility, neither of which is put on or forced. I've said it before, but she's the type of person whose arrows go outward, not inward.

How are the two of you the most alike and most opposite?

We seem to really value similar things, in the way we see the world and how we interact with people. We are both ridiculously short humans, which we laugh about a lot. We're opposite in the way we decorate, maybe? I live in a postmodern house in California that's all white…and at one point, Hayley's house had an octopus chandelier in the dining room, scratch-and-sniff cherry wallpaper in her hallway, and a giant dinosaur next to her pool.

What's been your favorite memory with Hayley?

Whatever the next one is going to be, because all the others have been pretty awesome leading up to now. ✏

BRAIN MAP: LORDE

☆ charting a constellation of influences, by our queen bee ☆

Illustrated by Isabel

"That slow-burn wait while it gets dark!"
— a lyric from "A World Alone"

I remember this super vividly. ☆☆
It was the night "Royals" went #1 in New Zealand for the first time — I didn't know what that meant then, my producer called me to tell me and also had to explain what it was. I wore a Blue dress, so that song's color world has always been blue and kind of a weird red. We went out to a dress-up party — it was a girl from school's birthday. Maybe it's a New Zealand summer thing, but it gets dark sometimes at nine or ten. So I remember lying on my boyfriend's bed watching something, and that feeling of the wait. It never felt cool to go to a party when it was light out, there was a self-consciousness there.

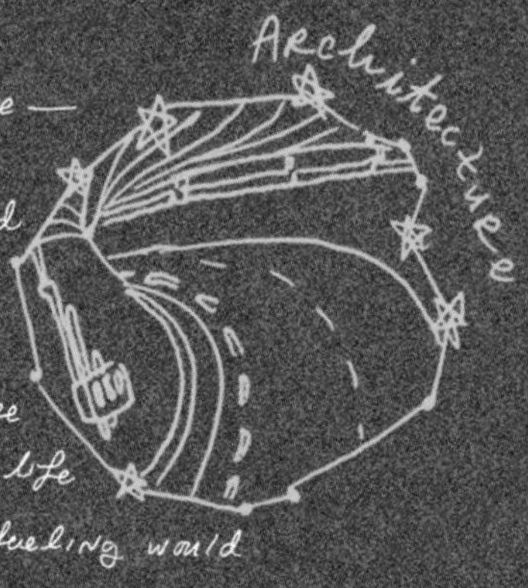

☆☆ I've talked about the white tunnel before, but I wanted to expand on it here — it's the tunnel that connects the city to the area where I live, and my boyfriend. James (Lowe) and I drive through it a couple of times a day. The whole thing is painted white. and it feels to me like going through one of those simulation blizzard tunnels at aquariums. My dad was actually involved with the construction, and before it opened, he was invited to a dinner inside it — they put out a table and a white cloth and silverware right there in the tunnel, which is the coolest thing ever in my head! It was a big part of my life and that record. — everything slows down and brightens up in that tunnel; however I was feeling would become immediately clear to me whenever I went through it. It helped me to identify a lot of emotions behind songs like "Buzzcut Season" and "400 Lux."

Architecture

"Magnolia Mountain" by Ryan Adams

My first really visceral, intense reaction to a piece of music, I was 12 or 13. I had this guitar teacher. He was in a band locally, and in our house he was a rock star. We would do these lessons in my very sunny/hot, very squashed, very "TEENAGE" bedroom, and each time I had a lesson I would fall more in love, lol.

He played me this song on guitar at our very first lesson, right at the end. Something about the melodies, the chorus lyric, "lie to me, sing me a song," that coating of the sun on his face and his hands on the guitar and the physical closeness of this music being sung at me a half meter away, was so overwhelming. I burst into tears, and I remember kind of being amazed, because it was the first time music pushed me somewhere I didn't necessarily want to go (bawling in front of my hottie teacher/him thinking I was a creep). Since then, I've had intense reactions to music much more as I've tapped into that part of myself and that involuntary emotion is something that I know means I'm almost destined to write songs... — it's coming from somewhere so deep down; it's wrapped around all the other parts of my brain like a softly pulsing chain. I know that I can never get rid of that. ✴

ANOTHER time when I remember being like,
"WHOA, MUSIC RULES,"
quite early on was when I was on a school trip.
I was sitting up on my knees down the back of the school bus,
losing my mind to this song, dancing around. I definitely
would have died if we had, like, crashed into a ditch
or something. I had never heard anything like that vocal
delivery, there was something very dumb about the song,
which I loved.

★ "my Generation" by The Who ★

[James Blake] Another moment of total discovery, feeling
like I was out in the wild while something alien played
around me, was hearing James Blake for the first time,
maybe at a party? I ran to the next room and put my ☆
face up against the speaker....

The Threat of the World ending... (December 2012)

This hung quite heavy in my world. I felt like the final months
★ of that year, all I could think about was the moment
everything was going to come apart, and what we would do.
People started to really irk me around that time, too, like,
"D-day is in two weeks and you're doing 'this'?" I stopped going out
at night because it was so irritating for me. I started working on
★"Glory and Gore" at my bach (a beach-house shack-type thing) out
in the garage, in January, and that line,
"You've been drinking like the world was gonna end (it didn't),"
drips with disdain for the people I knew who weren't
doing anything significant with what I thought would
be our last days on earth (although, come to think
of it, I probably wasn't doing jack either).
🪐 There's relief there, too.

[Finding new music] When I was in school a huge part of what kept me happy was finding music. Surfing YouTube or SoundCloud, taking chances clicking on stuff hoping to find gems. We'd burn mix CDs for each other, mine with very elaborate cover art and my (dude) friends' with just the track lists scrawled on a couple pieces of paper — and they were our treasures. It was the most informative time for me as a listener, being exposed to all this awesome stuff through the internet and my friends. I'm not sure I remember so many of the songs — maybe I have a couple of the CDs somewhere, but there was definitely a remix of "Skip Divided," a Thom Yorke song — I listened to that a lot walking around school. And "Satellite of Love," by Lou Reed.

"Feed" by M.T. Anderson I was a theater kid growing up, so how words sound read aloud is huge to me. I would lug around a collected Shakespeare book, a real brick, and sit alone at lunchtime reading softly to myself, getting inside and between the lines and figuring it out. A book I remember having an effect on my relationship with writing/words early on was "Feed". I had read it and half-understood it when I was 6 or 7, but I persuaded my teacher to assign it to us in 9th grade to read as a class, and that's when I really got to live inside it. The rhythm of the words in that book is really special — it's a dystopian novel about having a chip in your brain that streams adverts into your consciousness, so there are a lot of crazy passages, which I guess are supposed to overload you, and stimulate that feeling of not being able to control every thought inside your head. There's one scene in particular, when the main character, Titus, meets the girl he's going to fall in love with, Violet. He's in a club, and there's sensory assault coming from all angles, and it builds up and up in the prose and the intonation of the words until he sees her, and it all falls away. Please, please read that book if you haven't. I'm going to reread it right now.

"bullet in the Brain" by Tobias Wolff

"This short story is about a guy who gets shot in a bank robbery, and his memories leaving him as the bullet travels from one side of his head to another. It's really well done, you can really see the story, and it reads perfectly. There were many hours spent reading that one aloud in my room.

Ray Bradbury

My teacher in 7th grade used to read his stories to us, which I think was my 1st exposure to short fiction. The fact that they were read aloud helped them feel like huge billboards in my head, like movies. I think they're the reason I'm a sucker for really grand, powerful science - fiction imagery in film, like the giant wave in ¬ Interstellar ¬ that they think is a mountain, or Sigourney Weaver moving through the ship in ¬ Alien ¬ once she realizes she's alone...

New Zealand + Nature

All this stuff I'm talking about is very retrospective, so I thought I'd include something more current. I spent my summer in New Zealand this year, the whole summer, and I got to fall in love with nature again. My year had been spent almost exclusively in the biggest cities in the world, so I wasn't taking anything for granted. I would wake up really early in the morning, walk around the rocks, touch the walls of succulents and water plants growing up the side of the mountain, sometimes I see dolphins. I'd drop my towel at the beach by my house, and let this incredible, cool-warm silver water swallow me up. I'd walk or swim up the beach, and feel the sun on me and just marvel at that ¬ BEAUTY ¬ I'm not religious, but it felt as close to recognizing the existence of a god as I've ever come. And it wasn't, like, supermodel - intimidating nature beauty, but more like creeping; like when you see someone across the room at school or at work and realize for the first time that they look like a Michelangelo painting. A lot of my summer was spent in the water, either with those early morning swims or evening ones at a different beach around the corner. The light is totally different there, the water is a dark green, to me it feels like secrets. I'd go there at 8 or 9 pm with whomever I could convince (it was kind of colder at that time), and we'd lie on our backs and float, watch the cruise ships glittering past, watch the moon. When you float like that, it's like your body's being held by up little invisible hands, keeping you there. In that moment. When you float, it's pretty hard to feel anything but alive. ♥

FRIEND CRUSH:
TYLER FORD AND ARIANA GRANDE

When a pop star and a poet bond for life and belt out duets at Thanksgiving.
By Tavi. Illustrations by Mithsuca Berry.

TAVI **How did you two meet?**

TYLER FORD She was 12. We met three days after my 15th birthday.

ARIANA GRANDE Me and my friends were in a group called Kids Who Care, and we would sing at different galas and fundraisers to raise money for charity, and Tyler was the newest addition to the group. We would sing musical-theater songs, pop songs—really only one Christmas song from 'N Sync.

TYLER I was Justin Timberlake.

ARIANA Of course.

Was there one song or musical that you shared a particular passion for?

TYLER "Rent," and everything from *Rent*.

ARIANA But especially "What You Own." We love a Roger—

TYLER A Roger and Mimi duet. At Thanksgiving, there was a piano and we got up in front of everyone and did "Take Me or Leave Me."

ARIANA With Star playing piano! My bodyguard, Star, is also the greatest pianist you've ever heard in your life.

[Editor's note: A week later, Tyler texted us, "'ONLY' BY NICKI MINAJ IS OUR FRIENDSHIP SONG. BUT ONLY THE FIRST VERSE. TEXT TAVI THAT.—Ariana"]

Can you each describe a moment when the other was there for you?

ARIANA Tyler's usually the first person I go to when something is not 100 percent, you know? If I'm anxious or whatever. One of the first things that comes to mind is when my grandpa got really sick. Toward the end, Tyler came to Florida to spend a lot of that time with me when I was up all night taking care of him/anxious/crying/trying to wrap my head around it all. Tyler makes me laugh harder than anyone on earth, but there's also something very comforting to me about Tyler. Even though it was the hardest time of my life, it was beautiful, because I got to spend a lot of time with my grandfather, and be there for him and make sure he was comfortable, but I also had Tyler with me. A lot of love helped.

TYLER I wrote about this for Rookie. When I first went off hormones and didn't know where I stood gender-wise and was trying to figure myself out, I was living with Ari and was spending every day with her, 24/7. She was always the first person to just be like, "All right, you do you. I love you, and I still think you're the most amazing person, no matter who you are, even if you don't know what pronouns you're going to settle on." Every day, she would ask me, "How are you doing, now that you're off hormones? Do you feel OK? What pronouns are you feeling today? What pronouns do you want me to use?" Even though I was struggling with who I was, I always felt comfortable with her, even if I didn't feel comfortable with myself or anyone else.

ARIANA Wow! I love you.

TYLER I love you. That was so important and crucial to me at that time, and made me so much more confident and comfortable with myself. Though, literally, when is there a moment when she's not here for me? She's here for me every day and vice versa.

In what ways are you most alike and most opposite?

ARIANA Our humor is very identical.

TYLER I don't ever laugh more with anyone.

Do you feel you're different in a way that you balance each other out?

ARIANA I feel very balanced with them, but I don't think it's the way that we're different. I think it's our energies, they're compatible. Deep, right? [*Laughs*]

Do you have nicknames for each other?

TYLER We just call each other different things in different moments, random things.

ARIANA Sometimes, it will be [*falsetto*] Sweet Pie.

TYLER Babe of My Heart.

[*Simultaneously*] Princex of My Heart!

TYLER Cutest Person in the World. And Ari.

ARIANA Baby Sun from the *Teletubbies*.

When did you go from being good friends to being best friends?

TYLER We spent so much time together in our formative years. She was 12. I was 15. We were rehearsing two times a week for like four hours. We had dinner together two or three times a week. Or, before a show, four times a week. I, like, LIVED at her house. Even if we weren't close and calling each other up—because that's a big age range at the time, 12 and 15—she's always been my family.

ARIANA I remember being so young, and being like, "Tyler. Have you ever kissed

somebody?" And they were like, "Um, go to bed."

TYLER We really started spending every second together, like, August of 2013? She came to New York for a show, and I was like, "Hey, can I work on your tour?" And she was like, "Sure."

ARIANA That's not even what happened! This is the best part! I came to NYC for a show, and they came back to see me, and I was so excited to see them, because it had been a while since we'd seen each other, at this point. Next day, I'm at a different venue, and I'm like, "It was really nice to see Tyler yesterday. I'd like them to be by my side for the rest of my life." I called them, and I was like, "Do you want to come work on my tour?" And they were like, "Yes. Doing what?" And I said, "I don't know, but I'm willing to pay you, and we're leaving tonight. Can you pack a bag now?"

TYLER "The car is coming in 30 minutes! Pack a bag!" I literally ran around my apartment.

It's great that you've been in each other's lives through such formative experiences.

TYLER It's not an average life…there are a lot of really rad experiences that are very rare. I think the best part, for me, is not really what I get to do with her or in her company, but to watch her do what she does and share what she does with the world, and be there to witness her growing process.

ARIANA And help me through it!

TYLER And watch how she affects so many people's lives. I was watching her at *Jimmy Fallon* today. I know she's funny and smart, but it's nice to watch other people get it. She does or says something in a skit or an interview, and they're like, "Oh, she can do these things," and I'm like, "Fuck yeah, she can!" It's not "I got to be on set at *Jimmy Fallon* today," it's "I got to watch everyone fall in love with my best friend."

ARIANA Cutie pie, wow!

Normally, when we do these interviews, we do them separately. I usually end with "What can I ask your friend to make them laugh?"

ARIANA Can I whisper something? Tyler, go away! You could say, "For a present, would you ever get Ariana a blanket with a huge picture of your face on it?" They'll know what that means. Tyler! Hasten hither!

TYLER What's happening?

Would you ever get, as a present for Ariana, a blanket with a huge picture of your face on it?

ARIANA [*Laughs*]

TYLER Oh. My. God. I can't deal with you! I can't believe that's the thing you just told her!

Now you have to explain it!

ARIANA You didn't tell me we had to explain it!

That's OK, we can leave people guessing.

ARIANA I have a blanket with Tyler's face on it!

You do?

TYLER I didn't get it for her! I would never do that. [*Both laugh*] EVER!

ARIANA It was our friend! Our friend gave us a blanket with all three of our faces on it.

TYLER With life-sized pictures of us, and it was really weird.

ARIANA It was the funniest thing that ever happened in my whole life. She gave it to me, and I was staring at it, thinking, *Oh my god. This is the creepiest/funniest/greatest gift I've ever received,* but *creepiest* is the most prominent word in my mind.

TYLER There was a line in our show that we used to sing in retirement homes. [The line] was inappropriate to sing at a nursing home, but we never remembered until 20

seconds before we were going on stage, and then we were like, "Oh my god, can we change it?" And we never [did].

What was the line?

ARIANA "You're dying in America." We were in front of all the lovely old people. We were singing our usual set. This was our first gig at an old-age home, and halfway in the song, it goes from "You're living in America" to "You're dying in America." We all look at each other, and we're all [*mock sings*], "You're dying!" *I guess we just go ahead! Got nothing to lose!* We all looked at each other with such cold, blind terror. We so easily could have kept on singing, "You're living in America." But we didn't!

TYLER We were very young. Just middle schoolers and one high schooler.

This was very special.

TYLER Thank you.

ARIANA If you want really embarrassing pictures of us, let us know. Thank you for doing this. We had so much fun! ✎

CHANNELING MY 15-YEAR-OLD SELF:
AN INTERVIEW WITH SOLANGE

The Grizzly Bear artist chats with our new life guide on getting vocal about your truth.
By Ed Droste. Illustrations by Alyssa Etoile.

ED DROSTE How are you, boo?

SOLANGE I'm really good. I'm happy to be back in New Orleans. As soon as I get off the plane, I feel like I'm in my safe happy place.

Tell me how you came to discover New Orleans as your place, and what it does for you creatively.

When I was in L.A. there were definitely things I loved. But it didn't click as my homestead. My journey to New York was mostly motivated by the fact that my entire family was there. Julez was getting older and I thought it would be incredible to raise him in the same city as grandma and auntie and cousin. And my life partner, Alan [Ferguson], was practically from there. He'd lived there for 20 years before we moved to L.A. I found that the Big Easy was the perfect slow vibe! I needed to feel like I was never missing out culturally. It was like, "Let's try this out and see how we dig it." A lot of folks don't know this is where my mom is from—Louisiana. My dad is from Alabama. I'm kind of a true Southern girl.

I wanted to live in a black city, which I had never experienced. And I wanted to connect with black culture in a different way. There's such distinctive and rich and preserved regional culture and food and music, and that has been super inspiring. It's pretty magical.

You've always been very in tune with the speed at which you wanna do things. But you manage to multitask and be a mogul of sorts, where you're running your own label and a store. You're releasing music. You're involved in fashion. How do you manage to do all that and yet also seem so chill? [*Laughs*] You *are* chill.

The biggest key in all of that is balance.

I didn't even mention that you're a mother.

I have included Julez in my life in a different way than maybe a lot of working moms have. I feel really lucky that I'm able to travel with him and have him come to shoots and gigs. I don't ever take that for granted, 'cause I know that is not a typical working-mom situation. That alleviates a lot of tension and stress in terms of the mom-and-work balance.

On all other fronts, all of the different things that I have my hands in, there's nothing that's not an extension of me directly. I look at everything I do as all under the umbrella of—and I really hate the context and the pretentiousness of using these terms—being an artist and a creative. There's not anything that feels like work, because I've made my work what I love to do. Sometimes it gets tough. I will not paint the tale that it's just smooth sailing. I'm extremely lucky that Alan and I are able to say, "Where are you gonna be? What projects are you working on?" to figure out how to balance it all with Julez.

And, as you know, I'm a terrible texter. I'm a terrible email responder. All of our friends curse me out on a pretty consistent basis.

When the times are tough, you reply and are there, always. [*Solange laughs*] It's true! Whenever I've been through a crisis, you've been there.

I really do try my best to be a devoted friend and balance that part of my life, too. But in terms of, like, day-to-day cackling, LOLing via text, sometimes that shit suffers.

A sense of humor is also how I maintain my sanity. You have to laugh, you have to be able to laugh at yourself, laugh with people. That's a huge saving grace in my life.

When I became friends with you, you had just released your last full-length album and were touring. Your profile's grown tremendously. But there's also this other side of you, before I knew you. I was watching *Bring It On: All or Nothing*, and all sorts of things from your archive. How have you evolved, and what helped you grow and change? You've managed to have your own voice in a world where that could be very difficult.

It's really interesting, because my very first record was released when I was 15. And [because of my age] it's always been contextualized as teenybopper, pop music. Which is totally fine, and during that time I loved that shit like the rest of them. Being almost 30 now, I'm still incredibly proud of and connected to it. I wrote most of it on my own, with the exception of one or two songs. I hadn't quite figured out, as a teenager, how to express who I was in a way that didn't have to be so literal.

I went to Jamaica when I was about 14, and I came back and felt so connected to Rastafarianism—but I lived in the suburbs of Houston. I became a vegan, I cut off all of my hair, I went natural. I only wore clothes from the secondhand shop, because I didn't believe in commerce and spending money on material things—but I was such a walking contradiction, in terms of what my lifestyle was outside of those things. I needed to express all of these deep feelings and emotions that were so, so, so strong, and at that point, pretty radical. So it's interesting to look back and listen to *Solo Star*, because some of the lyrics that I wrote then I could never write now. They were so raw and unfiltered and second nature for me. As you get older, you tend to overthink them. Although it's truly what you feel, there's an analytical part of your brain that wants to make sure that you're articulating [those emotions] carefully.

When I think back on that time, one of the most important things that happened was when I was 13 and stepped in as a background dancer for my sister. Those two years were probably most crucial to my development, because every day we'd wake up in a new city, new country, new continent. And my mother was very trusting, so I'd get to roam a lot. We were in Europe for probably eight months straight when the Chemical Brothers, Portishead—all of these super-innovative electronic bands—were doing great stuff on pop radio and MTV. I was exposed to so many different types of people, cultures, music, art. I lived in museums. We'd have soundcheck at three or four o'clock, but until then, if we were in Australia, I'd go and see the Opera House. If we were in Tokyo, I'd see all the Harajuku girls and hang out. I was extremely lucky—I wasn't in a classroom, but I was in probably the biggest classroom ever, being able to travel and experience things.

Also, we didn't have cellphones, so I had to use maps and get lost. That was really magical. It grew me up a lot. I still lived with my parents, but they instilled a great sense of responsibility in me: "If you're gonna be working and making money, you need to learn how to manage your money. You need to cover these expenses, and you need to start saving money for college or a car."

After my record release and tour I felt burned out, by the age of 16. I wanted to be home. I wanted to have more consistency, and I would've been as fulfilled if I wrote songs for other artists and didn't have to perform, tour, and promote them. So I started writing for Destiny's Child and Kelly [Rowland]'s solo projects and my sister [Beyoncé]'s solo projects. And some commercials. [Writing] truly was, and remains, my favorite part of the creative process of being a musician and an artist.

One of the contributors to Rookie asked if you felt any stigmas about being a teen mom, let alone a famous teen mom.

I had been with my son's father off and on from 13 to when we got married, when I was 17. At that age, having a four-year relationship is really major. It feels so permanent and so real; that was the entirety of high school. A lot of people give me the eye roll when I say this—but I mean it: We probably would've run off and gotten married anyway, whether I became pregnant with Julez or not. We were just so passionate and everything felt so serious. It was also this contrast of life. There were two sides of me: performing at the NBA All-Star Game or on the Grammys as a backup dancer, and then going to the fall dance at his high school.

Did you feel any criticism?

Oh, absolutely. At times it was a big deal that I was 17 and getting married. People, of course, were like, "Duh, she's pregnant." [I was] like, Fuck all of you guys, you know? This is clearly a decision that I've made and that I feel strongly about. And at that age especially, it's so much easier to tune out the world when you have a partner in crime. It's the whole "You and me against the world" mentality. So [criticism] was definitely there, but I don't think it caused a lot of pain or stress or confusion for me.

What strengthened me was having a newborn in a town in the middle of nowhere [in Idaho], with no family or friends, having to wake up every two hours in the middle of the night to breastfeed.

I've met some incredible mothers who were super young. I've met moms who made some really bad decisions that were teenagers. Then I've met incredible mothers who started in their 30s, and some mothers in their 30s who made really bad decisions as moms. I've been the only one in the crew with a kid for a long time. Now our friends are starting to have kids. I feel great about my role as a mother from 18 to 28.

Julez is one of the most polite, engaging, fun kids I've ever been around. I've seen him when he was still at an age when he might've thrown tantrums or whatever, and he's always been so gracious and wonderful and loving.

Out of everything you could tell me in the world, that means the most to me. It makes me smile the hardest, and it makes anything else that is a priority kind of just fall through the cracks when you hear that, as a mother. So thank you, so much.

As someone that's not even sure they wanna have kids, when I hang out with you and Julez and Alan, it makes me be like, "Maybe…if I could have a kid like Julez!"

[Julez and I have] grown up together. Something that I constantly talk to Julez about is being a family as a village. What can he contribute? Even on the tiniest scale, as a family, as a unit, what can he contribute as his part in the village? There are a lot of sacrifices that we've both made. And I think that's one of the things that came from having him so young. It's been incredibly important to have a career and to maintain a social life and to have friends and all of that. Probably the hardest [thing about] having him at such a young age was always feeling that I had to do everything on my own, otherwise people would feel like it was a consequence of me being a young mother. I've let so much of that go over the years. But that was one of the alluring aspects of moving to Idaho, 'cause I felt like it'd just be us. I wouldn't have my mom, my sister, my friends, my cousin, everybody telling me what to do or how to do it. I wanted to trust my instincts and listen to my maternal voice, no matter what age I was. When I look back, that time was isolating and hard. But my time as a mother and my commitment to Julez and our connection— that was invaluable.

My family and friends were pretty vocal about what would happen with Julez's dad and our relationship. And they were right, [it ended]. But it didn't matter. I still had to go through it myself, to know what to look for, what I wouldn't tolerate again, what I might take with the bad and the good, etc. It's one of those annoying things, like when you're a teenager and people are writing your story for you. Who cares if shit happens or not—you still have to go through the journey. That's something that would've been nice for me to hear, you know? "Yeah, he's gonna do this, you're gonna do that, but these are still your decisions to make."

What is the biggest challenge you've faced trying to get your voice out there— whether it's being a woman, a minority, whatever—and what advice would you give to people facing similar challenges?

There are some really awesome things that happen through your journey as an artist, and then there are some really sucky things, too. I try and take them with as much context as I can. I'm transitioning into a space that I wasn't even at a year ago, where I see the relativity in all of this.

You have to walk the line of being tough and assertive to protect yourself and the way you present yourself to the world, but also be careful you don't let paranoia and constant tension affect your fluidness and the vulnerability it takes to achieve your best self…whatever it is you're doing.

We, women especially, have progressed so much, but there's still an incredible amount of work to do, especially when collaborating. I read an interesting, funny piece [on Pitchfork (January 2015)], where Björk discussed taking a picture in front of a soundboard in the studio, touching the knobs, and what that would do visually for people's [perception of her as a female] producer. I understood that completely.

Starting off as a songwriter at such a young age, that was my pride and joy. I had a publishing deal when I turned 18 and wrote for all these artists and projects. On my last project I was much more open to collaborating than in the past, and to see my voice kind of get lost in the space of how it was received was really heartbreaking. For me, things took on an entirely

different spectrum of issues, including culture, sex, and race. A particular audience might not have known the scope of my work as an artist or songwriter before. But there was an audience that did, and they wouldn't have thought twice about my role in the work.

I'm incredibly proud of my last album, and as an artist all you can do is make your work, and be so extremely grateful to those who receive it with love. But I have to admit it was a bit weird that it was always said to be my most successful record, when it only sold barely a quarter of what my previous album [*Sol-Angel and the Hadley St. Dreams*] did. We all have our own interpretations of success, and record sales couldn't be more on the bottom of the list for me. But it was really dismissive of my previous audience for some people to essentially say, "This is more successful and relevant because *we* know about and like this one," when the actual facts, in terms of how many people it reached, did not align with that narrative. When those audiences were so clearly defined by race, it became tough for me to understand, but it all goes back to what I said earlier about protecting yourself and your values and ethics and not being afraid to be vocal them.

These are predominantly white male music critics that you're talking about?

Yeah. One critic actually said, in response to me speaking out, "Does Solange not know who's buying her records? Don't bite the hand that feeds you."

There were a lot of times when I saw certain responsibilities for us as humans— to be sensitive to each other and one another's cultures and racial backgrounds—being challenged. At the end of the day, all I ask for is sensitivity and kindness, and that was not being reciprocated.

It feels great that these conversations about appropriation have been had, about subcultures and how we have to be respectful and treat them with kindness. Azealia Banks has been incredible, speaking out on some of those issues. The young actress Amandla [Stenberg] from *The Hunger Games*, who's 16 and incredibly smart, produced a great piece about appropriation. Zendaya opened the conversation about black hair that really needed to be addressed. I think people feel more comfortable and brave having these conversations, knowing they're gonna be protected and that there are like-minded people that have these same issues. This was a huge source of inspiration behind starting the website Saint Heron, which has been my passion project about celebrating the diversity and innovation between young creatives of color who are doing all types of things all over the world, and to keep those conversations going.

It's better now than it was two, five, ten years ago, but it's still not perfect. What would you say to readers who struggle with these issues?

One of the biggest things for me was to stop seeking validation from people who I didn't feel understood me—as a woman, as an artist, as a black woman, as a creative. When you stop seeking validation from outside sources who are not understanding you and have been vocal about that, you gotta move on. Create your own platforms, your own forums, to have that celebration, to meet like-minded people. One of the other things that society has done, especially for young black women who are creatives, is pushing an undertone that there can only be one or a couple of us celebrated at one time. Opening up that support system and camaraderie becomes a force—it's invaluable.

It's especially interesting within fashion, where there are all these opportunities to have brand partnerships or gigs as a performer or DJ. There's an underlying quota that you start to see. You notice the same people fulfilling [this quota]—Token Black Girl or, it gets deeper—Token Black Girl with Afro. That should be inspiration for people to create their own forums, their own brands, their own sources, so that this type of stuff stops happening. There are so many wonderful, creative, insanely talented people; the more and more independent platforms people create for themselves, [the better]. If you're complaining about

"not seeing enough of [X]," well, start your own. That's my response: I don't feel comfortable representing this brand, but I'm starting my own brand, you know? That's where my head is and where I see myself encouraging people with those same types of issues.

I made comments on Twitter and NPR about two years ago about the state of journalism when it comes to black culture, black music—specifically R&B culture—about the way black music was being contextualized and written about, and its voice within the indie music landscape. At that time, there was a wave of people kind of coming after me, making a joke out of what I was saying. There was a hashtag, #DeepBrandyAlbumCuts, which I thought clearly identified the issue I was speaking about—the constant satire and irony associated with the way black music and black artists were approached. It seemed, to some people, really annoying or bratty that I was speaking out about it. It's wonderful, a few years later, to see these issues being addressed more openly. It's so awesome that these are times that we can actually speak about these things, and have mutual love and respect for each other, for who people are. But two years ago, I didn't feel it as much.

We're all continually growing and learning. I really appreciate your fearlessness when it comes to speaking your mind. You've taught me a lot, and I appreciate those types of voices being out there. I can't imagine, if you've inspired me so much, how much you inspire someone younger who's facing more difficult issues than I ever will.

Aw, boo!! Thank you so much. I've always appreciated being able to have healthy, unfiltered, but still respectful, open conversations about race, sexuality, life. That's one thing I would also give advice on— have open and honest conversations with friends and people you love, no matter how uncomfortable it might be. As long as it's done in a respectful and kind and sensitive way, dialogue is what pushes us to grow and evolve.

I feel so much closer having shared so many challenging conversations with you, whether it is from your perspective or mine. On a less serious note: When will we hear new music?

Super, super, super psyched to be in the final stages of the record. It has been my livelihood for the last year and a half or so. One thing that's been challenging this go-around: Julez is a lot older, so being able to get away for a month and write and produce and work on songs while maintaining his schedule has become a little harder. It's about taking time when it comes, and shutting off my brain and going to places that allow me to do that, from Jamaica to Ghana to Cajun Country in the outer regions of New Orleans. The other [challenge] has been wanting to produce this record on my own. I've always co-produced my music, but from start to finish, having my hand in it that way, that was new for me.

It's truly been my most emotionally and historically [driven album], connecting a lot of dots with family and where I come from—being in Louisiana, where my grandparents are from, to write a lot of the music—the work has been incredibly personal. Where *True* was a very thematic album sonically, I was channeling or writing about other people's experiences. It was more about the sonic importance of the record. And this one is really about the subject matter. I'm really, really excited about it. I'm really ready for it to be over. Real talk.

One of the things that a lot of people don't talk about is how hard it is to complete a body of work. How much time, how much emotional drain, how many layers and evolutions, and how self-critical you become during the process. I've tried to exorcise, and not fall into, the self-criticism, the overanalyzing, the starting and redoing and starting and redoing. [I've tried to] capture the true essence of the emotions in the lyrics, channeling my 15-year-old self, when I wrote those songs and didn't think twice about what I said or how people reacted. That's where I've been with this record, trying to channel that space. And it's been a ride, for sure. ◬

FORMATIVE TUNES

By Solange. Artwork by Kendra.

Here are some jams that were heavy on my brain between the ages of 14-17 and that I identified strongly with and helped influence my writing style. I also thought it could be cool to include some songs I wrote for myself or others back then. :)

1. **Provider**—N.E.R.D.

2. **Smoking Cigarettes**—Tweet

3. **The First Taste**—Fiona Apple

4. **This Could Be Love**—Solange *(I wrote this about my son's father and almost exploded when he heard it. I was so nervous.)*

5. **Aqueous Transmission**—Incubus

6. **Inspiration Information**—Shuggie Otis *(When I was 15 and got a pet Chihuahua, I named him Shuggie, I was so influenced by his music.)*

7. **Green Eyes**—Erykah Badu

8. **Slow This Bird Down**—Boards of Canada *(I later ended up recording a song for my second album using this instrumental.)*

9. **Everytime**—Britney Spears

10. **It's Whatever**—Aaliyah

11. **Obsession**—Kelly Rowland *(Wrote this when I was 15, and almost passed out when Brothers Johnson played guitar on it.)*

12. **Destiny**—Zero 7 feat. Sia and Sophie Barker

13. **3x5**—John Mayer

I SEE MYSELF AS MORE OF AN ENTITY THAN A GENDER, MORE GETS DONE THAT WAY! —WILLOW SMITH

THE ADVENTURE THIS LIFE COULD BE IF WE JUST LET OURSELVES BE FREE

— WILLOW SMITH

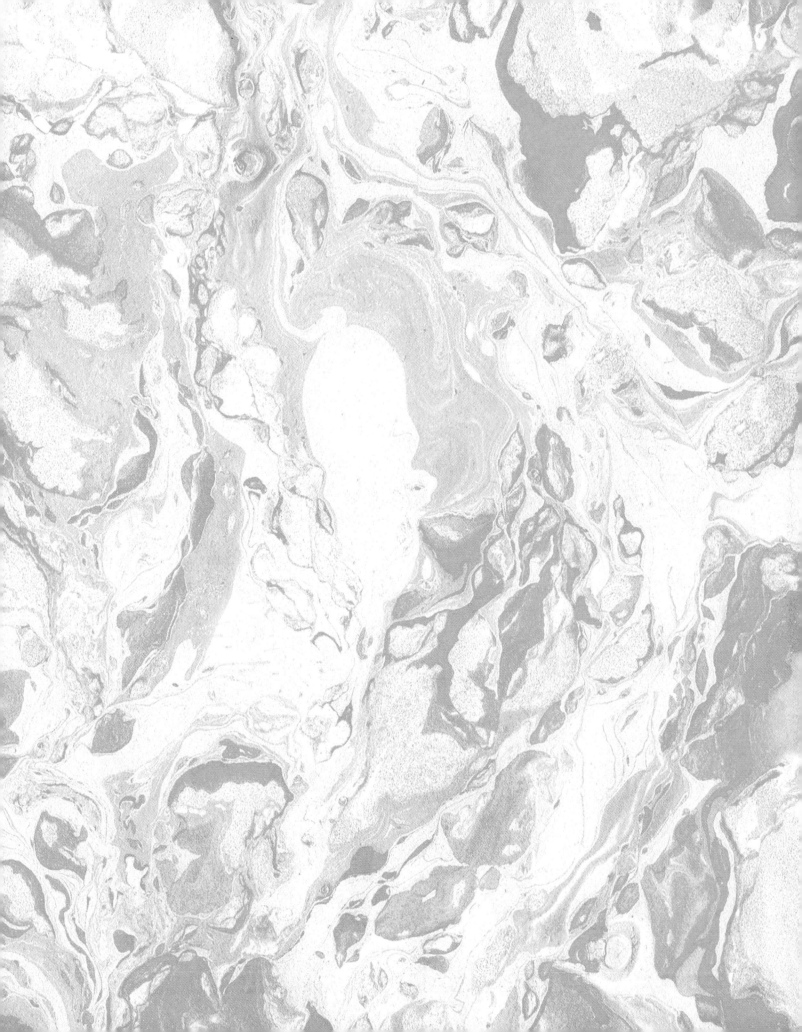

TEENAGE BEDROOM DIORAMA

By Leanna

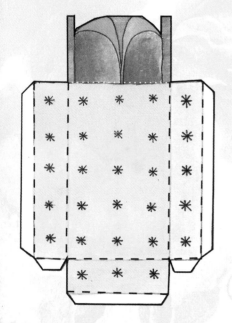

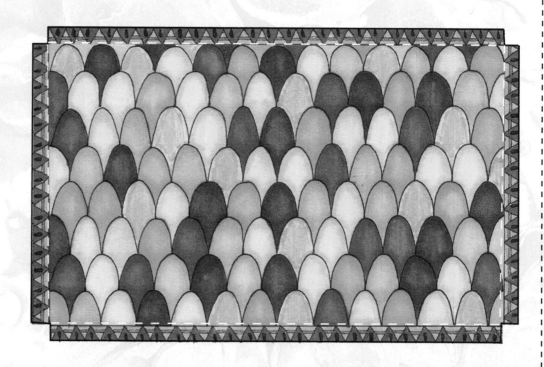

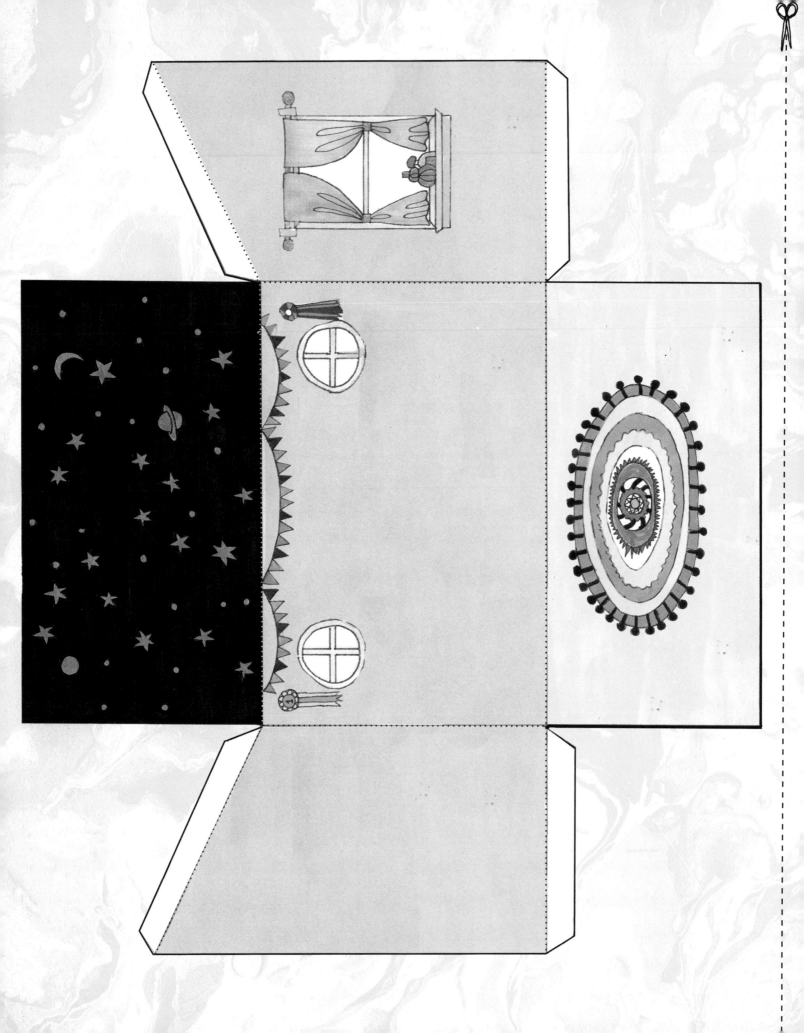

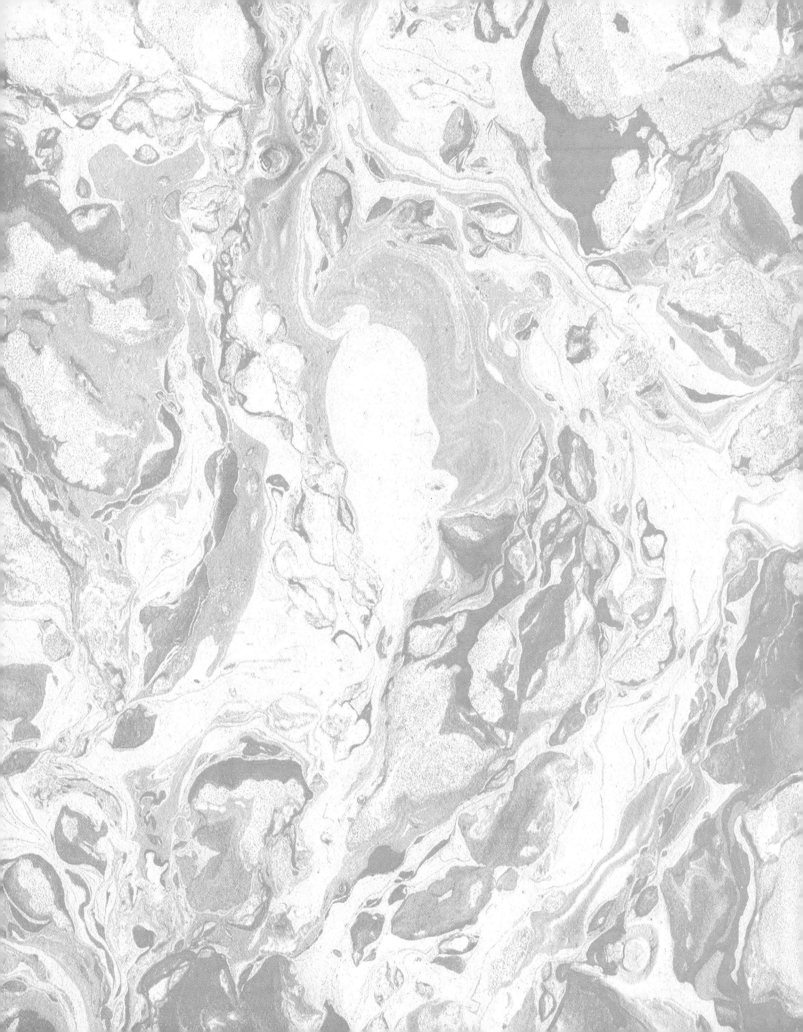

COLLAGE KIT

By Emma D.

ROMEO y JULIETA

ABCDEFGH
IJKŁMNOP
RSTUWYZ

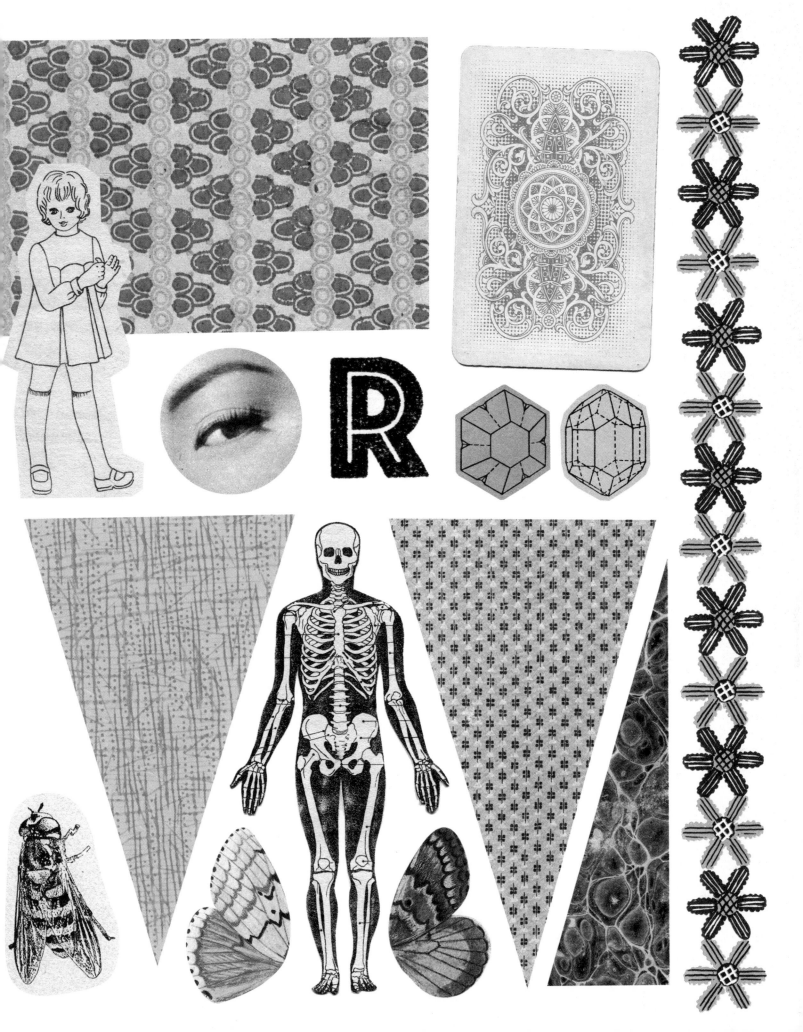

INSPIRATIONAL PIZZA BANNER

By Allegra

JEWELRY BOX

By Kendra

YOU ARE THE STARS

DIY INSTRUCTIONS

TEEN BEDROOM DIORAMA Materials: Scissors, glue or rubber cement, toothpick, clear tape.

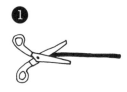
1 Cut all pieces along solid black lines. Don't cut off any tabs, but if you do, reattach with clear tape.

2 Fold inward along dotted lines.

3 Fold outward along dashed lines.

4 Run glue along inside of tabs on interior of the room. Fold tabs under floor and above ceiling. Hold in place until dry.

5 Wrap exterior of room around back of interior. Glue in place.

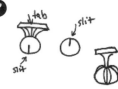
6 Glue roof on top of room.

7 Lantern: Cut slit halfway through each circle. Slide one into the other. Using a toothpick apply a dot of glue to back of tab and affix to ceiling.

8 Bed: Apply glue to tabs on end of bed and tuck behind foot of bed.

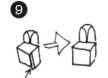
9 Chair: Apply glue to front of each tab and tuck behind front of chair.

10 Vanity: Apply glue behind drawer and fold it down to meet legs of vanity.

11 Dresser: Apply glue to tabs on sides of dresser, fold top of dresser over them, and hold until dry. Apply glue to long side tab and join it with edge of dresser to form a box.

12 Lion: Glue tail to back of lion. Curl around a toothpick to add shape and help lion sit upright.

13 All furniture: Once you find an arrangement you like, glue furniture in place using bottom tabs.

14 Posters: Use stickers on back of this sheet to decorate!

INSPIRATIONAL PIZZA BANNER Materials: Scissors, hole-puncher, string, tape or push pins.

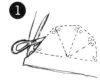
1 Cut out flags along dotted lines.

2 Hole-punch two upper corners of each cut-out flag.

3 Choose order of flags.

4 Cut string according to how long you want banner to be.

5 Pull string through each punched hole so it runs along the back of each flag.

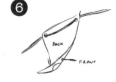
6 To make sure each flag stays in place, loop string back through each hole a second time before adding next flag.

7 Repeat for each flag.

8 Hang banner using tape or pushpins.

PAPER FAN Materials: Scissors, stapler or yarn.

1 Cut out along dotted line.

2 Start at one end of fan and fold paper over about half an inch.

3 Flip paper over and fold again.

4 Continue folding until entire sheet forms equally segmented waves.

5 Pinch left and right corners together, making ends meet.

6 To make a handle, staple or tie ends together with a piece of yarn.

JEWELRY BOX Materials: Scissors, glue or rubber cement.

1 Cut along outlines. Don't cut off any tabs, but if you do, reattach with clear tape.

2 Fold each wall up around "You Are the Stars" so it becomes the inside bottom of box.

3 Fold glue tabs inward, making sure "glue" side is visible.

4 Apply glue to "glue" side of tab. Connect to inside of adjacent wall. Hold in place until dry.

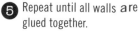
5 Repeat until all walls are glued together.

6 Cut out box lid.

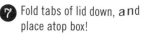
7 Fold tabs of lid down, and place atop box!